The Life of Helen Stephens

The Life of Helen Stephens

The Fulton Flash

For allie —
decorating genius
and friend —

Sharon Kinney Hanson
With a Foreword by Bob Broeg

Sharon Kinney Hanson —
12/16/04

Southern Illinois University Press • *Carbondale*

Library of Congress Cataloging-in-Publication Data

Library of Congress Cataloging-in-Publication Data
Hanson, Sharon Kinney.
The life of Helen Stephens : the Fulton Flash / Sharon Kinney
Hanson ; with a foreword by Bob Broeg.
        p. cm.
Includes bibliographical references and index.
1. Stephens, Helen, 1918–1994. 2. Track and field athletes—
United States—Biography. 3. Women athletes—United States—
Biography. 4. Olympic Games (11th : 1936 : Berlin, Germany)
I. Title.
GV697.S694A3 2004
796.42'092—dc22
ISBN 0-8093-2559-4 (hardcover : alk. paper)   2004010706

Contents

Illustrations

Foreword

*A*s a writer, one who has enjoyed putting one word after another profession-ally for more than a half-century, I'm almost as pleased with biographer Sharon Kinney Hanson as I am with the Queen of the Kingdom of Callaway County: Helen Herring Stephens. And I'm entirely flattered that dear Helen, with whom I ran a photo finish on the calendar, asked Ms. Hanson to have me write this introduction. Although I know fairly well the Kingdom of Callaway (as Helen's hometown county haughtily described itself from Civil War days), I've always regarded the Fulton Flash as internationally special. And not only because she *oopt* and *ahhpt* right in Der Fuhrer's face, as did Spike Jones and his band insult the Nazi leader in playschtik-music at a time when we Americans needed a good laugh. World War II wasn't funny, of course, but Helen's brief yet interesting meeting with Hitler before the Holocaust aptly is documented in this biography. As I write this intro early into the first decade of the twenty-first century, I hope the former little Austrian paperhanger will wind up being voted the number one villain in the Twentieth Century's Hall of Infamy.

And, I think Helen's biographer, using Miss Stephens' thoughtful diary, flushed out with professional research, assiduous interviews, and adequate travel, thor-oughly recaptures the amazing 1936 Olympic games.

My first boss at the *St. Louis Post-Dispatch*, John Edward Wray, to whom I reported from 1945 and onward, thought that the 1936 Olympic Games was the most glowing experience of his career—which began as far back as 1897, inclu-sive of his reportage on Ruby Robert Fitzsimmons relieving Gentleman Jim Corbett of the heavyweight boxing championship at Carson City, Nevada. As a well-traveled man, born three years before the establishment of the National Baseball League (1876), and before Custer's command was cut down at Montana's Little Big Horn, Mr. Wray—*always* addressed as "Mister"—was born on the east bank of the Mississippi in Alton, Illinois. At age twelve, Wray saw the smolder-ing ruins of Geronimo's last raid in Arizona.

Why bring up Ed Wray, as only his non-office intimates called him? Because he was the most knowledgeable sports writer, all-around, that I and friendly rival Bob Burnes of the old *St. Louis Globe-Democrat* ever saw! Wray was especially adept at writing about boxing—saw every heavyweight title fight from Fitz-Corbett to Joe Louis—and combined with the *Post-Dispatch* printer to achieve a remarkable statistical aid. Just for their own information as racetrack buffs, they "invented" the turf's past performance chart but didn't bother to copyright it. See?

Sports writers' wisdom doesn't cover financial things, else they might have lived a different, more affluent life.

But—and this is the point about dwelling on Mr. Wray in a book about Helen Stephens—he would have missed his greatest thrills. The ol' boss was "at" the 1936 Olympics; present during the shipboard episode by which swimming ace Eleanor Holm was cashiered (as Hanson notes and about which Helen was counseled and concerned) because gruff-stickler Avery Brundage saw Eleanor sip champagne and perhaps over-indulge herself with it. And thanks to the persistence of Kansas' great basketball coach Forrest (Phog) Allen, the Amateur Athletic Union scrimped together fare for the inventor of Phog's game, retired KU professor James Naismith, and basketball became an official Olympic sport at Berlin. (When I say I met Doc Naismith a year later at the rival university atop Mount Oread at Kansas' Raw River, please don't act as if I'm too old to remember, most certainly from my past and Mr. Wray's.)

To the venerable *Post-Dispatch* sports editor who lived until age eighty-eight, dead then only because of surgery in 1961, by which he wanted to improve his vision to write again, Helen's accomplishments ranked with Jesse Owens in Berlin as the highlight of a long, colorful career. If this sounds like a second-hand compliment, I hope you'll forgive me, but especially Miss Stephens, who was the Fulton Flash when baseball's swift Bake McBride (also of Fulton) wasn't even the gleam in a couple of Callaway school kids' eyes.

Unfortunately, I saw Helen as an athlete only briefly, before she joined Ed Wray in the Missouri Sports Hall of Fame and, of course, more handily was recognized in the National Track and Field Hall of Fame. I knew her best, early, as an avid boyhood reader in college. Ever since, I've known her as a great person with class. Make that championship class with a capital "C" or, better still, twin capitals. She's been not only a model citizen but a glowing model for kids to whom she has talked, unselfishly, often at her own expense. She was also standard-bearer catalyst for the Senior Olympics. The greatest disappointment would be if anyone anywhere, especially in Mizzour-ah, as I like to pronounce our home state, forgot the dear lady resident of St. Louis' flourishing suburb, Florissant. Now, because of Sharon Kinney Hanson, it won't happen. Thanks to Helen and her biographer for giving me a chance to say a few (or windy) words of admiration.

—Bob Broeg

Preface

*H*elen Stephens' name is etched in the monolithic pillar at the entrance of Berlin's Reichsportfeld, among the names of other 1936 Olympic gold medalists. But unlike Jesse Owens, whose record was bested within a year, and many who hung up their track shoes shortly thereafter, Helen's track and field records held for twenty-four years, and her athletic triumphs and personal trials remain important keys to the advancement of women's sports in the United States. Labeled a she-man in the Neanderthal Age of women's athletics, this unlikely farm girl from Missouri was active in sports for fifty-eight years. She was enshrined in seven sports Halls of Fame. Generous and fun-loving, she was a dynamic personality, a good sport, a gracious winner, a long-lived celebrity exhibiting the old-time values of competition and athleticism.

Helen Stephens excelled in what once was considered an atypical career for a woman. She was the first woman in the world to own and manage a basketball team. She was a parade marshal in the Olympics and off-shoot Olympic games, was a women's college track and field coach in the 1970s, and an engaging spokesperson and sportswomen's advocate in the 1980s and 1990s.

In the 1930s' entertainment arena, she ran in exhibition races against men (clocking in a second behind Owens); she plopped astounding distances as a discus thrower and set spectacular marks in the standing broad jump. When hecklers taunted her with, Hey, tomgirl, where's your beard? this larger-than-life lady came through with characteristic lip, firing back: Same place as yours—you're sittin' on it! She turned professional in 1937, signing with the barnstorming All-American Red Heads Basketball Team, playing men's rules, men's teams. In 1938, she started her own team, the Helen Stephens Olympic Co-Eds, which won over 50 percent of its games. Once during the 1940s in a Michigan bar and grill, she decked a drunk who, targeting her newly permed hair, stumbled toward her saying something like, Why don't you quit masquerading like a woman? Helen said, "I was mindin' my own business, sittin' in a booth trying to eat a meal in peace in the company of my cager-girlfriend 'Onse,' when this boozer made a big mistake." He put his hand on Helen's coiffure, whereupon, she said, "I stood up and knocked him down." The two ladies "threw the bum out and the bartender thanked us for it." Such incidents occurred early in her career when she had a penchant for wearing jodhpurs, men's shirts, and ties and probably led her to limit this attire, especially after taking a nine-to-five job. Her down-home friendliness usually won over most people, though her manly size and substance and occasional bark could overwhelm frail egos. Mostly she charmed everyone with her gregarious, witty self.

Booked by Abe Saperstein of Harlem Globetrotters fame, her Olympic Co-Eds traveled across the United States and Canada for five years before World War II; after the war, she reestablished her team and toured during much of the 1950s. Because Babe Didrikson advised her against golf, she took up bowling in the 1940s. Throughout the 1960s and 1970s, Helen was a reliable Olympic committee worker, fund-raiser, and legislative supporter; in the 1980s and 1990s, a consistent gold medalist in the national Senior Olympics and Missouri Show-Me Games.

In sum, on the track and on basketball courts, on the ball fields or bowling lanes, at podiums or in boardrooms, and in the world at large, Helen Stephens was Olympian in every way; she was an Olympian torch runner both literally and symbolically.

This biography of Helen Stephens documents her amazing, lifelong athletic career. It includes excerpts from her 1936 diary (in italics throughout) and gives a framework of professional and personal gender issues pertinent to her life that are relevant to women athletes today. It is an authorized biography that stems from over seventy interviews with Helen (beginning in 1987 and ending a few weeks before her death in 1994) and correspondence and interviews with her coach, basketball and bowling teammates, co-workers, friends, relatives, and others. Unless otherwise noted, the words of persons that are quoted or paraphrased in this book derive from these extensive interviews. Because Helen's personality drew upon storytelling, some pivotal moments are presented in an as-told-to mode; others come directly from her extensive archives that, with the publication of this work, become available to researchers in the Women's Collection of the University of Missouri's Western Historical Manuscript Collection. Within Helen's archives are her 1936 diary, her 1936 passport, an original copy of the 1936 Anti-Hitler Manifesto, a multitude of letters received and carbons of letters she sent from 1935 to 1993, accounts, agreements, authorizations, broadsides, clippings, contracts, cartoons she drew, invoices, ledgers, legal opinions, civil and school newsletters, notebooks, notes and scripts of speeches given by or associated with Helen, score books, promotional fliers, permits, photographs, proclamations, programs, publications, receipts, schedules, scrapbook ephemera, and more. My own correspondence with Helen and tapes of all interviews during the research and writing period will be placed in the Women's Collection upon my death.

There was unique magic in Helen's life; by not shrinking from public view because of rumored innuendoes, she above all unlatched the gates that widened the vision of athleticism for American track women. If not Helen Stephens, who achieved this? Was it the pretty 1928 world sprint titleholder, Betty Robinson? Betty quit athletic competition before World War II. Was it Helen's nemesis, the unfortunate Clevelandite Stella Walsh, whose amateur career spanned longer? No. Stella sprinted for Poland; was defeated by Helen every time she ran against her, four races in all. Was it Babe Didrikson? Babe abandoned track for the then neophyte game of golf. Indeed it was Helen Stephens—Helen Stephens who faced and foiled the outrageous insult of gender slurs—and kept running toward greater fame. Helen herself said it best, borrowing a phrase from her contemporary Yogi Berra: "I might not've been the best, but I was among 'em."

Acknowledgments

*F*oremost, thanks to Helen for allowing me to be her biographer and for permitting access to her personal archives. Also, thanks to her discovery coach, W. Burton Moore; Olympic teammates Elizabeth Robinson Schwartz and Annette Rogers Green; Helen Stephens Olympic Co-Ed Helen Onson, Lillian Merkel Woodsmall, and Virginia Durham Dellamo; Sam Snead and Dona Bailey of the PGA of America; Julia Spearman, John C. Harris, Rev. Isham Holland, Martha Sue Faucett, Leona Kemp Sampson, and Bonnie Lammers; alumnae sisters Myldred Fox Fairchild and Shannon Chenoweth Graham; Helen's cousin Thomas Thornton Meloy; Charles Guenther, her DMAAC supervisor; Dr. Glynn Clark, his wife Carolyn, and Oscar Hartmann, Helen's Senior Olympics colleagues; Bob C. Paul of the USOC; Sandra Fritz; and Bob and Betty Stephens. I especially thank archivist Pam Miner who volunteered her expertise and Missouri State Archives Director Ken Winn; my research assistant Karen Wells, Lincoln University; archive assistant Laura Malzner; and Michael Thompson. Thanks to William Woods University President Dr. Jahnae Barnett and her staff, Edie Maxie, Melody Jarrett, and Amy Richardson Bradshaw; Ann Morris, Nancy Lankford, Laura Bullion, and David Moore of the University of Missouri's Western Historical Manuscript Collection; Kris Kleindienst of Left Bank Books; James Downey of Legacy Bookstore; biographer/reporter Terry Ganey; athlete/author Mariah Burton Nelson; scholar/author Blanche Wiesen Cook; attorneys Grant Kang, Jerry Venters, Martha Brown, and Kylan W. Broadus; friends Gloria Overfelt and Bill Newcomb; author/historian William Barnaby Faherty, SJ, for constant support; authors Peggy Peterson and Betty Cook Rottmann; Madeline Matson of the Missouri Center for the Book; librarians Frank Pascoe, Patt Behler, Mrs. Gerry O'Halloran, LaDonna Justice, and Carolyn Branch; Dr. Melvin M. Grumbach; Missouri State Tourism's Steve Kappler; Don Howard of the Missouri Division of Aging; Missouri Show-Me State Games' Gary Filbert and Gene Madden; Jim Coleman of the Missouri Highway Department; sports writers Bob Burnes and Bob Broeg; sports cartoonist Amadee; sports commentator extraordinaire Bob Costas; Helen's co-worker Eleanor Sikorsky Cullinan; Phyllis Tucker, Jan Watson, Bruce Woodward, Judy Savage, and Sharon Koehler.

For permission to include material derived from their correspondence or from interviews, I gratefully acknowledge Bud Greenspan, C. Robert Paul Jr., Charles J. Guenther, Shannon Chenoweth Graham, John C. Harris, Helen Onson, and Julia Spearman. I also wish to express gratitude to the Thanks Be to Grandmother Winifred Foundation and its president, Deborah Ann Light, for financially supporting the research and collation of Helen's career papers.

Except where noted otherwise in captions, all illustrations for this book were provided by Helen Stephens for use in this authorized biography, including studio portraits and professional shots secured for publicity and promotional purposes and personal snapshots.

Special thanks to Kimberly Fritts, my sister-in-law, for photo-scans; biographer/professor Dr. Stephen Archer for editorial direction and solid encouragement; Illinois Hall of Fame director and manuscript reader Fred Huff; University of Missouri professor emeritus of German, Dr. Adolf E. Schroeder, for guidance with conversational patois; biographer Marilyn Cannaday for patient support and advice; and the Southern Illinois University Press staff, especially Liz Brymer, Jonathan Haupt, Kristine Priddy, Carol Burns, and my rigorous editor, John Wilson.

Lastly, my gratitude to spouse Richard Hanson for his unflagging support of various kinds.

The Life of Helen Stephens

1

Childhood of a Champion

They didn't think I was wrapped too tight in Fulton forty years ago.
They thought I was a little bit strange.
—Helen Herring Stephens, 1979

*N*estled in the coil of Callaway County, Missouri, in America's midland, is a little town called Fulton. It is a hundred ten miles west of St. Louis, a hundred fifty miles east of Kansas City, and some thirty miles east of Mizzou (the University of Missouri, Columbia), the first state university built west of the Mississippi River. Several tributaries run atwixt Callaway's foothills and forcefully sweep toward the Missouri River, a major water corridor in the state.

In 1820, when Fulton became the county seat, it was a burgeoning little hamlet. Townsfolk bore a two-hour buggy ride to the metropolitan City of Jefferson, some thirty miles south. State government once had operated out of St. Charles, but in 1826, legislators were steamboating to a more centrally located site or arriving by way of the Missouri-Kansas-Texas Railroad (aka Katy Trail). Jefferson City's capitol dome could be seen from great distances, sitting high on a hill alongside the swift, frequently flooding Missouri River. The four-story Carthage limestone edifice, a creation of New York architects Tracy and Swartwout, replicated the grandeur of America's White House.

During Helen Stephens' youth, rural roads were rudimentary, one or two lanes of blacktop or gravel. But motorists in love with Henry Ford's Model T traveled the foothills of Callaway County in such numbers that folks saw their piece of country as a crossroads of the world. Just outside the city, a sign long declared it so. Today, two main highways (Missouri 54 and U.S. 70) crisscross the county, and a marker in the nearby berg known as Calwood still proclaims that notoriety.

Fulton's origins decidedly influenced a dominant characteristic of the community, a strong composite of opinion, pride, and disarming friendliness, bolted together by a hardy streak of the state's show-me attitude: traits that outsiders interpret on occasion as plain-old, brown-paper stubbornness. Historians have noted that tempers flared over naming the little town, which in a short hundred years or so would become best known as the home of the Fulton Flash. The dispute tested friendships when Robert "Bob" Dunlap took his stand against naming the town Volney.

Monsieur Constantin-François Comte de Volney was a friend of Thomas Jefferson; he was a French statesman and man of letters whom Dunlap marked as an infidel—a monarchist enemy of Christianity. Dunlap petitioned county court justices, arguing that the American who built the first successful steamboat, Robert Fulton, deserved the honor.[1] Some folks, consequently, began to call their hometown "Bob Fulton." Some simply called it "Bob," in honor of their spokesman, Bob Dunlap. With time, the brouhaha fizzled; by the late nineteenth century, city fathers were boasting that their little town of Fulton, mapped out on fifty acres of land, "was half-grown before Chicago was thought of—before San Francisco ever amounted to a thing,"[2] which suggests great progress had occurred for the little burg once called "Bob."

The town incorporated in 1859, one year prior to the Civil War. For many years thereafter, Fultonians stubbornly hoisted the Confederate flag as a stronghold for "the grays," renaming it the Kingdom of Callaway. It is a designation still used during Fulton's annual Kingdom Supper, a gathering to honor accomplished sons and daughters.

For some, Fulton held an uneasy reputation as the site of the State Lunatic Asylum and the Asylum for the Deaf and Dumb, both established by Missouri law in 1851. Suggesting that someone should be "sent to Fulton" insinuated mental instability. But the town attained distinction and acclaim through its two prestigious, private institutions: Westminster College for men (1853), and the Female Orphans School of the Christian Church (1870), which was reorganized as William Woods College in 1890.

At the twentieth century's turn, a census showed Fulton's population near six thousand and Callaway County with over twenty-five thousand residents. The city bustled with a variety of businesses and civic organizations: several banks; racially segregated schools and churches (Disciples of Christ, Methodist, Presbyterian, and Baptist); a blacksmith shop and livery barn; veterinarian H. C. Ward; a doctor's office–drug store; C. Fischers' Tomb Stone on Asylum Street; the International Shoe Factory; the firebrick and clay businesses of W. K. Holland Company and Luther Nichol Company on Westminster Avenue near the freight lines; McIntire's Flower Shop; an ice plant and delivery wagon; Central Dairy Store; various mercantiles (Henderson's, Pitcher General

Store, Berghauser Hardware); a newspaper and a post office. The Fulton Garden Club, the Fulton Country Club, and the Gem Theatre medicine shows provided additional social opportunities for Fultonians with extra change in their pockets.

The twentieth century brought World War I and "aeroplane" production to Missouri, to St. Louis in particular. It was an industry that would provide employment for both the Fulton Flash and her brother during World War II.

Politics surrounding Helen as she grew up were electric. During her birth year, banner headlines leaped from the pages with reports on the activities of the County Council of Defense: POLICE HELP PATRIOTIC ORGANIZERS GO AFTER IDLERS. Draft-age "Loafers . . . are being rounded up and either made to go to war or to work. . . . use of a rawhide . . . whip is a powerful antidote for laziness."[3] That September, the council, stolidly secure behind its war slogan, Work or Fight, Black or White, felt vindicated when five members of the Klicks family were arrested and charged with disloyalty under the Espionage Act. One can easily imagine the chatter that that caused.

Among this struggling community rose a certain crowd-amassing preacher (pre–Father Coughlin) who shepherded the Presbyterian Church. The Reverend Dr. Abbott explained to his congregation and the local paper aired his views on why America declared war on Germany (April 6, 1917): not because it wanted to, but because it was the only honorable thing to do. Some German-descent parishioners cast their eyes to the floor or looked nervously upon their neighbors when he said Americans fought not for gain but for the underlying principles involved: to suppress a nation that had the most diabolical system of spies the world had ever produced. Germans, he said, were trying to establish a German empire in our own American republic.[4]

Everyone knew that as early as 1914 patriotic Callawegians were assisting the war effort to win victory "over the Hun hordes in France" by supplying good old Missouri mules. Chauvinism and xenophobia rode feverishly high in those years. Full of patriotism, composer John McDonald of Fulton wrote the song "I'll Fight for Every Star in the Flag." It was published by a New York firm in the year of Helen's birth. His tune was sung during school programs for many years prior to and after the war. Helen learned it while attending Middle River School. On August 22, 1918, the newspaper tracked the prevailing anti-German feelings of the community: "Acting on a suggestion by the County Council of Defense, members of the German Evangelical Church of Fulton voted unanimously to discontinue use of German language in its services."[5] Another news item that day centered on the anniversary of the execution of "Emmett Divers, a Negro fiend who was lynched on Auxvasse Creek Bridge . . . 5 minutes before 1:00 o'clock in the morning . . . [on] August 15 . . . and again hung on a telephone pole in the courthouse yard. . . . thousands of people viewed the horrible, ghastly body with black disfigured face, with tongue protruding, and stiffened limbs."[6]

At home, in church, in town, talk of politics and social injustice became commonplace for the Stephenses, the Herrings, and the Meloys. When World War I ended, November 11, 1918, Helen was a nine-month-old toddler. It was a time filled with anxieties. Americans still were focused "over there." Bedraggled families were careworn for news about their doughboy sons who battled against the Kaiser in what was a worldwide war.

Such was the setting into which Helen was born. Her birth occurred in the year a smallpox epidemic swept the state (some 548,000 died of it in the United States). "Spanish flu" also struck down hundreds of people in Callaway County. Drawing upon the concept of quarantine, the city physician closed the public library, for he thought that if a book chanced to be in the hands of someone ill with these diseases and it was returned to the library, it harbored and passed along those germs.

When Helen Stephens was born, on Sunday, February 3, 1918, Fulton was an ethnically rich community of Irish, German, English, and French descendants. Residing on the east ("dark") side of town were descendants of slaves. Helen's maternal great grandparents (Snow) were English, and her maternal grandparents (Meloy) Irish, and Helen's middle name (Herring, her grandfather's name) imparts a German strain. One of Helen's ancestors had married a Cherokee woman from Oklahoma, but that was all Grandmother Meloy would reveal about the proud, dark face in the family photo album. The somewhat affluent uncle in the textbook business in Kansas City, where Ford Motor Company had established a new plant, was the relative Grandma Meloy talked about. Helen saw in her grandmother a woman with a strong sense of social propriety. Helen claimed to be "a bit afraid of Granny's hands. She had a quick long reach—if you did something you shouldn't have."

The Stephens family followed the tenor of the times as translated by their ethnically mixed community. In those postwar years, unemployment loomed high, incomes plummeted and stayed low. Times were hard. In some households, reading was a necessity and a pleasure, much as television viewing is for some families today. Seeing "a swell movie" at the Gem Theatre in the early 1930s was a rare novelty and luxury for Helen. But the Stephenses, the Herrings, and the Meloys were readers, primarily. Most likely, Helen's folks and a large sector of Fultonians had read *Petenera's Daughter*, authored by Henry Bellamann in 1926, for he was a hometown boy who landed a Harcourt, Brace and Company publishing contract for his first novel.

Bellamann's 1940 best-seller, *Kings Row*, drawn from childhood experiences, unflatteringly portrayed Fulton as a Peyton Place and drew the Callaway Kingdom's ire that rankled townsfolk for years. They recognized themselves in the book. The 1942 movie *Kings Row*, starring Ann Sheridan, Bob Cummings, and Ronald Reagan, perpetuated hard feelings and rage that Fultonians fostered toward a native son who had exposed the town's underside. But all seemed forgiven in the mid-1950s when Fulton hosted movie star Ronald Reagan and played *Kings Row* all day and night at the local theater. Likewise, in 1980, Fultonians invited California governor Reagan and his second wife, Nancy, to give a speech at Fulton's Churchill Memorial, which city fathers had coupled with Christopher Wren's famous St. Mary Aldermanbury Church, recently imported piece by piece from England.

The town thus built pride by inviting dignitaries and public figures and by reconstructing nonautochthonous sites with which to mantle fame and lure tourists to the locale. Over the years, responding to the call to come to Fulton were George Washington Carver (guest speaker for the opening of a new "colored" school), and Hillary Clinton (campaigning for her husband's first presidential term), and Mikhail Gorbachev (who made the pilgrimage after the fall of the Berlin Wall). There have been many others. Just as they had transplanted Wren's masterpiece in total, townsfolk ingeniously appropriated a sizable slab of the Berlin Wall and resurrected it on the campus of Westminster College.

Fultonians read *The Inside of the Cup*, a novel written in 1912 by Winston Churchill, not the British political giant but a St. Louis native of similar vintage. Published by Macmillan's Grosset and Dunlap, the novel enjoyed a second printing in 1913; his other books came long into the 1930s. Some confused the two Churchills; their confusion was compounded when the British Sir Winston Churchill came to Fulton in 1946. Margaret Maunders wrote, "Plans are shaping up for the biggest historical event to hit Fulton since Jefferson Davis spoke here in 1875—an event which will put the town in the world spotlight and cause reporters, photographers, newsreel men and upwards of 50,000 spectators to converge from all directions on the tiny metropolis."[7]

Fulton provided the platform from which Churchill gave his "iron curtain" speech. Consequently, Fulton's Winston Churchill Memorial contains memorabilia of Sir Winston Churchill and books by the American author of the same name.

Helen Stephens' contribution to Fulton's fame, however, preceded Sir Winston's and likewise loomed worldwide.

As a kid, Helen enjoyed popular, cheap pulp fiction, such as the crime-fighter "Doc Savage, Man of Bronze" stories by another Missouri author, Lester Dent. The Stephenses read the rugged yet refined hometown paper, the *Kingdom Daily Sun Gazette*, as well as the *Missouri Telegraph, Kansas City Star, St. Louis Globe-Democrat, Ladies Home Journal, Farmer's Almanac, Reader's Digest,* and *Coronet*.

From these sources of information, their German and non-German relatives and neighbors found cause for debate. They aired their stance on whether a woman, Jeannette Rankin, a Republican from Montana, elected in 1916, should be in Congress; they discussed the rights and wrongs of the women's suffrage amendment passed in 1919 and what caused the stock market crash that same year. The fine points of Roosevelt's New Deal were rehashed, as were local matters of contention, racial segregation, and especially war issues as editorially slanted to them in their newspapers. An adage of the day, that little peepers had big ears, elucidates Helen's upbringing. By the time she began school, many such discussions had filtered in, and they were not lost on the only and precocious child of Bertie Mae and Frank Stephens.

In the first five years of her life, Helen was doted upon, attended to, talked to, and treated as though she were a person older than her years. She was instructed and disciplined by a bevy of relatives, especially on the Herring side. They were devoted grandparents. Grandpa William T. Herring, together with family friend Fred Schraen, was a devout founding elder and builder of Little Dixie Christian Church in southern Callaway County in the early 1900s. This girl child was the center of her grandparents' and her mother's world prior to her brother's birth.

As the postwar recovery years unfolded, the Stephens kids—sitting near the crystal radio set or scooted around the supper table—listened to talk about those hard times and heard speculations on what President Coolidge might do in his second term to help the farmer. Helen said, "We kids didn't feel poor 'cause everyone who farmed was in the same boat. Some folks got things from the Sears catalog, but we farmers mostly had to make do for ourselves."[8]

From that cold, gray Missouri morning when Helen's life began, people opined about her appearance, her behavior, and her talents, and they voiced various expectations for her. As she grew into a towering, self-conscious adolescent, friends and neighbors said that when she ran, this rough-and-tumble tomboy's large feet flapped like wings and her arms pumped like steam pistons. The best thing Helen did with her hands was to play the harmonica, although it wasn't considered a feminine thing to do. Later, she would say, "The music that I play may not sound very sweet, but I get a lot of amusement out of playing cowboy songs on the thing, hill-billy numbers too."[9] Back then, by playing the harmonica, Helen already was emulating her idol, Babe Didrikson, and her favorite radio personality and newspaper columnist, that Indian flyboy from Oklahoma, Will Rogers.

Mrs. Stephens wanted her daughter to learn to play the piano, but Helen said, "somehow I just couldn't sit still that long. I had a hankering to get outdoors too much, I suppose, for me to learn to play the piano. Much to my mother's dislike . . . for it was unladylike. . . . I did the usual farmhand chores, riding and herding cattle, sheep, and so on, helping garden, plant corn, and pitch hay of course. In the process, I was developing a strong healthy body, working in the fresh air and eating solid, no-frill food grown on our own farm."

When she became "a young lady" with a yard-long sports record, folks assessed her as an oddity, though within sports circles, she was viewed as a champion among champions. Girls—females—ladies—in those days were not supposed to be interested in, and certainly should not excel in nor be equally gifted in sports as boys were.

Helen's father, Frank Elmer Stephens, worked for firebrick companies in Fulton and in Mexico, Missouri. He hauled clay for V. E. "Jake" Reed, the owner of a strip mine company off Highway F, near Fulton. But he turned to farming after he, at the age of twenty-seven, married Bertie Mae Herring, twenty-three, who had graduated from William Woods College in the spring of 1916.[10] Their wedding occurred at the old Herring homestead among family and friends on September 2, 1916. It was officiated by the Reverend Mervill Hutchinson of the Christian Church (Disciples of Christ) of Fulton. Bertie's father, William T. Herring, and sister, Sallie B. Rice, signed the marriage certificate as witnesses.

Scant information about Frank's side of the family has been uncovered, even with the research skills of a professional genealogist. Among the bridegroom's relatives at the wedding were three brothers, Charles, Oliver, and Ray, and their sister, Laura. Frank's father, William Isaac Stephens, was known to enjoy his drink and (according to what Helen had been told) was chased off by his sons once they had reached the age of maturity, which in those days occurred with puberty. Said Helen, "Frank didn't take a drop, except on special occasions, during Thanksgiving dinner or on New Year's, or in the company of friends who offered it." Drinking alcohol (the genesis to their domestic fights) was one thing a Christian lady like Bertie Mae, brought up under the strong influence of churchgoing parents aligned with the temperance crusade of Carry Nation, did not capitulate to easily. Unhappily, Bertie did not get along with her mother-in-law, Elizabeth Shaw Stephens, a poor farmwife of lesser education and greater sufferance; yet Lizzy allied with Bertie's antiliquor stance, for good reason.

The Herrings urged their hardworking son-in-law to quit his seasonal delivery job in town and become a farmer, to work rather than go to war. By 1917, Frank Stephens was working for himself as a farmer and stockman. He was one of seven children (two girls, five boys) and well accustomed to the hard work bequeathed a dirt farmer's son. Being his own boss better suited his strongly independent nature, a trait he would pass down to both his children. Farming during the Great Depression and war years might try his strength and perseverance, but he meant to be at home with his family, rather than travel on uncertain country roads and be subject to the fluctuating brickmaking industry. As a married man, and now a tenant farmer, he could expect the children he fathered to help make his farm a success. By the summer of 1917, Frank's young wife Bertie Mae was expecting a baby. The new farmer and soon-to-be father wanted and needed a large family of sons.

The newlyweds rented a farm in Callaway County east of Business 54, west of the Illinois Central Gulf Railroad. Here, Frank Stephens harvested crops of wheat, barley, corn; he tended apple, grape, and cherry orchards; he marketed pigs, raised chickens, and hired the help of a farmhand, at five dollars a day, when he could afford it. It was a farm of 140 acres of fertile land located where the William Woods campus stands today. It was wintertime on this tenant farm-land when Bertie Mae gave birth to their first child.

Frank Stephens took the chubby, nine-pound infant into his arms and said he really had hoped the first one would be a boy. He looked at the birthmark, about the size and color of a large, ripe plum on Helen's forehead just above her eyebrow and rubbed it with his thumb. Their conversation went something like this: "What's this?" he asked. Bertie said, "Just a birthmark. She's okay, see? What'll we call her?" And he said, "Whatever you want, Bertie, but I want our next child to be a boy." He put Helen into the cradling arms of his wife and left the room.

Blaming herself, Helen's mother accepted the birthmark as explained by an old wives' tale. She thought her child's marking had been caused when, a month before giving birth to Helen, she had been startled by a cow that broke through the fence and ran amok in the front yard. Surprised and frightened, Bertie had raised her hands to her own forehead, touching the exact place on her brow where Helen's mark appeared on hers. Her baby's birthmark, she felt, was her fault. Concerned for her child's "life-marking," as she called it, Mrs. Stephens consulted the family doctor, who assured her it was nothing to worry about. It was too near the baby's eyes, he said, to be removed.

Eight years later, still worrying about the embarrassment the blemish would cause Helen, Mrs. Stephens tried a folk remedy to remove it. During Grandpa Herring's funeral in 1926, Mrs. Stephens lifted her father's hand from his coffin and touched it to the purple spot on her child's forehead.[11] But the birthmark remained.

By the time Frank got his wish for a son, Bertie had endured two miscarriages, and the family had moved again, to the east side of the Chicago–Alton railroad line, on property not far from the Herring homestead. Their second child, Robert Lee Stephens, arrived on April 16, 1923, in the house where Grandma Herring had given birth to Helen's mother. Bertie Mae and Helen had situated themselves at Grandma Annie's so she could help with the birthing of the child and look after Helen as well. Frank stayed home to tend to the farm animals.

According to Helen, with his son in his arms, Frank was a happy man: "We're going to have more boys like this healthy little scrapper," he said, smiling and pulling a tiny fist. Now he could put his hope in this son and have a farmer's expectation that this child one day would work the fields alongside him. But no more sons or daughters would follow. Only two children would be born to Bertie Mae and Frank Stephens. Frank's joy was short-lived, and his inner turmoil magnified when the doctor said that his wife was too frail to bear more children.[12]

Bertie asked her five-year-old what she thought of her baby brother, and Helen said, "He ain't got no hair," and questioned, "Why can't we keep a baby pussycat in the house, instead?"

Sibling rivalry emerged once Robert was old enough to follow after his big sister and as the two vied for their parents' attention. Robert soon adored his big sister, for she ran faster, jumped farther, and played harder than most of their friends. Helen felt protective of her little brother, whom she called "R. Lee." She played school with R. Lee, read to him, and taught him to read, and when she fished for bluegill or crappie, R. Lee tagged along.

The children mostly relied on each other for play. Their nearest playmates lived several miles from the Stephens farm, and there were only two girls among them for Helen to play with. All seven Haymart children (Clifford, Homer, Ralph, Clayton, etc.) were boys, and it was under their influence that Helen tried smoking corn-silk cigarettes. She lunged headlong into other boyish adventures. She pretended she was Annie Oakley. First she carried a BB gun, then a .22-caliber rifle, shooting crow in her daddy's cornfields and rabbits in her mother's garden, and in the woods, she banged gray squirrels out of oak trees as easily as any of the boys could.

Though she understood the necessity of killing crop pests and hunting wild game to put food on their table, she never grasped nor forgave the cruelty she saw in her father. She was sickened by one particular task he had given her. Just before supper, he made her get the six new kittens from the barn, put them in a burlap gunnysack, take them down to the creek, and drown them. Too many mouths to feed, he said; too many cats in the barn. She told him she didn't want to do it, but he told her, "Don't come to supper 'til you've done it." Afterward, forlorn and sad, her eyes tear-reddened, solemnly she came to the table but had no appetite.

Theirs was a modest house surrounded by pastures, meadows, woodlands, and fields of corn and grain that Frank tilled and harvested without the luxury of a tractor. Neighbors used John Deere equipment, but not Frank; he could not afford them. From their small, two-story frame, almost hidden under elm, cottonwood, and oak trees, she watched her daddy walk behind a plow pulled by mule or horse. Helen could see one of the tributaries of Middle River from the kitchen window, if she strained a bit. A main thread of that river ran through Frank's fields as though it owned the land. The mouth of the Middle

River opened about five miles northwest of town; its waters bore tributary springs that created two creek beds, which joined the main flow, running toward the Missouri River before spilling out somewhere between the settlements of Cote Sans Dessein and the little town of Mokane.

Just three miles southwest of Fulton, this second farm that Frank worked was on hilly slopes, and while the land was fertile, it was rocky, and the creek beds running through it were seasonal afflictions for a man tied to the land the way Helen's father was. Each spring Frank's crops seemed cursed by if not lost to flooding. Helen remembers her daddy's wistful longings for the flatlands northwest of Fulton, land he called the prairies, land he couldn't afford. And though the Stephens kids worked long, hard hours to help make the land produce a living for the family, they found time to play, as children always do. But their parents' lives were difficult, made lean by devastating droughts and vanquishing floods. Leisure hours were too few for Helen's mother, who was timid and shy but craved more from life than farmwork.

In contrast, Helen's father was a gregarious man who had to be his own boss. In spite of its difficulties, he loved farmwork, and he loved to talk about it. Short, about five feet seven inches and sinewy in build, Frank Stephens was quick-tempered and often in disputes with his neighbors, many of whom viewed him as odd. One neighbor nicknamed him "Flake." Helen's childhood friend Julia Spearman said Flake tended to be argumentative and wasn't well liked at all. Some said he especially enjoyed the company of the women. At butchering time, for instance, Frank could be found in the kitchen "sometimes supervising the canning or helping with some other woman's chore," while the menfolk gathered outside on the porch or somewhere in the farmyard. Another neighbor said Flake charmed even the stock animals and told how "Mister Frank led a boar runnin' wild with romantic intentions, somehow guided the animal, rope-tied at the leg, down a footpath through the woods."

Not an easy feat, and it was a feat some perceived as supernatural.

Everyone knew Robert Lee was Frank's favored child. "Bobbie Lee was the spittin' image of his dad," the neighbor said. "He was hard on the boy hisself, but when talkin' to others, little Bob couldn't do no wrong."

But Helen had a different slant on the boy.

"I treated him like a pet," she said. "Being five years older and so much bigger, things got a little rough for him. Those were proverbial times." Like the time when, roughhousing, she accidentally closed a closet door on his hand. But as he got older, he gave back a measure of what she put out. Once, with a horseshoe toss, R. Lee broke her thumb. As a means of tormenting a pesky little brother, she said, she would stroll by R. Lee who was sitting, maybe reading something, and flip her hand over the back of his head "and ruffle up his new bowl haircut, then I'd run like mad. I could be pretty much of a terror," Helen admitted. "I was rough as a cob and preferred wearing denim overalls. Mother would always say, 'Helen, slow down! Quit rippin' around.' Or she'd say to me, 'Act like a lady. Cross your legs.'" Helen could slow down, could concentrate no matter what was going on around her, when she decided to read something. She read "advanced literature for a child her age," according to friend Julia. "She read any newspaper or magazine at hand" and could be seen sitting somewhat quietly, if only occasionally, in the pews of Fulton's Methodist Church. Julia recalls Helen's mother as mild-mannered and indulgent of her daughter. Julia overheard a friend's telling remark: "The only time I ever see Helen sitting still is when she's readin'."

Helen's mother also loved to read. She dressed neatly, was trim, and given to a pleasant manner for anyone who showed up at her doorstep. Julia said Mrs. Stephens was considered by some to be too refined a lady to be a farmer's wife, "soft and gentle spoken, prim and proper." She was one of four children of William T. and Annie Meloy Herring; the others were Sally B., Nolan "Jack," and Otis Paul, whom everyone called "Tommy." Bertie was taller than her husband by a few inches. She was musically gifted, as were others in her family; she had large, graceful hands, perfect for playing the upright Wurlitzer piano she brought with her when she married Frank. She also brought her Irish harp. Not many rural homes were furnished with a piano; the expense could be as much as several hundred dollars. But the Herrings and the Meloys—and a few members from the Stephens side of the family—were accustomed to Sunday afternoon musical gatherings. Pulling Bertie's pride and joy out from the wall, various family members joined their mandolins, violins, banjos, harmonicas, and their voices; it was a day that gave Bertie Mae a few hours of pleasure. Joining in on the fun, Helen gravitated to the harmonica. Bertie wanted both her children to play piano, and so she gave them lessons on her Wurlitzer.

The period during the mischievous ages of eight through eleven was one of rapid growth for Helen. For a time, she seemed accident prone. She fell from a pear tree while doing acrobatics. Once, "just racin' back and forth" through the wagon barn, Helen ran a pitchfork right through her big toe. Hearing screams, Helen's father came to help. With a quick jerk, he removed the fork. To prevent infection, he sucked blood from the wound and filled it with moistened tobacco, a homespun remedy that worked, but he scolded her for being so careless.

Another time, nine-year-old Helen entrapped herself in an ownership dispute with her little brother. According to her version, the two children jointly saved tinfoil and built up a ball of the silvery paper wrappings from chewing gum, Hershey bars, candies, her father's store-bought cigarettes, and other sources. Perhaps they saved tinfoil because, like string during the Depression, it could be put to other uses. Perhaps they saved it for fun because it looked pretty. In any case, they played in the house that day because it was raining, and for some reason, Helen wanted R. Lee to "divvy-up" her share of the tinfoil. R. Lee held back, saying the tinfoil ball was all his. They scuffled, and then for picking on her little brother, Helen's father banished her to her upstairs bedroom. The nine-year-old protested, "That's unfair!" and warned that she wasn't going to stay put in her room for rightly trying to get back what belonged to her. One strong will recognized another; Mr. Stephens padded up the stairs behind her and locked her in her room. But then R. Lee came tiptoeing upstairs "just to taunt me," Helen said, and their conversation went something like this: "Now what're you going to do, Hellie? Huh? Huh?" Yelling through the door, she advised him, "I'm slippin' through the window. I'm standin' on the porch roof. I'm going to escape! I'm going to jump off . . . and run away from home." He answered, "You won't neither, you can't. It's too far down!"

And so Helen jumped. She landed on wet ground with a thud and, letting out a banshee wail, put terror in R. Lee's imagination. Her left wrist snapped. Fortunately, Helen said, "the little snot told on me," and her father found a wet and wounded Helen lying on the grass. As night fell, he fashioned a homemade arm splint, then hitched up the wagon. Soon, in a heavy downpour, they were driving into the darkness of the night to visit a doctor.

One summer when Helen was still a preadolescent, a more serious accident happened to her. Having finished lunch, Helen stomped outside. "Doogie," a shepherd-collie mix, awoke from his snooze on the shady porch, ready for action. From the porch floor, Helen quickly grabbed up a piece of wood shingle that she had carved into an arrowhead. She noticed Doogie's teeth marks on the carving. She stuck it between her teeth and bit down to hold the arrowhead firmly; a tie-string threaded through a hole carved in the arrowhead dangled down the side of her mouth. She shook her head at Doogie as if to say, Try to get it.

"I don't know why I did it," Helen said, "it was just something a kid would do." Doogie rose swiftly and galloped toward her. Instantly, as Helen jumped off the porch to escape, her foot caught on something. She tripped and fell. Her chin hit the dirt first, and somehow the wooden arrowhead lodged into her throat. It punctured and ruptured her larynx. Blood gushed from her mouth down her neck and chest. Helen pulled on the tie-string, trying to pull the arrow from her mouth, but it would not dislodge, and pain almost made her swoon into unconsciousness. She struggled to get upright and staggered into the kitchen. R. Lee was the first to see his blood-splattered sister. He screamed, "What happened, Hellie? What's wrong?" But Helen couldn't answer.

Soon he and Helen were standing, holding hands, next to their mother, while their father hitched up the wagon. Doogie, leaning mournfully quiet against R. Lee's leg, sensed something was wrong. Mrs. Stephens had thickly wrapped

Helen's neck with towels. And she told Helen a second time—as she helped her daughter step up into the wagon—in a voice firm yet reassuring, "Hold the towels together and don't, for any reason, loosen the wrappings." She and Mr. Stephens had agreed that leaving the arrowhead in place would help to prevent a hemorrhage. "Is Hellie gonna die this time?" six-year-old R. Lee asked. His mother answered, "No, Ollie" (her nickname for R. Lee). "She's just going to visit Dr. McCubbin again."

Dr. McCubbin, an eye, ear, nose, and throat specialist with Fulton's School for the Deaf, told Mr. Stephens that a surgical procedure was immediately necessary to extract the object from Helen's throat, and he feared that an on-coming infection might cause serious damage. Helen tried to hold back the tears trickling down her cheeks; but pain and now fear took charge of her.

A month passed before Helen could talk. By the time school commenced in the fall, she spoke without pain in her throat, but she spoke hoarsely. Her voice from then on would carry a low and raspy quality. In adolescence, her low, mannish voice seemed to stigmatize her with another kind of birthmark, and it became yet another source of embarrassment.

While Helen was recovering, Mrs. Stephens thought this would be a good time to renew her efforts to teach her to play the piano. But "the lessons never took," Helen said.

Middle River School was west of Fulton on County Road H and about a mile from the Stephens farm. It was a little, one-room country schoolhouse that served the community's first through eighth grades, some twenty-five pupils in all, and more than 60 percent were girls. In all kinds of weather, Helen trotted alongside her cousin Thornton Meloy, who always rode horseback to school. Holding onto the stirrup, Helen kept pace with Thornton, jumping ditches, crossing streams, and racing down dirt paths to arrive on time. When Thornton broke his horse away from her grasp, she imagined Pegasus. Pegasus—her competition. Sud-denly her feet took wing and she ran ahead. "Well," she said of that horse, "he was windbroke, wasn't very fast."[13] Thornton, two years younger than Helen, confirmed the story, remembering Helen as a big, muscular tomboy who not only outran his nag but outran all the boys during recess and, unlike the other girls, played schoolyard football with the boys at lunchtime.[14]

Helen's favorite place on the farm was a spot known as the salt lick, a place twenty feet in diameter where nothing grew. Her father plowed a reasonable berth around it when he cultivated his cornfield. In midsummer, ripening stalks of corn created a privacy wall for reclusive or adventuring children scaveng-ing for flint stones and arrowheads. In frontier days, the salt lick attracted deer, the deer attracted native Indians, and Indians hunted there with bow and ar-row. Hellie's and R. Lee's prized possession was not the ball of tinfoil they squabbled over but a gallon-size canning jar filled with "real, live arrowheads!"

On one occasion, wearing overalls that Uncle Jack had given her, Helen lay daydreaming in this nook of seclusion. She clutched several arrowheads in her hand. She stuck a foxtail weed between her teeth, chewed on its sweetness awhile, and stretched her arms lazily, then tucked an elbow to cushion her head. In the warm summer afternoon, her thoughts drifted among the clouds where she imagined figures and faces changing shape slowly. She watched the sun burst forth, then disappear behind clouds again. It was a peaceful place, a place where the eight-year-old child easily drifted into a dream-filled sleep. Soon, she felt herself racing, not alongside cousin Thornton on horseback, but in a real race! She heard thunderous applause as she broke the winner's ribbon, and someone handed her a silver winner's cup. A rush of emotion pumped through her heart as she lifted the shiny victor's cup over her head. Colorful flags waved everywhere. She felt a flush of breeze. Again she heard thunderous applause as a ring of people surrounded her.

It was a dream so vivid that, awaking from it, she sat up abruptly. Then she bounded through the tasseled corridors of her father's field, dry cornstalks rustling as she ran. She wondered, could her dream come true? Could she ever run a real race? Would her mother be proud of her if she did?

Mrs. Stephens wasn't impressed with Helen's dream as she told about it. She listened to Helen, breathless from running in from the fields, chattering about a silver cup, the winner's prize, applauding crowds of strangers. "Slow down, Helen," she said. "Slow down. Settle yourself." Mrs. Stephens warned her daughter to tend the henhouse and to get on with her chores before her father came in.

She promised she would, right away. Disappointed, Helen vanished like a breeze from the kitchen, its screen door banging behind her.

Her mother called after her, "You've got to weed the garden some!" Her voice carried a melody in it even when it told her what she had to do, Helen said.

As a young woman, Helen later explained, "Perhaps my dream was a premonition of what was to be. I didn't know anything about clocked running times, but I knew I sure could run before I turned ten." In a letter to Brenda Chiles, Helen told how she spent her early years on a farm in the Middle River community, doing what farm kids do:

> herding livestock (cattle, horses, and sheep) either on foot or on horseback, fishing, working in the garden, taking care of chickens, turkeys, ducks, etc. I had one brother, R. Lee, who was five years younger. We played ball and did lots of running equally enjoyed by our dogs. I attended a rural country school [District No. 57] that no longer exists. . . . It was there I excelled at playing games with the boys and especially out-running them and out-hitting them in baseball. . . . as a group of us walked to and from school together, we had a daily contest in trying to see which one of us could

jump a particular fence, the widest ditch, etc. In other words, from an early age I was enjoying that clean country air, eating good wholesome food, and building my body with a lot of exercise.[15]

Helen's father, badly needing her help, treated his strong, strapping daughter much as he would have treated a stepson. By depending on her to do a sizable share of farmwork, he conveyed trust in her physical capabilities, though he never praised her for what she accomplished. Helen later said that her early athletic training came in the guise of a 140-acre spread about five miles southwest of Fulton on the Stephens family farm. She ran, she said, just for the fun of it, just for the joy of running.[16] To a tomboy whose imagination ran ahead of her feet, cornfield ditches became tracks, and field pits substituted as pads for the standing or running jump. Five-foot wooden fences formed hurdles. Beanpoles and horseweed shoots magically turned into javelins when Helen and R. Lee played Indians—aiming these at each other. Cow piles and rocks curiously transformed into discus platters. It was fun. Carefree. And Helen loved it more than anything.

She was misquoted as saying, "My brother [cousin Howard McAllister] was the state high school hurdles champion. At family gatherings, he'd put up bean poles for hurdles and I'd try right along with him and the other boys."[17] There were no organized sports for grammar school girls, but Helen heard that the high school coach sometimes let girls who could run fast try out for a Missouri State Athletics letter. She told R. Lee that she was going to bring one home.

By that age, Helen's awareness of the difficulties and differences between her mother and father had become clear. She placed her allegiance with her mother, always taking her side when disagreements raised her father's voice and turned her mother into a somber pillar of silence for long periods of time. She saw the power of her father's temper, imprinted the sharp effectiveness of his tongue, and, like her mother on occasion, she too felt the quick heat of his hand. Fighting with his wife, he yelled so loud Helen easily heard him from her room upstairs: "If you wanted things different, well, you should've hooked Ollie, not me!" He yelled and complained at Bertie regularly, Helen said, for not fulfilling his idea of a farmwife.

Frank's younger brother, Oliver, was inclined toward books and music. "Ollie" was well liked and quickly embraced by the Herrings and the Meloys. Helen early on developed a special fondness for quiet and patient Uncle Ollie. Soon after her brother Robert Lee's arrival, little Hellie took to calling the baby by his first initial and middle name, "R. Lee," which when spoken with a full midwestern twang, sounded to Frank like she deliberately was saying "Ollie." It only confirmed in his mind the fondness his wife and daughter felt for Oliver; it played out as a rejection of his own rough-hewn qualities and deepened the rift between husband and wife, father and daughter.

As Helen raced toward adolescence, the world's rawness and confinements descended upon her. Like most children of farm life, she knew how animals reproduced before she attended school. Lessons in human sexuality, not taught at home nor in school, were learned when she was in the fourth grade. A relative (now deceased, whom Helen would not identify) whispered to her while they were playing in the schoolyard that he wanted to show her something. He said it was in the barn. Up in the loft, a hundred yards or so from the schoolhouse, the teenager unbuttoned his work jeans and showed Helen his erect penis. He told her to touch it. Then he said, "Show me your thing." When she pulled down her overalls, he shoved her back against a wall and pushed his penis into her vagina.

"It hurt like blazes," she said. "I almost passed out. I don't know how long we were there, maybe ten minutes." When the school bell rang, they climbed down from the loft and went on to school as though nothing had changed. He told her, "We kin do it again, tomorrow. Want to?" She was naturally curious at nine years old and said yes, she wanted to. The two kids went up to the loft several more times, before and after the school bell rang, until their teacher discovered them and told Helen's parents. "I don't think she told *his* parents," Helen said, "but when Dad visited them, that put a stop to it." Her parents' reactions were at both poles: Bertie had asked her to explain the stains on her clothing; Frank grabbed his rifle and made a heat-of-the-moment call on the parents of the molester. He threatened, "I'll kill 'em if he ever touches my daughter again."

When later she was asked how she felt about it, Helen spoke of being enticed into the barn, sexually violated, and overpowered by a sixteen-year-old. She told of it almost as an afterthought, saying it was a pleasurable experience that hurt and frightened her and turned her away from boys from that point on.

Another sexual incident happened when her teacher stayed overnight with her family. As was the custom in those days, teachers were hosted several nights by the parents of their school children. Helen remembers that the teacher slept in her bed, and she herself on a pallet on the floor. She said her teacher "paraded to bed in the nude, which excited me somehow, but I didn't know what it meant. In the dark hours of the night, she let me feel her pussy and that got me very excited and interested."

In childhood, Helen had been happy. On the farm, as the eldest, the first born, the big sister, the bright child, Helen had been given freedom and responsibility that she took to easily. Grandparents and uncles doted on the child whose quick and eager mind caught the thoughts in conversations across the kitchen table "of a Sunday afternoon" when all the family gathered together. Her mother, too, doted on Helen, and those first five years of adoration firmly grounded the girl child with a self-confidence that complete acceptance and unconditional love underpinned. So, when her brother arrived and removed Helen temporarily from center stage by his crying, fussing, and bed-wetting, Helen's generosity of heart was tested. She was accustomed to getting what she wanted, and it was a trial to share parents and grandparents and toys and friends with a newcomer.

Helen grew up in an environment of rural poverty, of racism and social class divisions—the old money wealthy families and the very poor that Bellamann had described in *King's Row*. But she said she didn't know the bridlements of her family's status. She lived as though she wore blinders, like those strapped onto the head of her father's strongest workhorse, forging straight ahead to the end of the long, long row. She had the high metabolism, darting impatience, speed, and spirit of a quarter horse.

Even though her father seemed distant, a small man with big worries, his Goliath mercurial temperament rarely unsettled her, for she was equally strong-willed and uncommonly stubborn. Though confident, rowdy, and rambunctious in grammar school, Helen as a high school freshman would soon bridle herself into an uncharacteristic shyness and awkwardness—confronting cliquish city kids, bounding headlong into the manners and puppy-love behavior of adolescence.

Sexually aware, sexually awkward, teenage Helen began journeying toward self-acceptance.

2

Popeye Becomes the Fulton Flash

The kids up here hardly know my first name, they called me "Popeye" so long. "Popeye—the spinach eater"—that's been my name all through high school.

—Helen Stephens, April 4, 1935

*I*n fall 1931, the Middle River School tomboy entered Fulton High School at age thirteen years and seven months. She was a self-conscious teenager, peaking physically and racing into the last stages of adolescence. As a freshman, she was taller and stronger than her classmates, including most of the boys, and she looked "country." Dresses made her feel awkward; she preferred bib-trousers, felt more natural in denim overalls with shoulder straps and work shirts. She wore her hair bobbed short to keep it out of her face and liked going barefoot, but school policy didn't allow it. To understate it, socialization hit hard upon this poor farm girl as she made her own way among 256 other high schoolers.

Student newspapers shed light on what Helen experienced in her first year at Fulton High. Enrollment was up—45 seniors, 66 juniors, 45 sophomores, 100 freshmen—the result of the state's making funds available to needy families. This made it possible for the Stephenses to rent a room in town for their eldest child. There were no school buses then, and for some students, the distance to the school could be twenty miles. Borrowing Uncle Tommy's Ford or using their own buggy to transport Helen to school would have been inconvenient, expensive, and time-consuming. During the week, like most country kids, Helen stayed in town in a boarding room, the base from which she pursued a high school education. Helen shared a room with several girls. They brought food, clothing, and supplies to get them through the week and returned to their farm homes on weekends to help with chores.

Helen first lived on Sixth Street in the home of Miss Humphreys, an English teacher whose residence was about three blocks from school. Miss Humphreys resided with and cared for her father (a retired judge); her cousin, Miss Warene Clatterbuck, who was also a teacher, also lived there. Helen later moved to Miss Sadie Herford's house on Court Street. Both subleasers were respected spinster ladies who rented rooms only to worthy country girls determined to earn a high school diploma.

Two sisters, Charlene and Irene Carlton, shared a room down the hall. Helen initially shared a room with sixteen-year-old Bonnie Lammers. Bonnie's family lived about two miles from the Stephens farm; she had completed Phillmore Grade School by age fourteen and two years later began high school. As a sophomore, Bonnie moved in with a family who gave room and board in exchange for light housework, but at eighteen, she quit school to work in town at International Shoe Company. In the mid-1990s, Bonnie recalled that while most folks struggled through the economic depression, Helen's shoes had to be custom-made because her feet were women's size twelve.

At Miss Herford's, Helen cemented friendships with "later" Herford girls Leona Kemp and Louise Sampson and her distant cousin, Bonnie "Blue" Gooldy. Sarah Phillips stood apart from the more popular kids because her parents were hearing-impaired (graduates of Fulton's "deaf and dumb asylum") and were viewed as odd. The quiet, shy Julia Spearman soon became Helen's best friend. Straight-as-an-arrow "Julier" (as Helen called her) was an only child and had the distinction of having a stepfather. Julier excelled in French and math; Helen shone in history and English. The two girls exchanged homework in study hall. Julia remembers that their French teacher, Mr. McClannahan, reassigned Helen's seat in class, moving her away from Julia when Helen's long neck inadvertently stretched over Julia's shoulder during a test.

Helen said, "Unconsciously, I looked for and had friendships with kids who had good minds, those who were broad-minded and understanding, and all-around good scouts." It was natural that most of Helen's school friends were country kids. Citified Katherine "Katy" Jones, the best-looking girl in school, had hoards of friends, but Helen, Sarah, and Julia weren't among them.

In four years, the school would graduate 52 of 100 entering freshmen: 22 boys, 30 girls. In time, Helen would shine above them all as Fulton High's star pupil, academically, athletically, and, oddly enough, socially. But as a freshman and sophomore, she hardly glimmered among the student body. Though she stood out, it was for all the wrong reasons. Her large-figure rambunctiousness was viewed as a social *méfait*. Towering over classmates, she had nearly reached six feet tall by age fifteen. When she spoke, her low, gravelly voice made her seem all the more strange. She felt lucky just to be able to talk and too embarrassed to tell of the accident that caused her voice to turn husky. Also she was self-conscious about the raspberry birthmark on her forehead, tried hiding it with bushy bangs. Speaking of those early teenage days, she said, "I died a thousand deaths."

In the first week of Principal Newbolt's math class, classmate Isham Holland gave Helen a nickname that stuck. His own first name created spitting matches for some kids. Isham aspired to be—and became—a preacher (Church of God Holiness). His story in 1994 was that "big, old lanky Helen" strode hastily into their classroom, arriving after the teacher had called roll. As she took her seat in the back with other tall kids, Isham spoke up, saying, "There's Popeye now— hey, Popeye!" Holland said Helen was always willing and prompt to return any slight. She pulled an eraser from the chalk rack, slung it hard with retaliation in mind, and loudly greeted, Hi, Isshhhh! He ducked but got hit anyway.

The "handle" fit, for she was stronger, leaner, more muscular, and faster on her feet than any kid they had seen before. Ish thus forever tagged her to the then-popular but funny looking, spinach-eating cartoon character. True to form, Helen fought back, parroting the comic book sailor, proclaiming, "I yam what I yam!" So, what classmates espied was a jokester's pose and plain indif- ference to their assessment of her rough-hewn physique and giant, ungirlish strides. Helen said, "I didn't like that nickname, but I didn't let on. I acted like I liked it, joked around with it, and called myself Popeye the Great!"

No notice of "La Grand Popeye," however, occurred in the student paper as she caballed her way through the year. But she squirreled away each issue of *Hi-Life* and the once-yearly rag sheet called *Lo-Life*, both bearing news about Fulton High's popular kids, those who shunned her company.

What caused a stir that freshman year was the fact that Principal George P. Newbolt (some kids accented the "P," some the "bolt") had moved into his new house, on Nichols and Ninth, and invited everyone to a housewarming—and there would be dancing! Dancing? Was it a typographical error, or a joke? Religiously fundamental, George P. did *not* approve of dancing. It must be a mistake—the word *not* dropped from copy by a student editor! George P. was the older brother of Helen's childhood playmate Myra. Their farm was near the Stephens place, so Helen knew firsthand how strict the Newbolts were. In Prin- cipal Newbolt's eyes, Helen was nothing but a Middle River School roughneck, and he had good reason. Some years earlier—she couldn't remember why and she didn't know exactly what provoked her—she had torn after little "M'randy" in the schoolyard, swinging, punching, scratching, and pulling her hair, with a strong "urge to scalp her." Perhaps, she said, it was the influence of her un- known Cherokee relative. This outburst and unladylike behavior was not eas- ily forgiven and certainly was not forgotten.

The student paper also noted that twenty-seven girls under Miss Nellie Mae

Morrison's baton had tried out for Glee Club; the football squad had been entertained by seniors from Mexico, Missouri. It named those scheduled to address the student body: school board member Dr. Franc McCluer; Mayor Frank Baker; and William Woods College president Egbert Cockrell, speaking on the subject of higher education *for girls*, with Miss Jasper and *her* William Woods girls. The screed told how some teachers spent their summer vacations, most significantly, Coach W. Burton Moore, who had rooted for the St. Louis Browns in Sportsman's Field in St. Louis and also had trekked to Chicago's national track and field meet.

Moore was in his third teaching year at Fulton High. He had learned what he knew about track at Westminster College from Missouri-born Brutus Hamilton, the Olympic trackman who left Westminster to coach at the University of California. The deliberate, well-mannered, twenty-six-year-old Moore carried himself erect; his step conveyed the confidence of a young man at the threshold of his career. He was strikingly handsome and unmarried. Dozens of girls, including Helen, "carried crushes" for him.

Organized sports for females was a moot issue for the administrators of this small rural school; a girls' basketball team was nonexistent. Female students were expected to take P.E. (physical education), while boys engaged in various sports. In fact, many a mother wrote notes for their daughters to excuse them from gym class, and one sure way to do it was to pen a declaration of the female discomforts of puberty. The school's black and gold athletic letter *F*, proudly worn on school jackets, gave high status to the guys who won them. Boys, not girls, sought to win their school's letter and the state letter *M*, as well. Boys ran fifty yards in seven seconds flat to qualify for an *F*. Helen thought she would like to try for a track letter, just to see. It was an odd goal for a girl, and an improbable one, even if she had the speed for it.

That year, Helen played basketball with the Methodist Church girls, along with Martha Sue Faucett, Ophelia Squires, Bonnie Jo Gooldy, Martha Yancy, Gladys Rice, Louise Harrison, and Elizabeth Blattner. Coach Moore first spied Popeye in her junior year playing forward on this team and was struck by her aggressiveness. Like a tigress, she never let up—she was after the ball all the time. He wondered just how fast the tall tomboy could run.

The Depression hit the rural Midwest especially hard, and Helen's folks struggled to hold onto the Herring-Stephens family farm. Just after Christmas 1933, they defaulted on the deed of trust signed thirteen years earlier, secured by L. E. Gooldy, a relative of one of Helen's schoolmates. W. Ed Jameson, trustee and editor of the *Missouri Telegraph*, posted the news January 26. The public sale of their 115 acres (S35, T47, R10) on February 18 was a substantial abasement for Helen, who turned fifteen that month. D. P. Bartley paid $4,000 cash for the property. But a few weeks later, Helen's destiny lay at her feet.

That spring, Moore put her with several other girls at a starting point on the school's cinder driveway—just to clock them in the not-too-strenuous 50-yard dash. As he watched the fifteen-year-old move toward the starting line, he saw a shy, somber-faced kid. Her head slunk down so that her neck was barely visible, her eyes steeled straight ahead. She wore baggy pantaloons, the gym suit her mother made, and dirty sneakers. She didn't know a thing about running form. Said Helen, "I just ran, and when I finished, Coach kinda looked at his watch, puzzled-like, and asked would I mind runnin' it again. He said he didn't quite get my time."[1]

Moore was skeptical, having clocked her at 5.8 seconds. When she ran it that fast a second time, he knew he had something. A newsman weaving the story into mythic proportions wrote that Moore was so stunned at first by such talent that he wondered if his stopwatch was working right, so he took it to a jeweler to check it. According to Moore, that didn't happen, though it was an incredible moment, he said, to watch the untrained sophomore match the speed of champion girl sprinter Elizabeth "Betty" Robinson.[2] Robinson held the outdoor 50-yard world record at 5.8. And now, this greenhorn, natural-born athlete, ran it as easy as a breeze! He had found a likely new champion in this hometown girl. He recognized natural ability when he saw it, and it clearly had materialized in front of him—in the form of a gawky farm girl!

Helen said, "Coach knew he had a tiger by the tail, but he didn't know exactly what to do about it at that point."

Moore told his fiancée, Mary Lou Schulte (William Woods College graduate and Fulton High's music department head) about Helen's record-tying speed. He told Mary Lou that he didn't want to notify anyone just yet, because he didn't want to put false hopes in the girl but would work with her awhile to see what happened and to teach her some running form and technique. But how? Fulton High had no program for girls' track. He consulted a Westminster buddy, in confidence, to help him decide what to do about this girl. But the girls Helen out ran straight away told their parents, and within a few days, the local paper carried a few inches about Helen's feat. Some folks scoffed at Moore's claim. Some believed what they read but wished Helen's speed had been found in one of their boys. Some hardly noticed it, for news of President Roosevelt's New Deal captured their attention.

Mrs. Stephens wasn't sure just how she felt about having Helen's athletic achievement publicized in the paper. Herself an alum of William Woods College, Mrs. Stephens had urged her daughter to enroll in typewriting classes and hoped her daughter would qualify for a college scholarship, knowing their farm income couldn't afford college. She was proud of Helen's academics, proud that for the third year in a row she was an honor roll student. Despite a keen hatred of algebra, Helen had done well, though she was not as fast with figures as she was with her feet. Math was simple drudgery, but history, English, and social studies were her favorites. Helen now had cause to add athletics, sprinting in particular, to her list.

By the end of basketball season, Helen had scored the highest number of points in any one game of the girls' church leagues. In April, Moore had Helen sprinting on a straight dirt strip at East Elementary School at Bluff Street and St. Louis Avenue. In order to overreach the imaginary tape that marked a hundred yards, she ran into weeds. Soon, he had Helen running laps on Priest Field's cinder track at Westminster College and training with high school and college trackmen. He pounded into her eager mind to run *through* the tape, not *to* the tape, to run another ten yards past the finish line. As Moore put her through the rigors with his boys, he watched in amazement as she excelled in throwing discus and javelin and shot put, and in both broad and high jumps. "She's Amazonian," he said, "outrunning my boys even when she gives 'em a 100-yard lead in a 1-mile race."[3]

Fathers of some of these boys objected to Moore's efforts with Helen as an unwarranted intrusion because their sons lost races *to a girl*. Even so, several track boys felt chummy toward Helen, especially John C. Harris, who helped Moore line her up, trigger the starting gun, and clock her. Curiously, Helen laid off track practice during her junior year (fall 1933–spring 1934) and for part of her senior year. In mid-January 1935, she was back on the track. This hiatus may have been a result of the flack Moore had received for turning the athletic program coeducational. Or it might have been something else. In any case, many hearts were broken when Moore married Mary Lou Schulte over Christmas break.

Though "Helen Stevens [*sic*]" was listed as one of two joke editors that year, the January and March 1935 issues of *Hi-Life* awarded scant space to Popeye and her clique's activities, though Popeye's wit and quick turn of phrases become apparent by comparing issues of *Hi-Life* published before and after her graduation. These papers offered missionary C. F. McCall's words about Japan's moral superiority to the United States and its athletic inferiority; the mayor's address, excerpted, told of his experiences in the Great War "over there." *Hi-Life* reported that German-language students at Westport High, in Kansas City, were corresponding with pupils in Germany, that track practice began March 4 and several students were working toward athletic letters *M* and *F*, and that Coach Moore had six track meets scheduled for his boys. But Helen found no reference to the upcoming girls' National Amateur Athletic Union championships held in late March at the St. Louis Arena.

Moore wanted to seize this opportunity for Helen but needed two things: permission to enter Helen in the meet, and her two-dollar entry fee. He approached school superintendent J. Tandy Bush, then in his late forties, with

these requests and was told no, that Fulton High essentially would be embarrassingly represented by only one girl. Stern and wiry, Bush pointed out that
entering only Helen amounted to Fulton High's debut appearance in girls'
competition—begun at a national level. Not a good idea. Moore persisted.
Helen would make the school proud, he said, she was a sure thing to win second or third place in the 50-meter dash and might win several events.

Bush held firm. He said Moore was being foolhardy. He wasn't for it, and
he wouldn't spend school money on something likely to embarrass them. He
noted that not everyone was as keyed up about the tomgirl as Moore seemed
to be. He asked what her folks thought about this. Moore said he just couldn't
see passing up this once-in-a-lifetime opportunity. He said he spent considerable time thinking about Helen's prospects and several months getting her
ready for this meet. He told Bush that Mrs. Stephens wanted a college education for Helen but her father wanted her to quit school to take a job at the shoe
factory. But "sir," he said, "my wife will chaperone. I'll pay the entry fee myself."
So, Bush gave reluctant approval—saying something like, "Okay, go! Go and
come back quietly. I don't want another word about it."

"Friday. March 22, 1935. It's a date permanently chiseled in my memory,"
said Helen.

A hopeful Helen squirmed in the backseat of Moore's clanky old Ford; this
was her first real step toward the Olympics and she knew it. Helen's track buddies, John Harris and D. W. Herring in particular, and others loaded up in
another car to create Helen's first cheering section. It was raining in the early
morning as the cars caravaned northward on the two-lane blacktop from
Fulton to Kingdom City. At Highway 40, they sailed eastward three hours, exited
at the Red Feather Expressway, and then on to the arena.

In spite of stormy weather, over four thousand people filled the newly built
domed structure. Some seventy-five other hopefuls with chaperones and
coaches also had wended their way to St. Louis, coming from New York, Chicago, and Toronto.[4] Among the expected notables were two senior Olympic
titleholders, Betty Robinson, from Chicago, and Stella Walsh, a "foreigner." St.
Louis–based athletes coached by the city's 1928 Olympic sprinter, Dee Boeckmann, were the Ferrara sisters, Kathleen and Evelyn, Gertrude Webb (also a
1928 Olympian), Evelyn Hall, and Harriet Bland, the redheaded spitfire and
1932 Olympic "qualifier."

For the most part, Helen was an unknown quantity pitted against world-
class sprinters. But since Robinson was a no-show, Stella Walsh was the prospective winner. Walsh had lived in Cleveland, Ohio, since childhood, but her Olympic
wins were claimed by her native country, Poland. She was widely known as the
first woman to run 100 yards in less than 11 seconds. Stanislawa Walasiewicz
(repenned Stella Walsh, aka "the Polish Flyer") won track and field events in

1930 in Prague, in 1932 in Los Angeles at the Federation Sportive Feminine Internationale Olympics, and a gold medal in the 60 meters in 1934 in London. Everyone wanted to see Stella run; they had never seen nor heard of Helen Stephens, who just had her seventeenth birthday some two months earlier.

At the starting line in one of several trial heats, unbeatable Stella crouched confidently, a veteran competitor seven years Helen's senior. Helen took a side glance and thought, There she is, there's Stella. Helen knew Walsh's records well. But this was the first time she' had seen her in the flesh.

The fledgling Helen looked awkward and harmless as a newborn foal. She had a thatch of hair, cut blunt and short, that brought to mind a soft brush used too frequently for buffing shoes; her fast-growing bones forged her face into a block of angles and planes that only a pencil-sketch artist like Tom Benton would latch onto—and immortalize. She had no track uniform, no track shoes of her own. To dress appropriately for this, her first public competition, Helen borrowed sweats from Johnny Lutz and running spikes from T. J. Neukomm, two Westminster "men."

"I couldn't wear my gym suit and sneakers to a national competition!" Helen said. "Aw, I really looked like a hayseed." Helen the Hayseed. But Helen grabbed the crowd's attention and won their devotion anyway. It didn't matter how she looked. For, in her first competition, the shot put, she tossed up first place, heaving the eight-pound iron ball 39 feet 7¼ inches, easily beating out district titleholder Theresa Wiesler. Then, with her mind set to win the standing broad jump, she leaped 8 feet 8¼ inches strong. This victory was hers, too.

Now with two events in her pocket, she was ready at the mark in the trial heat of the 50-meter sprint (her favorite event); she felt sure she could take on any competition, Stella included. When the gun went off, her friends froze momentarily, astounded as Helen faltered. For an instant, the small crowd of supporters who put their hopes in her thought all was lost. She'd gotten off with a poor start but in a split second kicked up speed and was foot to foot with the St. Louis favorite, Harriet Bland. Helen sped like an arrow shot from a bow and with a desperate lunge at the tape, broke it and took victory away from the petite contender, in 6.6 seconds!

Next, the final heat, and the bets were on. Did Missouri have a new record holder in this newcomer, this Stephens girl, this country kid from nowhere? Could she beat Stella?

This time running against the Polish Flyer and Faye Epstein, Olive Hinder, Thelma Norton, and Marie Cottrell, Helen made a good takeoff. She took the lead, broadened it, and victory was hers, again repeating her 6.6 time, some say a full four feet ahead of second-placer Stella Walsh.

Spectators went wild. Sportswriters went crazy, bolting onto the track, passing by the former titleholder, pushing toward the kid who had just stomped Stella, immediately penning sobriquets: "The Missouri Express," "The Fulton Flash."

St. Louis Post-Dispatch cub reporter Damos Kerby screamed in her face, "Do you know what you've just done?"

Helen, panting for breath, pulled her thoughts together. "I . . . thaank . . . I wunh," she drawled in her midwestern tongue.

"You, you just outran Stella Wala-sie-wicz!" he shouted, fumbling Stella's surname.

"Who?" Helen said, grinning broadly, tossing a quizzical look. "Stella who?" Her dry wit, which she comfortably practiced as joke editor for the school paper, spread out a reporter's picnic. She knew who Stella was. Sure, she knew. She had Walsh's picture hanging in her room, stuck full of darts.

After things quieted down, her buddies crowded around to congratulate her. David "Swede" Herring lumbered forward, handed his program to her, and asked for her autograph. He already had Stella's on the cover; he wanted Helen's next to it. She took his pen and wrote her name in large letters right across Stella's signature. Pal John Harris stood quietly nearby, watching it all. He remarked, "Well, *that* pretty well cancels out Stella!"

Within moments, St. Louis AAU president Norman F. Rathert sent word to Coach Moore, asking if he could make dinner reservations for him, his wife, and Helen. Like many of the men holding AAU offices, Rathert moved among wealthy, old-money members of the Missouri Athletic Club; most were doctors, lawyers, political Indian chiefs. Rathert, a dentist, was the young (in his thirties), new club president and a member of the board of governors of the national AAU.

At Garavelli's Restaurant, a very fancy place in Helen's eye, Rathert grasped at a glance Helen's circumstance and expressed interest in helping. He offered to back Helen, to provide free dental care *if* she came to St. Louis. If she would align with the Missouri Athletic Club, he could get cash support from others in the area—*if* she proved herself the kind of kid worthy of it, *if* she trained diligently and listened to her coach. The men lingered in the parking lot, talking about what to do next, while Helen and Mrs. Moore waited in the car. Good-byes were said several times before Rathert withdrew, satisfied that Moore would apprise him of each move.

During the drive back to Fulton, Helen explained her "Stella who?" remark. She said she was so happy that she was trying to compose a joke in her mind. And with those words, Coach Moore said, she had diminished her competition even more.

Helen's glibness became the fuel that the media used to inflame poor Stella, who just wouldn't believe her competition didn't know who *she* was, hadn't heard of the world-famous Stella Walsh! When newsmen quizzed Stella on how she felt about taking second place to an unknown seventeen-year-old who didn't even know her name, she quipped, fairly flabbergasted, "Oh, it's . . . just a fluke."[5] They goaded her on with the "Stella who?" gibe, provoking her to strike out. Helen was just a greenie from the sticks who jumped the gun at the starting line, Stella said. "I can beat her anytime I try," she boasted.

Reporters rang up Helen Saturday morning to ask about a rematch and tell her what Stella said. Helen laughed, "Swell! Tell Miss Walsh I shall be delighted to race her anytime, anywhere, even over plowed ground."[6] As far as a rematch, they would have to talk to Coach Moore. But Helen had slung down the gauntlet, and the spat between the two sprinters began appearing in various newspapers. Reportage became a kind of she-said-then-she-said. Finally, Stella said she would beat the upstart on April 5 in a series of races—the 50, 60, and 220 yards.[7]

Helen retorted, "I guess my beating her, burned her clean to the dirt on the bottom of her spikes."[8] Helen meant to prove to the Flyer and to the world that her St. Louis victory was no mere fluke. She made a vow right then and there that Stella would never see anything but her heels in any future race. In her debut appearance before the sports world, Helen had taken first place in all three of her chosen events: the shot put, the standing broad jump, and the indoor 50-meter sprint. The last American girl to set an indoor record in the 50 was Tidye Anne Pickett in 1932. Until now, Pickett owned the current American record for this indoor event with a time of 6.7 seconds. Even though girls could only compete in three events, when the points were tallied, Helen had earned second place for her school with what she alone had scored.

Track official Barth Rossfield attributed Helen's victory to technique, saying that Stella "dug into the soft, sandy clay . . . whereas Miss Stephens more or less ran with foot, leg and knee frontward, giving a sort of flat-footed motion that didn't make her feet sink into the clay as was the case with Miss Walsh."[9] Lengthy coverage swamped sports pages all across Missouri, and Helen's exuberant coach frequently was quoted. He said Helen had the grace of an antelope, an effortless eight-and-a-half-foot stride that combined all the elements of perfect sprinting form. Some dubbed what they saw in her upright running technique as imitative of the erect and high Callaway style of Moore's former track coach, Brutus Hamilton, a Westminster man who now trained quarter-milers. Moore admittedly had passed on to his female speedster every trick he had learned from Hamilton.

How did Superintendent Bush react to Helen's sudden fame? The man who didn't want her to go to the meet in the first place? He was as busy as the devil ensnaring souls with party trays of temptation. To start with, Bush himself was running agog that morning, smoothing a path for reporters from the *St. Louis Star Times*—setting up photo opportunities and interviews with the fast-moving "Missouri Express" and her parents. And moreover, Coach Moore was his man, the best coach Fulton High ever had! Before the day was out, Bush made sure that news of Fulton's star athlete would ink much of the next student paper. To make the most of it, he authorized a celebration on Monday. He now gave full authority to Moore to work with Helen and the use of Westminster's track to push her toward greater sweeps. Helen's favorite running distance might likely not be the 50 but the 100 or the 200! With double the distance in the yard or meter sprints, Moore, he felt sure, could get Helen really hopping!

One-inch headlines told the story: "From Farm to Fame on the Cinder-track: Surprise Star of Women's Track Meet: Olympic Sprint Hope." "Fulton Girl Becomes Famous Over Night: Helen Stephens, 17-Year-Old High School Student, Beats International Entrant in One of Three Victories in St. Louis." Sportsters romanticized her—she was a poem of grace from the moment she left the starting line 'til she hit the tape. Columnists wrote ditties to her and jabbed at Stella:

> All hail to Helen Stephens
> The Swift Missouri maid
> Who met Stella Walsh at evens
> And left her in the shade.

Another one defended Helen's unconventional running form:

> Young Helen took the crowd by storm
> A clever leg she shakes
> She may not have athletic form
> But she has what it takes.[10]

Across the nation, Sunday papers carried meters and yards of copy on the Helen Stephens story. Even so, no one in Fulton was prepared for the commotion that swept into town Monday morning. Helen was supposed to be in class, but before 8 AM, Superintendent Bush had called Principal Newbolt to find out what he and his staff were doing and told him to get busy setting up a downtown display of the medals Helen had won.

At 9:30, the principal declared it was Helen Stephens Day and planted Coach Moore and Helen in his office.[11] And there they sat, answering questions thrust at them by reporters and others who wanted to see and talk to Helen and her coach. Flooded with phone calls, Newbolt felt trapped in his office as a stream of walk-ins crowded and clamored about. For a time, it was impossible for his own staff to reach him by phone (because some pressman had "the durn thing" stuck to his ear) or in person (because local merchants and other folks were crushing his suit). Newbolt got nothing done outside of talking about Helen's victories and speculating on her prospects. Finally, he announced a special assembly so that students and teachers could participate in the parade that city fathers had organized for the afternoon.

At 11:00, everyone moved into assembly for a program designed to honor their distinguished athlete. First on the program was school fidelity, which meant, we all will now sing. Someone stepped forward to lead the chorus:

> We're loyal to you, Fulton High.
> We're faithful and true, Fulton High.
> We'll back you to stand
> 'gainst the best in the land,
> for we know you have sand,
> Fulton High!

Some kids pondered, what did *sand* have to do with it? Was it a reference to the cinders and sand on the track? No, someone explained, it's about having grit.

Having endured all nineteen lines of their school song, the students let go with ear-piercing exuberance: "Chee hee! Chee hi! Chee ha ha ha! Owski wow-wow." Newbolt stepped forward to introduce reporter Horace Carr, who spoke of his excitement watching the event in St. Louis. Carr said the town should get behind Helen and send her to Berlin, for they had an Olympic athlete in their midst. When Coach Moore stepped up to the podium, a reverent calm rippled over the crowd. He spoke of Helen's world record-breaking achievement and Olympic potential. Clearly she'd displayed a God-given gift in St. Louis, he said, and she, "a fine and modest person," had truly proven herself to be Fulton's heroine. When he stepped back, the kids let go more eruptions. Applause rose to a deafeningly pitch as our heroine rose from her seat and Moore stepped aside for her.

A hush again fell over the assembly.

"Who," she paused, "is Stella Walsh?" This triggered uncontrollable screams, shouts, foot stomping, laughter, applause. When quiet fell again, she spoke of her goal of getting a job as an athletic coach *after* college. She expressed gratitude to her coach and to the boys' team for letting her use their field and loaning a track outfit. When she finished, track cocaptains Joe Thomas and Carl Mertens and lettermen Clyde C. Herring and Tom Wes Pasley stepped forward, full of praise for her accomplishments. Joe spoke of their hopes for her future. Carl handed her the school letter and said every member of the team would consider it an honor if she would agree to be an honorary track team member. She said that she would consider it an honor to wear the black and gold colors. Then, dressed in pep-squad sweaters, Betty Reid and Ralph Hammond jackknifed like puppets from the front row onto the stage and led two cheers, one for Helen, one for Coach Moore. Joe Thomas pinned Helen's three championship medals on her dress. Then, assembly ended with a heartfelt melody: "Once again . . . we fain would lift our hearts . . . to our high school, dear Alma Mater, let gladness our moments prolong."

With afternoon classes canceled, it was indeed Helen Stephens Day!

Heading a parade to Court and Fifth Streets, Helen waved to a crowd of screaming well-wishers, some calling out, "Hey, Popeye! Popeye!" Monday night's paper explained the excitement: "Feats of Fulton Girl Athlete Make Study Impossible." The front page recounted the fact that Mussolini ordered a recall of Italian troops, but more space was taken up by Helen's feats: "Fulton Girl Becomes Famous Overnight: Helen Stephens, 17-Year-Old High School Student Is Olympic Certainty." The Fulton Daily Sun-Gazette's windows soon held five life-size photos of the hometown girl provided by the *St. Louis Star-Times.*[12]

On Tuesday, Helen played basketball in a special Sunday school league game in the Missouri School for the Deaf gymnasium. Pitted against coaches and physical education teachers, Helen's team of girls (picked from five teams) won 34 to 23. Helen scored 12 points; the newspaper noted that the largest crowd of the season had come just to see the Olympic hopeful play. Along with Ophelia Squires, Elizabeth Blattner, and "Pinky" (formerly "Blue") Gooldy, Helen was All-Star Six. By the end of the season, she'd set a record as the highest point-scorer in any one game. And Moore was quoted as saying she was the most determined girl he'd ever seen, "but don't get the idea she's not stable."

Friday night she spoke of her victories, sharing the Dorsey Literary and Debating Society dais with college president Dr. Harmon. The front page of April's *Lo-Life* reported its financial status, showing $6.35 expended for new track shoes for Helen (men's size ten) and $1.19 for autograph pencils for Helen's use. It listed her as joke editor, still misspelling her name as *Stevens.* The misspelling occurred again in the April 19 *Hi-Life*, whose front page was dominated by her graduation photo, placed smack-dab in the middle of the paper.[13]

Student writers, editors, and faculty advisers, it seemed, were fully focused on news about the Fulton Flash. Some wit of a person writing about the senior play in the April 19 *Hi-Life* worked in a reference to Helen's speed. A three-column ad announced Fulton High's track meet, highlighting a special 100-meter exhibition by Helen at Priest Field, on Saturday, April 20, with 10¢ and 25¢ admission prices. Another reporter wrote about Helen's track honors and fame, mentioning the fact that she had won Fulton High a bit of fame, too, with its second place in the AAU meet. The fifteen points she tallied for the school were exceeded only by the Chicago team's twenty-five points. Fulton's one-girl track team certainly did not bring embarrassment to her school. Lacking restraint, *Hi-Life* also printed an easy poem, titled "To Our Champion":

> H is for Happiness, coming her way
> E is for Earnestness, shown every way
> L is for Loyalty, unceasing friend;
> E is for Endurance is there till the end,
> N is for Natural, can never pretend.

S is for Shyness, wherever she goes;
T is for Tireless as her laughter shows,
E is for Excellent, grades do agree;
P is for Pleasant, such nature has she,
H is for Hasty, when she's on the track
E means Exalted, when she comes back,
N is for Notable—watch everyone stop;
S is for Sensible—she is the top.

Page 2 further lauded Helen. In "Girls Play Carnival at William Woods College," we learn that a team of five girls and one faculty woman competed among forty schools in the state: "our athletic department" players were Martha Sue Faucett, Helen Harris, Ruth Holman, Anna May Shryock, Eleanor Smith, and alternate Vera Beamer. Helen was invited as a special guest and "permitted to participate in all the events if she wishes to." Page 3 ran "A Story of My Life," in which the All-Star explained: "My grade school days were filled with my attempts to beat the boys at their own games. I think that my natural ability, of which the press speaks, is due to my early hard playing. Of course, people thought that just because I liked games, especially running, that I was a tomboy. Maybe I was, but I think if those people had had any understanding of athletics, they might have chosen a better term."

Plucky in print she was—could write one way (proper English) and speak in another, depending on what the circumstance called for. She confessed: "Naturally I love sports of all kinds. Ever since I can remember, I have had a secret ambition to get in the athletic world, in some way, however small. Above all I never expect to get 'big-headed' or 'stuck-up' over anything that I have done or, if something more than luck is with me, that I might do later."

Her athletic gift was indeed something more than luck. Along with Pinky Gooldy and Ophelia Squires, the star forward played on the girls' all-star basketball team and was selected captain of the Methodist girls' team. Fulton's fast-track angel also sang in the Methodist Church choir.

Helen's English teacher, Miss Georgia Richardson, purchased a dime-store scrapbook for safekeeping news clippings for Helen as she pursued her dream. Her beauty shop was now doing Helen's hair without charge. Miss Richardson asked Mrs. Stephens to let her pay for Helen's senior class picture. Bertie accepted the offer but asked that the negative be retouched to remove evidence of the birthmark prominent on Helen's forehead. Richardson understood the sensitivities of a girl in her teens and agreed to have that done. Mrs. Stephens worried that Helen's speaking and exhibition schedule would badly affect her final grades. Never mind that, Mr. Stephens said. He expected his high school graduate daughter to help him with spring planting and other farmwork and help his wife around the house, as well. And maybe take a job at the shoe factory.

During assembly on the last day of class, Helen's classmates presented her with a traveling bag and their good wishes that she travel far as an athlete.[14] *Colliers Magazine* (May–July) carried a story of Helen's meteorlike ascent. Now that she could practice on any track field she wanted, she began working out four times a week with her personal trainer. Coach Moore bought Helen a pair of track shoes and a discus. Within days, she clocked in at 8.1 seconds running 70 yards, and the papers headlined it: "Stephens Betters Mark in 70 Yards." Helen-watchers noted that on May 11 she would run the 50 and 200 meters and throw discus and shot put at an event in Washington, Missouri, sponsored by Wright City High.

In June, she received the Leacock Trophy, a national award for outstanding athletics. Local folks now grappled with the issue of financing her, while Rathert pushed Helen to join the St. Louis team, knowing she could help it win the national meet and put his Ozark AAU on the district map. After an exhibition in Maplewood (a St. Louis suburb), reporter Horace Carr nailed Fulton's city fathers for seeming indifferent to Rathert's pleas and for not doing anything except offering congratulations to Moore and his prodigy.[15] He wrote that Moore continued to bear Helen's trip expenses from his own pocket. Since Fulton was getting worldwide publicity through Helen's achievements, Carr wrote, the least Fulton should do would be to organize its own athletic club to bear the expense of the big meets.

Indeed, with Moore's help, the country tomboy had translated herself into a self-assured athlete of substantial marketability with offers of numerous speaking engagements and several scholarships, all within in a few months. In March, she had won a national track title; in May, she was sought by professional and amateur athletic scouts and was pursued, however covertly, by a boyfriend; and her girlfriends—old and new—were looking at her in a new light.

Popeye, having undergone the tedium of a "permanent wave," complements of Miss Richardson's beauty salon, now wore a fashionable bob of curly straw-blonde hair; a store-bought manicure and painted fingernails drew attention to her long graceful hands. She slipped her large feet into their first set of sleek high heels, thanks to Brown Shoe Company, and her mother had bought Helen's first garter belt and girdle, though Helen's slim, narrow hips needed no reduction. Mrs. Stephens adapted Butterick dress patterns, keen on something tailored yet stylish for her daughter, who measured extra-large, extra-tall, and was unusually long-limbed. Good-wishers gave Helen a store-bought coat, a jacket, and certificate notes with which to buy several dresses in St. Louis, where, free of cost, Dr. Rathert examined and took care of her teeth. Mrs. Harris, a banker's wife and the tall-statured mother of a track mate, gave Helen one of her own gowns, a beautiful silver-gray knit with sufficient stretch to fit Helen perfectly, for formal occasions.

Still, there was no Helen Stephens athletic fund in Fulton.

In her school scrapbook among graduation cards, programs, and announcements, Helen pasted a poem by Dinah Mulock, revised into prose form and containing typo flaws, which she or someone hastily typed, that expressed her feelings at this time:

> Oh, the comfort, the [in]expressible comfort of feeling safe with a person, having neither to weigh thoughts nor measure words,,—but pouring them all right out—just as they are, chaff and graintogether, certain that a faithful ~~friends~~ hand will take and sift them, keep what is worth <u>kiiping</u> and then with the breath of kindness blow the rest away.

A serious-minded girlfriend had declared herself to Helen in the spring of 1935 and may have given Helen this philosophical note. Helen tucked away in this private scrapbook several handwritten notes. One postmarked June 23, Illinois, closed with "Love. Lots of Love. S." It referred to shared interests and revealed that "S" didn't like her temporary stay in the land of Lincoln, of about six months, "so it won't be too bad." S admonished Helen to write another nice long note and said she had read that Stella had run away again: "Stella's quite a quitter, isn't she? I can't see her object—you know the whole world is laughing at her. I would rather be beaten than called a quitter, wouldn't you? I'm glad you finally got a rest. You deserve it. How's your knee? You'd better watch it because it might cause you some trouble. Dancers have their legs insured. Why don't you?"

Something more than girlish friendship transpired. After Thanksgiving, S again wrote "Dearest Stevie" and spoke of a long-distance call from a boyfriend who went to Columbia (Missouri) to see a girl during Thanksgiving; S said she had written him an angry letter, hoping to get "results." One of her several letters sent in December spoke of receiving Helen's class portrait and Helen's exhibition in Louisiana: "Stevie, honey, I want you to try your darndest to come by here on your way home—you know how your plans can work this. . . . Gee! I'll sure be glad to see you, if and when I can. Don't worry so much—you know it'll work out—someway. The vic is playing 'Basin Street Blues'—you know how it goes 'down in New Orleans'—wish I could be there to watch you show them how it's done." Their love, coursing here on these pages, could not be fully in the open.

Love embers blazed again, in a perfectly typed poem that may have originated from S or from a second girlfriend smitten by Helen's charm. Without date or attribution, the poem conveys more depth and sophistication than S seemed capable of, judging from her writings. Titled "Anti-Suggestion," it reveals a keen mind and a heart flushed with profound feelings. One line of grammar seems intentionally colloquial. Helen safeguarded this poem in the same scrapbook.

I do not ask if you are true;
Faith leaves such queries proudly mute,
Content to claim my trust in you
Is absolute.

Swear not by any stars above!
Such vows I'd rather be without
Than cloud the mirror of our love
With horrid doubt.

Though fairer maids with subtle art
Vie for your favors, they shall find
My humbler image fills your heart,
Your steadfast mind.

On such stanch base is built our bliss.
Always, I've firmly made it known,
I rest serene, secure in this:
You're mine alone.

Nor do I tease to find you fond,
Or if that's but a pleasant myth;
I never blurt, "Who was that blonde
I seen you with?"

The question's one I pass right by
With eyes unseeing and unwinking.
You're never going to say that I
Started you thinking.

In essence, Helen had apperceived a total makeover. For love had made its changes inside her, as well, and love had vaulted toward her from both genders. Many still called her "Popeye." But some special friends called her "Steve." But not would-be boyfriend John C. Harris. He used her "proper" name.[16] In the busy, romantic spring of 1935, as editor of the last issue of the student rag, John corrected the spelling of Helen's last name, an error no one had caught in three previous issues. He was newly impressed by Helen's transformation after March 22, and like all others, was now viewing her in a different light. John thought that Helen was extremely graceful, feline in her movements. Lately he saw a neatly groomed, almost-pretty girl holding herself proudly erect and confident before groups of people. He admired her ability to speak forthrightly and intelligently. In informal situations, he perceived a sense of lighthearted gaiety in her. She could slip naturally into a Will Rogers mode with razor-sharp wit and warming insight or move up to a composed, beguiling charm. To him, Helen seemed more mature for her age than other girls. In his mind, she was a person of considerable substance. And she laughed at the things he laughed at.

May's *Hi-Life* lists the seniors' activities. Popeye's were similar to John's: Carnival, Play Day, *Hi-Life* Staff, Who's Who, 2, 3, 4; Pep Squad, Christmas Program, Honorary Track Team 4, Honor Roll, 1, 2—all indicate the hectic pace of her last two years of school (3, 4).

A prevailing dictum in those days was that kids weren't worth a nickel without nicknames. John was one exception to this rule; John was simply John. John was a leader among the school's most popular boys as was his track buddy David W. "Swede" Herring (no relation to Helen). The Swede was an enormously big, not just tall, guy who played football *and* sang in the Glee Club. Also popular were Martin Crowson, class vice president and active in debate and Latin clubs, and George "Bud" Fagley, an easygoing track letterman. Bud's father was superintendent of the school for the deaf; he would become an enthusiastic Helen supporter, moving quickly to help raise money for her Olympic trip. Bud's older sister, Elizabeth, a student at the University of Berlin, had already ordered their stadium tickets for the 1936 Olympics.

These boys early on admired Helen's athletic abilities and made no apologies about it. Several other football *and* track guys were Tom "Kong" Pasley, Fred "Hardware" Carr, Howard "Doug" Douglas, and Joe "Sleepy" Thomas. Others who paid no attention to the girl or the athlete in Helen were Gayle "Eddie" Edwards, Billy "Hoosier" Haden, Carl "Killer" Mertens. Perhaps without popularity and not worth a nickel were Doyle Miller and the brothers Joe R. and Ray Shryock.

Miss Richardson, in her role as student adviser, supervised all budding journalists. Her two joke editors were Helen and the "locally celebrated ballroom dancer" Martha Sue Faucett (her father was Judge Faucett; her mother was active in the Methodist Church that Helen attended). The girls shared two mutual interests: dancing and joking around. Literary editors were Ovid H. Bell (whose family owned the largest commercial printing company in town) and Anna M. Shryock (voted the smartest girl in class).

The column known as "The Will" prophetically claimed that Helen had bequeathed gold medals to the high school for exhibition purposes, that Julia Spearman while confessing to a math-teacher crush was "leaving Mr. Garrett" to Fulton High School, and that twice-blessed Bonnie Jo "Blue" and "Pinky" Gooldy (who had given it freely elsewhere) had given her love for the Gables (a popular romantic venue) to Eden Byler. "Swede" Herring offered his size-sixteen shoes to Winn's Grocery "to deliver groceries in."

The nicknameless yet popular boy who mustered up his nerve to be Helen's Junior-Senior Banquet date, John Harris, was president of the senior class and a track letterman. He was a tall, skinny kid (six foot four before he stopped growing) who played Second All-Star basketball for the Presbyterian Church, and like Helen, he was smart. He made the Honor Roll, 1, 2, and if he had serious intentions about Helen as a girlfriend, to use his words, "I never made a commotion about it." He truly liked and admired her because she was bright and funny. Together with Martha Sue, Helen was "to blame" for the silly, mind-twisting "Intelligence Test" John edited, as senior editor of the school paper: What is the name of George Washington? How big is a piece of paper 1 foot square? Name the colors red, white, and blue. How hot is heat? If 10 men move 10 locomotives in 10 hours, how long does it take for 10 men to move 10 locomotives? What is the weight of a 200-pound man? And what is a board walk made of?

John was also a quick-witted student who took his studies seriously; he, too, admired their English teacher and faculty adviser; he thrived on the discipline she required of students, the many composition assignments and demands of proper grammar. John and Helen actually liked to diagram sentences! He was a Latin Club member, in the Mixed and Boys Chorus, active in Carnival 4, as was Helen, and was listed in *Who's Who*, too. Any love interest he may have had was lost on Helen, for she thought the class president had been told to escort her to the banquet. Besides, her heart was elsewhere.

In spring, the thoughts and hearts of soon-to-be high school graduates will bud. Independent of any influence, except the thought that by all rights Fulton's brightest star ought to go, John Harris rang up the boarding house where Helen lived (in the 800 block of Court Street in Miss Herford's home) and asked her to the banquet.

Helen politely accepted.

John's handsome face and figure didn't go unnoticed by other female class-mates. He was quite a catch for a date. But Helen didn't jump or squeal with delight after his call, as happened several times in Miss Herford's hall that April when some of the other girls put phone receivers back into their cradles. Helen didn't think the good-looking boy from a wealthy, prominent family could be *really* interested in her; she assumed easy-natured John was just being a good pal. Besides, by then she had another interest and outlet for her romantic feel-ings. Other than her lingering crush on Coach Moore, Helen felt no romantic feelings for boys, John included. Instead, the *girl* friends who professed amo-rous intentions toward her stirred something inside her that drew her more toward them. Society, she understood, required cloaking such private feelings in order to not betray such forbidden intimacies.

Adeptly wielding double entendres, her public declarations emerged tongue-in-cheek in "An Ode to My Old Pal—the Typewriter" in the student paper. She used what she had seen in her parents' relationship and what she felt about the treatment she experienced in school before her stardom. Leaving it all behind was heady stuff for the formerly unpopular, poor farm girl. Here she divulged one early source of solace (writing, self-expression, i.e., the typewriter) and admits the cause of all her troubles (her self, her Popeye-self):

> I certainly have pecked on you old friend, but yet
> I know that you shall have only one regret
> About the bruises that I have dwelt upon thy breast
> So now I want to leave with you one request.
>
> Even though I may never peck upon you ever
> I will always hold your name in holy rever
> And in the future years to come;
> I may still call you a lousy bum.
>
> Pardon me, if your dumb self can
> And extend to me your short steel hand
> While I ask you to oil up your gadgets and
> Next year be much more speedier on paper land.
>
> Speed and endurance, some have more than you
> For you act as if you had only one screw.
> So, at least I have found you to be
> But I expect the trouble is just with me.
>
> So I bid to you au revoir and lots of luck
> Because I know you are fed only the world of chuck
> Yet I know that you will not extend to me any greetings
> For you know, as well as I, who got the cream of the beatings.

On the night of the banquet, John Harris drove his daddy's car, a sleek, dark-blue 1934 Buick, to the house on Court Street where Helen stayed. He knocked on the door and waited several long moments before Helen emerged. She was, that night, a vision of femininity, her hair permed, her lips bright with fire-red lipstick, and John, closing the car door, noticed a faint scent of perfume. She wore a Scandinavian blue formal her mother made, choosing the color to flatter Helen's aqua eyes. Helen slipped like a gazelle into the front seat, and when he had settled in and started up the car, she complimented him on it. She did not know how to drive a car, she admitted, but it couldn't be much different than Uncle Tommy's tractor.

The details disappeared with the years, but John remembered what happened when he took her home. Being the gentleman that he was, he helped her out of the car and was careful to not slam the door. Moving swiftly onto the sidewalk, skirts ruffling, Helen strode ahead of him, up the stairs and onto the little stoop. Standing there above him, she shook his hand and thanked him for a nice evening. Perhaps nursing a minor crush on her, John may have thought about kissing her good-night on the cheek, but she didn't give him a chance. She swung around and vanished into the house, its screen door slapping behind her.

By then, Helen was a young lady with a future. She had become a determined person with serious Olympic aspirations. All she wanted was a chance. The route included full-speed pursuit of a college education.

To many, it seemed as though this all happened overnight. Indeed, it had. Class prophecy shows Helen "living a life of ease and comfort" on the money received for running exhibition races. Other predictions suggest that Margaret Dunlap would become principal of Barnes Hospital nursing school in St. Louis; that Helen Craig would turn into an advice columnist for the lovelorn in the *McCredie Sunday Chronicle*; and that the Pope sisters, Mary and Mabel, would be featured dancers in the Monte Carlo Ballet Russe.

The kids were pretty much on target in Helen's case. With much pride, Helen's mother placed the AAU trophy on the dining table and put the other commendations, medals, and awards on the fireplace mantel. Her kid brother, now twelve years old, appointed himself monitor of her latest (and for public view) newsprint scrapbook of local and big-city newspaper clippings. Proudly, but with some hesitancy, R. Lee broke into short-running monologues, speaking to friends or reporters, telling of his big sister's record-making performances. "She don't milk the cows nomore," he said. "Hellie says that's man's work. I hav'ta do it, now."[17]

Helen "Popeye" Stephens, the Fulton Flash, the Missouri Express, had gained the respect of classmates, teachers, friends, and family. Popeye the Great was now the Great Fulton Flash! The last half year of high school had been totally contrary to her first three and a half years. As wind separates wheat from its chaff, her physical differences initially set her apart from the group of popular kids with nice looks and nice clothes. Too broad of shoulder, too large, too tall, too unfeminine for a girl, thus peculiar (meaning odd, compared to the majority of kids), this rural farm girl had incurred scoff and scorn and met instant unpopularity. Being smart had merely distanced her farther from average classmates. Until Coach Moore saw and validated them, her unique abilities marked her as being too oddly different to be accepted by a society proscribed with unbending feminine roles. Several teachers saw beyond Helen's circumstances and appearance and accepted her as she was—a likable kid who was eager to learn, who made good grades, liked to read, was friendly and helpful when asked. And if initially she had been reticent in certain social settings, she had plunged in wholly passionate about athletics.

The next few months of hard work, of speaking engagements and exhibition races, could sweep the seventeen-year-old world-record indoor champ onto higher plateaus of celebrity. In August, she might enroll at William Woods College.

Life was absolutely wonderful now. One special classmate proclaimed undying love and devotion. Their relationship would be tested and either surge upward by world wind currents or capsize. But they promised to be true to each other, like Elizabeth Barrett and Robert Browning, to fashion a life together of their own design.

3

Stella Who and Who Else?

Sure I'm going out for the Olympic team, and nothing less.
—Helen Stephens, quoted in *Columbia Tribune,* May 5, 1935

*T*he Callaway County lass kicked up three titles for herself in her first try at competition. Burt Moore had discovered something more than a fluke. He found a champion. It was impossible for him and impossible for her to fall back into the usual routine. After March 22, 1935, reporters, promoters, sports impresarios like Norman Rathert and Earl Reflow, or just the curious began hounding both of them.

Without brag or false modesty, Moore told what he had, what he knew Helen was: "She's a natural. She's out sprinted every boy in school and she trains religiously. Good wholesome food, with no pastry. Regular hours for eating, and plenty of sleep—particularly the sleep—and she works out several times a week."[1] Lacking a girls' track program in central Missouri, and using the only avenue available, Moore planned to put Helen under his personal training, at least for the summer, and perhaps set up an exhibition race.

Helen herself said she would settle for nothing less than the Olympics. But Stella bluntly took whacks at the country dilettante, and Moore realized Stella spoke the truth. In spite of her celebrity in Missouri, Helen *was* a nobody. An untested, virtually untrained, certainly untried newcomer. All right. She was what she was, a greenie from the sticks who had never, until recently, traveled beyond Callaway County. As she gushed, "I'd never seen such a big building as that arena,"[2] photographers captured an image of the bucolic novice at her home wearing a denim jacket and overalls, rabbit rifle in hand. They depicted her idyllically in the kitchen, wrapped with an apron, sitting in a rocking chair near a potbelly stove, sewing. Nevertheless, inexperienced Helen had grabbed first place among a small group of sports molls who ran pretty fast that day—on an indoor track in the big city of St. Louis. A hayseed she might be, but thus far she was the fastest hayseed they had ever seen. Her incredibly wide gait and unstoppable desire to be the fastest woman in the world indicated enormous promise.

In Moore's mind, there was little doubt Helen could overtake Stella in a rematch. Moore saw no reason to work Helen in Stella's 60, 70, or 80 yards *or* meters because those distances were not regulation events in American meets. But Moore arranged for the two to race in Columbia's Brewer Field House during the boys' state high school track meet in April. But Stella had no intention of coming to little towns in Missouri. She stayed in Cleveland on the day of the proposed rematch, countering with her own press splash, setting a new record (8.2) for the odd distance of 70 yards. Instead of a Stephens-Walsh match, spectators paid 25¢ to watch Helen run against Westminster's finest male sprinters, John Lutz, Frank Brown, Don Sartor, Phil Toney, and Loren Wolfe. There, the Fulton Flash cracked the women's 50-yard world indoor record.

The next day, Dee Boeckmann, the first woman to chair the AAU's Ozark District Committee, was astonished by the raw talent she saw as Helen dashed five yards ahead of St. Louis athlete Gertrude Webb. Bolstered by old money from the Missouri Athletic Club, Webb was a strong runner who had competed in London's 1934 International Games and had her sights on the Olympics. Helen outran her at 6.4.

One of Missouri's few athletic programs for girls was in Wright City.[3] So, in April, fifty miles west of St. Louis in another exhibition race, Helen vanquished all contenders, including two school friends, Martha Sue Faucett and Eleanor Smith, and Wright City's Etta Mae Schaper and Naomi Wood. Afterward, promoter-interloper Marion Plake announced that Stella and Helen would race each other and he would say where and when as soon as he had written acceptance from both stars.[4] But the aggressive Dee Boeckmann already had talked with Moore about setting up a match between Helen, Stella, and a few of her St. Louis girls, in particular her protégée, the petite redheaded firebrand Harriet Bland. Dee scripted a contract and issued a press release: "If the Olympic star (Walsh) accepts the opportunity to run against Miss Stephens again, it will be in a special 80 meter race, an event in which Miss Walsh set the world's record of 9.8 in 1933."[5] The place? Maplewood, Missouri. The date? To be determined.

When the day arrived, the weather had turned rotten. The hard downpour had stopped, but a spitting drizzle settled in. In spite of contract, publicity, and promotion, Stella didn't show, so the 80-meter option fell to the wayside. Helen had to run against the clock. Both coaches knew the conditions were against her, yet Helen surprised them. On a muddy track, wearing her honorary Fulton

High track suit and using starter blocks, she ran 100 yards in 10.8, setting an intercollegiate record. In the 50 yards, she ran 5.9, once again tying Walsh's world record. Boeckmann had observed the lanky youth take the spotlight away from eight hundred boys at Priest Field in record time at Helen's personal best: 10.8 in the American standard 100-yard sprint—equaling Walsh's 1933 record.[6] Boeckmann understood Helen's speed was no fluke. She herself clocked the child with her own timer. She offered to train Helen, to get her situated in the private girls school of Loretto Academy in St. Louis, but Helen said no. She was deaf to any coaching offers except Moore's.

The local press showed up May 7 at Priest Field where Helen was practicing. Helen ran 70 yards (not meters) in 8.1. The next day, papers headlined, "Stephens Betters Mark in 70 Yards." At the May 18 Missouri College Amateur Athletic Union Men's Meet at Priest Field, Helen ran 220 yards in an exhibition race against two adult men, Coach Moore and Westminster College Coach Gene Kimbrell. Admission price had jumped from 25¢ to 35¢. In spite of having a strained thigh muscle, Helen gave the crowd a good show, hitting the tape ahead of the veteran track men. Later she confessed she had been working out too enthusiastically and had run the 100 meters against the clock in 11.6 despite nursing strained muscles just above the knee. She had bicycled all over Fulton "yesterday, nearly paralyzing my legs, and . . . high jumping the day before. I think I weakened these muscles some," she said. She didn't think it would prevent her from giving an exhibition in Fulton Memorial Park's "brand new, electrically lit ball field" during the Columbia Merchants versus House of David ball game.

Appearances like these were crucial. They established Helen's predictable speed, however unofficial, and generated interest, which ultimately would glean financial support to get her to Berlin. She needed to establish records plus lay claim to an institutional affiliation. During the state interscholastic meet, Helen achieved a new, unofficial world indoor record and tied the 50-meter outdoor record of 6.4. In Mexico, Missouri, at the Military Academy invitational, she ran the 100 yard at 11.1, and at the state high school meet in Columbia, set a new world high school record for the 50-yard dash (5.9) and equaled the 100-yard world record (10.8), another new high school record. So far, she had surpassed Stella's 70-yard speed, equaled the Olympic 100-meter record, made a good run in the 200 meters, pitched impressive distances in shot and discus, and set a new yet unofficial American and world record in the 220-yard race. But because her times and distances were exhibitional, all were unofficial.

Though accepted as one of the boys on the high school track team, technically Helen was a graduate and no longer entitled to school facilities or training. Superintendent Bush and the Westminster athletic director now accepted Moore's purpose and allowed access to school facilities. Moore was confident that if he coached Helen and got her ready this summer for the Olympic trials next year, he would win the support of others who would help her financially. And now that he had solidly aligned Helen with Westminster men, he felt he could get its sister college, William Woods, to give this honor roll student a scholarship. He sought financial backing for Helen's Olympic trip from civic groups and private sources. He scheduled Helen to speak before Rotarians, where she told about her St. Louis race and exhibition experiences. Personally spreading news about her accomplishments and showing herself worthy cemented her chances for gaining the support she and her coach needed to pay their immediate expenses. Two AAU events where her times and distances would be official were the Ozark District Meet in St. Louis and the Mississippi Valley Meet in Kansas City. Moore also set up exhibitions in central Missouri, then talked to her parents about the AAU meets in June. Not only could these meets prove Stella wrong about Helen's win being a fluke but these meets would supply official records and ready her for the nationals. After that, they could move toward the Olympic trials.

What he might accomplish during the summer depended on Helen's father. Moore needed his permission to release Helen from farm chores to train on the outdoor track and to travel to out-of-state meets. Moore readied himself for debate against an old-fashioned farmer's objections.

Frank Stephens' expectations were that Helen-the-high-school-graduate would get a job in town and bring home some money to help the family. Moore had to convince him of the benefits of this once in a lifetime opportunity. If successful, he assuredly could convince certain William Woods board members to award Helen a full scholarship. He knew he could rely on Mrs. Stephens to press her husband on that score. Moore felt sure that Helen would ascend Mount Olympus if her father would relinquish to her the summer of 1935. Frank consented reluctantly, on a meet-by-meet basis. If she won these races, he said, he wouldn't argue with success.

Reporters pursued Helen relentlessly; they wrote folksy stories on how the poor, homespun speedster chased after and bare-handedly caught rabbits nibbling in her mother's garden. They wrote that the barefoot, would-be Olympian raced after and rounded up livestock for her father. They quoted her as saying, "I'm a pretty fair typist, too! But it seems as if I do better in things where I have to use my feet."[7] She liked Will Rogers because he said he liked everyone he met. Rogers' column appeared in the local paper, and she clipped it, sometimes, for her scrapbook. Quizzed on the country's state of affairs, she used Rogers' words, saying that reading newspapers gave you the idea that our whole defense force "is sorta Mickey Mouse." The great "Babe" Didrikson was her idol, she said, and if a Texas tomboy could win a gold medal, well, she thought she could too. She already was emulating Babe by playing the harmonica (cowboy songs and hillbilly numbers), but her music interest came from her mother's side of the family. Helen avowed that she had read about Adolf Hitler, Huey Long, Benito Mussolini, and other men of her time in high school.[8] She was a bright kid with a lot of gumption and belief in herself. Genial and frank, given to droll quips, her face lit up with quick smiles during interviews. Responding to probes, she might say, "Nope. Nope." When asked if athletic ability was something she inherited, she would shoot out a short remark perfect for radio sound bites: "My dad never did anything in athletics. Too busy, I guess." And leave off with that. Of her twelve-year-old brother, she said R. Lee was just an average boy, "interested in athletics, a little, I guess."[9]

Moore prophesied that in time her career would parallel that of America's then most versatile female athlete, Babe Didrikson. Sportswriters soon were writing their own Babe/Flash comparisons. Moore felt he could ready Helen for Berlin but that it was unlikely he could accompany her there as her coach. Boeckmann was in a better place to do that. She had both the qualifications and connections, as district AAU chair and newly appointed Olympic women's track and field coach. Dee had planted her own seeds in higher places. Hanging in her office was a national Olympic fund drive publicity photo of herself at the White House with First Lady Eleanor Roosevelt (honorary chairman of the National Women's Track and Field Committee), Dr. Sigurd von Numbess (ambassador of Finland), and athlete Lucille Brackett (of Washington, D.C.).

Boeckmann's influence as a role model for Helen began immediately. Helen's rural and poor origins were in stark contrast to Dee's urban-privileged, upper-middle-class status. Her father was a mining engineer, while Helen's, of course, was a farmer. But the coach and her soon-to-be student athlete had similarities, too. Measuring just a bit shorter than Helen, Dee Halpin Boeckmann, barefoot, was five foot nine. Born in 1904 (in an Olympic year in an Olympic city), she was fourteen years Helen's senior when they met. Like Helen, she was the older child and only daughter in her family, and she also "suffered" a little brother. She was dark in hair and eyes, a strikingly beautiful feminine-female. She carried herself proudly erect. Boeckmann emphasized her Catholic Irishness with a trademark, the lucky four-leaf clover. She collected and wore the green talisman of good luck, in jewelry pins of the proper shape on her lapel and on stylish hats (another trademark), and for luck, she stuck real four-leaf clovers in her shoes or those of complying protégées during competition. She gave Helen one at the time she interviewed her for *Amateur Athlete* magazine and another one in Berlin, prior to the 100-meter sprint.

Like Helen, Dee was a native Missourian of German and Irish heritage who knew and shared firsthand experiences of prevailing anti-German sentiment in the 1920s and 1930s. She covertly dealt with national chauvinism by using two passports, one bearing the German spelling, *Boeckmann*, the other bearing an abbreviated American form, *Beckman*. For this and other special urgencies, FBI chief J. Edgar Hoover said Dee was more trouble than a movie star or a criminal and nicknamed her "The Duchess of Sports."[10] It is not hard to imagine Boeckmann suggesting that Helen underplay her German lineage by omitting the use of her middle name on her passport. But being abstruse was never Helen's style or intent. By the time J. Edgar Hoover personally fingerprinted Helen, she already had several fitting nicknames. Though occasionally she used her middle initial *H* (for Herring), Helen never dodged or downplayed her heritage. She was the proud namesake of her maternal grandfather, William T. Herring; still, Helen touted neither her German, English, or Irish ancestry. She never proclaimed or publicly touted the Methodist sway of her childhood, except in reference to her basketball linkage, though she remained a tithing, nonattending member to the day of her death.

Like Helen, Dee had Olympic stars in her eyes and a sports career long and distinctive. At sixteen, Dee had many first-place track victories before she participated in the 1928 Olympics. An errant discus paralyzed her arm temporarily, hindering her performance in the 800 meters; she finished behind a girl she had outrun several times. Also injured (with shinsplints), a distracted Helen would place poorly in her Olympic discus event in which she had excelled previously.

Both women earned college educations when it was unusual for women to progress beyond high school. Boeckmann's career included basketball, as did Helen's. Dee captained Curlee Clothiers women's world champions, beating out the Canadian titleholders. Helen also captained a champion Curlee Clothiers municipal team. During wartime, after achieving international prominence in amateur and professional sports, both women enlisted in military service. Dee traveled with the Red Cross as athletic adviser and coach and worked with General Douglas MacArthur, setting up women's national athletic programs in Japan, Alaska, and elsewhere. Helen was a Marine for a short period, which gave her inroads to a federal defense job among high-ranking officers. Helen organized federal employee athletic programs, clinics, and meets and officiated at AAU athletic competitions. They both coached track and field at private girls' schools, Dee at Loretto Academy in St. Louis, Helen at William Woods College, Fulton.

Both women had long service records as officers for amateur and Olympic athletic organizations and attended postwar Olympic and Pan-Am Games in official capacities. In retirement, Helen was elected president of a bowling league; Dee was president of a fencing organization. The Associated Press chose Helen as best American athlete of 1936; Dee was chosen all-around American sportswoman of 1948. Both died in their seventies, having excelled in an era difficult and discouraging for sportswomen. They exhibited opposite styles, one viewed as blazing and confrontational, the other posturing as a jovial, good-ole boy, but both cleared paths for future women athletes. Finally, neither woman married, though they enjoyed long-lasting and somewhat closeted love relationships throughout their lifetimes.

While some Fultonians stayed cool in a darkened moving-picture theater enjoying W. C. Fields buffoonery or Bing Crosby crooning, sports-minded residents and merchants (the Blattners, McIntires, Backers, Fagleys, Nolins, Wests, and others) moved about in the summer's heat, building up the Helen Stephens Booster Club to send their rising star to the preliminaries: the Missouri Valley AAU in Kansas City in June, the Canadian Carnival in Toronto in August. Some went door-to-door, selling thumb-sized cardboard Helen Stephens stamps; the item carried Helen's name and face. If all went well, come February she would compete in the 1936 district indoor meet in St. Louis and again defeat Stella Walsh, and then on to Chicago in March, and then, yes, it was *Providence*—Providence, Rhode Island, for the national Olympic trials, July 1936. And then, bon voyage from the Big Apple!

Finally, headlines announced, "Stephens Ready to Meet Walsh June 1" in a special 80-meter race in St. Louis arranged by the AAU Ozarks Division and Dr. Rathert. Stella Walsh, as of May 4, held a new 80-meter record time of 8.2 seconds. Again, Stella was a no-show, and Helen ran anyway. She ran the 200 meters in 24.4 and set a new U.S. record; she ran the 100 meters in 11.8, tying the world record; and she threw the discus 129 feet 1 inch, setting a new Ozark District record.

In Kansas City, days later, Helen cut two-tenths of a second off her 100-meter record, running 11.6 at the Mississippi Valley AAU district meet. Two exhibitions followed: a Tuberculosis Day benefit in St. Louis in July (where Helen ran the odd 150 yards in 15 seconds flat) and the Missouri State Fair in Sedalia in August (where she ran 100 yards in 10.9). The important events that would put Helen's new speeds and distances on the books came near summer's end: Canada's National Exhibition for girls under eighteen, in Toronto on August 31; and the National AAU Women's Meet, September 14 in New York. Before departing for Toronto, she gave reporters a sketch of her tentative 1936 schedule, as she knew it, if things went according to plan: First, St. Louis in February; second, Canada again in March (Hamilton on the eighteenth and Toronto on the twentieth); then, Chicago on March 25; maybe Iowa in May; then the district trials; and finally, the Olympic trials in Providence, Rhode Island, in July. "And oh," she said, "I just might go to Memphis in May, to run an exhibition race at halftime during that Cotton Bowl game down there."

In Toronto on August 31, 1935, Helen ran the 100 yards in 10.8, tying the Canadian and world records. By then, Helen and her parents were comparing scholarship offers from Washington University in St. Louis, Northwestern University in Illinois, the University of Missouri in Columbia, and elsewhere. William Woods College appealed to Helen's father now; he wanted her nearby, where she at least could do some farmwork on weekends. His wife agreed, but for different reasons. She wanted Helen to have the advantages of a private college, preferring her alma mater, and to be close to home. Amazingly, all three of them were in agreement on this.

As Helen had written in her school biographical sketch, it seemed something more than luck was with her. For who would have wagered that this dirt-farmer's daughter ever would be aligned with eighty young ladies of privilege from the upper social class? But this was the reality of it. In the fall of 1935, she enrolled at William Woods.

Although its name and mission had changed five times in less than fifty years, "The Woods" had a reputation as a fine private women's college. Founded and supported by men, historically its presidents all had been male graduates of divinity schools who once served their communities as ministers. While the seat of administration and the governing board were held by men of high moral conviction, character, and connections, the majority of instructors were well-educated, young, unmarried women. Female members of the faculty, with few exceptions, were "let go" if they accepted marriage proposals.

Named after Dr. William Stone Woods, the school sprung up after the Civil War under the influence of the movement and time that encouraged refinement in women. The Woods' progenitor emerged in 1870, not in Fulton, but at Camden Point, Missouri, spawned by the Disciples of Christ Church as the Female Orphan School of the Christian Church of Missouri. In 1889, when fire destroyed the facility, all seemed lost. But several men of the church who recognized a prospect for growth when it "appeared" to them, and a wealthy Callaway County businessman by the name of Daniel Matthew Tucker, persuaded the governing board to rebuild and relocate its venture in Fulton. The Old English rendering of the name *Fulton*, meaning "town near a field," was not lost on these founding fathers.

Daniel Tucker was a teetotaler. Though not a churchgoer himself, he had given the land on which stood Fulton's Primitive Baptist and Episcopal Churches. He had contributed property at Tenth and West Avenue for the site of Synodical College, a Presbyterian school for girls, which closed in 1928. The ground Tucker proposed for this new school was a few blocks from Westminster College, a prestigious, private men's school. His reasoning for backing this development rested on a desire to protect his townhouse residence (his "Highland Place" estate) from encroachments by buyers of uncertain status or racial origin. In his mind, a church-related, private institution set amid his 580 pastoral acres offered the right kind of neighbor to impart the buffer zone he wanted. Westminster supporters aligned with Tucker, seeing the advantage in having a girls' finishing school nearby.

Tucker gave the land in 1890, and the new school was named the Christian Orphans School. But the charity concept of a school for orphans became a liability. About a third of admissions were orphans boarding on the campus without sponsored pay. The balance were paying students from families with the means to send one or two daughters to the school. To change the image, the board in 1899 renamed the school Daughters College of the Christian Church of Missouri. To pay off mounting debts a year later, the board wanted to liquidate some of the property Tucker had donated. Dr. William Stone Woods and his wife, Albina McBride Woods of Kansas City and Excelsior Springs, came to the rescue. The doctor was a physician, a banker, a real estate developer, and guardian of his grandchild—a little girl whose recently divorced mother was "abroad." School officials were keen to crush rumor when possible, but the present scandal created by Dr. Woods' only daughter, Julia Woods Davies, focused on her recent searches for a new husband. It was noted before her death in 1923 that Julia had found a naval captain at large to replace husband number four, an opera singer known as Giorgio Salvatore "of the Opera and Concert Stage."

Woods' vision was molded to some degree by his desire to see his granddaughter and her friends instructed in a manner suitable for young ladies of distinguished background and sensible ambitions. Woods proposed to elevate the school to a plane aligned with America's best educational institutions. He gave money and suggested improvements. While coeds attending Bryn Mawr or Radcliffe sought to make in four years its women equal to the students of Cambridge and Harvard, Dr. Woods readied his charges for proper marriages, family, and the home. When he pledged his ongoing financial support in 1901, Daughters College was renamed William Woods College for Girls.

Woods funded each year-end deficit thereafter and set up a $500,000 endowment fund, effective upon his death. In 1908, the college's name was shortened to William Woods College. High school preparatory curricula continued at the Woods until 1930, in accordance with his idea of a combined curriculum. And a few boys under the age of ten were admitted for awhile; but this practice was discontinued upon his death in 1915.

By the time Helen passed through its gates in 1935, the campus had changed considerably but was still a two-year "finishing school for young ladies." Its architecture still conveyed an old-world, turn-of-the-century feel, and its administration still sought to embody Christian morality in faculty, staff, and student body. At its south entrance, a flower bed "charmed" the base of a five-foot fountain statue—a laughing boy holding a swan in his arms, water flowing from its bill. The focal point along a paved motor drive was a three-story offices and classrooms building with tall, formal, solid-oak doors.

Architects designed the stone and brick Academic Building both to serve and to impress. Nearby was the chapel, in Jameson Music Conservatory. Dulany Memorial Library and Auditorium were adorned with stained-glass windows bearing the faces of three early benefactors, Daniel M. Dulany, William H.

Dulany, and B. L. Locke. Tucker Dining Hall held an attractive clock tower. There were three student residences (Edwards Hall, built in 1891, Jones Hall and Booth Hall, in 1919), a presidential residence, infirmary, and Equestrian Arena and Stables. Placed picturesquely amid the now eighty-five acres of rustic glades and glens were two lakes, supplied with boats and bathhouses, canoes, and sunning decks.

Turned out each year on these grounds were the pomp and circumstance of a joyful spring graduation ceremony. Newly alumnaed girls in their white dresses, each holding onto a portion of a far-reaching ivy chain, fathomed completely that their selves indeed had been changed by the Woods experience and that they would forever be entwined as alumnae sisters.

Although Helen was given the promise of an athletic scholarship at William Woods, sports were not seen as suitable subjects of study for young women. Rather, physical education at the college aimed more toward recreation—golf, tennis, archery, boating, and equestrian arts. McBride Gymnasium offered an indoor swimming pool and a court for volleyball or basketball (employing girls' rules, of course). McBride also served as the site of formal balls, events designed to introduce the "girls" of William Woods to Westminster men.

What lured Helen to this place? Why hadn't she taken the offer from the distant but exemplary Northwestern University, or the close-to-home University of Missouri, both of which offered bona fide women's athletic programs? What made the decision for her, she now told the press, was the offer from her discovery coach. As a part-time assistant to Westminster's athletic program, Moore would take her on as a special student and train her for the Olympics. He would put Priest Field at her feet as the training ground, personally manage her events schedule, and teach her what she needed to know. For seventeen-year-old Helen, there could be no other choice. It had to be Coach Moore; therefore, it had to be William Woods. What she privately felt, and only admitted to her trustworthy friend, Julia Spearman, was that the training and attention he gave her had kindled her crush on him into a blaze of "true love." But it was to no avail—he was unattainable, having married Mary Lou Schulte on December 27, 1934.

To Helen, the little campus was breathtakingly beautiful. In the spring, the grounds were lovely, all trim and green, with dogwood and redbud, oak and maple. And this was her mother's school. As the daughter of a William Woods "daughter," she automatically was admitted to the Lineage Group, a club open to only those whose relatives had attended the school.

The college president had arrived on campus about ten months earlier. Thirty-three-year-old Dr. Henry Gadd Harmon began the task of filling the shoes of the Reverend Egbert Cockrell, who died in office in the summer of 1934. Harmon set out to expand the college health program, to create the office of business manager, and to add a dormitory or two. Harmon had headed the Department of Education at Culver-Stockton College in Missouri but seemed naturally bent toward institutional promotions. Like his father and several relatives, he was a minister (ordained 1924) of the Christian Church and earned a college administration doctorate from the University of Chicago in 1935.

In his first year as college president, Harmon established a budget for a student newspaper, the *Green Owl,* and latched onto Helen as prime recruitment property. He put the world-renowned athletic star on the *Green Owl* ad-sales staff and named her advertising manager for *Echoes,* the yearbook. He likewise used another William Woods athlete, the beautiful, 1933 national archery champion from Tulsa, Anna May King, in the same way. Harmon's secretary, Miss Georgia Schulte, was a person incessantly busy and harried—a condition caused by her boss's furor of activities. Schulte's plight was not lost on Helen. Helen cloaked her opinion of the president in a 1937 *Echoes* back-page filler titled "Truth Will Out":

> *Teacher*—Jeannette, please tell me where your father works.
> *Jeannette*—Oh, he doesn't work; he's president of William Woods College.

Helen was elected treasurer of her junior class but held no class office in her senior year. As a "Willies-In" junior, Helen settled into Edwards Hall. She became representative of "Willies-Out" in her senior year, for she was moved off campus under problematic circumstances. Hilda Guenther, the secretary-treasurer of Willies-Out juniors and president of Willies-Out seniors, knew all the whys and wherefores. But Hilda was not a gossip.

But living on campus that first year, Helen struck up with the twin Sutter sisters, whom she met in typing class, the Alpha Iota sorority Bluhm sisters, Eleanor and Evelyn, and Lineage Group member Lorraine Killingsworth, of Clarinda, Iowa, who was also a member of the YWCA, as was Helen. Another Fultonian, thus a Willies-Out member, Betty Sue Reid, was already Helen's pal and a member of the Lineage Club and Campus Players, as was high school buddy Bonnie Jo Gooldy.

Being unencumbered by in loco parentis rules of campus-bound life, Willies-Out girls were envied, but they, too, were supervised, that is, sponsored by Mrs. H. Lee Whitlow and Mrs. Elizabeth Maughs. Willies-Out girls enjoyed monthly meetings in the Academic Building, and their annual Junior Class Christmas Party was an event everyone attended. By that time, in that season of the year, under the spell of the holiday cheer, many a young person vowed a commitment of one's heart. Helen was as vulnerable to it as anyone. During the 1935 Christmas party, Helen gave a friendship ring to her favorite coed.

Several faculty women now played prominently in Helen's campus life. Among them was a relatively new faculty person, Elsa Wade Williamson, in her second term when Helen arrived. Williamson taught English composition (Helen's second-most favorite subject) and world literature, and she was the *Echoes* faculty adviser. Always the educator, Williamson encouraged all her students to enter literary contests. A tad strange herself, she had an unreasonable fondness for black cats; it was said that her chief activity was scouting out campus poets and that she had a strong affinity for sweetened cornbread and the color red. She insisted on using both her maiden and married names, but irrepressible Helen flat-out nicknamed her. In the safety of other students, she called her "Wide Wad," because, in Helen's logic, the youngish prof was a bit hefty in the beam as well as "something of a dark beauty."

"Wide Wad" was academically demanding, but she showed special devotion and attention to Helen. She advised that, especially as Helen would be traveling a great deal her first year of higher education, it would be taxing but crucial to her future that she keep up her studies, first and foremost. To win over her new charge and gain trust, she bought a dime-store scrapbook, newsprint size, and told Helen she was keeping pictures and articles about the star athlete's exploits and showing it to colleagues, pupils, and family. She, too, was interested in sports, from a spectator's standpoint. Wide Wad would mold Helen, but she, too, would be influenced by her pupil; she became a member of Helen's fan club.

Most dominant of all the women's faculty was Miss Fannie Willis Booth, formerly the dean of women, dean of faculty, and college librarian. "She knows more about WWC than any other," claimed the *Echoes*, and every "old gal" who returned to visit the campus "goes first to Miss Booth." Miss Booth taught science, government, psychology, ethics, and Helen's favorite subject, history. Arriving with the first faculty in 1890, Booth had no intention of resigning and was not interested in marriage or retirement. By 1931, she was the official alumnae hostess; in Helen's day, she sponsored the Lineage Group. She was unusually tall for a woman, close to six feet, thin, and prim. Lanky, flat-chested, and bespectacled, the spinsterish woman was fond of long, blue crepe dresses and dark, sensible heels. Afternoon high teas were held on the occasion of her birth. Very few students could slip past the purview of this ancient plank of the school's foundation.

It was Miss Lessie Lanham, however, who became Helen's history teacher. According to the yearbook pronouncement, Miss Lanham expressed a passion for contemporary life by regularly attending the movies. Movies allured Helen as well. Martha Alexander was the head of the physical education department, and her assistant, Miss Betty Shelly, was a Woods graduate hired as a P.E. instructor that year and assigned to sponsor the Pepper Club. Miss Ruby Dean Harris sponsored the Women's Athletic Association. It was Miss Alexander, along with Coach Moore and Superintendent J. T. Bush, who appeared in the news photo announcing "The Track Flash" had enrolled at William Woods.

Another faculty personality in Helen's circle was Mrs. Hedvig Marcum, the typing and shorthand instructor, whose interests included the organ and horse-back riding. Her picture in *Echoes* shows her face as plain, with an unfortunately high forehead, suggestive of male-pattern balding. Her students felt free to josh her in print: "We are pleased to report that Mrs. Marcum now knows where to find the brake on a bicycle. You need no longer hold your breath when she goes tearing down Court Street."

Coeds who lasted through the two-year program encountered most of these teachers and one or two of the college dormitory hostesses, a nurse, and the dean of students. The nurse cared for the physical health of the student body; a dormitory or house hostess supposedly was available at all times to attend to the girls' residential needs.

It was said that all eyes shifted in Helen's direction when she came and went about campus. But it was Helen's dormitory hostess whose vigilance rose to the extreme. The elderly Mrs. Fannie Longmire was the hostess of Reid Hall, where Helen was installed for one term of college, sharing a room with another junior. Perhaps Longmire was a widow, for according to *Echoes*, "The only rival that her girls need fear is Dickey Bird." She had a pet bird encaged in her room. Evidently, she was devoted to it and talked to it, perhaps, if not about it to the girls. Helen formed her own opinions and misgivings based on several personal encounters with her. Longmire was, she said, "bony framed, thick eyebrowed, tightly thin faced with small bird-like piercing eyes, a crooked mouth and a smirk poured in concrete, topped with an inflexible crown of finger waves." Helen did not like her at all.

The dean of students was there for consultations with students on any type of problem or concern about etiquette, social conduct, or academics. As the sponsor of the Student Co-Operative Government, an organization designed to settle disputes over student violations of college regulations, Dean Marie Gragg Shafer played a major role in Helen's life as it unfolded on and off campus. She taught life careers and orientation courses. *Echoes* reported that her interests ranged from the latest books to chicken ranches and silver fox farms. Shafer was a pleasant looking, stocky woman with kind eyes behind wire-rimmed glasses, eyes that seemed to pierce into the very soul of her students. Her short-cropped hair never fell forward and always appeared to be freshly combed. She seemed to like her job and took her work seriously, and she was well liked and trusted by students, other faculty, and administrators alike. She approached her girls with the attitude that their particular brand of individu-alism enriched everyone, but certain social standards were expected. She pos-sessed, according to *Echoes*, "a rare understanding of the modern girl and her problems." She became a Helen supporter. When calamity struck Helen at the turn of her senior year, Dean Shafer (like classmate Hilda Guenther) closed her eyes and refused to contribute to the problem. Her reprimand was to merely advise Helen to be more careful in the future.

Within a few weeks of beginning classes, Helen headed for New York. At the National AAU Women's Outdoor Championships, September 14, 1935, Helen rose above a number of strong contenders. In the 100-meter race, she out-matched May Brady, who came in second, Harriet Bland, in third, and Josephine Warren, who trailed in fourth. In the 200 meters, Helen dethroned Boston's Olive Hasenfus and bested the German American Marion Thomson and Brooklyn's Agnes Gerrity. (Brooklyn's Alice Arden was forced out of the 200 when she injured herself during the high jump; but she qualified in another event.) Helen came in second in the discus to Margaret Wright; she beat out Evelyn Ferrara of Lake Shore Park Club and Rena MacDonald of Albineton, Massachusetts. (Rena tossed the shot put 38 feet 3⅞ inches, keeping her title in that event.)

The 400-meter relay winners were Dee Boeckmann's St. Louis girls: Harriet Bland, Jane Santschi, May Brady, and Gertrude Webb. The 1933 champ in the 50 meters, Louise Stokes, of the Onteora Club of Malden, Massachusetts, re-tained her title with a time of 6.7. Considered the best girl athlete in New England, "the Malden Meteor" was the first African American to win a national track title; she held the Eastern AAU titles in the sprints and high jump.

With Helen's help, the St. Louis Athletic Club earned first place for the Ozark District with 14.5 points. Helen single-handedly won 13 points, making her the highest individual scorer of the day and assuring the district first ranking. Boeckmann chose a photo of the champ taken during this race for the cover of the October issue of *Amateur Athlete* to illustrate her article titled "The New American Sprint Champion." The fact that Helen's William Woods running shirt lacked the college's letters disconcerted key college administrators; they immediately set out to correct the oversight.

Back home, Helen was treated like a campus hero. Wide Wad saw to it that a full-length posed picture was taken of Helen dressed in a new *WWC*-emblazoned sweat jacket and trousers. It was used prominently in the 1936 *Echoes*, with Helen's athletic prowess acclaimed and her new track records noted in a sidebar.

Next was the indoor AAU nationals, scheduled for two days before Valen-tine's Day at the St. Louis Arena. Helen was welcomed as America's national amateur champ returning to the scene of her acclaim. Her delinquent foe, Stella, being a Polish national, didn't need to compete here, unless she wanted to try for an American record. Word was that Stella never again would set foot in this arena because a friend of hers, known in sports circles, had measured the track and discovered a shortage of three meters! Stella also claimed that St. Louis officials used only one stopwatch, which was like having a farmhand measure off the distance with his feet, or relying on city hall's tower clock as a timer. She further jabbed that Helen had used starting blocks, which was against the rules. Everyone except Stella knew that none of it was so, but the gloves were off. Helen would have to wait. In five months, in Berlin, Helen would have an opportunity to call Stella's bluff.

The program flyer pictured Dee, as an Olympic committee member and the chairman of the Women's AAU Track and Field, and sports promoter Earl Reflow, also known as "the Earl of Reflow," the man who brought midget-auto racing to St. Louis. Eighteen girls were aligned with the Missouri Athletic Club, most notably May Brady, Jane Santschi, and Harriet Bland. Also at this meet were a trio of star runners from Chicago's Park District, Kathleen and Evelyn Ferrara and Evelyn Hall. From the Illinois Club for Catholic Women came past Olympian Annette Rogers, seeking an Olympic replay. Alice Arden represented St. George's Dragon Club of Brooklyn, and Harriette LaMertha, the University of Missouri. Tidye Pickett was the only "unattached" athlete.

This time, Helen was up against Canada's star sprinter, Roxy Atkins, who represented the Supreme Ladies Athletic Club of Toronto. But Roxy proved to be no threat at all (though later she would loom onto the stage, in Helen's words, as a proverbial and perennial sore loser). Helen ran the 50-meter dash in 6.4, equaling the world record. She threw the shot put 41 feet 7 inches and set an impressive distance in the standing broad jump, 8 feet 8 inches.

Now, for the paperwork. In Fulton, Helen scooted into Dr. Greene D. McCall's office to get a physical-exam slip required of all Olympic trial competitors. She waited while the secretary typed the certifying document, attesting that on March 16, 1936, the doctor "examined Miss Helen Stephens of William Woods College, Fulton, Mo. and find no defects, and in my opinion she is in perfect physical condition, and meets all requirements physically for competitive track activities." That same day, she applied for a passport at the post office.

In blustery winter weather, family friend Mrs. Warren Tuttle Williams drove Helen, Mrs. Stephens, and Coach Moore to St. Louis Union Station, where the threesome hopped a train and headed for Hamilton, Canada. Helen hoped she would, at last, race against Stella on March 18 in Stella's favored 220-yard dash. But Stella was not there. Perhaps it was better that she hadn't made the trip, for Helen splintered Stella's 220-yard record (26.4) with a time of 26.3 to establish a new Canadian record. Annette Rogers came in second. In a special invitational 50-yard dash, Helen came in at 6.0, tying the 1932 speed of Canadian Myrtle Cook. "Everybody expects her to break a record every time she runs," Moore told reporters, though people failed to consider that "she has been able to train none at all out of doors because of [Missouri's] weather."[11]

They sloshed through nine inches of snow in Toronto, where Helen ran for the first time on board tracks. On March 19, she set a new Canadian record in the 60-yard dash (first running in 7.1 and then in 6.9 seconds). She brought home four trophies, a gold medal set with a diamond, a solid silver fruit basket and silver relish tray, and a copper and silver desk lamp. Crowds encircled her, seeking autographs at the King Edward's Hotel where she and her coach participated in a CFRB radio evening broadcast. On air, Moore said that though Helen won, the Canadian runners had broken from the starting line after the "Get set" and before the gun went off, a procedure Helen was not used to, and that consequently, she had made a poor start.

Back home, Coach Moore, Mrs. Stephens, and Helen took a rest for a few days, and then Horace Carr drove them to Chicago, where Helen ran in the indoor relay race sponsored by the *Chicago Daily News* and the AAU Polish-American Union on March 25. Event planners asked Stella to compete against Helen there, but Stella volleyed, "Tell her, I'll beat her in Berlin." While there, Coach Moore learned that his wife was about to give birth to their first child. He remembered, "I took off for home, my first ride ever on an airplane." But before leaving Chicago, he scribbled on a slip of paper and gave to Helen his list of things to do and remember. It was full of support and advice:

Principle [*sic*] look out before meet—get all rest possible. Stay off of feet before and during meet when possible.

Be very careful about eating too much—take laxative pill each day on trip. No ice water.

Physicians examination.

Find out when prelims are. What time meet starts. Get best discuss throws in prelims when fresh—they count in finals.

Find out how many throws in prelims, how many qualify & how many throws in finals.

May pass a throw any time. Sit down while waiting for turn. Loosen up in ring—forget about trying to stay in ring.

Take time going to marks. Ask photographers to wait.

Wait until final race to open up.

In 200m prelims start with field and ride on nose of wedge.

Ask how many qualify.

Watch starter start races before you run. It's better than asking.

Remember the best always get beat—prolong it as long as possible.

Stretch well before running.

Watch side lanes—they are soft & loose sometimes. Get number & pin it on well.

Races already won & all medals & cups in the world will not win a subsequent race.

If you can, practice with the starter off to one side as he starts some other races.

Among those Helen outran were Chicago's top come-back Olympian champs, Betty "Smiley" Robinson (1928 gold 100-meter sprinter and silver relayer) and Annette "Nettie" Rogers (1932 gold relayer and 1933 American record holder in the 200 meters). Betty and Annette had decades of experience and excellent training between them. According to reporters, they were cuter and prettier, smaller in stature, more delicate in structure, and older than Helen, but they weren't faster or stronger. Helen ran the 50 meters in 6.4 and threw the eight-pound shot put 41 feet 11 inches. She was the most likely to succeed in all the individual races. The base of friendship between them began at this meet, unfolding in their special talent and mutual love for running. If the top two speedsters with Olympic experience couldn't outrun the new 100-meter champ, they at least hoped to be part of the Olympic 4 x 100-meter relay with her. Sports fans expected as much.

In Fort Madison, Iowa, on May 30, in much better weather, Helen ran the 100 meters a bit slow (12.6) but threw the discus 129 feet 7 inches, a bit farther than her previous record. In June, the Kansas City newspaper headlined her two unofficial world marks set at the Cotton Carnival in Tennessee, at Fargason Field—running the 100 meters in 11.5 and the 200 meters in 23.6.

Helen's funds were still insufficient for her Olympic trials and trip, so the mayor of Fulton declared Thursday, June 11, Helen Stephens Day. He scheduled a fee event in Fulton so the hometown girl could once more "show her stuff" to earn her way to Berlin. Helen ran the 100 meters in 11.6, faster than the world record. Robert Morrison of the *St. Louis Post-Dispatch* wrote, "She ran on a track hard as glass . . . without blocks, without foot holes. And a faulty start caused her to strain a muscle in her left leg." But Helen pledged, "I'm gonna beat her! I'm gonna beat her!" It sounded like a chant. "I'd rather beat Stella Walsh than do anything else at the Olympics." Coach Bill Hargiss, from Kansas, told the reporter he "never saw a better running form than Helen's. . . . for a woman . . . she has plenty of arm drive and her leg movement is sound. Whatever is natural is usually best, and Helen's natural style has power."[12] Moore's daily workouts kept her weight at 155 pounds, but he thought she needed help with her start off.

Gate income for the Helen Stephens Day event was substantial. It exceeded the $500 budget for women athletes. Now, Helen headed for the Olympic trials in Providence, Rhode Island. *Providence.* To Helen, the name of the place seemed prophetic and right. And she was to run on Independence Day before a crowd of five thousand. How American, how patriotic could it be? Before leaving for Providence, she saw the movie *It Happened in New York* and got a preview of the sites she hoped to see in the Big Apple.

Mrs. Moore and Helen checked into the Rhode Island Crown Hotel while Burt Moore registered Helen for three events—the maximum allowed. Proudly wearing William Woods jerseys, Helen would compete in the shot put, the discus throw, and her favorite, the 100-meter sprint. When (not if) she qualified, these might be her events in Berlin—if the International Olympic Committee (IOC) admitted the shot put for women. Otherwise, she might compete in the 4 x 100-meter team race.

Helen's running gait now measured well over nine feet—twice that of the girl Dee Boeckmann had coached for several years. Now teaching physical education at Loretto Academy, Boeckmann was strongly backing another Missouri girl, twenty-year-old Harriet Bland. Five foot five and feisty, Bland had qualified for the 1932 games, but members of the American Olympic Committee (now known as the USOC) claimed that funds had limited them from sending all the girls who had qualified. Harriet was told she wasn't among the cut selected to go to Los Angeles. But Boeckmann was in the AOC loop now and was convinced that this 108-pound, strongheaded sprinter would make it this time. Weather permitting, Bland worked out daily year-round at Sherman Park near her home on Washington Avenue; she trained indoors in several St. Louis facilities. Bland was ready and hopeful. And Dee Boeckmann was in the right position to get her there.

Helen stepped up to the mark in the trial heat of the 100 meters, pitted against the consistently fast sprinters Annette Rogers, Louise Stokes, and Harriet Bland. Helen took it easily in 11.8; Stokes trailed in second at 12.2; Rogers and Bland tied for third at 12.4. In the final heat, Helen again won, this time clocking 11.7, beating out Rogers, Bland, and Olive Hasenfus. Then, she threw the discus 121 feet 6½ inches, less than what she had accomplished before, but far enough to win first place. She threw the shot put 41 feet 8½ inches (her record distance) and won first place in that event, also. On that day, 115 women competed for an Olympic berth in track and field. Only 18 qualified. Helen was the best of them all. Boeckmann was the prime mover behind at least 4—2 Missourians and 2 Illinois natives—and within days, she was appointed the women's Olympic track and field coach.

With the winnowing process over, America's outstanding prospects were Betty Robinson (all-around athlete), Evelyn Ferrara (third in discus), Harriet Bland, Tidye Pickett (second in 80-meter hurdles), Betty L. Burch, Olive Hasenfus, Anne O'Brien (winner of 80-meter hurdles), Annette Rogers (winner of high jump), Helen Stephens (winner of 100-meter dash, discus, and shot put), Gertrude Wilhelmsen (second in javelin) and Louise Stokes.

Helen had a sure-thing ticket to Berlin. She had twenty-seven records and fourteen AAU titles. Rhode Island's newspaper headlined her as "A New Didrikson."[13] She had broken Stella's 11.8-second sprint record and was first in two other events. Boeckmann was privy to the AOC's event selections by this time. She told the press that as Helen's Olympic coach she would capitalize on

America's speed queen and use her only in the sprint event and maybe in the relay. The Moores resituated Helen in the Lincoln Hotel, Gotham, New York, where she was to wait for the July 15 bon voyage to Berlin. Helen's first, foremost, and most favorite coach and his wife then returned to Fulton, carrying tales of current victory and future glory. As they left, Helen felt a little heartsick. Once home, Moore tethered-in more funds for the Fulton Flash. He told townsfolk that Helen needed stay-over funds plus a minimum of $500 cash for living expenses abroad, travel, and miscellaneous "touring" costs that she would incur once she had won a gold medal. The Fulton Chamber of Commerce and the newspaper office quickly assumed the task of collecting and managing the Helen Stephens Olympic Fund. Not knowing where to reach her during this limbo period, Senator Harry S. Truman sent a good-luck and good-wishes telegram to Helen's parents. News of this served to spur on the fund-raising effort.

Stressing a fund deficit of $150,000, U.S. Olympic officials announced July 5 that they were sending only four qualifiers to represent the women's track team. Harriet Bland wasn't one of them. Though she had qualified in the 100 meters and the 4 x 100-meter relay, Harriet had been dropped again! Stranded in Providence, she told reporters, "[AOC president Avery] Brundage will hear from me on this."[14] She said she was going to wire St. Louis and would not sit quietly by and let them cheat her out of a place in 1936. "Why didn't they tell us what they intended to do, so we could have made our plans?" she complained angrily. During the press interview, she lapsed into silences to fight back tears. She had spent $70 getting there to qualify and didn't intend to spend any more. "Why do they pick on me?" she asked. "I won a place in the final tryouts in Chicago in 1932, and yet Tidye Pickett, who fell in the hurdle heats and didn't finish and Evelyn Furtsch who quit, were placed on the team ahead of me. I don't know whether it's because some of them come from Chicago or not, but I do know that Mr. Brundage and Mr. Steers will hear from me on this." (Fred Steers was then the U.S. women's team manager.) She pointed an accusatory finger at Avery Brundage's hometown. She had sent him a telegram about being passed over in 1932 and he didn't even reply, she said. He wouldn't get away with ignoring her this time, she declared.

Sportswriters noted that because Helen placed so high in her performances, no limit of funds could possibly rob her of a place on the team. So, Helen was "sitting by, taking it all in, in grim silence." She, too, was disappointed by the cutbacks in the women's team. What did she think about it? "It's a terrible thing for the girls who qualified and now won't be able to make the trip. There's disappointment in sport enough, without this. I feel terrible to think that some who qualified for the team won't be able to go. It looks to me like a plain case of discrimination in favor of the men against the women on using the available money. There's been so much log-rolling that I'll believe I'm in the

Olympics when I actually take the mark in Berlin." Pretty testy stuff, coming from a girl.

Others weren't so lucky. Margaret Caswell of Los Angeles and Mabel Blanche Smith from Tuskegee Institute were left behind due to a lack of funds—or was it logrolling? They had no Dee Boeckmann fighting for them. Or was it another kind of discrimination?

Dee Boeckmann said nothing was certain "after all that's gone ahead," but with *her* help, Harriet got to Brundage. Bland complained in this letter to him that it was unfair for her to be cut out after qualifying for two Olympics in a row. Dee sent copies of the letter to newsmen. In no time, newspapers carried a photo of the pitiful little girl sitting on her luggage, thumbing a ride home from New York.

On July 8, the Olympic committee announced its decision to send five women track and field stars, noting that in December they had haggled over whether to send a women's team at all.[15] Finally, after releasing an account of funds, the committee said it would accommodate eighteen women, if each secured the minimum $500 ($1,000 would be ideal, they said) to pay for her trip to and from Berlin. Interest in women sprinters was strong in the Midwest. The *St. Louis Globe-Democrat* and Boeckmann came to Bland's aid and raised money for her trip, while other sports enthusiasts in other states solicited money for their star sprinters.

The American Olympic Committee widely publicized Dee Boeckmann as the Olympic women's track and field coach. But she was on board without salary; the committee agreed to pay only her travel expenses. Dee got her due in print, however, when John Wray wrote the story as he saw it: "No money, no team, no hope. . . . Today she is working hard to condition her squad of 16 [*sic*] athletes, 12 of whom she, almost single-handedly, financed on this Olympic tour." It was largely through her effort, Wray said, that local communities came to the rescue with funds to send the women to Berlin. Wray's other slant was that without Helen the American team wouldn't have a second-rate chance.[16]

Helen sat tight in New York City while Fulton's paper tracked the protégée's every step. It noted that the hometown girl had written home to tell her mother that newsreels had been made of her running the races in Rhode Island. She wrote that these reels were showing in movie theaters across the United States and that she had been invited to make a movie picture in Hollywood, once she returned from the Olympics in Berlin.[17] She thought she ought to accept the offer.

Missouri journalist O. K. Armstrong wrote at length about "our dashing young lady" in a weekly magazine.[18] "When Helen Stephens gets closely pushed in a race," he said, "she simply turns on more speed, and that usually means a new record." He asked if was she trying to set a record when she ran 150 yards in Sportsman's Field in St. Louis. And true to form, Helen gave him something coy and quotable: "Why, no. My rival just stepped out with all she had and I ran just fast enough to beat her." Helen explained her training routine and diet: "Just plain food . . . very little sweets and pastries. Regular hours for everything. Of course, I don't drink and I don't smoke. And I sleep eight and a half to nine hours every night."

With the exception of falling in and out of love, Helen was stepping into the most transforming experience she would ever know. Armstrong had asked the inevitable; drinking and smoking were habits she would admit to later. For now, all his readers needed to know was that she was only interested in sports. For she was being told what to say and what not to say to the press by the savvy Coach Dee Boeckmann.

4

From Fulton to Berlin

I do not consider Hitler to be as bad as he is depicted. He is showing an ability that is amazing, and he seems to be gaining his victories without much bloodshed.
—Mohandas Gandhi, May 1940, *Letters to Raj Kumari Amrit Kaur*

*B*y the spring of 1936, Helen had come to the end of her first year at William Woods College. Her grades were acceptable yet disappointing, especially to her mother. It had been difficult for Helen to keep up with class work. The reasons for her less-than-glowing academic performance were that she was preoccupied and often had been excused from classes and had a multitude of social diversions. For one thing, Coach Moore kept Helen busy, training her with the men's team at Westminster College. To get competition experience with women athletes, he scheduled Helen in special exhibition races out of town, hence out of class. Gleaning all recruitment potential from his most renowned student, President Harmon committed Helen to speaking engagements in town and out. Harmon worked the star freshman on the yearbook advertising staff, knowing the magic of persuasion would couple with a prospective buyer's interest in meeting the Flash and, perhaps, getting her autograph. Autograph collecting was "all the rage" then, and Helen had purchased her own pocket-size autograph book for her trip to the Olympics.

Over the years, William Woods College molded itself to suit the cultural needs of elite members of society and operated with a certain noblesse oblige. Any idea of physical education as a career choice was, at this private haven for girls, "a foreign notion." In lieu of a bona fide program, the college offered recreational activities—indoor swimming and fencing in a gymnasium, archery, tennis, boating, and equestrian studies. Fresh off the farm, Helen viewed horse riding as neither recreational or educational; however, the other physical outlets mentioned appealed to her. Young women sought acceptable physical outlets through the Women's Athletic Association led by Miss Martha Alexander. In past years, basketball, also called hoopball, was an on-again, off-again thing.

Though its institutional structure did not provide athletic scholarships per se, its doors of higher education had opened wide to Helen by way of a two-year scholarship. She declared modern history as her major. And she earned some money for the necessities of life by taking a student job in Dulany Library. If she stayed on campus for the weekend, she enjoyed a Saturday matinee in a back-row seat of the movie house and stayed up after-hours talking and smoking Chesterfields or Camels. She and her clique of friends—Betty Sue Reed, Evelyn Bluhm, Kay Killingsworth, Mary Griffith, and a half-dozen other Woodsies—went to college concerts or plays in which friends played a part. She rarely refused diversion from study for a quick game of tennis or a slip down to Senior Lake to row a canoe in the moonlight.

As a consequence of too many track events, career commitments, extracurricular activities, and several glorious but torrid love affairs, Helen's grade point average sagged lower than what her abilities could accomplish in a less complicated, less frenzied academic and social climate.

She had gained entry to this place solely by the fact of her talent, her Olympic potential. She was an enigma in those days, insofar as she was a jock and brainy. She had been a grade-A high schooler, thus Woods trustees claimed they had awarded the scholarship based on her need and academic excellence, but it was Helen's athletic prowess that brought her, her hometown, and her college national attention. Acting in loco parentis, the college would benefit from the limelight Helen would bring her alma mater during an Olympic year. In this case of noblesse oblige, there was something to be gained all around. In developing Helen's talent, it was agreed, Coach Moore melded William Woods and the Westminster College track program into a purposeful alliance.

"Miss" Stephens—from the moment she stepped into the Academic Building—was in the news almost weekly, with something about her training, her home life, her appearances, or her exhibition races always referenced to her amazing speed. Also reported in the summer of 1936 was the fact that Harmon had appointed one of Helen's favored teachers, luckily in New York during summer recess, to act as her chaperone.

Dean of Students Shafer intuited that her unusually gifted student was embarking on an excursion that would push her swiftly into adulthood. Journeying to and from Berlin afforded an education far beyond what any history class offered. Shafer expected her students to learn from such experiences, and to assist this purpose, she bought a bon voyage gift, a little something—a travel diary—to give to Helen at the dock, but she attached to it an assignment that sounded more like a mission. Helen penned her own name on the first blank page in ink and below it wrote: "William Woods College, Fulton, Mo., American Olympic Team '36, Berlin, Germany." Her diary entries, presented in this and the next four chapters, show the innocent character of a youth molded by a wide and strange world. Passages name people and record events during her flight to glory that would change her life forever.

July 15: Day One, Boarding SS Manhattan, New York Harbor

Helen awoke shortly after six o'clock and ate breakfast quickly. She had stayed up most of the night. Staying in a New York City hotel was cause alone for sleeplessness. She was a country girl, after all, a long way from home. Coach Moore's words kept popping into her head: "When you win that Olympic medal, don't let it swell your head, Helen." She kept hearing her mother's voice: "Make us proud, Helen. Make us proud." She had talked endlessly to her roommates way into the early morning hours. Somehow, President Roosevelt's objections to Olympic participation had been quelled. With a margin of a single vote, the American Olympic Committee's winning teams were on their way now.

It was about eight o'clock when Helen and the other track girls handed the gate attendant their boarding passes for the SS *Manhattan*. Among their send-off crowd at the gate, Helen saw in the corner of her eye, "old piano legs" charging down Pier 60. Dean Shafer, Helen's ex officio New York chaperone. Originally a New Yorker herself, Dean Shafer embodied every bit of what yearbook scribes wrote about her: "a woman of rare tact and charm who possessed the fundamental qualities—a love of truth, hatred of prejudice, loyalty to one's convictions, charity, and reverence toward the spiritual."

What transpired between teacher and student on this day went something like this. She most likely said, "Here, Helen, take this with you," and thrust a small book into Helen's palm. Gold lettering on pitted leather branded the cherry-red volume as a travel diary. Now, amid the scrunching crowd, the dean of students had waited for the *Manhattan*'s final moment of departure before giving Helen this farewell gift. She told Helen to write down every exciting thing that happened to her during her stay in Berlin but to be careful what she wrote. Helen thanked Dean Shafer and promised, "I will! I'll use this. I'll write about everything. I'll write in such a way that anyone can read it, out loud. Whenever they want!" She waved good-bye, smiling excitedly.

By eleven o'clock, the sun brightly shinning, Helen and 382 American athletes set sail. In a few weeks, she would be competing on an Olympic track, in the magnificently new, $30 million Reichsportfeld. The ocean liner so impressed Helen that she jotted on the first page of her travel diary: *A floating hotel. Very nice indeed.*[1]

Though she had traveled before, she had never traveled by ship. Just days ago, by car and by train with Coach Moore, she traveled to Rhode Island for the Olympic qualifying trials on the Fourth of July. And last year, she had competed in AAU track meets in Chicago, in Memphis, and in Toronto. But this trip was the reason for it all. Now en route to Berlin aboard the *Manhattan*, this was what Helen had dreamed about and waited years for. This was the trip to make her childhood dream come true—or render it false. She stashed her passport safely in the inside pocket of her brown-and-white checkered jacket. Her passport carried all the required stamps and signatures, the official Nationale Olympische Komitee XI stamp, and the markings of America's Olympic committee president, Avery Brundage.[2] Helen's expression in her passport photo evinced dogged determination, a kind of edgy eagerness. Challenge was there, a pouty dare in her pulled-down, full lower lip.

Helen wrote: *Had no difficulty in getting settled. Betty Robinson, Kath Kelly & I have Cabin 35 on Deck 6. Had a grand send-off & had many, many pictures taken. Got flowers from D.S.* [probably Dean Shafer] *& Mrs. Fagley from George.* Fagley was the director of Fulton's School for the Deaf; her son George was a Westminster track pal of Helen's; their daughter Elizabeth attended the University of Berlin. Dozens of bouquets awaited the girls, for hopes in America's Olympic athletes ran high. Helen did not write about the letters from American Jews asking athletes to boycott what they called the Nazi Games to protest restrictions on Germany's Jewish athletes and to secure amnesty for Carl Mierendorf, Kurt Schumacher, Carl von Ossietsky, and other political prisoners of Hitler's regime.[3] At the close of her first day aboard ship, she wrote: *Everything O.K. Meals good.* [Kathlyn] *Kelly,* [Louise] *Stokes and* [Tidye] *Pickett sea sick.* [Stokes and Pickett were the only black American women on the team.] *I am fine, now. 8 laps of walking after dinner. Night just wonderful.*

July 16: Day Two, Aboard Ship

On her second day out to sea, Helen was blissfully happy: *Betty and I lapped deck before breakfast. Feel grand. Kelly, Pickett, & Stokes still under. Our group had work-out on deck—stationary running and exercises. Pictures were taken. Got our track outfits and suits and hats this afternoon. Mine were about O.K. Nice weather all day. Had mail distributed in lounge & then President Brundage gave talk and introduced some of the other members of A.O.C. After dinner went on deck for game of shuffleboard with Evelyn* [Ferrara] *& some boys—boxers. Turned watches up an hour at dinner. Bed at 10:30. Sea is a little rough—boat rocking some.*

Upon awakening, Helen peeked through the tiny cabin porthole; her spirits high among the puffy clouds drifting by. She relished the rocking of the wood floor beneath her feet and felt eagerness flowing through her legs. When bright sunlight broke from the clouds, a tingle ran through her veins. How would it feel, she wondered, racing on an Olympic track, wearing her red-white-and-blue Olympic uniform? Could happiness hold more than this?

In the afternoon, Avery Brundage, a man who had near dictatorial power when it came to America's Olympic policies and affairs, spoke to a full assembly of athletes. His words rippled into Helen's heart. He said this would be an Olympics long remembered, for there would be exemplary accomplishments. There were rowdy shouts from the men's track team standing near Coach Lawson Robertson. Their applause halted his talk momentarily. When they quieted, his serious voice reminded them that the Olympic Oath would be required of each of them during the opening ceremonies. He paused to command silence, then recited the oath: "We swear we will take part in the Olympic Games in loyal competition, respecting the regulations which govern them . . . participating in them in the true spirit of sportsmanship for the honor of our country and for the glory of sport." Helen murmured the words under her breath, "for the honor of our country, for the glory of sport." "We can't give every one of you a private coach," Brundage continued, "but you know your routine. Follow it to the best of your ability. And good luck!"

Helen felt wonderful. An official moved through the crowd distributing a list of conduct rules and mail from home full of encouragement and pride. The girls—Betty Robinson, Harriet Bland, Annette Rogers, and Helen—were told to get into their Olympic running shorts and tops and come back on deck for a press photo. Helen's were a little snug, but "O.K." What exhilaration she must have felt opening the box with her name on it and putting on the Olympic armor. She traced a finger around each of the five overlaying rings, lifted the satin to her face, and closed her eyes. She looked herself over in the vanity mirror on the door of her narrow locker. She couldn't be happier.

July 17: Day Three, Aboard Ship

On the third day, Helen wrote: *Spent short time in sun on deck. Took work-out with team. Most of us dressed in new uniforms. Everyone seems to be occupied. Went above to see pictures taken in New York harbor. Got lost & wandered about exploring ship. Played game with Mrs. Wray and her friend. Saw 3 ships in distance. Saw picture above.* She finally found the right port, where the women's track team, in a huddle with Coach Boeckmann, was looking at publicity photos. Helen thought Coach Boeckmann seemed tense and preoccupied. Soon, everyone gathered in the "commons" to watch a film of the Olympic trials. Helen wrote: *Later met boy from Mo. U. Pictures of Olympic trials shown. Saw myself from screen for first time. Heavy fog & horn busy. Had meeting in Dee's room at 10:30.*

When Dee singled out Helen to stop by her cabin, Helen knew something was up. She wondered what her coach (now on a first-name basis) wanted to talk about. Diet? Training? No, that wasn't it. Dee pumped Helen for information on Eleanor Holm, a swimmer enjoying her third Olympic year. She wanted to know if the girls were caving in to the boycotters, which, if they were, would mean serious trouble for them in Berlin. She wanted to know what Helen thought. Helen remembered that the conversation went something like this: "Eleanor's not influencing any of *my* girls, is she? I'm depending on your help, Helen. Our girls must use their time aboard ship wisely—eat right, get their sleep!" Dee insisted that Helen relinquish the protest letters she had received, telling her that Steers and Brundage wanted them. Dee's manner intimidated Helen, who demurred, dropping her eyes to her feet to give herself time to think. Helen told her she didn't think the girls knew much about German politics, that they seemed mostly interested in boys and having fun. Of herself, Helen said she had read an abridgment of *Mein Kampf*, "But I don't think the others know, or care. Besides, a boycott would mess up our chances."

Dee pressed, "I can count on you, then?" Helen said yes. Dee gave her a copy of *Amateur Athlete* and told her to read the piece written by the Reich sports commissar about the controversy surrounding two German Jewesses, fencer Helene Mayer and high jumper Greta Bergmann. The commissar claimed they would be treated like any other Olympic candidates, that Germany acted in the Olympic spirit, that the commissar had invited Mayer and Bergmann to be on the German team, and that IOC member Charles Sherrill had gained confirmation of Germany's nondiscrimination after lengthy consultations with Reich leaders.[4]

Bergmann won her Olympic trials with 1.65 meters, but the German Olympic Committee judged her mark as "mediocre," which was meant to discourage her from competing. Mayer had won a 1928 Olympic gold medal in fencing in Amsterdam; in 1932 in Los Angeles, she had taken only fifth place but was hopeful that she could regain her title in 1936.

That night Helen scribbled in her diary: *Found my blue coat in Stokes' possession. It was a mistake. Cutting up in* [Alice] *Arden's and Bland's room.* She wrote nothing about meeting with Boeckmann or about the *Amateur Athlete* article.

The introductory pages of her travel diary advised that departing ships are "overrun with visitors, occasionally pilferers, therefore, put baggage in stateroom and keep it locked." She thought she had locked her room, which she shared with two other girls. Sometimes they didn't bother to lock. When the weather turned cooler after three days at sea, Helen searched for her coat. Bunkmates Kathlyn Kelly and Betty Robinson swore they hadn't seen it. But Harriet claimed she saw one of the "colored" girls wearing a coat that looked like Helen's and told her to check with them, which she did. When Helen asked about her missing garment, she met an upswelling of anger. She had unknowingly crossed a line, blundered into a sensitive area, and ostensibly accused "a black girl" of stealing. Once she realized what she had done, "the much celebrated white girl" apologized, but tempers had flared quickly and ignited a fire in the minds of her segregated teammates, Tidye Pickett and Louise Stokes.

As it turned out, Helen had taken all but one of her belongings into the safety of her cabin. She had carelessly thrown her coat on a pile of baggage and forgotten it. Louise owned a similar, dark-blue wool coat, and three days earlier, seeing "her" coat slung atop a collected group of baggage, had taken it to her cabin.

With the missing coat matter settled, blithely Helen bounded onward, "cutting up with older girls" Arden and Bland, whom she had competed against at qualifying events but never socialized with, until then.

Friday, July 17, was the day a Mr. Maybaum invited Eleanor Holm to a party in the A-deck bar and lounge. Partying lasted until about 6:00 AM, which was about the time that Eleanor, the only team member invited, was seen being carried back to her cabin.

July 18: Day Four, Aboard Ship

Cabin 35 got up late for breakfast. But I got mine piecemeal. Walked around deck for most of my work-out. Back of legs and back were stiff. Lunch was more than a dinner. Our team was given white tams [dress hats]. *Went to see pictures, walked & sat on deck and fooled away time. And the harmonica! The Gala dinner or Captain's Ball was lots of fun. The noise and bright hats were swell as well as the music and songs. The Dance was afterwards. Most of the day was damp, misty & cool.* [Kathlyn] *Kelly is getting over her spell* [of sea sickness?] *& getting out some.*

Contrary to Dee's directions, our promising athlete was staying up late with revelers and losing sleep. Bedded down in third-class quarters, Betty, Kathlyn, and Helen relived every little goings-on of the late-night, early-morning parties. Betty (Boeckmann's peer in 1928) asked what Dee wanted, and Helen "told all." The girls agreed that the boycott wasn't something they would do, having gotten this far, and they wondered if Brundage would kick Eleanor off the team. None of them believed that would happen, because she was favored to win several gold medals. Eleanor held the 1935 record for the 100-meter free style swim and recently had broken the 200-meter record.

Defending Eleanor and showing off, Helen read aloud from her traveler's companion, which advised various remedies for sea sickness and hangovers: black coffee, mineral drink as a relaxant, or alcohol (the hair of the dog); lying flat, fresh air, quietness accomplished by plugging the ears with wool or wax. The guide advised: "If you do not care for wine or beer, drink bottled mineral water which can be bought anywhere." To our homespun girl traveling on a budget, the most basic necessities of safe water and hand soap were extras, as cruise cabins were not supplied with these items. Travelers purchased or brought with them such consumables. Some girls generously shared theirs or bought them for Helen, the youthful, up-and-coming star athlete.

JULY 19: DAY FIVE, ABOARD SHIP

Arose too late for breakfast. Dressed for pictures on deck. After dinner I started getting autographs & wrote about 5 letters. Day mostly cool but the sun shone. However, I spent little time on deck. Headache bothered me a little during most of day. Major Bowes' Amateur Hour was staged. It was very, very good. More laughs.

Among the autographs she collected were Alice Arden's, who wrote, "Best of luck in all your endeavors, to the kind of teammate that makes a trip worthwhile," and Jesse Owens' fluid-flowing hand, "Best of luck and all my good wishes. Jesse Owens, Ohio State." The amateur hour parodied the number one American radio show of 1936. Major Edward Bowes' well-known clanging gong signaled a performer's strikeout. In Olympic translation, all imitators of competing countries were gonged routinely. The builder of New York's Capitol Theatre and one-time Goldwyn Films vice president, Major Bowes showcased impersonators and personalities, tap dancers, and other entertainers (Charlie McCarthy, Edgar Bergen, W. C. Fields, George Burns, Gracie Allen, Mae West, etc.). Shipboard fun included mock weddings, mock funerals, and mock wakes. Life at sea was for living and play! But as Helen found out, there was a price to pay: nausea and headaches from drinking too much and staying up too late.

Helen wrote: *Bill Cunningham, sports reporter from Boston, spoke. We had to go to bed before the program was completed.*

Stifled by the sexually and racially segregated third-class staterooms, the wife of nightclub singer and big band owner Art Jarrett, Eleanor Holm, was one of the last to leave the party. Brundage had warned her against "smoking and the use of intoxicating drinks." The swim team chaperone, Mrs. Ada Taylor Sackett, tattled that Eleanor was lounging in upper-class quarters with reporters and drinking alcohol. But Helen's entry that day carries none of the scuttlebutt that chafed "old tight-lace Sackett and stiff-neck Brundage," which was how Helen described these two officials to her biographer in the early 1990s.

JULY 20: DAY SIX, ABOARD SHIP

Arose early & watched sunrise from porthole. Got up at 7 & Kath & I walked about, watched sailors clean boat, played ping pong & enjoyed early morning sun & air. Took usual work-out. Wrote letters, walked & sat around, etc. most of day. Had venison for lunch. Saw show "Green Pastures." Ship took Betty's iron. Enjoyed movie pictures of athletes shown in dining room. And Bob Mitchell!!

With her sleep pattern shattered, a restless Helen stepped onto the deck to watch daybreak. Workout aboard ship meant sprinting around the deck a time or two plus calisthenic exercises designed to strengthen leg muscles. Track coaches of men and women alike did not proscribe weight lifting or other body-building routines that are now thought to be essential for training runners. Jogging on the ship's hard boards, in fact, injured Helen's legs. Her daily routine caused painful shinsplints that required treatment and rest at a time crucial to her conditioning. Although her diary reveals no anxiety about it, Helen's legs bothered her greatly. The ship's captain had confiscated Betty Robinson's flat iron because she had violated fire safety regulations. Passengers were not to use travel irons in their cabins. Robert Mitchell had Helen and all the other girls swooning; but who Mitchell is (whether an athlete or actor), Helen never explains and could not remember when asked.

July 21: Day Seven, Aboard Ship

Arose with rest of group about 3:15 to see Ireland. The lights from shore were beautiful in distance. The biting breeze was cold. Boat came out & got passengers, mail & cards. The land & houses were very pretty in early morning sunlight. No trees. Rode most of day near land & got to Plymouth, England mid-afternoon. . . . a scattered town but picturesque—the green hills, homes, low buildings. 2 boats met us. Saw the show, "Spendthrift." The "Mock Wedding" was more than ritzy—hot stuff! Had to leave early. Will probably awake in Le Havre, France. Sent off mail at last. The straw hat.

Alan Gould transmitted the news from ship that they had touched Côbh and skirted the Emerald Isle: "the athletic argosy was impatient to complete the eight-day voyage and exchange sea-legs for a brisk workout on terra firma. . . . officials are keeping their fingers crossed after an eventful wielding of the disciplinary big stick, and a mild epidemic of sore throats. . . . athletes are anxious to resume conditioning ashore, especially the runners and hurdlers, who have been cramped aboard ship."[5] Gould said that Coach Robertson denied that the 4 x 100-meter relay team was composed of Sam Stoller, Mack Robinson, Foy Draper, and Marty Glickman—whom the track and field committee had named the previous morning—but said that, with the possible exception of Robinson, this was the most likely combination. Helen was happy to mail her letters written days earlier; she cryptically notes the tossing of someone's hat into the sea.

July 22: Day Eight, Le Havre, France, on English Channel

Spent the day until 4:30 in afternoon in port of Le Havre, France. Officials were allowed off boat but not the athletes. Packed things during morning with 2 [Olympic] boxers in the room. The buildings had tall chimneys & there were many bicycles. Most of town was on hills. Very pretty indeed. Saw show in afternoon and prizes given to winners of various contests. Cashed one of my cheques for [Deutsch] marks. Sent several cards from France. Weighed 162 lbs today!! Just passed Dover, England.

Eleanor Holm was in the news again. The AOC had voted her out, and team manager Herbert Holm (no relation to Eleanor) had the task of informing her, carrying the message that she was charged not only with inebriation but gambling, for she had won $100 in a game of craps.

"So what?" she snapped. "I'm free, white, and over twenty-one!" During the stopover near Cherbourg, she had attended a champagne party, and Ada Sackett, once again, "discovered" her with a young man, staggering back to her room. Eleanor was in deep slumber, according to her roommates, Olive McKean and Mary Lou Petty, when Sackett pounded on her door, in the company of the ship's doctor, J. Hubert Lawson. Dr. Lawson diagnosed the swimmer's condition as "acute alcoholism." In telling her side of the story, Eleanor disclosed, "The day before the boat was scheduled to dock . . . newsmen threw a humdinger of a party. . . . Everybody got pleasantly soused."[6]

When the ubiquitous chaperone, Sackett, caught America's star swimmer slinking back to her third-class quarters, she reported it to Brundage, who decreed that Miss Holm was off the team and would be sent home ASAP! To show what happened to girls who ignored the rules, Dee Boeckmann paraded her team into Eleanor's stateroom. Eleanor was "laying in" that morning, less than shipshape, and recovering from "a headache." Helen was horrified that her coach humiliated Eleanor that way. She commiserated with Betty, who also was sympathetic with Eleanor. They grumbled to each other, asking why their coach and old tight lace were being so hard on her.

July 23: Day Nine, Baltic Sea and Elbe River

Arose early and walked around. Spent morning in line getting land passes, inspection, inspection of money by customs officials and baggage checked. And who stole my tags? Had picture taken in afternoon. Took work-out. Played 1 game of deck tennis 6 times in order to train. Some fun! Terrain scenery very swell. Dutch mill, light houses, canals, flags, ships, red roofs, & homes very pretty. Alice Arden had birthday—party-doll. Danced little after dinner. Bed at 9:00 (?) Will be in Hamburg in morning. Ship sailed slowly all day & stopped some.

She retired early but couldn't sleep; made a brief entry in her journal, bridging the gap between nights that ran into days, using a three-word sentence and a *code* question mark to remind her later of the jolt she felt when walking on deck in the dark of night. She thought she was alone, but she wasn't. She heard whispers and muffled sounds, something banging against wood, coming from a lifeboat. The canvas stretched over the length of the boat and tied down by rubber straps was moving. Somebody was under there. Helen moved into the shadows and waited. Minutes passed. Then she saw Jesse Owens swiftly step out from under the covering and vanish into the darkness. More minutes passed. Helen started to leave when another person, a girl, slipped out and padded lightly by Helen. The girl whispered good-morning. Who she was, Helen didn't know.

July 24: Day Ten, Hamburg to Berlin, Germany

Stayed up most of night watching boat dock in Hamburg. Very Pretty. Rousing welcome along river. Arose early for 6:40 breakfast. Had speech on board. Went ashore & took buses to City Hall of Hamburg. City was in flags. After ceremony there we took train to Berlin. Received wonderful welcome in Berlin Station & had same at City Hall. People lined streets and buildings by thousands. And the flags!! Passed Unter der Linden—the great arch. Came out to beautiful new dorm & had dinner. Group of us went over to the great Olympic Stadium.

Using antique cut crystal glasses to propose toasts to the young American athletes, who had not eaten much en route, the Germans wined them at Hamburg City Hall. *Prosit* here, *prosit* there, and when it was time for the group to leave, some of the glasses left with them. In the afternoon, the athletes were told that if those glasses didn't reappear pronto, they were all going to be *prosit*-ed in a German jail.[7]

At Lehrter Railway Station, Helen waved good-bye to forlorn Eleanor, waiting in vain to board a train festooned with huge swastikas. Brundage had invalidated her ticket to Berlin. She was on her own. Thousands of people had gathered, and amid the amplified brassy notes of a Sousa march, they pushed and bumped her as they tried to catch a glimpse of Olympic hopefuls. Helen was ushered to a berth separate from the other girls. She would be with CBS reporter Bill Henry, *Post-Dispatch* sportswriter John "Ed" Wray, swimmer Dorothy Poynton Hill (who, like Helen, had qualified in more than one Olympic event), Glenn Cunningham, Jesse Owens, and Avery Brundage. America's star athletes were to broadcast to America from the train: *first time in history!* she wrote, her mood exhilarant.

The city of Berlin, arrayed with swastikas on blood-red fields, heralded the arrival of Olympian athletes, while the young woman whom Brundage had installed in the Avon Hotel, with a chaperone, hung onto a thin thread of hope that she might be reinstated to America's swim team. The Associated Press announced that the American team had circulated a petition, signed by 220 athletes, urging Eleanor's reinstatement. But Brundage refused to budge.

Anti-Hitler Germans sent a manifesto to potential medal winners, especially targeting the women.[8] Somehow it passed through the mail system and entered the Olympic village. Written in Dutch originally, translations appeared in Spanish, French, and English. Helen's copy was waiting for her on the first day she settled in her room:

> Hundreds of Germans will be unable to [attend the Olympics] because they are political prisoners, confined to concentration camps for two or

three years, because they are pacifists or against National-Socialism. . . . It is hoped that Hitler, the champion of German national peace, will be seized by the chivalrous Olympic sporting spirit, and that he will liberate his innocent political prisoners. . . .

In the first place we appeal to all women participating in the Games. What would the Olympic Games be if the women athletes were to refuse to take part? Whether the German political prisoners will be released depends to a very great extent on the girl athletes, for they can exercise their powers of persuasion to induce their male colleagues to join forces. . . .

German authorities will start by being very displeased, but they cannot punish anybody. The worst thing they can do is to send home those athletes who stand up for Mierendorf and his comrades. . . .

Germans will threaten to do so, but will not carry out their threat, or else all newspapers throughout the world would write about it. Especially the women in the Olympic Games can come to no harm.

Evidently, the Dutch viewed women athletes as essential components of the Olympics. American officials had asked for all political letters and postcards received when the *Manhattan* docked, but Helen kept the manifesto for her scrapbook. She hid it among her belongings, knowing it was a solid, little piece of history.

Mystery shrouds the quick exit from Berlin of two men on America's team who, in seven days' time, would be sent back to the United States. Some papers reported incorrectly that two U.S. "boxers" set sail for home due to homesickness. Others speculated that politics were involved in Coach Robertson's selection for the 4 x 100-meter relay and the early return of two sprinters. Robertson replaced two Jewish American track men, Sam Stoller and Marty Glickman, with two "black auxiliary" teammates, Ralph Metcalfe and Jesse Owens.[9]

JULY 25: DAY ELEVEN, OLYMPIC WOMEN'S DORM
AND SPORTS FIELDS, BERLIN, GERMANY

The Flash was limping a few days before her main event.[10] Dee Boeckmann told Helen to be careful around snoopy reporters, to guard against letting her shin-splints be the focus of a media story. Helen made no mention of this malady in her daily journal, except for references to treatments she sought and cutbacks on her workouts, and there is no mention of the boycott. But she used language that would flag what she held back in her mind: *It rained at intervals during the day. Cloudy weather dampens the spirits. Did our washing during morning & straightened our bare rooms. Loud echoes & no hangers. Received our competitor's badges & the Olympic Memorial medal from Mr. Steers. Took light work-out.*

Many people came to watch & get autographs & the photographers took pictures. Pictures taken at all times of the day, from every angle. Gertrude [Wilhelmsen] & I took walk around the fields & enjoyed the beauty of the huge fields, stadium, and towers. Only thrills come as you gaze upon it all.

Since Helen's reputation as America's best and youngest sprinter preceded her, streams of media men hounded her. Under scrutiny, she appeared to be in stride and projected a natural, casual manner. Nothing seemed to be ruffling her. She diverted reporters: "I'm not worrying a great deal about my shin splints. I think I can beat Stella [Walsh] even though I'm handicapped by injuries."[11] But she *was* worried about her affliction hindering her performance and had not followed Coach Boeckmann's advice on handling the media. Walsh, on the other hand, yet to arrive, had fanned the flames by telling reporters she had made a vow: "Helen will never defeat me again, in this or any other race."[12] Naturally, the press tunneled Stella's bravado into Helen's face. "We'll see about that soon, won't we?" Helen replied.

As to the Spartan conditions of the Frauenheim, the women's facilities, she was jovial. In Popeye-mode, she quipped about cold, damp rooms, renaming their building "das Freezin'haus." She likened the sounds of thunder to Hitler's boots stumbling across wood planks, lightning claps could be distant pistol reports, the steady patter of rain slapping against windowpanes recalled the vigorous hands of her German masseuse.

Soon, their breakfast of dark bread and green apples was converted to a hearty and familiar American diet of bacon, eggs, cereal, and juice. The evening meal left a hungry growling in their stomachs, for the German custom was to eat a hearty midday meal and lighter fare at suppertime. It felt like fasting to Helen. Within a short time, Helen had a liaison with a German waitress in one of the village restaurants, Ruth Haslie. Ruth began giving Helen large portions and food varieties not served to other girls. Those sitting at the table when Ruth was on duty observed that Helen got partial treatment from this fräulein.

The dormitory lounge had a floor-console radio. At first the girls thought it would be "swell" to be able to dance to big band music. But the radio was receptive to one station only, airing Wagnerian operas, German marching songs, and Hitler's daily *volks sprechen*—addresses to the people. There was nothing Ruth could do about changing that.

July 26: Day Twelve, Frauenheim, Berlin

Some of group went in to town to church. Betty [Burch] & I went over to the swimming pool & watched swimmers. Newspapers carried accounts of Eleanor Holm. Day was very bright after rain. The German people milled about all day— flag-carrying youth practicing for some festival—others for flag-carrying in Stadium. Very pretty. We went for walk around Berlin. Took subway. Berlin very pretty. Buildings not too large. People stared & stared. Many hadn't seen any Negroes. Made record & then heard it. Wrote home.

As Helen and Betty L. Burch (of Allston, Massachusetts) toured the streets of Berlin with Louise Stokes and Tidye Pickett, Berliners gawked and whispered, *"die Amerikarinen . . . schwarz Frauen,"* curious about the black American women. Betty Burch's appearance may have also provoked whispers, although among the cabaret set, her "look" was commonplace. In an interview, Helen described Burch as "a small gal who wore her hair cut short like a boy and often was mistaken for a boy. . . . [She was] a quiet type, wasn't into conversation." Tidye hailed from Chicago, "a very petite and pretty gal, full of fun," with a light skin complexion, "a high yellah Negro." Louise "was on the quiet side and dark."

By this time, the spat Helen and they had aboard ship seemed forgotten, and they had learned that Eleanor Holm was not to be reinstated. Brundage intended to banish her from Berlin. He withdrew all amenities except a ticket back to New York as punishment for "repeated infractions of training regulations." But the lady was from Brooklyn. The five-foot-two woman who swam as gracefully as a porpoise wasn't without resources. Six years earlier, this eighteen-year-old glamour girl had turned down Florenz Ziegfeld's invitation to join his Ziegfeld Follies; the petite plum wanted Los Angeles and the 1932 Olympics, instead. For at the tender age of fifteen, she had landed fifth in the 100-meter backstroke at the 1928 Olympics. Eleven days after winning a gold in the same event in 1932, Jack Warner signed her to a seven-year, $500-per-week contract, which she broke nine months later when he tried to push her into a pool-act part for Warner Brothers. It would have compromised her amateur status, so she quit! She wanted the Berlin Olympics in 1936, instead. By the summer of 1936, Eleanor successfully (some said inevitably) had mixed a tantalizing concoction of swimming and show biz.

This eye-catching doll of a nightclub entertainer was the wife and costar of the Coconut Grove's feature act. She was "Mrs.," not "Miss," when she boarded for Berlin, and Mrs. Eleanor Holm Jarrett gave Brundage a wrestling match he never could have dreamed of. Publicly accused of training infractions, Eleanor fired back, charging that he and other officials of the American committee were guilty of misconduct en route to Berlin themselves, that they had neglected their responsibilities, and that the mock marriage and trial given as entertainment aboard ship were *shocking.* Remonstrating through his official spokesperson, Gustavus Kirby, Brundage denied it: "There was nothing to offend anybody. The whole thing was done in the spirit of fun without anything offensive whatsoever."[13] The sure-winner backstroke queen got numerous cablegrams and messages of sympathy and a gift box of handkerchiefs from the women's swim team, with the note "Keep your chin up!"

But she didn't need the hankies, for soon newspapers announced that

Eleanor had acquired a job as a broadcast columnist. She would work along-side some of the best writers in the world, with her own by-line and amid an army of sportswriters assigned to report on the Olympic Games: Paul Gallico and Alan Gould of the Associated Press, Bob Considine, Jimmy Powers, and Charles MacArthur (Helen Hayes' husband). Eleanor would be in the swim of things after all, poised in the press booth behind Hitler's box, hobnobbing with notables, and attending all VIP parties, much to Brundage's chagrin. Her emerging journalism career so enraged Brundage that he later banned her from other amateur competitions, faulting her for profiting from her Olympic suspension. (Eleanor turned pro in 1937, signing a $30,000 contract to star with Olympian Johnny Weissmuller in Billy Rose's Aquacade. In 1939, calling Eleanor his "Nijinsky in a bathing cap," Rose divorced Fanny Brice and married Eleanor shortly after she divorced Art Jarrett.)

July 27: Day Thirteen, Olympic Dorm, Berlin

Rained last night & at times during the day. Quite cool. Left for tour of shop at 9. Dee, Betty, Kathlyn & I had one guide, Ilse. I bought pair of Bavarian shoes—tan & green. Expect to buy more later. We had grand lunch in German place. Came back & Betty & I went to sleep until practice. Took quite a work-out. Heard Stella was doing 11.6. Had grand dinner of lamb chop, carrots, potato, fruit cocktail, milk, & cheese. Bland stole my bathrobe! The little guide who had to get out. Cashed my marks. Saw balloon put into air with Olympic rings on side. Gave myself rub-down.

Brundage's moves against Eleanor Holm hit the papers in full bloom on July 27, but Helen camouflaged it when she wrote about the German anti-Hitler organization's spy: *The little guide who had to get out.* She may have been the one who slipped the manifesto into the athletes' rooms and when found out was forced to leave.

July 28: Day Fourteen, Olympic Dorm

Rain as usual. I wrote cards most of the morning but didn't finish. After lunch, I fooled around until 3 o'clock. Had picture taken with [illegible]. Had hard work-out on damp track. Threw discus about 123½'. Hope to do better.

Helen practiced discus that day without Dee's supervision. She worried but didn't write about the modification in her running style that Coach Boeck-mann wanted her to make. Helen's getaway from the starting line—a kind of flying leap she learned from Coach Moore—threw Helen off stride, according to Dee. Men, with their considerable strength, might find that kind of start beneficial, she told Helen, but the structural frame of women hinders the bal-ance needed for a flying leap takeoff. Helen was reluctant and unsure about any changes to what Moore had taught her, especially at this late hour. But

Boeckmann insisted on what she thought best and told Helen to discard her old way of placing her feet and reaching out her arms. She had her practice running with her toes turned inward (pigeon-toed), and Helen said she felt and probably looked like a duck. After a few tries following instructions, Helen flatout refused. Finally, they compromised; Helen would concentrate on setting down her feet and hands and would lean in such a way as to, said Dee, maintain starting balance and get her in stride quickly. They practiced for hours on this, agreeing to limit it to starts only, fearing aggravation of Helen's injury. At night, Helen applied ice packs to her ailing left shin, while each day, bulletins reported on her condition.[14]

She concluded: *Came back after practice & got hot bath. Then Betty & I got in on another record. After dinner, Bland, Kelly & I took short walk. Some of boys outside gate. Got negatives from Evelyn. We got nice lamp for room.* A diversion of great appeal to the girls was recording one's own voice on vinyl audio-platters. The teammates chipped in to furnish their room with a light fixture. Though directed by a baroness (Johanna von Wagenheim), das Freezin'haus not only was dreary and dark but still cold and damp, and on this day Dee Boeckmann lodged a written complaint about the lack of heat in the women's dorm and the odd evening diet provided for her girls. Meanwhile, her girls slipped out for a short walk at night, unescorted, and tarried at the gate, chatting and flirting with some local youths of quick acquaintance. The athletes and their new friends stayed out too long, and the girls had trouble getting back into the dorms. Harriet Bland's and Kathlyn Kelly's German boyfriends lingered at the gate and caused a ruckus trying to get in.

Now fully smitten by Helen, Ruth Haslie quickly had claimed Helen as a "dear, dear, American friend." The two passed notes to each other, like schoolgirls do, saying when to meet at a certain place at a certain time. Ruth left little baskets of food and drink, fruit, cheeses, beer, and wine in Helen's room and promised in a note she wrote to Helen "to be friends and to write, after the Olympics ended."

July 29: Day Fifteen, Olympic Dorm

Group of us went shopping very early after breakfast. Anne [O'Brien], Gertrude [Wilhelmsen], Betty R. [Robinson], Betty B. [Burch] & I bought-out Berlin. I picked up most of my trinkets, etc. Had very enjoyable & busy time. Rushed back for work-out at 3:00. Took good starts & discus throws. Barely got in for dinner. Quite a few of us, including China & Finland, went to the Winter Gardens [an exhibition attraction]. It was a nice place & show was good. Came in about 12:00. The beautiful blue lights were focused over the Stadium & it made a very, very pretty sight. Some other countries were coming in, including Poland & Stella Walsh. Got letter from Mildred Meyers.

Mildred was a voice from home. A plain-looking but nice first-year student from Lucern, Missouri, Mildred sent well-wishes to Helen, who was now counting down the days before the big event. Helen did not make the mistake of being overconfident. She was buying souvenirs and small gifts for her family and having fun with her friends, but she did not overlook or forget her workout. Her main competitor in the 100-meter race had just arrived and had commenced her training in the Olympic practice field nearby.

July 30: Day Sixteen, Olympic Dorm

Back in the Midwest, a long stretch of days exceeding 100° led to an officially declared drought. But in Germany, sports reporters wrote about the persistent wet weather, noting that the tracks offered dangerous gullies and muddy stretches. Daily grappling with the hazardous field conditions and the drizzly cold, Helen gave her two cents' worth about *der sturm*. She wrote: *Gertrude* [Wilhelmsen], *Evelyn* [Ferrara] *& I went out to practice discus before noon. I got some good heaves. In afternoon I took a light work-out. Got good rub-down from the new lady. My shin splints were worse today & have slight cold. Received letter from Mother. Wrote a few letters. Food much better. Dee put the dope on my legs at last. It didn't rain—for once.*

In addition to an infirmary, the Olympic village had several eateries, a library, a theater, swimming pools, a post office, office space, and other necessities of life. Some 150 German youngsters served athletes as guides and errand runners. Ruth said that some of the guides who came and went into the athletes' rooms might not be guides; they could be secret agents. Helen hid her diary among her clothing and kept her luggage locked. Dee's analgesic balm was the same solution Moore used for his athletes, a blend of rubbing alcohol, oil of wintergreen, and olive oil. Helen used the services of a German masseuse who promised, "Give me a few days to work on you, and I'll have you good as new." That day, she wrote a short thank-you note on Olympic letterhead to John Mertens (a relative of high school chum Carl Mertens) who was handling donations to Helen's Olympic fund, saying she hadn't signed the Holm petition, was suffering from a slight cold and shinsplints, but expected to be "in the pink" by the time her races were scheduled.

July 31: Day Seventeen, Olympic Dorm

Was extremely happy to get letter from Someone. Heard from several Fultonians. Leg hurt me rather badly. No work-out. Had 4 or 5 interviews with various news men & women. Had my portrait painted. Looked like Caesar.

Remembering Dee's advice, Helen diverted reporters by talking about the wet condition of the red cinder track and the belief among Germans that it never rains on *der Führer*. She told them she didn't like the tinted portrait of herself because it made her look like Julius Caesar. She again declared to the press that she wasn't worrying about her shinsplints. "I think I can beat Stella Walsh even though I am handicapped by injuries."[15]

Via Atlantic cable, columnist John Wray told St. Louisans that Helen was confident that she would win. He reported that she had gotten shinsplints running against Annette Rogers and Betty Robinson "in 60 meters (7.8 sec) who pressed closely behind her. Only eight of 17 team members were able to workout on July 30 due to 'colds' and [Harriet] Bland suffered a lung attack [asthma]."[16]

Helen wrote: *Laid around in sun while not taking treatments. Very nice & warm day.* In truth, she was fraught with ascending feelings and destabilizing touches of self-doubt. She was aware that Stella Walsh was working out nearby and was unsettled by rumors of Stella's most recent top speed. She worried about how slowly her shinsplints were healing and applied frequent ice packs on the tendons of her leg. But her spirit lifted, finding solace with a piece of mail from home. The first line Helen wrote in her journal that day acknowledges a letter from capital *S* "Someone." The message from this anonymous person warmed Helen's heart and repaired her mood. "S" had posted her letter on July 18, just a few days after Helen left New York. Helen's closing passage, *Was extremely happy*, prominently acknowledges she had a very special person back home. This letter, arriving during a low point, uplifted her at a crucial time.

5

Winners and Losers

I saw Helen getting ready to surrender to a slice of lemon chiffon pie,
but I headed her off. "You can't beat Stella Walsh that way," I told her.
Believe me, it worked.
—Dee Boeckmann, quoted in *St. Louis Post-Dispatch,* July 11, 1936

*P*romoted as the games of peace between nations, the Eleventh Olympic Games
commenced during a time of international turmoil. Mussolini had invaded
Ethiopia; Germany spied on all its neighbors (using the Hindenburg blimp);
Franco ravaged Spain; Japan invaded China. Across the waters in America,
Roosevelt's New Deal was struggling against a staggering economic depression.
Striding before this trembling political backdrop, the contests began, hosted by
Germany's fledgling National Socialist Party, which only a few years earlier had
ousted the Weimar Republic. Its Olympic stadium presented itself as a testa-
ment to Germany's new regime. North of Munich, situated on Heerstrasse, not
far from Spandau, Berlin's Olympic sports complex still stands as an historical monument.

August 1: Day Eighteen, the Reichsportfeld, Berlin

Eight days earlier, crewmen had been madly at work paving concrete seats for
the stadium and finishing other tasks. On this day, their labor was done. The
stadium's seventy-three tiers accommodated 110,000 spectators. Walls of the
upper section rose forty-eight feet above the sports field, approximately 325
acres in area; its lower ring burrowed some forty-two feet below ground level.
Inset at the top of the gate's pillars, two gigantic clocks informed of the exact
Olympic time and seemed to command spectators to synchronize their

watches. The inscription on the bell in the Olympic Tower read: "I Call the Youth of the World."

Helen wrote simply: *The Olympic Games are declared open. It was a very thrilling day in many ways. I spent the morning getting treatments, etc. It was cloudy, damp & cool. Before the time for the opening ceremonies, the "Von Hindenburg" passed over the fields & stadium, a very impressive sight. After marching to our places on field, we waited until time to march in. The Fuhrer marched from Bell Tower to Stadium. The march into stadium, the throng of people, the torch runner from Greece, Hitler's declaration of the Games to be opened, the ringing of Olympic bell, loosening of pigeons* [some accounts say doves], *booming of canons* [sic], *& trumpets will long be remembered.*

The Hindenburg transatlantic passenger airship drifted overhead showing its colors, a large swastika adorning each tail fin; a pristine white (for purity) Olympic flag waved heavily below it. Opening day and the following nine days brought wet, cold, overcast, dreary weather.[1] Climate like this was inhospitable to achieving excellence in outdoor sports. Still, the spectacle of the first day of the Olympics stirred a brighter mood. The stadium filled to capacity. Distinguished visitors sat waiting in the reserved section. The telegraph office, the press workrooms, and the glass cubicles for broadcast media were above the grandstand; below it was the track judges' box. Two fifty-foot stone walls, where the names of Olympic victors were to be carved as spectators watched, served as an impressive west gate, through which some 5,300 athletes paraded.

But first, in full military attire, descending from the tower as if an Olympic god himself, the chancellor came, signaled by a solitary trumpet sounding "Deutschland über Alles." Adolf Hitler entered, strutting alongside Count Henri de Baillet-Latour, the International Olympic Committee president, and Dr. Theodor Lewald, president of the Games Organizing Committee—both wearing silk high hats and tuxedos. Other IOC members followed. Then came "Horst Wessel," played under the baton of Richard Strauss and sung by a chorus of 10,000 voices bursting with national pride. After the Olympic hymn and a slow tolling of the Olympic bell, the crowd roared into a frenzy, inflamed by swaths of color and pageantry.

Parading in first were the Greeks, according to custom. Greece's Olympic officials led, and squads of athletes followed in distinctive native costume, circling on the 400-meter track, saluting as they passed their host, Hitler, and IOC officials, now seated in a bullet-proof box. Sitting beside Hitler were his first and second cabinet ministers, Third Reich deputy Rudolf Hess and Reich Marshal Hermann Göring. Then 250 French athletes stepped out in dapper blue berets and coats and white trousers; then came turbaned Afghanis and Indians; then Argentines and Australians, sporting naval caps and cricket caps, respectively, and the colorfully garbed Chinese, with their straw hats. Canadians strode in wearing snappy red blazers and white trousers; then Egyptians, unique with their elegant red fezzes; Italians, in smart national caps; and of course, the exotically imperious Japanese, flowing in stunning silks.

All aligned in alphabetical order by country, some goose-stepping, some with simple walking strides. Group leaders hoisted banners that carried their nation's colors, and following behind each group, marching bands played their national anthems. Color guards held flags high as they directed their groups to circle the field. They dipped their flags to show respect as they passed the führer's box. Athletes, coaches, and officials saluted; some used the Nazi salute, some tipped caps. Every group saluted in this fashion, except one.

When the team from the United States of America entered the stadium 382 strong, the crowd shouted enthusiastic cheers and derisive jeers. The men braced forth wearing white shirts and trousers, navy blue jackets with embroidered Olympic emblems, red-white-and-blue ties, dapper white sport shoes, and jaunty straw hats. Similarly, Helen and her American compeers wore blue tailored jackets, white skirts and blouses, white felt caps, and white shoes. Led by Avery Brundage, Graeme Hammond, Joseph Raycoft, Frederick Rubien, and Gustavus Kirby of the American Olympic Committee, the American coaches and athletes gave a simple but official Olympic eyes-right; the men held their straw hats over their hearts as they passed Hitler's viewing stand. Flag bearers Alfred Jochim and Frank Wykott were instructed to follow the military custom of not dipping the Stars and Stripes to anyone other than the president of the United States, and this provoked some to titter nervously. Some disapprovingly whistled at the nonconformity on the part of the United States, others shouted *Nike! Nike!* (Greek for "victory").

True to tradition, the host country's team appeared last, resplendently decked out in white yachting caps and white suits, with an eagle emblem on their jacket pockets. Marching last, behind the U.S. team, the German team of some 500 athletes goose-stepped eight abreast in military precision. Stretching arms out and upward in the Nazi salute as they passed their führer, they shouted, *Sieg Heil! Sieg Heil! Sieg Heil!*

Each squad, having marched the full stretch of track, stood at attention on the field behind insignias and flags, facing the Tribune of Honor. As the International Olympic Committee and others semicircled the athletes, Theodore Lewald spoke in German for some twenty minutes, officially welcoming the athletes.

A sixty-trumpet fanfare sounded. A distant battery of cannons boomed eleven times, for the eleventh Olympiad, and slowly the Olympic flag rose on the central mast. Suddenly, from one hundred ramparts, flags of the nations swirled and intermingled with masses of white silk Olympic flags, displaying five colorful rings entwined. With a burst of flutter, thousands of "doves" winged into the air in waves of rhythmic beauty over the field, symbolically proclaiming the goal behind the Olympic Games: peace among nations. All eyes lifted to the sky.

Within the moment, high on the east platform, the last of 3,000 torchbearers appeared, carrying the Olympic flame. The first one had enkindled the sacred fire at midnight, July 21, from the ruins of the Temple of Zeus. Others, waiting at various points along the route, had reached out for it, night and day, and brought it across Greece, Bulgaria, Yugoslavia, Hungary, Austria, Czechoslovakia, and finally into Germany. Now, the last torchbearer appeared. Down the platform came a lithe, blond-haired German youth, an ephemeral haze of blue smoke trailing behind him. Across to and up the west gate stairs, swiftly he sped, then paused to ignite the Olympic chalice and light the way for international goodwill. Once flames leaped brightly from the Olympic font, he disappeared.

Solemnly, the flag bearers formed a semicircle to face the Olympic committee and stood at attention as Germany's Rudolf Ismayr (1932 middleweight lifting champ) recited the Olympic Oath in behalf of the athletes clustered on the field. Raising right hands, each athlete expressed assent to the oath. Guided by spotlight, thousands of bodies turned toward the host's viewing stand. Hitler sat waiting as Greek athlete Spyridon Louis approached him. The crowd stirred. Dressed in his nation's traditional uniform, the 1896 Olympic Games marathon winner gave Hitler an olive branch. When Hitler rose to his feet, the masses fell silent. Loud speakers reverberated his thunderous voice: "Let the Games begin!" The audience roared, and then, with a signal from the field marshal to strike up the recessional music, in reverse order the parade of athletes filed out of the stadium, bringing opening day ceremonies to a close. This grandiose show-of-shows would long be remembered by Helen and anyone who saw it. Such splendid ceremonial array, the competitions themselves, the intrigue, and the glamorously outrageous scenarios that marked the Berlin games would make it the most written about, most discussed, and most memorable of Olympic Games.

August 2: Day Nineteen, Olympic Dorm, Berlin

For Helen, Sunday in Berlin was another day to be spent singularly focused on her purpose for being there. Once she had achieved her life's goal—her sole reason for being in Berlin—*then* she would see some of Germany's ancient, inspiring churches, the Church of St. Nickolas, Cathedral at Gendarmenmarkt, Berlin's Eosander Chapel, and the Cathedral at Cologne. But for now, other concerns pressed upon her.

Another Sunday during which I didn't attend church. . . . [The] day bright & dark by spells. I took my treatments at the hospital in the morning. Stella was there getting her muscle massaged. Rogers, Bland & I were not allowed to attend the Games as we have to run tomorrow. Yes, the strain of waiting!!! Gertrude, Martha & Betty lost in the javelin. The victors were certainly honored upon arrival home.

Bland & I twitted about, doing little or nothing most of afternoon. Our treatments continue & the sick list grows, but we wait until tomorrow.

Some two hundred yards from the women's housing facility, the training fields, wet from three days of intermittent rain, still hampered athletes as they tried to stay in good physical condition. Diligent about getting treatment for her worrisome ailment, Helen ran into Stella at the infirmary. Stella was nursing a similar concern. No words passed between them, though their eyes locked onto each other. "Stella glared at me," Helen recalled. Both sneaked glances at one another. They hadn't seen each other since the AAU meet in St. Louis when the "greenie from the sticks" had stomped the great Polish Flyer. With deliberate piquancy, Helen wrote of Stella's *muscle*—being singular. Treatment now involved camergesic (heat) packs applied to reduce swelling shin muscles, used day and night, for at least four days in a row.

Helen conscientiously kept track of her teammates' efforts. Gertrude Wilhelmsen, Martha Worst, and Betty Burch placed inconsequentially (seventh, ninth, and twelfth) in the javelin throw event; Germany took top honors (Tilly Fleischer won the gold and Luise Krüger nabbed the silver). This "team defeat" on the first day of competition dispirited Helen's teammates, for these victories seemed to confirm Hitler's boast that Germany had the best women's track and field team that year.[2]

August 3: Day Twenty, Olympic Dorm and Stadium, Berlin

After spending most of the day in a sort of mental agony, Annette, Harriet & I went to the stadium at 3:00 o'clock.

The day of the 100-meter trials finally arrived. In the prelims, Helen's roommate, the short but spunky Harriet *also-ran* Bland was scheduled in the first heat. Bland placed fourth and, therefore, was eliminated early. In the second heat, Helen ran and qualified, clocking 11.4, leaving Canadian Mildred Dodson in second place some 10 meters behind. With "a favorable wind" at her back, Helen's 11.4 speed was four-tenths of a second better than the world record held by Stella Walsh. Holding back, Stella won her match with 12.5, running in the third heat. Two other U.S. teammates ran prelims: "pretty" Nettie Rogers ran the fourth heat and qualified, but "butchy" Betty Burch, who ran in the sixth and final trial, did not qualify, nor did Louise Stokes, whose hopes and dreams of a second shot at an Olympic medal in this event were crushed.

In the semifinals, Helen finished first with 11.5; Stella finished her semifinal again with 12.5. Fans said Stella was conserving her strength for the finals; others said she was off form due to a sprain she had gotten while training, as reporters had speculated.

Helen knew Stella's speed that day was not her best. She later said of her own semifinal that she had run four yards ahead of the competition, while Stella seemed pressed by her opponents. Helen figured Stella indeed had held back, to disarm her into overconfidence, but her diary reveals none of this. She wrote: *I ran in the second heat and made 11.4! The rub-down was agonizing. Coming back for the semi-finals, I made 11.5. . . . [The] applause was great. For the first time I ran before an endless mass of humans—over 100,000 people. Tonight . . . graciously received by everyone & am happy in my success over those of my equal- ity. Owens won. My legs didn't bother me at all. Saw Crown Prince of Italy.*

Helen mentions Prince Umberto, seen by others as he sat in the chancellor's box, but whom she met when he came to the girls' dormitory, "He said just to meet me." Addicted by now to collecting autographs of athletes, movie stars, celebrities, and political figures, she added the newest and most notable sig- nature she now had in her little black autograph book, that of Prince Umberto.

Annette Rogers qualified for the finals, having placed second and third in her trial and semifinal heats. If Helen or Annette couldn't win medals in the finals on the following day, America's women would make a poor showing all- around, for almost everyone thought Germany's team would sweep the relay. And as far as the other events (discus, hurdles, javelin), the American women's team was figured as having no chance at all.

That day, in the cold, wrapped under a wool blanket and sitting on the side- lines, Helen cheered as runner number 733 (Jesse Owens) won the men's 100 meters in 10.3 seconds. She went over to Jesse afterward in the area where the track and field group gathered and congratulated him. He wished her good- luck on her race. As they sat on the ground chatting, a photographer snapped a shot of the two star sprinters together.

Helen was curious about the woman directing cameramen on the sidelines. She watched this woman whiz by on the contraption that had tracked Jesse's record-winning pace. Who was she, this woman behind the man operating three lenses while riding on a rail? At that sublevel, the woman was more vis- ible than the cameraman whose face pressed into the eyepiece. Shouting orders while standing on the speeding device that ran in trenches paralleling the track, she was just about five feet from the runners.

"That's Hitler's favorite movie star–filmmaker," Jesse said.

"I hope I get to meet her," Helen said. "She's beautiful."

"Most likely you will," he said, "if you win your race."

Independent filmmaker Leni Riefenstahl was not part of the official German film crew, nor a Nazi party member, but Hitler himself called upon her to film his Olympic Games.[3] He wanted a truly German "artiste" for his Reich films. Because Riefenstahl had easy access to Hitler, Propaganda Minister Joseph Goebbels resented her from the start. He saw her as a threat to his authority and a usurper of his domain. She saw him as an interferer; she had experienced his meddling while documenting the 1934 National Socialist German Workers' Party convention (for *Triumph of the Will*) and tenaciously fought him for its artistic integrity. In *Olympia*, she documented more than just physical strength; she captured classic athletic movement. She succeeded in unveiling the art and grace of sports on film. Although Riefenstahl kept him at arm's length, Goebbels pressed her to comply with progress reports and other procedural tasks. Lacking tolerance for that, she entreated Hitler to give her free reign.[4] Which he did, thus launching rumors that she was Hitler's mistress. Her reputation was maligned further by America's decathlon athlete, Glenn Morris. In evening shadows, when Morris stepped down from the winner's podium, he grabbed her, tore her blouse from her shoulders, and kissed her breasts. Her friend, Germany's Erwin Huber, had introduced them earlier on; zodiac enthusiast Riefenstahl (a Leo on Virgo's cusp) said she felt something inside stir when their eyes first met.

Riefenstahl was born August 22, 1902, into a family of affluence. Some said she was part-Jewish. Energetic and spirited Leni was unmarried and would turn thirty-four years old a few weeks after the Olympic Games. She was beautiful in an unusual way, exceptionally strong-willed, single-mindedly career-motivated, and substantially gifted in the arts. Some called her driven. In her teens, under the influence of Isadora Duncan, she had a brief career as a dancer, much to her father's dismay, and having reached her prime in that field and endured leg and foot injuries, she moved easily into stage and film acting. There she excelled in what was known as the adventurous, German mountain genre. It was on the silver screen that the hauntingly attractive Riefenstahl caught the eye of Hitler, a man fanatically addicted to the relatively new motion picture industry. But by the early 1930s, Leni had moved behind the camera, established her own film company, and had ongoing film projects throughout Europe at the time Hitler demanded that she film the 1936 Olympics.

The film's prelude is a masterful mix of chiaroscuro visuals and inspiring music. Her slow-motion, underwater sequences, for which she engineered innovative cameras, are breathtaking. Helen's friends on the diving team had spoken of Riefenstahl after she had filmed their "air ballet." While harsh weather created a hellish nightmare for sprinters on the track, the overcast, cloudy sky with occasional bursts of sunlight magnificence, staged a filmmaker's heaven of contrasts. Riefenstahl's palette of moods showed every shade of the gray scale, from the purest whites to blackest blacks. Her eye captured the drizzle and drip of intermittent rain; her film canvas is a masterpiece of an unexpected liquid beauty and sensual drama. She was the first person in history to create a complete documentary film of the Olympic Games. And Helen wanted to meet this woman, but she would have to wait a few days.

What began as a light mist soon tore into the Olympic stadium as a downpour. Though modern in composition for its day, the track had been made with a mix of cinders and red clay, and it lacked sufficient drainage, which is essential to outdoor events. The American press didn't lead with the day's weather, as in earlier reports. Instead, they referred to this day, August 4, as "Black Tuesday"—not because of dark, stormy weather and deplorable track conditions but because the United States' "Black Auxiliary" (as the German press referred to our black athletes) swept up many gold medals from Germany's most likely victors. The international press soon referred to them this way, also.

Though America's Fulton Flash was a likely win, its press focused more on the men's track team. Helen was not thinking of this slight as she took her track outfit from the locker. Muscles in her legs still ached as she pulled up her trunks, and her sleeveless tank top fit too tight. The American insignia and ribbon of red and blue stretched taut across her flat, broad chest. It was cold in her room, colder outside. She put on the sweat pants, then her shoes, carefully double-tying the black strings of her leather spikes, and pulled over the heavy, navy blue jersey. Bold, block letters identified her as a U.S.A. team member. At that instant, a buoyant mood came over her. Something lifted her feet. It was a feeling hard to describe, hard to explain. She sensed that she was ready, ready to face her destiny. That evening, she wrote: *At last the great day arrived! Gertrude* [Wilhelmsen], *Evelyn* [Ferrara], *& I were beaten soundly in discus after marching upon the field. Cool & excitement of coming events, etc.* She was excited yet calm and ready.

Germany's women took the gold in the discus. Gisela Mauermayer tossed the platter an incredible distance of 156 feet 3¾₆ inches. The Germans were sports-smart, said Helen later, "they had one spike in the ball of their shoes, so they spun around a lot easier than we did in the wet muddy cinders."[5] The Americans threw the discus in track shoes. Evelyn Ferrara, a Chicago girl of Italian descent, was, according to Helen, on the stout side, friendly, full of fun, and powerful, but she failed to qualify for the discus finals.

Helen qualified, however, throwing 121 feet 6½ inches, but her performance during the final competition proved far less than what she had shown herself capable of. Her mark (112 feet 7½ inches) put her in tenth place for this event. At an AAU district meet two months earlier, she had thrown 129 feet 6½ inches, which, if she had been able to muster it in the rain that day, would have put her fourth, just one foot shy of the third-place Olympic mark. Interestingly, four years later at a meet in St. Louis, Helen threw the discus 140 feet. But today, she was nervous, readying each throw but watching the track, feeling riddled and distracted by the possibility that she might miss her main event. The discus event was finishing up just as the 100-meter race was about to begin.

"I could see Stella digging in over there," Helen said, "digging her hole, getting ready to run against me. I really was beside myself with anxiety; I just didn't concentrate on the discus the way I should have." She admitted, "I didn't feel I had any chance since I had never been really trained with the discus." Neither of her coaches—Boeckmann nor Moore—had concentrated on Helen's field techniques; they focused on her running ability almost exclusively.

All Olympic sprinters in 1936 competed without starting blocks. Each, with trowel in hand, dug his or her own footing hole prior to each race. The psychological pull of seeing her only real competition—Stella Walsh—readying herself for *the race* that Helen expected to win was nerve-racking for Helen, who was in the discus competition, her third allowable event, only because she qualified for it. Of the six events that track and field women could choose from, the discus held little appeal for her. She would have preferred the eight-pound shot put, for she had set a 1936 American shot put record in March in Chicago with 41 feet 7½ inches. But a women's shot put event did not exist in 1936. Hurdle running was not a choice for Helen, nor were the running high jump or the javelin events, because Coach Boeckmann wanted to eliminate any additional chance of injury. Since women were limited to competing in only three events, Helen followed Boeckmann's direction. She qualified for the discus, the relay race, and, of course, the 100 meters.

Helen threw her last throw, adjusted her trunks, and as she sprinted for the track, told herself, I can do it. I'll make my dream come true.

It was the worst kind of weather, and the worst kind of track conditions, and certainly the worst everything for setting any kind of record. Cold, blowy rain had drizzled onto the track all day. The track was a gooey mix of clay and dirt. Globs of slippery mud clung to number 737's spikes and stuck on her trowel. Helen had arrived with just enough time to get settled. She pushed her trowel point in exactly were she wanted it and pulled it out. She placed the toes of her size twelve foot into the gully she had carved and patted the ball of her foot hard against the red clay dirt, telling herself, Put it exactly as Dee said to. Now, let's beat the time I clocked in the trials. No wind right now, just a slow steady drizzle. She was thinking 11.4, her speed disallowed due to an aiding wind. As she bent forward, she swayed her shoulders forward and back, as if loosening them. She shook her arms. She dropped down on all fours, let her short, wavy hair fall forward, checked her form, then snapped her head up, bending her neck back a bit, tipped her haunches. Her large fingers, like ten uniformly cylindrical monopodes, supported her sturdy frame, her blue eyes steeled straight ahead. The winner's ribbon is only 100 meters away, she thought. Let's go!

When the official's gun went off, Helen shot from the mark like a kid's bottle rocket, leaving behind nothing but the awed expressions of onlookers, the strained and smoky configurations of her would-be contenders. She flashed light yards ahead of cocky Stella, left way behind Kathe Krauss, Marie Dollinger, and her teammate, Annette. Emmy Albus was hardly an afterthought. She was far ahead of all of them.

New Olympic and world titles were hers—the moment was hers, once her foot left ground.

Those who penned her "The Missouri Express" said she looked like a human locomotive, with her arms and legs pumping like pistons, speeding faster than humanly possible (they exaggerated). Some said her figure—in white silk running suit—blurred in motion. They said she became a quick, phosphorescent blaze, ignited and extinguished in an instant. (Was this truth?) One hundred thousand voices cheered, hands clapped like lightning, feet pounded seats with thunderous applause when Helen Stephens snapped the ribbon. And as before, and embarrassingly so for Stella, trailing some two meters behind Helen, the Polish Flyer ran a sad distant second. Kathe Krauss of Germany lagged in third. Roars again pierced the air with the announcement that a new Olympic record had been set. By three-tenths of a second, Helen Stephens had set a new record—speed-balling 11.5 seconds. And again, deafening roars exploded throughout the stadium as the announcer proclaimed that Helen's preliminary wind-aided time of 11.4 would be recorded, after all.

In her unpublished career notes, Helen wrote that she "got off to a bad start but took command of the race mid-way," that after their race, Stella Walsh congratulated her for winning it. But that day, in her 1936 diary, modestly she but sketched her victory: *Then in the 100 meters—I won the Olympic crown (11.5). Walsh (11.7) & Krauss (11.9) came in that order. Yes, the applause was grand. The thrill of seeing the American flag raised for me & the crowning of the victors was marvelous.*

Before taking the stand to receive a gold medal, Helen extended her hand to the now former Olympic titleholder. As they shook hands, the crowd cheered for the sportsmanship spilling from their new champion. Thrills of emotion stirred Helen as she stepped to the top height of the victor's stand. Some medalists, she said, wax on and on about the thrill of being on the victory stand, others fall into silence. She said she had a lump in her throat, that chills ran up and down her spine, that the hair on her neck stood up, her skin was goose bumpy, and her knees knocked so much that "my feet felt like they were dancing. I was so glad, proud, humble to have been able to do this for my country, my team, school, coach, plus family and friends and last of all for myself."[6] In the instant that the laurel wreath crown was placed on her head, she said, she thought, Somebody will come along someday and make me look like I'm standing still.

As she bent forward to receive the prized gold medal, with the national anthem playing and Old Glory flying overhead, it was for her, she said, a once-in-a-lifetime peak experience of patriotism and pride. Stella stood on the second step, with a silver in her hand; Kathe Krauss had the bronze. (Germany's Dollinger took fourth; the United States' Annette Rogers came in fifth; Germany's Emmy Albus was sixth.) Then an official handed Helen the gift of an oak tree sapling and said, "Grow to the honour of victory! Summon to further achievement."[7] Swell, indeed! she thought.

These simple words carried great import to Helen at this time in her life. They anointed her, implored her to live purposefully, to seek maturity and greatness, like an oak, stately and strong and symbolically appropriate for dreamers like her.

She wrote: *Spoke to U.S.* [via CBS radio]. *Hitler met me privately & congratulated me. I also got his autograph & another official's. Received at dormitory by team. Flowers from team & Baroness. Dee, Kathy* [Kelly], *Betty & I crashed an International Banquet—met & had hand kissed by Goering, the Minister president.* Flowers and congratulation notes sent jointly by the women's team and dorm directress Baroness Wagenheim brightened Helen's room.

What occurred during her private visit with Hitler became ammunition for the IOC. On August 2, the first day of the games, Hitler had called Hans Woellke, Germany's gold medal shot put athlete, to present himself immediately upon stepping down from the victor's box. Dutifully, Woellke complied, and the games were delayed as the audience stirred, and the confounded officials waited while Hitler orchestrated what looked like an official Olympic act—the honor of the victor meeting the Olympic host. The next day, Hitler called two more gold-winning athletes (a German and a Finn) to present themselves before him, which again held up the games. IOC officials, dismayed by these unapproved, unscheduled time-eaters, sent a message to Hitler, asking him to please not continue this disruptive practice. Officials realized that Hitler might ask every gold medalist, or only select ones, to march forward for a pat on the back, which could lead to further problems.

Press reports on Helen's meeting with Hitler tied in Black Tuesday's events. They claimed the führer shunned Owens by leaving the stadium after yet another black won gold (the 100-meter race). U.S. weight lifter John Grimek said, "A group of us were sitting about two tiers below Hitler in the stands watching Jesse run and we could see he [Hitler] was real mad." But Owens himself refuted the media's chauvinistic, racist interpretations.[8]

When Helen won her gold medal, Hitler ordered one of his aides to fetch her. He wished to meet the towering speedball who, he said, looked like a true Aryan woman. His aide called out, *"Sieg Heil!"* to Helen and Dee as they were walking off the field, Helen recalled. He had a trimmed mustache like Hitler's and was short, much shorter than Helen. He spoke in a mix of broken German and stilted English, saying *der Führer* wanted to see her immediately in the chancellor's box. *"Kommen Sie."* She should follow him, now.

Helen told him, "But first we must go to the telegraph office. . . . Radio expects to interview me and my coach . . . broadcast to America." Then, "*Verstehen Sie?* Understand?" He seemed perplexed. Dee shook her head no, he didn't want to understand Helen. She said to him, pointing, "We go now . . . to broadcast office." Though coaching her first Olympics, Dee Boeckmann was no novice. She knew the high-handed maneuvers of governmental interference and was not going to let this little Hitler imitator ambush Helen from world-wide coverage of her record-breaking victory.

But he persisted: "I tell *mein Führer* 'no'"? His voice peaked. "*Ya!* You must *kommen . . . kommen Sie mit!!*"

Helen said, looking down into his puffing face, "He won't shoot you. There's too many people around." Then Dee chimed in, "*Wir kommen* later. After broadcast. Can't come now. Tell your führer we'll be there *after* broadcast!"

Helen saw fear seize his face. He saluted quickly, swiveled around, and marched off, and they rushed on toward the stairs leading to the broadcast office. The women stopped at the convenience room, combed their hair, applied lipstick, adjusted their sweats so the large U.S.A. letters were straight, and then set off to meet press photographers and reporters. Afterward, they saw Hitler's messenger nervously waiting for them on the stairs. Quickly, he ushered them to Hitler's private room—a small glass-encased room behind his seating box. There, the three waited. Within minutes, the heavy red drapes covering the doorway parted and a dozen Blackshirts (bodyguards) entered. They circled the room, posting themselves at the entry and along the walls, and then began unholstering their pistols. As they stood at attention, Helen and Boeckmann glanced at each other and at the troopers, wondering what would happen next.

"Lugers?" Helen asked. No one answered.

Then two armed soldiers stepped in ahead of Hitler, who was followed by two more. In dress military uniform, with five-inch swastikas on each sleeve, black boots, and brass buttons, Hitler crossed the crowded room, faced Helen, and saluted. "It was sloppy," Helen said, "like he didn't really want to give me one." She extended her hand for a handshake. He grabbed it and pulled her toward him, patted, pinched, and hugged her. "Of course, wearing that hat, he looked taller," Helen said, and he behaved in an uncomfortably familiar way. She thrust her autograph book into Hitler's hand, and his interpreter, Deputy Rudolf Hess, explained that she wanted his autograph. Helen gave this account of what happened as Hitler signed her book:

> A little guy wearing a uniform and a press identification tag snaps a picture. I never saw a man change his disposition so fast as Hitler did. And as the camera flashed, Hitler jumped about two feet in the air. When he landed, fists flaying, he bellowed something like, "*Was fällt Ihnen ein?* Get

him! Destroy the evidence!" Hitler's face turned red, and his eyes fumed hatred and rage.

Dee screamed back, "Don't you dare!"

While guards restrained the photographer, Hitler slapped his leather gloves across the man's face, then punched him and kicked his shins, all the while screaming in German.

Dee pulled me back a few steps out of the way and whispered, "I think he just set a new high jump record." In the scuffle, the camera fell to the floor, and Hitler booted it like a football against the wall. Then, guards hiked the guy—one, two, three—through the door. One guard picked up the smashed camera and tossed it after him. Another retrieved one of Hitler's gloves that lay near Dee's feet. Hitler calmly turned to me, smiled sweetly as though nothing had happened. He wriggled his body as if to shake himself back into composure. Hess said to me, "I thought Miss Boeckmann didn't understand German." When Hitler spoke again, his eyes fixed on mine, and his sentences came soft and controlled. Hess's voice quivered. "Fräulein should consider running for Germany. Fair hair, blue eyes. Strong, big woman. The Chancellor says you are a pure Aryan. Yes?"

"Nein, Danke," I shook my head and smiled back at Hitler. Still looking at me, Hitler asked through his interpreter what I thought of Germany and its progress. "You like Berlin better than Fulton homeland?"

I said, "Yes, Mister Hitler, Berlin's very, how do you say, nice, pretty? *Schoen?* Even in the rain." I kept my comments short, positive. Hitler beamed. What I had seen in Hamburg and Berlin looked good—the Third Reich made sure Berlin had put her best foot forward for her international visitors. I didn't want to discuss the heck of a depression we were experiencing in the 1930s.

"Fräulein Stephens, no one will ever break your record," Hitler said [through Hess], but I told him that records are meant to be broken.

"You would like to spend the next weekend with Chancellor Hitler at his villa in Berchtesgaden?" Hess asked.

Dee spoke up again, "Tell your führer Miss Stephens is in training. The relay's next Monday. Thank him for her, but Miss Stephens can't." When Hitler realized the answer, he turned to Dee. Again his face broadened into a smile as he waited for the interpreter. "Would *she* join him in Berchtesgaden?"

And Dee said, "Thank you, Chancellor. Duty demands much, no?" addressing her refusal this time directly to Hitler. "Thank you, but no, I too can not accept your kind offer." Hitler seemed to understand before his translator gave him her answer. Then he reached behind me, pinched, then saluted us both, and marched out.[9]

The following day, a picture postcard of Helen getting Hitler's autograph was sold at vendor booths around the stadium. Helen bought a half dozen of them. On August 6, she returned to buy more, but the vendor said he didn't sell them. "But you sold me some yesterday!" she told him. He denied it adamantly. Had Hitler or the IOC demanded their removal? She didn't know.

Helen was the only American athlete who met Hitler privately. The photo was reprinted throughout the world. Because of this, some people thought Helen was a Hitler supporter, but it was not true. The encounter with Hitler, alarming though it was, didn't frighten her, she said; before setting sail to Berlin, she knew she would meet this man who held the world's fate in his hands. She had no fear, she said, because she felt the American flag protected her.

Helen's mother, Bertie Mae Herring, with Helen's grandparents, William T. and Annie Meloy Herring, ca. 1880s

Helen's father, Frank Elmer Stephens, with one of his workhorses, Fulton, Mo., date unknown

Helen, age nine, wearing a dress her mother made, and her only sibling, Robert Lee, age four

Portrait of Coach W. Burton Moore, ca. 1930s

Eleanor Roosevelt (honorary chair, National Women's Olympic Committee) with Dee Boeckmann (Olympic track and field coach and chair of the National Olympic Track and Field Committee), Dr. Sigurd von Numbess (ambassador of Finland), and athlete Lucille Brackett at the White House opening of the national fund drive. Interestingly, President Roosevelt favored boycotting the 1936 Olympics. White House photo.

AAU meet in Chicago, July 4, 1936. *Left to right, kneeling*: Betty Robinson, all-round athlete; Evelyn Ferrara, third place in discus; Harriet Bland; Tidye Pickett, second place in 80-meter hurdles; Betty Burch; Olive Hasenfus. *Standing*: Anne O'Brien, winner in 80-meter hurdles; Annette Rogers, winner in high jump; Dee Boeckmann, women's Olympic coach; Helen Stephens, winner in 100-meter dash, discus, and shot put; Gertrude Wilhelmsen, second place in javelin; Louise Stokes

Helen's 1936 passport showing Avery Brundage's signature and other authorizations

Chancellor Adolf Hitler congratulating Helen, who set new Olympic and world 100-meter sprint records, Aug. 4, 1936, Berlin

Gold medal–winning 4 x 100–meter relay team in the field, Aug. 9, 1936. *Left to right*: Annette Rogers, Helen Stephens, Harriet Bland, Betty Robinson.

Helen shaking hands with "the Polish Flyer," Stella Walsh, August 6, 1936, Berlin. Snapshot by Dee Boeckmann.

The 1936 U.S. Olympic Women's Track and Field team aboard the SS *Manhattan*. *Left to right, back row*: Manager Fred Steers; Martha Worst, Annette Rogers, Kathlyn Kelly, Gertrude Wilhelmsen, Louise Stokes, Betty Robinson, Coach Dee Boeckmann. *Kneeling*: Evelyn Ferrara, Helen Stephens, Harriet Bland, Alice J. Arden. *Sitting*: Tidye Pickett, Simone Schaller, Josephine Warren, Olive Hasenfus, Betty Burch. *Not shown*: Anne O'Brien and Chaperone Katherine Dunnette

Helen (*center, kneeling*) and the House of Davidites Baseball Team, 1937. "Ham" Olive stands behind Helen.

Buster Connors's promotional poster for Helen, ca. 1937

Poster for All-American Red Heads Basketball Team versus the Warner Brothers Studio team, featuring Helen Stephens as a sports exhibitor, Jan. 13, 1938

| SUNDAY MAY 26 FIRST GAME 1:00 P. M. | **BASEBALL** (THE AMERICAN GIANTS) **COLORED WORLD CHAMPIONS** ====VERSUS==== **THE FAMOUS HOUSE OF DAVID** | SUNDAY MAY 26 FEATURE GAME 3:00 P. M. |

BASEBALL
(THE AMERICAN GIANTS)

SUNDAY MAY 26 — FIRST GAME 1:00 P. M.

COLORED WORLD CHAMPIONS

SUNDAY MAY 26 — FEATURE GAME 3:00 P. M.

====VERSUS====

THE FAMOUS HOUSE OF DAVID

at NICHOLS PARK --- JACKSONVILLE, ILL.

Admission Adults 55c   Children Under 12 - 25c

Queen of the cinder paths · Holder of 14 world's records is now on nation-wide tour with the House of David baseball club ·World's fastest woman sprinter · Olympic champion will give exhibitions between games at Nichols Park · Sunday May 26th · She challenges any man, horse or auto for a distance of 100 yds. Never beaten in her life.

Helen Stephens

Norman Cross

Ace of the Colored Champs pitching staff · won 31 - lost 5 games last season in Professional Colored League. Probable pitcher against House of David Sunday, May 26th, at Nichols Park, Jacksonville, Ill. Ham Olive · one of baseball's greatest showmen · Center-man in the famous House of David Pepper-Game.

Ham Olive

FIRST GAME STARTS AT 1:00 P. M.   BROWNING VS. STATE REPRESENTATIVE ANDY O'NEIL'S BASEBALL TEAM

DON'T MISS THE FAMOUS HOUSE OF DAVID PEPPER GAME
WORTH THE PRICE OF ADMISSION ALONE

Helen featured in exhibition between Colored World Champs versus the House of David, 1937

All-American Red Heads Basketball Team in Phoenix, Ariz., ca. 1937–38.
Left to right: Helen, "Lily," "Ozzie" (Ruth Osburn of the 1932 Olympic
Track and Field Team), Gladys, Kay, Peggy. "Vic" took the snapshot.

Helen's brother, Robert Stephens, in
World War II uniform, ca. 1940s

John Emmons's publicity photo of the reorganized Helen Stephens Olympic Co-Eds, 1946–47. *Left to right, standing*: LaVern(?) Hempen (aka Sally Hale), Mary Margaret(?), Virginia Merkel Summers, Irene Bles, Helen Stephens. *Kneeling*: Iva White, Mary Schierbaum, Bert Herald, Lillian Merkel Woodsmall. Photo courtesy Mrs. Lillian Merkel Woodsmall.

Helen's sports memorabilia exhibited at William Woods College administration building shows her with Babe Didrikson and J. Edgar Hoover, Sept. 12, 1936; on stadium field with Jesse Owens; a souvenir swastika; etc. The exhibit was relocated to the Helen Stephens Sports Complex in 1993. Photo by Sharon Kinney Hanson, 1990.

Coach Stephens with her William Woods College track and field team and Carl Meinke, Westminster College student assistant, 1977–78 season

Helen Stephens (*left*), age sixty-five, running the 200-meter race in the rain during the National Senior Olympics IV, St. Louis, Mo. Also shown are Wilma Hise and Mary Jane Klerlein. Photo courtesy of Gary Brady and the St. Louis Senior Olympics.

Helen Stephens with the Show-Me State Games torch and the American flag flying in background, August 1983. Photo courtesy *Rural Missouri*.

6

In the High Callaway Style

German guides were polite and gracious, but they made it plain they were out to avenge the Treaty of Versailles.
    —Helen Stephens, quoted in *St. Louis Post-Dispatch,* July 25, 1976

*S*he had done it. She was now, officially, the fastest woman in the world, and everyone wanted to meet her. The U.S. women's team manager, Fred Steers, boasted that "by the time she turns 21, she'll come closer to the men's mark than anyone dreamed possible."[1]

By asking for Hitler's autograph, she had facilitated a photo opportunity for that sorry photographer who became the brunt of Hitler's ire. Smiling happily, Helen looked pretty, standing shoulder to elbow with Hitler. But it wasn't admiration for Hitler that she felt, for she knew of his brutal tactics, his prison record, his backdoor-revolutionary entrance into Germany's highest office. She had read his book, read about his beer hall putsch and the Ernst Röhm blood purge of June 30, 1934. She loved history. Like most people, Helen was intrigued by this forceful character who had become one of Europe's most powerful heads of state. She later, in the 1990s, said, "I was aware of how Hitler rose to power, had read news accounts of the warfare going on in Europe then. And I thought that if I qualified, if I made the Olympic team, I might somehow meet him. I knew it was a long shot—with hundreds of athletes on the U.S. team and thousands more from other nations. But somehow I felt . . . that is, I had a sense that I'd meet him."

Hitler's role was choreographed by the authority of the IOC; as both host and head of Germany's Olympic committee, his booth was situated in a prominent place in the stadium, but he was never given the role to "meet" or "greet" gold medalists. When he, of his own volition, began calling the winners to his booth, complaints quickly came in to quell him. The IOC was disgruntled by the disruption and time delays that Hitler caused each time he singled out an athlete for a special audience with him. IOC officials sent word to the chancellor to stop meeting publicly and privately with Olympians.

August 5: Day Twenty-two, Olympic Dorm, Berlin

Harriet Bland, suffering from a cold that she had caught aboard ship, told Helen about the German guides and officials who were asking her out on dates. Helen warned her, "I wouldn't trust 'em if I were you. They'll try to sabotage our team somehow. Keep you up all night to fatigue you out, or get you into some kind of trouble with the officials." Harriet ignored her, so Helen pressed harder, reminding her that the nurse told her to rest. Harriet thought the kid from Callaway County was both silly and naive.

Germany's notables celebrated long into the night, but Helen wrote little about the gala. She, Harriet, Kathlyn, Betty, and Dee were invited to the evening's celebration, where they partied with the Deutschland's version of the Fortune 500—the state's social and political elite. They mingled among Germany's privileged class, seemingly oblivious to the stormy downpour. As the evening progressed, Dee treaded off with a duke and duchess from somewhere and a Bürgermeister So-and-So. Their German guide disappeared for a time; Betty and Kathy drifted off with revelers, and Harriet skipped onto the dance floor with any chap who invited her—an athlete, an officer, an attendant. Helen noticed Avery Brundage, happily mingling among high-ranking figures. He lifted his glass in a toast proposed by Gretl Braun (according to Helen's guide) for her sister Eva and Herr Hitler. She saw him tilt back his head and bring a cocktail to his lips, but did he take a sip? Had he winced? His blue eyes flashed. Mr. and Mrs. Art Jarrett crossed paths with his group, in tandem with Helen Hayes and her spouse. Eleanor (Holm Jarrett) broke into laughter and threw a smile back at them. The Jarretts paused to greet Conductor Richard Strauss, standing near cameraman Walter Frentz, and Leni Riefenstahl, all of whom now moved en masse within earshot. Helen heard fragments of what Leni was saying, a mix of German and English, explaining, perhaps, how music is the essential component of aesthetic mood, "a conveyance welded . . . indelible . . . cinematographic art."[2]

Trying not to stare, Helen gazed over their heads and listened. Suddenly, Leni pirouetted and captured the hand of an officer Helen had not noticed. Leni pulled him onto the dance floor, abruptly excusing herself. She had seen the minister of propaganda ambling toward her group and thus escaped from her club-footed adversary, Joseph Goebbels, who, Helen had heard, was a consummate womanizer. Gracefully, Riefenstahl avoided what may have become unpleasant for everyone. Goebbels stepped between the composer and Eleanor and made customary greetings, but his attention was elsewhere. Helen scanned the room in the direction of his gaze and saw the dark, sunken-eyed Martin Bormann nodding his head at Germany's so-called unbeatable prize boxer, the massive Max Schmeling. Reichstag president Hermann "Jolly" Göring, second in power to Hitler, flopped by in white riding pants, brown military jacket, and brown leather boots that met the curve of his knees.[3] Treated for narcotic addictions at Langbro Asylum years earlier, Göring lived a kind of bachelor's life since his wife's tuberculosis had made her an occasional invalid. He was an imposingly powerful figure.

Helen wasn't the only one engaged in surveillance that night. Many foreign eyes swooped in her direction, watched, and listened as the towering American girl mulled about. The most sought-after member of the U.S. women's team stood alone for awhile in this crowd, until her bilingual guide reappeared and led her to a group of people that included Göring.[4] Göring instilled no fear in youthful Helen, nor was she impressed with him. Eleven days later at the party he cohosted with Rudolf Hess on Goebbels's island estate, he would make an unforgettable impression on her.[5]

After today's party, however, Helen wrote: *The newspapers carried accounts of my victories. Received "congrats" from Dr. Harmon & others. Reporters, etc. Quite relieved to be the champion at last.*

The president of William Woods College telegrammed Helen; he and many other Fultonians had seen Olympic newsreels in movie theaters and photo finish stills that the Associated Press cabled to the United States to illustrate Helen's victory. And amazingly for some, her own voice had spanned across the ocean via CBS radio airwaves.

Speeding roughly two meters (about six feet) ahead of Poland's favorite, Helen tabbed an Olympic and a world record in the 100-meter race that would last for twenty-four years. (A sprinter from Tennessee, Wilma "Skeeter" Rudolph, finally ran faster in 1960.)

Helen's running stride was well over nine feet, and her speed just a fraction less than Jesse Owens's. Polish news writers, disheartened by the defeat of their former record holder, sullied Helen's win by printing scathing accusations that she learned about from bilingual reporters, village staff, and others. Immediately after the outcome of the race was announced as official, the Polish press claimed that Helen was a man. They wrote that Helen had bad running form, that she ran too upright, and that her arm action was faulty. Helen told reporters that her form was in the high Callaway style.[6] She sloughed off the derogatory remarks, which Boeckmann said originated with Stella Walsh's coach and members of the Polish Olympic committee.

European pressmen read translations of the Polish papers to Helen and asked her, "Are you really a woman? Are you disguised, a man running in women's races?" She told them to check the facts with the Olympic committee physician who sex-tested all athletes prior to competition. It's just sour grapes, she told them, not showing what she felt. It upset her, but she did not write about it in her diary; she put this ugliness out of her mind and kept it out of her diary. Helen explained to reporters that her discovery coach in Fulton had instructed her on how to use her arms, that he taught the value of a positive competitive attitude. "Good sportsmanship's part of the high Callaway style, also," she said.

Much later, Paul Gallico nailed the Poles for not being sportsmanlike in his book *A Farewell to Sport*, in a chapter titled "Farewell to Muscle Molls, Too." He told of two cases in Europe in which a manly woman engaged a surgeon and was transformed into a man. He said the Poles claimed they saw another such case in Helen, but that the AAU had confirmed that, before allowing her to board the ship, the Olympic committee had "La Stephens frisked for sex and had checked her in as one hundred per cent female. With no thought whatsoever for the feelings of the young lady . . . [these] findings were triumphantly if ungallantly aired in the press. Somehow there seems to be a rather far-reaching and complete criticism of the muscle moll per se when, immediately after a lady succeeds in sprinting a hundred meters in 11.4 seconds, a world's record for girls, she is suspected of being a man. The men do the same distance in 10.3."[7]

The Associated Press picked up the August 5 Polish story, and shortly thereafter, the *New York Mirror* blamed Stella herself, claiming that she put "before the Polish Sport Tribunal a charge that Helen Stephens . . . is a man. The Polish Committee will forward Miss Walsh's accusation to the International Amateur Board."[8] Helen couldn't remember who put this article into her hands when she arrived in New York, but when she got home, she pasted it in her scrapbook.

Trained some in the rain. Bland & I went to stadium to see Games. U.S. won several first places. Our girls were forced out of hurdles—Tidye's accident—Simone's finish (pictures). Arden, Bland & I went to see fencing bouts. It was fair—very good for the men, I suppose. I was given a large bottle of wine by the dining room service with their congratulations. Much feeling running about over relay position.

The Americans—both men's and women's teams—were unskilled in fencing that year; the event was dominated by European countries. Gold medals for five of the six women's track and field events were won by four countries: The United States, thanks to Helen, won the 100-meter race, Italy won the 80-meter hurdles, Hungary took the high jump, and Germany sank both the discus and javelin events. Californian Simone Schaller, America's most promising hurdler, lost out, as did Tidye Pickett. An electric photo-device documented her placement. Helen faithfully recorded the performances of her teammates in trial races.

The Americans thought the sixth and final women's event, the 4 x 100-meters, was within their grasp, at least a silver medal. Initially, it looked pretty good, for many had qualified. The "negress from Chicago," Tidye Pickett,[9] and Harriet Bland were very promising candidates. Both girls had relay experience, but only one could fill a vacant spot, for the three other chosen relayers—Betty Robinson, Annette Rogers, and Helen Stephens—had the fastest speeds and had won their Olympic heats. And there were several other fourth-line girls who wanted in. Louise Stokes, of Malden, Massachusetts, was a likely contender, as were Anne O'Brien of Los Angeles, and Josephine Warren of Massachusetts.

But Harriet fought the hardest to get the last available leg of the relay. Not the slightest bit timid, she saw this as her last chance to prove herself. She harangued and pestered with every breath, trying to persuade Dee to put her, not Tidye, in this race. Though less mouthy than Harriet, Anne and Josephine, Louise, and Tidye wanted the relay event just as badly.

As fate would have it, Tidye Pickett incurred an injury. She had fallen during her second preliminary hurdles heat and was disqualified from one of the two events she expected to win medals in. Dee discussed this twist of fate with Tidye, then called a meeting with all of her girls. Dee stressed that a shoulder injury would hinder Tidye's speed.

Unlike the 100-meter race where a runner depends only on herself, relay running demands teamwork. Two of Boeckmann's sure picks—Robinson and Rogers—ran in previous Olympic relays and thus were seasoned gold medalists in this event. Robinson was a double Olympian, having won the 100 meters in 12.2 and a silver as a relay team member (49.8) in 1928; Rogers ran a leg of the gold-winning Olympic relay (47.0) of 1932.

Atop the heights of Mount Olympus for her first time, Helen Stephens was both the youngest on the team and the least experienced, but she was the fastest. Confronting the Polish accusation with humor, teammates affectionately now called her "Steve" or "Stevie." Without question, the even-tempered "Stevie" would run one of the legs in this race, probably anchor it. Her Olympic experience was limited to the 100-meter sprint race she had just won, and her relay experience back home was nil. Nevertheless, Helen was the speediest of the four sprinters, and indispensable, as Boeckmann saw it, for this competition.

On the other hand and not of the same Olympic caliber was Harriet Bland, whom some were now calling "the Brat." She had relay competition experience, was older than Helen but younger than Betty and Nettie, but she had no Olympic experience at all and also had the slowest speed. Tidye Pickett's self-promoting stance was that she ran faster than "the Brat," but that fact made no impression on Bland. Bland contentiously kept pushing her argument that she also had qualified in 1932 but was bumped from the team for political reasons.[10]

"Tidye's out because she's injured. She had her chance. . . . I deserve this race," she pleaded. "I'm not going to be cheated out of an Olympic medal again!"

All of the girls wanted in, and each of them ran at speeds so close that some of them overlapped. So the question for Dee was who was right for the fourth leg. She was puzzling over this and thinking about how to position the relay to achieve the strongest lineup order, as well as how to pacify, or at least calm, those who would not get a leg of the relay. For Harriet and Tidye, that meant the loss of a second, golden, Olympic opportunity.

August 6: Day Twenty-three, Olympic Dorm and Stadium, Berlin

[The] *mail was mostly autograph seekers. Worked-out twice—once in morning & in afternoon for relay. Posed for expression pictures in discus and running. Stella Walsh came out & took pictures & accompanied us to the stadium.*

Stella. Stella. Stella. Born in Poland in 1911, Stella Walsh arrived in the United States as an infant. She grew up in an ethnically mixed community in Cleveland, Ohio, and in adulthood remained a resident of Cleveland, living with her parents. She spoke without a trace of Polish accent. Her English carried the sounds and idioms of an Ohioan. In sports competition, however, the Polish American wore Poland's colors.

That morning, the five-foot-eight flyer sprinted onto the training field and struck up a conversation with Helen, who was working out under Dee's supervision. Stella was seven years Helen's senior and possessed a load of sports awards, medals, and trophies. Helen noticed a fragrant cloud of toilet water cologne hovering around Stella that day. She had heard that the former champ insisted upon and had gotten a room of her own in the women's dorm. "People said she was modest and shy but she wasn't shy with me," Helen said. "She was often alone, and we never saw her in the group showers. I think she tried to cover up her casualness about hygiene with all that perfume."

Stella came over to Helen and reached out her hand to congratulate her. She had a viewfinder with her and seemed friendly enough, but nervous, Helen said. Stella asked to take Helen's picture; Helen said okay. Dee offered to assist by taking the picture of the two of them standing together, then grabbed her own camera from her training gear and told the girls to pretend they were shaking hands.

For a year and a half, Dee Boeckmann and some AAU officials had tried to get Helen and Stella together in exhibition races ranging from 50 to 440 yards. Stella had reneged every time, canceling or failing to show. No time and no place was agreeable to her. But now, as a silver medalist, Stella had to run exhibitions set up by the IOC. There was no escaping it. In spite of her bravado, as expressed in news reports, she probably was fearful of losing again. Helen later said, "There was money to be made in exhibition races, and so we tried to arrange some with her in the forties, too. But she just wouldn't play ball. I ran in exhibition races against Jesse Owens, but Stella never agreed to any of it." The IOC's arranged exhibition events between many of the top Olympic medalists as fund-raisers for the committee's needs. Stella would have to compete in two such races—one in Wuppertal, one in Dresden—and face the Fulton Flash, who was her most formidable opponent now.

Helen notes: *Saw Cunningham beaten by Lovelock, Hardin win the hurdles, Owens win 200 meters, girls' hurdle race. Also men's javelin.* She saw Germany's Tilly Fleischer and Gerhard Stoeck win gold medals in the hurdles. America's Glen Cunningham took a silver medal, and Jack Lovelock (of the Netherlands) won the gold in the 1,500-meter run, an event that remained unavailable to women until 1972. Because she was interested in longer races, Helen noted Glen Hardin's 400-meter hurdles win, an event unavailable to Olympic women until 1984. Distances longer than 100 meters were, in the United States, still considered dangerous to women's health.[11] The much-discussed 200-meter event wasn't added to women's Olympic competition until 1948. In the 1930s, perhaps unsure of what best suited females, American and Canadian officials vacillated, using the distances of 200 and 220 yards *and* meters. Rogers set the amateur indoor title in the 200 meters in 1933 (27.9) and in 1935 (26.8); Robinson held American records for the 220-yard dash (25.1) in 1931. Helen set a new American record for the 200 meters with 24.4 in June 1935.

Helen wrote: *Had dramatic discussion about places in relay in Tidye's room. It seems everyone can't run & win too.* Helen and Tidye wrestled with the problem again. Helen told her friend that she had already won just by being in the Olympics, just being on the team. "That's easy for you to say," Tidye shot back angrily. "You've got your medal!"

"But you're injured!" Helen argued.

"Harriet's not in peak condition either!" Tidye countered. "Sick and coughing all over everybody. Coach is unfair and you know it." Tidye knew what she had to do. She would take it to a higher authority.

For weeks, eight women had trained for this event.[12] Two days of time trials identified America's fastest runners, but still the selection dilemma perplexed Dee Boeckmann, for two willful girls persisted in making their desires known. Tidye held on, knowing this might be her last chance. And though Harriet had failed to qualify in the 100 meters, she pleaded privately with Coach Boeckmann and lobbied for Helen's help, asking her to speak to Dee in her behalf. Finally, their coach announced her decision: Annette Rogers, Betty Robinson, and Helen Stephens would run this race; the fourth leg was Harriet Bland's. Naturally, the decision set off more ill will between the girls.

"Dee gave the race to her pet," Helen said later. "Tidye, who ran a fraction faster, was cheated out of her chance." Though no printed word in Helen's archives verifies it, Helen said she told reporters at the time that so much potential was there (in Tidye) that if black women were given more chances to compete in track and field they would soon dominate the sport.[13] Many athletes that year, including Helen, competed with physical maladies (shinsplints, head colds, cramped muscles, sprains). Just how hampering Tidye's injured shoulder might be was a judgment call, and the decision ultimately was the prerogative of the women's coach. Even so, Tidye threatened to take her cause to a higher authority.

Dee's choice came with remembrances from her own Olympic experience. On a hellishly hot day in New Jersey in 1924, she had qualified for the women's Olympic team. Her hopes and ambition readied her for the Olympic Games in Paris, but the IOC elected not to send a frail contingent of women that year. Olympic coaches during the 1920s were male volunteers from the professions—doctors, lawyers—often minus athletic training themselves but with the interest and time to devote to sports. In her own second try in 1928, along with Betty Robinson and fellow Missourian Catherine Maguire, Dee had sailed off to Amsterdam, where women competed in the 100 meters, discus, high jump, 4 x 100-meter relay, and the controversial 800-meter race. She was injured by an errant discus, and her sprint performances proved less than what she otherwise was capable of; and because women were poorly trained in those years, a few collapsed while running the 800 meters. The resulting public outcry quickly disallowed that event for women, a ban that lasted for thirty-two years thereafter. American track men (like the women) made a poor showing that year. It was said the men did poorly because they were overcoached, overtrained, overfed, and overconfident.[14]

Dee sympathized with both Bland's and Pickett's situations, but she caved in to the sociopolitics of privilege and gave the opportunity to Harriet. Her own affluence and the preferential treatment whites received at that time were probable influences on her as well.

Losing out fell hard on Tidye. Helen took on the role of placater, trying to boost the morale of all those not selected. Soon, they all turned their effort toward pulling together. For the sake of team spirit, Helen attempted to give the media the impression of having no quarrel with the decision. Always the diplomat, she much later told writer June Becht that Dee was an excellent coach, and that she herself "probably wouldn't have made the team without her help."[15]

The next task was determining the running order. Running order and the strategy behind it were as crucial as deciding who would run the race itself. Usually, coaches put the fastest runner in the last leg. But who would run first and who would run last was something that only Dee would know, for she intended to keep the girls and the German team in the dark about the lineup until the last minute. Boeckmann had the girls practice with Helen running the first leg and then changed the order, with Helen running the second leg behind

Harriet. Then she would change it around into some other arrangement, with Betty starting first, Helen second, and so on. She told them that the German coach would be watching them. Though the German team had favorable odds for winning, the Americans were expected to give the German girls tough competition. Dee wanted to psych the German coach into thinking she was uncertain about what lineup to use. She wouldn't tell a soul ahead of time what the final arrangement would be. Who best ran the first leg and who best ran the last could make the difference between which team would win and which would lose the race, that is, come in second. She knew it. The German coach knew it. And the girls, she said, had better know it, too! She told them that they all had better be ready to run their best regardless of what place they ultimately would run in.

Spats and hard feelings, and now the stress of their last chance to win a medal, turned the girls' moods uncharacteristically somber. Dee was resolute in making the team feel hopeful of bringing home at least silver, if not gold. The only thing to do, she told her girls, was to focus on their goal, focus on the task of winning. And don't let up!

Six days of events had passed, and Hitler's habit of appearing in the grandstand exactly at 1:00 PM and leaving about an hour later had become a subject of conversation for Hitler watchers. Some found pride in his punctuality. Clouds gathered overhead on the morning of August 6, but, they said, it never rains on the führer. When the clouds dispersed shortly before one o'clock and a nervously cheerful Hitler appeared in his private box, Hitler watchers conveyed their satisfaction with I-told-you-so's. And something else was in the air. A petition to boycott the games was being passed around the Olympic village like a relay baton, quickly and unobtrusively. And then a fury erupted. As the men's soccer game commenced, a fight broke out on the field, and the upshot of the brawl was that Peru withdrew its team. And word got out that two "homesick" American boxers had been sent home, the details of which went unreported in the media. Helen wrote: *It didn't rain. Hitler was in stands as usual & we came in after him.* That was her abbreviated way of noting and responding to what was touted as his habit.

August 7: Day Twenty-four, Olympic Dorm, Berlin

Felt better today in several ways. Spent some time in beauty parlor. Wrote some letters & received <u>one</u>. *Learned my record of 11.6 passed. . . . I snapped several pictures & took them to the studio. Spent afternoon trying to sleep. Have fun with the German girls as they attempt* [to open and to read] *some of my letters. Our dessert was absent & Betty & I went elsewhere for it. Improved working knowledge of French by talking with Evelyn and the older masseuse. It was cool & nice most of day.*

There was no mention of or reference to Helen's shinsplints for several days, but she alludes to feeling better. And a second letter from that special someone "S" at home is identified by underlining, but never by name. The July 23 postmarked letter was chatty and carefully worded so as not to betray the essence of the relationship. S wrote: "I imagine by the time you receive this letter you will already have my letter . . . mailed . . . on the 18th. Of course, I don't know how long it takes a letter to cross the ocean. . . . [It] has now been 9 days since I have heard a word from you." She mentioned having relatives by marriage in Berlin, that her aunt had been to see them two or three times, and that she had bought a new, dark blue dress and planned to borrow her mother's dark blue straw hat to wear with it. "[I am] very anxious to see you and to hear all about your trip," she wrote. "I know you will do great in the games and I'm yelling for you always—no matter what! Remember that."

No matter what? Did S mean win or lose the race? Or had the Polish outburst reached Fulton? Given the letter's postmark, Helen suspected that something had happened back home. Even so, on Friday night, her spirits were high because the letter had arrived and there was the prospect of winning one more medal. Come Sunday afternoon, she would have another chance to win another race. She practiced traveler's German and French and horsed around with the dorm attendants, who were curious about her mounting pile of letters from home; and she teased about the dessert stashed in her room: "Who *essen mein torte*?" she asked them.

But most of all, she made sure she would feel better and be in good shape—getting the therapeutic treatments of a skilled masseuse and having her hair done to look her best for photographers. She would avoid a repeat of one photo in which, she said, "I looked awful. I looked like Julius Caesar in the pictures they took of me right after I won the 100 meter." She wasn't going to let that happen again.

August 8: Day Twenty-five, Olympic Dorm and Stadium, Berlin

The outcome of the preliminary races confirmed what most people suspected: Americans were fast, but the more experienced Germans were faster. The Germans set the pace when they clocked in a world record but still were holding back. Helen detailed the outcome of the two relay teams in their separate preliminary trials. She wrote: *The day was bright & dark at times. Spent most of day waiting for the race to start. Met with Steers in the morning about relay selections. We ran in 1st heat & it was my first relay. We won and I ran anchor going away. The crowd roared & Betty said it was for me. The Germans came through in 46.4 beating the world record as compared to our 47.1. My leg felt tight. Played Rawls phonograph & danced some. Bad for legs, & tomorrow—the finals.*

Tidye had taken her complaint to the women's head coach and team manager, Fred Steers, who said he would look into it. When he met with the team, to give a pep talk and put an end to the bickering, he supported Dee Boeckmann's decision.

For the first time in her life, Helen ran as a team member. Her team won second place in the preliminary, and she was elated. Winning another gold seemed possible, if not probable. The kid from Callaway forgot about her strained leg muscles for the moment and *danced some* and danced some more. Only afterward *(Bad for legs, & tomorrow)* did she think of the consequences of cutting loose and enjoying herself on the dance floor with swimmer Katherine Rawls.

August 9: Day Twenty-six, Olympic Dorm and Stadium, Berlin

The seven-tenths of a second margin that the German team had yesterday would not be easily topped today. And though the crowd showed appreciation for Helen's talent, as Betty Robinson had said, a majority of spectators, assessing the odds, put their money on another victory for Deutschland. But a split-instant slip of the hand changed everything. She wrote: *I secured my 2nd Olympic* [gold] *medal! After spending most of day writing cards (30). It was very warm & pretty Sunday. Larson's friend came to see me . . . got warmed up to a glorious feeling. . . .* [The] *relay was fast & we about held our own until the Germans brought their last pass & dropped the baton. I pulled in first by yards. Got gold medals & crowns & 1 tree. I spoke for Fox Film* [producers]. *Stayed to watch high jump & marathon. Relay—Bland, Rogers, Robinson & myself. Went to Women's Club of Berlin for a grand dinner.*

"Larson" was the Reverend August F. Larson, who taught Bible studies and sociology at William Woods; he was known for his unfailing good humor and interest in all things Swedish. The Reverend's friend was a Swedish masseur who showed up at the eleventh hour and asked permission to apply an ointment to Helen's ailing leg. He proved to be a godsend, and the salve produced a tingling feeling of well-being, numbing her pain.

She walked calmly onto the track, gazed into the clouds, and whispered a prayer. She positioned herself just as Boeckmann had told her, in the third-leg spot, and then looked back at her coach, who nodded approvingly. Robinson was in fourth, the anchor position, and as directed, once the German girls assumed their places, the two quickly switched spots. Helen was now anchor, and the German coach and her girls appeared anguished by this last-minute change.

Bland, the lead-off runner, made a fast break from the starting line and darted ahead of Emmy Albus. She passed the baton to Rogers, then dropped back. Somewhere between the time Bland slipped the stick to Rogers and Rogers passed it on to Robinson, the German runner took the lead and was barreling ahead. At the three-quarter pole, just 100 meters away from the ribbon and a gold medal, Ilse Doerffeldt waited nervously for Marie Dollinger. Ilse was looking over her shoulder, keeping an anxious eye on her opponent, the Fulton Flash, the fastest woman in the world. She saw that her teammate ran but a meter or two in the lead.

When Marie thrust the baton in Ilse's outreached hand, Ilse took off like a shot. Helen watched it happen. Following her coach's instructions to look straight ahead and go with the touch of the baton, Helen held her head up and faced forward, eager to explode into a blur of speed. Worriedly, she watched Ilse widening the distance between them. Ilse was clutching the stick in her fist, her arms swinging up and back, up and back. But in an instant, Ilse made a fatal mistake. She pulled the baton across her chest, switching it to her other hand. It was an unnecessary time-wasting effort, and one that caused the wooden rod to slip from her grasp. By this time, Robinson had pushed her baton into Helen's palm, and Helen was hell-bent on closing the gap. She saw Ilse fumble her baton, saw her shorten her stride and, in agony, cover her face with both hands as the baton went bouncing underfoot.

The stadium crowd fell silent, disbelieving.

In seconds, Helen flew past Ilse, opening about an eight-meter chasm between herself and the trailing British rival. Ilse, in a state of shock, was now crying, staggering off the track. Her teammates hovered around her; their eyes searched fleetingly for the lost baton and darted upward to the chancellor's box. Stunned like everyone else, Hitler had risen from his seat. His mouth gapped wide, his face winced in defeat. His arm stretched out, his finger pointing to where the baton had rolled to a stop.

Many theorized that Helen would have caught up and overtaken Ilse anyhow. Ilse had feared this possibility; her nervousness, which caused her to fumble the baton, merely demonstrated it. She had looked back over her shoulder, which she shouldn't have done, for it divided her focus, and she had tried to switch the baton from her right hand to her left, which was unnecessary since she did not have to pass it on to another runner. The thought of running anchor against Helen had snapped her concentration, and she had forgotten all she had been taught and violated rudimental relay form.

And all was lost.

Helen again stepped onto to the winner's platform, accompanied by teammates, to receive the wreath of peace, the oak of honor, and the gold medal of victory. As America's flag rose ceremoniously, Gisela Mauermayer, the six-foot blonde beauty who had won the discus, turned her face away and saluted the Nazi flag. The stadium crowd roared. Within an hour, Hitler sent a Mercedes-Benz filled with roses to console his girls—women athletes who had dominated track and field events much like the American black auxiliary now dominated men's track and field events. In their preliminary heat, Albus, Krauss, Dollinger, and Doerffeldt had shown themselves to be superbly conditioned, smashing all previous records. But this slip of hand was something they deeply lamented, for they had lost a sure Olympic gold medal. It fell from their grasp the moment Ilse Doerffeldt let the baton slip from her hand.

The Americans not only set a new Olympic relay record but had taken both their gold and their place in Olympic history. Helen spent quite a bit of time afterward, writing thirty postcards, telling about her second victory to her many supporters and friends in Callaway County. Her team won 2 of the 24 gold medals America took home that year. The German team won 33. Forty-nine countries competed for 131 possible gold medals; there were 3,738 male athletes compared with 328 women.

In sum, the women's track and field record played out as follows: Americans won the 4 x 100-meter relay with a time of 46.9; Great Britain won second (47.6), Canada third (47.8), Italy fourth (48.7), and Holland fifth (48.8). Germany was disqualified from the relay. Americans, per "La Stephens," won the 100 meters (officially, in 11.5), while Poland won the silver via Stella Walsh (11.7), and Germany the bronze via Kathe Krauss (11.9); Germany's Marie Dollinger ran in fourth place; America's Annette Rogers came in fifth; and Germany's Emmy Albus was sixth. The 80-meter hurdles saw no American winners; the victors were Italy's Trebisonda Valla, Germany's Anny Steuer, and Canada's Elizabeth Taylor. Likewise, the high jump event went to Europeans: Hungary's Ibolya Csák, Great Britain's Dorothy Odam, and Germany's Elfriede Kaun. In the javelin event, Germany's Tilly Fleischer and Luise Krüger won first and second, and Poland's Marja Krasniewska, third. The discus proved to be the same story. No Americans emerged victorious; the Europeans set the records and took the medals: Germany's Gisela Mauermayer, Poland's Jadwiga Wajsówna, and Germany's Paula Mollenhauer.

In the end, Germany's women walked off with a total of seven medals. The American team won only two—both achieved by the enormous gift of a farm girl from Fulton who ran in an unorthodox way—in the high style of Callaway County—and showed what winning honorably is all about.

Two events in which Helen had demonstrated ability would be offered to women in 1948. The 200-meter race would be won with a time of 24.4; Helen clocked 23.9 during a 200-meter exhibition in Wuppertal just days after her 1936 Olympic victories. The shot put gold medal would be won with a distance of 45 feet 1½ inches; Helen threw the iron ball much farther—a documented 54 feet—in an exhibition later in 1936.

7

Running the Continent

Citius, Altius, Fortius [faster, higher, braver].
—The Olympic Motto, coined by Fr. Henri Didon

*T*he 1936 women's track and field competitions were now history, and the Olympic Games would be over in six more days. Now, Helen began the final leg of her journey. Crowned with Olympic laurels, she toured the city of Berlin and the countryside with her new friends—Canadian, Greek, Austrian, and Polish athletes. The American Olympic Association booked exhibitions for its medalists; Helen's itinerary entailed races in Wuppertal, Cologne, and Dresden. She would fly in an airplane, an experience she had desired since childhood. She sent a postcard to her mother from Dresden: "Writing from a cafe high in the Swiss Alps of Germany where you can see over into Czechoslovakia. It is a gorgeous view and stopped there for a short time. Ran Stella and others in Dresden last night—won in 11.4 or 11.5. Dresden is home of beautiful china & that was prize [a demitasse cup with the crest of the City of Dresden]. Having a grand time in a grand place. Well, I got the second gold medal in the Olympics—it was great fun."

AUGUST 10: DAY TWENTY-SEVEN, DRESDEN, GERMANY

Dee, Bright Eyes & I went to Dresden on train . . . were greeted by officials and shown about the city. After lunching with [Dresden] Mayor, we were shown about until meet. About 10,000 came. Ran Stella & Krauss in 11.4. & 11.5. Meet lasted until dark & I was smothered by autograph seekers. . . . we were entertained in the hotel. Some fun! The Bouraghmaster [sic] & the American Ambassador were there. The music goes round & round!!! We were given Dresden china as prizes.

One of Helen's gifts was a glazed porcelain figurine of a dog (reminiscent of the Ming dynasty), said to be the symbol of friendship. In the meet, Helen proved Stella wrong for the third time and also beat Germany's fastest sprinter. But who was "Bright Eyes"? Was it Betty Robinson? Or Alice Arden? Helen had dubbed someone with that nickname, a reference to Shirley Temple, the bright-eyed and innocent child star of the Hollywood movie *Bright Eyes*.

AUGUST 11: DAY TWENTY-EIGHT, DRESDEN AND GERMAN SWISS ALPS

[Took a] *bus trip through Dresden and southern Germany near Czechoslovakia. . . . Mayor came along & we had a very beautiful & enjoyable trip. . . . mountains were grand and the view wonderful. And the Japs were so tired! Dee, Bright Eyes & I came back 3rd class & I had big time. We attended a Japanese Club & had food served Japanese style—got pins, etc. More fun eating with chop sticks. The Austrian girl liked it too.*

With the Austrian competitor Hermine "Herma" Bauma (fourth in javelin), Dee Boeckmann, Bright Eyes (again), and others, Helen toured the Kaiserlauf and other places that day. Lapel pins were gift mementos from their Japanese hosts.

AUGUST 12: DAY TWENTY-NINE, OLYMPIC DORM, BERLIN

I didn't do much except fool around during the morning. In the afternoon I did much needed washing. I went out for the evening with Mr. Smiley & Mr. & Mrs. Platt. We had a very nice evening & at the House Fatherland. The various rooms were interesting portrayals of different nations. Collected several dogs. And the Goose! . . . I led a band too—a Bavarian band. I gave some of the kids a treat upon my arrival home. And how?

The Platts were wealthy Americans, and J. B. Smiley, the Platt's "eligible" friend, became Helen's escort. She dined in a fancy restaurant, enjoyed several night spots, and took much pleasure in her first beer hall, in Wuppertal. She was given the baton of a German folk band and became the center of attention. Tasting such adulation and strong brews were dizzying experiences for the youthful Olympian. Did she mean to be perplexing by using a question mark at the end of the page? Probably.

AUGUST 13: DAY THIRTY, OLYMPIC DORMS, BERLIN

Harriet, Alice, Louise Washburn & Alice's Ohio friend took us out to the Olympic Village. Came back & argued with gate keeper. After eating a late dinner, we went to swimming stadium. . . . Gertrude, Harriet, Betty Burch & I went to tea at the home of a famous horsewoman of Germany. Later we went to her sister's home & were given records of her singing. After dinner . . . quite tired but managed to find energy to dance & have big time in music room.

Arguments with the gatekeeper stemmed from the girls' ignoring curfews and forgetting their identification papers. Alice Arden's friend could have been Gertrude Webb (not Gertrude Wilhelmsen), whom Helen had competed against in AAU events. Webb (or whoever it was) introduced the girls to Hilga Bohnsteat, a German countess "absolutely nuts about horses." Away from home, friends of friends became friends, so the girls had a grand time. In the evening, in the dorm's music room, they danced cheek to cheek, doing the jitterbug and the Charleston.

August 14: Day Thirty-one, Olympic Dorm and Berlin

Betty & I went to town with a runner. Betty had difficult time finding her boy friend. I bought my shoes & had my picture taken. Came back in rain to lunch, then went to pool with some swimmers to see relay & Adolph Kiefer. Our relay 3rd. Received letter from Mother. Got gift in mail. Alice Arden left for London, England. Hope to make our trip.

Rainy weather was still with them. America's Kiefer won the gold medal for the 100-meter backstroke and a bronze in the 4 x 200-meter freestyle relay (Japan won the gold). In this, her briefest daily entry, she notes "Our" women's swim relayers, Katherine Rawls, Bernice Lapp, Mavis Freeman, and Olive McKean, placed third (4:40.2), and that she had experienced a disappointing jaunt in Berlin with Betty Robinson. She and Betty had set out with a runner, not named; Helen felt it was a waste of her time to wait and look for some guy Betty was infatuated with and to return to the dorm on her own. Helen was also disappointed to learn that Alice Arden had left; she worried that Alice had found another passage home, which would cut short their time together. No further mention of Bright Eyes occurs after this date, which suggests that Alice may have been the one given that nickname.

August 15: Day Thirty-two, Berlin

Kathlyn [Kelly], *Elsie & I went into the city for the morning . . .* [and did] *some shopping—as long as my marks lasted. After eating some downtown . . . lunch at the Freisenhaus. Attended swimming events . . . went to big stadium to see soccer game. Attended the Ball on the lovely island, given by Goebbels & the Air Minister. . . . a beautiful occasion &* more *than a good time was had by all. The fireworks & Ruth. And Bland + Mrs. Brown.*

Helen set about buying gifts, a leather purse for her mother and a meerschaum pipe for Coach Moore. Dr. Brown was an American physician in Berlin for the Olympics; his wife was the girls' escort. Using a plus sign *(Bland + Mrs. Brown)* suggests something, but Helen could not remember what; perhaps social waters seeking their own level. Ruth Haslie accompanied Helen to the Olympic farewell party featuring a fireworks show. Of course, bilingual Ruth was creating fireworks of another kind for Helen. They now were intimate friends, seeing each other frequently each day, as often as possible in the time left to them. Helen invited Ruth to go with her to Goebbels's party, and Mrs. Brown acquiesced to the arrangement. Mrs. Brown walked all three youths through the palace doorway but somehow lost track of them. Almost instantly, a palace attendant aligned himself with the girls, giving special attention to Helen.

It was a gaggle of upper-class people from all parts of the world, an event of the privileged and despotic German *haute monde*, hosted by the minister of Enlightenment and Propaganda, Goebbels, and the Reichstag president, Göring. The setting was a medieval castle once inhabited by Kaiser Wilhelm but now owned by Goebbels. Ruth told Helen that the party was worrisome for many reasons, particularly as "the Nazi chief denies himself nothing. Drinks flow like the Rhine."

Streams of men and women glided into Göring's private lair all evening. It was past midnight when a messenger appeared to say that Göring wanted to see Helen. Ruth was told to wait. The courier opened the door for Helen and slid a tall, large goblet filled with burgundy into her hand. He guided her toward Göring and said he would be outside. As Helen recalled it, "He sat dressed, or should I say, undressed, in a black bathrobe, which fell open, exposing his thighs, and he slunk back in a cushioned seat. It looked more like a throne than a chair. His sausage-fat arms draped limply over ornately carved armrests, and as I was introduced to him, several scantily clad women crawled out from under the head of the long table where he sat."[1] Göring rose to greet her, took her hand, and kissed it. Suddenly, the feeling of being trapped overswept her, with one hand holding the wine and the other locked in his. In English, he invited her to take their drinks to his private quarters for a little talk. He jostled her toward a huge double door.

Helen held back. Instinct told her something was *off*. She pulled her hand from his, thanked him, and excusing herself, explained that she needed to find her girlfriends. She said that they had to be in their dorm before curfew. "*Danke*," she repeated, "excuse me." She held her glass toward him, implying she was asking where to put it. She tried to beg off, saying she needed to return to Mrs. Brown. "*Bitte. Bitte*," he said, clamping onto her again, this time at the wrist. Someone interrupted them; he had a phone call. Would *Fräulein Stephens* please excuse Herr President Göring?

Immediately, an attendant appeared from nowhere, it seemed to Helen. He took her glass, took her arm, and ushered her out. "It's time to go," he told her. Ruth appeared and said something to him in German and then to Helen. "It's late! We must find Harriet," said Ruth, and off they went. They pushed through the reveling crowd and spotted Harriet dancing. Helen waved to her from the side floor, mouthing, "Come on, let's go. It's time to go." Harriet saw her but ignored her and stayed on the floor talking to her dance partner, though the music had stopped. Helen waved again, vigorously. The attendant now motioned to Harriet, but again she paid no attention to either of them. She was not going to leave her dance partner willingly, so their attendant shuffled onto the floor, seized hold of the petite athlete, and firmly pulled her by the hand. "We're leaving," Helen told her, shouting over the noise. The rescuer held onto Harriet, and Ruth grabbed her by the waist, and between them they ushered a protesting Harriet away. Helen followed close behind. They moved through various private rooms, until finally they were out, through a back gate, and into a beautiful, moonless night. Awaiting them was a chauffeur and a Mercedes-Benz. Their protector hurried them inside, and soon they were in the safety of their dorm. Helen's simple underlining emphasized that *more* than a good time was had by all.

August 16: Day Thirty-three, Berlin

It was a very warm & beautiful day. . . . [Spent] most of morning packing, etc. Had picture taken for Olympic film. Had big time at lunch with Dr. Brown. In the afternoon, we went over to see the equestrians or riders of different nations compete. . . . a very pretty sight. Had very difficult time packing & didn't attend the closing ceremony at night—the beautiful blue lights & music could be seen & heard. A GOOD BYE. 16 days of world sport has closed until 4 years will have passed.

Leni Riefenstahl did not have enough footage of the women's 100-meter event, so she set up some cutaway shots of Helen and the other sprinters she needed for her film *Olympia*. Helen's luggage did not hold all her belongings, so she gave some clothing along with a remembrance gift to her friend Ruth Haslie. She did not attend closing ceremonies, preferring instead to spend her final evening of the Olympics in her room with Ruth, who kept unpacking her luggage and begging her to stay. While beautiful columns of blue light lit the sky, sweetly triumphant music drifted through their window, and their room shimmered with flickering fireworks.

August 17: Day Thirty-four, Wuppertal, Germany

Arose at 6:30 & had breakfast. After goodbyes . . . took the bus to RR station . . . had to wait until 9:30 for train. Most of us were tired but in our car little sleep was had. Anne O'Brien, Harriet Bland, Gertrude Wilhelmsen, & Kathy Dunnette [chaperone] *had one swell time. It was a very nice ride through some beautiful German country. . . . at Wuppertal, we were greeted by the masses & escorted to Lake Kaiserhof by police. After reception tea, we got our large rooms—Betty & I. After dinner we went to a kind of tavern for drinks. And the crowd!*

The Olympic flame was extinguished. The winners' tour abroad began. Olympic champions would spend another four days in Europe. Now Helen shared a room with Betty Robinson, for whom such adulation and hero worship was nothing new.

AUGUST 18: DAY THIRTY-FIVE, WUPPERTAL

Had difficulty in arising from a soft bed. After breakfast, the USA's need shopping. We needed marks badly. Later we marched down narrow crowded streets to the City Hall. Here we were welcomed & given refreshments. We put our names in the gold book of the city . . . were taken to the Suspension RR & to the zoo & its gardens. After refreshing ourselves with tea, we walked about the zoo . . . sang songs during bus ride home. After dinner, I wrote some letters. The German boxing champion was welcomed home in the afternoon by the band +.

The plus sign again! Whom or what did she mean? There were two gold-winning German boxers: the super heavyweight (175-pound) champ, Herbert Runge, and the flyweight (112-pound) Willie Kaiser. Popular tunes such as "Red Sails in the Sunset" and "Good Night, My Love" flowed from the open windows of the tour bus, as jubilantly, joyously the "USA's," as Helen called them, sang to each other.

The girls ran short of German currency as well as time for choosing last-minute mementos. They toured Wuppertal's streets and sites, bought tea, meals, and celebrated. Amid the adulation and clamor, Helen sent news to friends and family telling of her record-making events and carryings-on. The suspension bridge—like today's speedy, elevated monorails—was an amazing engineering feat, far ahead of its time; it was a must-see attraction for any Wuppertal visitor, and Helen was no exception. She bought dozens of postcards depicting the places she saw.

AUGUST 19: DAY THIRTY-SIX, WUPPERTAL

Group of us went shopping with the usual crowd following. Packed some & looked over . . . purchases. Got our Swastikas. Slept little in apt. Betty had bad cold. Took bus to field about 4 o'clock in afternoon. Sang songs & feeling high. Went on field too soon. After marching on field before a packed field . . . Won the 100 & 200 meters in 11.6 & 24.1. Placed second in shot & anchored our relay to second place. Got huge box of candy. Swell prizes. Germans happy over relay. Went back to hotel. . . . Black cats. . . . went to city banquet ball. Swell time & drinks fine. Presented with tray for high points.

The girls received little swastikas to take home as souvenirs. Helen outran Walsh a third and a fourth time during the International Women's Sports Festival event. She was elated, winning both the 100- and the 200-meter races—the same 200-meter race that Stella had boasted Helen lacked the endurance for. Stella's 200-meter time was 24.2, compared with Helen's 24.1. (In the 1946 Olympic 200 meters, the Netherlands's Francina "Fanny" Blankers-Koen won the gold with a time of 24.4—three-tenths of a second *slower* than Helen's 1936 speed.) Stella lost in the 100 meters, too; her time was 11.8, compared with Helen's 11.6. Helen threw the shot put a distance of 39 feet 7^{13}⁄$_{64}$ inches, which placed her second to Japan's Fumi Kojima's 40 feet 2^{19}⁄$_{64}$ inches. The prize for second place was a small covered Bavarian china bowl; the first-place prize was a life-size bronze bust of Hitler. In this instance, Helen was glad she won second place. In the six events held that day, none of the other American girls placed, although Anne O'Brien came close to it, running fourth in the 80-meter hurdles. Stella took first place in the broad jump with 18 feet 8^{41}⁄$_{64}$ inches. Helen received a silver tray for scoring the most points. She was *the* female Olympian, running faster than all others. And in the next few months, she would prove also to be braver.

Olive Hasenfus (Betty's replacement) ran the relay with Annette Rogers, Harriet Bland, and Helen, who anchored. Harriet would never be an anchor, no matter how much she implored. These four were matched against the same German team who had flubbed the Olympic baton and, according to them, for that reason only had lost the gold medal. Seeking vindication, Doerffeldt held onto the stick, made no needless switch, and to a rousing, vengeance-seeking crowd of 35,000, beat the Americans by half a meter. With 46.06, they eclipsed America's Olympic record (46.90), but it was only in an exhibition, so it was not an official mark. The Americans, for their part, also ran faster than before: 46.07! Better track conditions and better weather were the likely reasons.

The black cats mentioned in Helen's diary were ones that the girls believed had been put in their room as a prank by some person, an associate of the German team perhaps, to cause anyone with a black-cat superstition to worry about bad luck.

August 20: Day Thirty-seven, Wuppertal and Cologne, Germany, over Belgium, in Paris, and to Le Havre, France

All athletes . . . given box of trinkets from Wuppertal. Bland, Rogers, Olive Hasenfus & I traded our relay trophy for other things at the store. . . . I chose toilet set & bracelet. Watch & compact taken. Went back to hotel. . . . Black cats—laughter—running & screaming in halls. . . . left by bus at 3:30 in morning . . . in Cologne about 5 AM. Got out & touched the cathedral—a beauty in early morning. Crossed Rhine. Ate breakfast at air field & took plane to Paris. Beautiful & thrilling ride—going up! Paris not so grand. Took special to Le Havre & got on S.S. President Roosevelt about 2:30. A good meal & sleep. Ship not quite as large as [the SS] *Manhattan.*

Helen thoroughly enjoyed airplane travel. Flying above the clouds excited her. Olive Hasenfus had placed poorly in the Olympic trials but was now running in the relay exhibitions. The girls claimed that they had reversed the black-cat curses to "good" luck, for they had lost the relay by only one-hundredth of a second. With the cats' help, they thought they would win if they had another chance against Germany's team. Helen took a quick look at the cathedral in Cologne. The guide section of her diary describes the *Manhattan* as the twenty-eighth largest of the fifty ocean liners in the world at 668.4 feet long, 86.3 feet wide, and 33.3 feet deep.[2] The *President Roosevelt* did not make the list. Having known one of the better vessels, Helen recognized a ship of lesser appointments; now an experienced cruise passenger, she notes its smallness.

AUGUST 21: DAY THIRTY-EIGHT, OFF WEST COAST OF ENGLAND

Dee, Betty & I have room they had in 1928—Cabin 3 with 3 portholes. Many bags arrived before us. Got up at noon. Ship docking at Southampton, England, made such noise last night. Alice Arden got on there. Fog made going bad & fog horn kept sounding. Played deck tennis, shuffleboard, and golf during day & night. Bland & I were close-by when the ship's officers found two Chinese stowaways down in pipes near top of ship. Von Hindenburg flew over us . . . on its return to Germany. I snapped it. Gertrude & I took in the picture show. Dropped several cards in Ireland. Danced most of night. In afternoon enjoyed phonograph. Drinks in room.

Having fun was Helen's foremost concern now. Driving golf balls into the sea—as she said, day and night—was one way to pass the time, since the trip back was not only on a lesser boat but a noisy one at that. It seemed momentous that she had the same room that two earlier Olympians had shared. She was happy that Alice was on the same return ship, though she liked Gertrude Wilhelmsen's company, too.

Her journal advises: "In foggy weather, ships underway blow a long blast on the whistle at frequent intervals. Anchored ships ring a bell for five seconds every minute. Modern passenger ships have other means of guiding themselves in the fog—submarine listening devices, radio-direction finders, etc."[3] But the ship's whistle was more like a horn to Helen, blasting daily at noon and blowing salutes to passing ships. It served as a signal for boat drills (drill directions were posted in each cabin), and the noise seemed excessive to our young traveler who celebrated late into the night. The Hindenburg's approach was announced by a blast, and so Helen grabbed her camera to get a photo of the blimp as it flew overhead. She mailed postcards when the ship docked in Ireland. Now comfortable having wine with her meals in the company of older women, she had drinks delivered to their room. If her teetotaler mother ever read her diary, she would have a word or two for her newly famous daughter who had abandoned the farmer's motto of early to bed, early to rise.

AUGUST 22: DAY THIRTY-NINE, SAILING THE ATLANTIC

Arose in time for lunch. Lapped deck about 15 times—11 laps to a mile. Dee filled our room with a Chinese laundry. . . . [Was] a rather cool day & misty. Ship ran

into fog & fog horn started in evening & continued at night. Had my "Goose" for
dinner. Saw picture show on deck. . . . Didn't go to dance but Betty & I wandered
about ship in the whipping wind & spray. And the "Chinks" didn't knife us either.
Listened to the Antioch College band on 3rd deck. Had coffee & sandwiches in
our room.

Some passengers worried about what desperate act the Chinese stowaways
might commit if they managed to escape. But Helen's indifferent tone and
reported ambling about the deck with Betty suggest she was not concerned at
all about it. She jogged a little more than a mile. For whatever reason, Dee was
either the beneficiary of clothing that the "stowaways" brought with them, or
Helen was "funning" around with her about the stowaways. Perhaps Dee gave
her a laundry list of dos and don'ts upon disembarking. Helen's notes are deliberately vague: Helen's portrayal of the fugitives as bloodthirsty, knife-carry-
ing "Chinks" seems to convey the "foreign" (chauvinistic) prejudice that some
Americans felt. And what about the "Goose" remark? Did she mean to imply
that her goose was cooked?

AUGUST 23: DAY FORTY, THE ATLANTIC

Still arising in time for lunch. Stiff breeze & fog all day. Ship rocks quite badly
tonight. . . . Spent most of afternoon laying around the rooms. With Alice. Eating
tea cakes. Betty's birthday. Had a formal dinner party for her & I gave her box of
candy. . . . [The] champagne was quite good. Had amateur athlete's night. Had
to play harmonica just when I thought I was through. Stiff breeze . . . salt spray
upon the top deck. A Sunday which didn't seem like one. Some acts were a scream.
Is life worth while?

Up just in time for lunch! Laying about eating tea cakes with Alice—what
does this convey? The top deck, evidently, was the place to be, day or night.
Always ready with wry humor, Helen wrote that she enjoyed Eleanor Holm's
preferred drink. She spent some leisure time with Alice and with Betty. She
celebrated Betty's birthday but seems to have become bored with sea travel and
thus pursued distractions. When asked to entertain, she was moody but played
her harmonica anyway. Shipboard intrigues and crushes and romances, with
their ups and downs like the waves, dampened her spirit, swayed her this way
and that. Sometimes, life proved itself to be very worthwhile; at other times,
she doubted it quite earnestly.

AUGUST 24: DAY FORTY-ONE, THE ATLANTIC

Had breakfast in bed—service de luxe. Betty & I took work-out on top deck.
Wrenched shoulder muscle. York, Penn. Still getting sun tan. Firing of small canon
on top deck. Missed lunch in order to lose my German goiter. Washed my sea blown
hair & Gertrude did her duty. Tossed the dice for the horse races. Got my pictures

from the ship photographer. Saw the two colored girls. Had my duck for dinner. Thought we saw iceberg during tea time. Costume ball on deck tonight. Windy & rainy some tonight . . . was cool & nice most of day. Can still type. Coffee & sandwiches in room. On deck alone.

One diversion offered passengers was horse racing—a game noted in her diary's advice section, "The Art of Travelling in Comfort." A roll of dice determined the progress of miniature horses; the ship's purser sold tickets to those betting on the races, and the winners collected "pro rata portions of the total amount of the bet (after deduction of a percentage for the seamen's fund or some other charity). On ships with plenty of deck space there is often a 'field day' organized, with potato races, etc., in great variety and abundance of prizes."

Three days away from New York, Helen takes a gamble, tries lady luck for the first time in her life, and wonders what people back home must think about gambling. She didn't write about winnings or losses; she was as unlucky in gambling as she was in love. Her shipboard infatuations had fizzled. Still offended about Helen's role in the relay decision, Tidye and Louise badgered her. Her goose (duck) was proverbially cooked during dinner by Pickett and Stokes. It was not a good day for Helen. She had gained weight, having slacked off her training exercises. She was snacking and eating more, but this lunchtime, she deliberately fasted. Gertrude Wilhelmsen's duty was to curl Helen's hair and, conceivably, mentally prep her for the New York welcoming. Her joke about being so out of condition but still able to type makes one wonder what she had done with or to her hands. Or perhaps she simply was glad that her typing ability was intact.

Helen saw *the* person from York, Pennsylvania, sunbathing on deck. Was it someone who broke her heart? She typed a lengthy letter to her special college friend and cards to family, and she posted them with the purser, whose office served as the smoking room and post office. She smoked several cigarettes while composing the letter to "S" and reread the letters she had received from S just before winning the first gold, and the one received August 7, before winning a second gold. Her shipboard love life had taken a final nose dive at the ball, and so Helen closed with another shrouded three-word sentence, *On deck alone.*

8

Victor's Return

But things like that, you know, must be
At every famous victory.

—Robert Southey, "The Battle of Blenheim"

*T*he SS *Roosevelt* was capable of turning up about fifteen knots per hour; but this morning, in this weather, in these waters, the going was rough and the velocity much slower. The captain issued an advisory for all to stay below, but three passengers ignored it, having agreed to meet before breakfast on deck. Powerful, thirty-foot, wind-whipped waves slapped loudly against the bow, causing the vessel to jerk and sway, much like a stuttering roller coaster. Leaning abeam of the ship's center, windward, and holding onto the ship's rail, Helen and Betty and Dee had sea spray up their noses and their clothes doused. Helen stretched her long arms and torso over the rail as far out toward the Atlantic as she could. Her short "permanent waves," frothing into a frizzy tangled net of yellow gold, snapped across her wet forehead. The strong, vigorous winds of Mother Nature were, as Helen recalled, "Bracing, indeed!"

Dee briefed the girls about the upcoming health inspection by the ship's doctor. Before being allowed to put foot on land, each passenger would be subjected to a general physical exam. "Do not misplace your landing ticket," Dee warned. "It must be presented at the gangplank." Betty, Helen, team nurse Kay Riche, and Dee would depart as a group, and Dee wanted no delays and no blown-out-of-proportion rumors going around. Scrutiny of gold medalists would parlay—especially for the individual gold medalist/world record holder—and Helen must be prepared for it.

A grand celebration was being inaugurated in New York, but Helen's mind drifted to the welcoming awaiting her at home. She spread open her arms and held them there, widely evoking all the world that lay before her. As her flaying arms pitched to and fro, a button popped from the waistband of her skirt, sprung off into the gusty breeze, and disappeared forever.

Once Dee had had her say, off they went, swaying arm-in-arm, toward the dining hall. The bonds of friendship seemed solidly cast between them. That night, Helen wrote: *Breakfast for three was served about 10 o'clock. Sea rough . . . boat kept pitching. Loads of fun trying to weather the strong wind and spray forward. Felt a little queer at lunch as boat kept pitching. After lunch slept & fixed waists. Read l.e.t.t.e.r.s. Made away with a good dinner. Saw the show—"My American Wife." Went down near bow to watch the big waves come in. Bland & I spent short time on top deck. Started a novel. We were given a mock Chinese funeral for the China man that was supposed to have died. Dancing was held as usual. Beer & sandwiches.*

Helen was letting out waistlines, seeing movies, watching waves come in. She flipped the pages of a book while resting on deck but lacked interest and concentration. She tied words into a sailor's knot, a flag of letters each separated by a period, having received three letters from friends back home, yet yearning for one from one particular girlfriend. She wrote nothing about the content of yesterday's conversation nor what she and Harriet on deck solo talked about. Harriet's tell-me, tell-me, me-too attitude had become irksome.

Officials seemed less concerned than they once were that intoxicating beverages were served to young athletes. The ship's press worked up a piece about poor diet, dank, cold Olympic dorms, head colds, shinsplints, constant rainy weather, and the slow, muddy track—all to slant an American-kids-overcome-odds story.

AUGUST 26: DAY FORTY-THREE, THE ATLANTIC

Had my 5 meals today!! . . . swell day and smooth sea. . . . Shuffleboard on top deck. Won one game . . . watched wrestling on mat. Betty B. & I went through our bout & I lost the bet long ago. "To Mary—With Love" was a good picture—& oh how true to life! Talked & listened to head of physical culture school as sun sank away below sea. Dressed as Japanese in Freezing House for little skit given. Was crowned as Gold Medal winner and given celery for flowers. Spent evening or early morning with Evelyn Ferrara.

Snacking and dining put inches on all the girls' waistlines, contributing to unused buttonholes, seasickness, and calls for steward assistance and remedies.

Evenings continued to spill over into morning hours. Helen had fun in a skit portraying a kimono-clad, white-socks-wearing Japanese Olympian, who flubbed each and every discus throw.

With less than two days left at sea, Evelyn Ferrara was showing interest in Helen, whose spirits ebbed when a "Dear Mary" letter arrived from Fulton. Conversely, serious-natured Betty "Butch" Burch harped on how teammates with no medals (i.e., herself) felt left out. Burch said that Helen should have been Tidye's advocate and should have signed the petition to support Eleanor Holm. (Three hundred out of four hundred athletes supported Holm's reinstatement.)

Other disgruntled athletes claimed that some things aboard ship and at the games were kept from the press. In a few days, the wireless made their complaints public. Mile-runner Gene Venzke called the American Olympic officials petty, aloof, and unfair to athletes. He said Al Masters was right about mismanagement, that officials squabbled among themselves. Platform diving champ Dorothy Poynton Hill claimed there wasn't one happy athlete on the whole ship. At the other extreme, a relay medalist, Harriet Bland, was happily bubbly about everything. Wine and beer, the "ruination of drink," were easily obtained by the younger set, and she enjoyed herself every minute, she said, "especially on the way back, when training rules were relaxed."[1]

AUGUST 27: DAY FORTY-FOUR, THE ATLANTIC

Had our breakfast in bed about 11 o'clock. Did my washing at last, partly in salt water. Filled out our landing slips. Had our pictures taken. Got paint on my hands & went in radio room. Dee & I took pictures on bow of boat. It was cool today & the ocean was as pretty as a picture. In late afternoon, a steamer was sighted crossing our pathway.

Gertrude Wilhelmsen now sat at Helen's table, with growing personal interest in the star. Helen's words are surprisingly calm and serene. She ran afoul of fresh paint, for the old ship was undergoing a touch-up amid preparations for the crowds and filming expected upon docking. Axioms rang true for Helen: Victory is sweet. Everyone loves a winner. But what might her parents do if they knew she slept until almost noon, shared breakfast in bed, and drank beer, wine, and mixed drinks?

Shenanigans, "festations," celebrations, and quickening kinships abounded for the youthful athletes heading homeward with songs in their hearts. At the end of the day, at the end of a page, Helen wrote: *No lunch & no tea. The captain's dinner was held—noise, novelties & fun. Ate a swell dinner & enjoyed it to fullest extent. Gertrude & I spent some nice moments upon the top deck in the cool breeze & wonderful moonlight.*

August 28: Day Forty-five, New York Harbor

Another nice day. Everyone anxious to leave ship. Wrote letter. Had breakfast for first time below. Sighted land. . . . Drifted in slowly to Quointine pier about 7 after the mail was taken off. Representatives [Stanley Howe or Howl and Jack Dempsey] *of the City of New York came on board to tell of the elaborate plans of entertainment through Sept. 3. Message from Mayor La Guardia. . . . Souvenirs in form of programs. Got all baggage off & inspected with little difficulty. Tree sent to Washington . . . for inspection. Met friends. Eddie Mayo took me to Hotel New Yorker. Room with Dee (# 1254). Telegram from Fulton. Got away from pier about 9 o'clock. Gertrude, Evelyn, Bland, Betty, Dee, Eddie & I were introduced from floor. Got in around 3. Detroit Tigers in room.*

Eating breakfast during breakfast hours? Amazing! She mailed her reply to the "Dear Mary" letter. Cleverly, she created hidden meaning by omitting the subject of her sentence, thus implying both she and her baggage got inspected: "[I] Got all baggage off & [I got] *inspected* with little difficulty." The dockside greeters were a New York educator/administrator for the public schools, and a famous boxer who owned restaurants in New York bearing his name.

The Olympic trees were transferred for a quarantine period to Washington, D.C. Helen used the word a second time, encoding *inspection* (hers and the tree's). As planned, Dee, Nurse Riche, Betty, and Helen left together, and there was only one hitch: In their haste to leave when the okay was given and the gangplank dropped, a heel from one of Helen's shoes snapped off. A platform set up at the pier served for introductions and welcome speeches. The hoopla lasted about two hours; then off she limped to the hotel.

Dee was now Helen's chaperone-roommate. When they arrived in their hotel room, a load of baseball players were encamped there, waiting to meet the star female athlete. Personal representative and licensed real estate broker Edward Mayo had talked the desk clerk into letting them in.

Many people made promises to Helen. Some, like the assertive and aggressive "Eddie" Mayo, accepted invitations and scheduled appearances for her without asking her. Mayo was a Madison Avenue booking agent and an acquaintance of Dee. According to Helen, he was a celebrity hanger-on who latched onto her almost the moment she put foot ashore. Mayo reached into Helen's life by wiring Dee and offering to line up some special introductions for them at the hotel. Small in size, little Eddie thought big and promised much. He talked too much, too fast, and now, according to Dee, was a little too vague on the details. Free of the ocean liner's confinement, Helen expected to have time to herself, disentangled from Dee and without engagements. She wanted unhampered time to be with friends. But Eddie had other ideas for her.

August 29: Day Forty-six, New York City

Arose about 11:30 . . . pictures taken in swanky room of hotel. Breakfast & lunch in coffee shop. Sent telegram home. Got shoe heels repaired & left Dee. . . . we met Eddie at Mount Clair Hotel. He could walk despite accident. Went to Yankee Stadium to see Yankees beat Detroit 6 to 3. Peanuts, ice cream, & cokes. . . . [Met] some of players. Got autographed baseballs. Met Bill Robinson & Pat McDonald. Went to friend's place for reception . . . went to Dempsey's place for dinner. Spoke over radio. Nice entertainment provided. More autographs secured. . . . Went to 3 big theatres & made reservations. Went to NY Times . . . [and] Paradise night club. A grand show. Pictures & introduction. Got home around 3. A great day. Bathed my watch.

Helen met personalities Bill "Mack" Robinson and Pat McDonald and was elated. She hit the sack around four, rose late in the morning, combined meals, and grabbed time for herself with the excuse of needing a cobbler. She found a closet-size shoe shop a few blocks away and then rejoined Dee and Mayo, who, running headlong to greet her, moving too fast for his own good, fell up some marble stairs and banged his shins.

At the newspaper office, she learned that Jesse Owens was being honored as the state's Olympic "Negro sprinter and jumper" on the capitol grounds in Columbus, Ohio. State offices closed for the afternoon so that fans could meet him at Union Station. Governor Davey, Mayor Gessaman, and Ohio State University president Lou Morrell had greeted him. Arthur Evans presented Owens and his wife Ruth with a gift (a chest of silverware) from the Junior Chamber of Commerce. Owens was to fly to New York for other honors on September 3.

Helen had a day of unchaperoned sight-seeing with friends and at day's end took a dip in the hotel pool, forgetting to remove her watch.

August 30: Day Forty-seven, New York City

Some athletes were to reach port on Thursday aboard the SS *Manhattan*; those who arrived earlier were hosted by the New York Hotel Men's Association and were accessible to the press while they awaited Thursday's official reception at Randall's Island. Reporters latched onto the titular head of the Olympic track team, Dr. Joseph Taycroft, and head track coach Lawson Robertson. These officials offered the media prewritten comments on how poorly the Germans treated their American guests. The *New York Times*, however, noted Venzke's criticism that the American Olympic Committee did little to make things easy or comfortable for its athletes. They were neglected, he said; some favors amounting to very little financially were denied, but officials "could not or would not see things that way. Several of us lost sweat shirts and when we asked for others we were turned down flatly. They don't mingle with us and spent a good deal of time squabbling among themselves."[2]

Newsmen asked Robertson to respond to these charges. He admitted that some improvements should be made. When probed about the removal of Stoller and Glickman from the relay, he said he hoped no one had misconstrued his decision, which was "made purely in the interest of the team and certainly was not a case of racial prejudice." Newsmen turned to the Eleanor Holm question, and the swim team chaperone stepped forward as if on cue. Said Mrs. Ada Sackett, Mrs. Jarrett "was warned three times. . . . the officials' action was the only course they could take. . . . It was a regrettable incident, which should be forgotten. I don't think Eleanor bears any grudge." Sackett did her duty, stepped back, and the media moved on to other officials and athletes.

Helen's diary held no trace of these accounts: *Dee went to mass early in morning. Kay Roche* [Riche] *came over early for dinner in hotel. Talk in Bland's room. . . . Kay showed us through Post Graduate Hospital where she is supervisor. Came back to hotel—Dee, Gertrude & I. Eddie & Poo came up to room. Wrote some letters. Eddie had us in for dinner to see ice carnival in our hotel after Dee, Gertrude & I returned from appearing at a temple. Show was good & we were introduced to audience. . . . Dee, Evelyn & her friend, Gertrude, Eddie & I went to Radio City Music Hall. . . . Saw Fred Astaire and Ginger Rogers in "Swing Time." Met George White. Walked through Radio City. Lovely clouds.*

Dee gave thanks for their Olympic victories at the cathedral that morning and in the afternoon joined Helen and Gertrude Wilhelmsen for a function at a synagogue. Helen toured a hospital and had dinner with the team nurse. Looking back later, she could not remember who "Poo" was. Helen went to Harriet's room to discuss plans for their trip home to Missouri. Dee had rented a car and would drive both girls to the St. Louis reception. They spoke of giving Dee the relay team's "Hitler oak" and planting it in St. Louis rather than Chicago, Betty's and Nettie's hometown.

After the Radio City show, Eddie, Gertrude, and Helen, walking arm-in-arm, strolled down the sidewalk, happily intoxicated by the sights of the city. Following close behind them were Dee, George White, Evelyn Ferrara, and Ferrara's nameless friend. On an impulse, Gertrude pulled away from Eddie, took Helen to a clear spot of sidewalk, and began dancing in the spirit of Fred Astaire and Ginger Rogers.

August 31: Day Forty-eight, New York City

Got up rather early in order to get to Police line-up by 9. Taxi missed & we walked back to correct address. Had very interesting tour of the department. . . . finger printed & had our pictures taken. Dee & I went to Times Building. Came back for rest & interviews about Olympics, etc. The Holm question. Dinner with a "screw ball" reporter. Saw "Mary, Queen of Scots" and the Olympic features including myself. Went to several other places too. Met Franklin D. Roosevelt, Jr.,

Al Jenkins, several famous detectives, & actors and dancers. Talked home to Mr. H. [illegible].

Folks at home telephoned and telegraphed, asking what her plans were; she wasn't sure herself. An administrator of Fulton's Chamber of Commerce and the president of William Woods College wanted to know what time to expect her. All she knew was that there were some exhibition races and appearances in New York and Canada, and that she wanted to see as much of New York as time allowed. Helen and Dee set out on foot to find the Federal Bureau of Investigation. Once there, Helen was fingerprinted and given a tour of FBI offices. Then she hurried back to the hotel for a press banquet.

Not satisfied with Sackett's official words, reporters asked Helen about the conflict between Jarrett and Avery Brundage. Eleanor should have played by the rules, Helen told them, at least until after the games. She said also that Coach Boeckmann had told her not to sign the petition to reinstate Eleanor. Over dinner, a "screwball" newsman tried pumping both women guilefully on the sex allegation made against Helen in Berlin. Dee intervened: Neither she nor Helen was the right person to discuss Eleanor's problem, and as for false accusations, they most likely would be settled in court; therefore, no discussion, no story.

September 1: Day Forty-nine, New York City

[We] went to Empire State Building for a tour through it. Very interesting & quite a dizzy height to climb. Met former [New York] Gov. Al Smith & had pictures taken with him. Bought cards & Dee & I shopped—swimming suit, rain coat, etc. Dee & I were unfortunately separated on the subway. Took taxi back at next stop. Went to Amateur Athletic Union office. Had dinner & Eddie took our group to show & went to get pictures at "March of Time." Shown below & pictures made. Evelyn Ferrara left for Chicago. Got letter from mother. Very pretty day & busy too.

While Eddie was pulling strings, Helen was enjoying full celebrity treatment. Dee and the AAU grew fearful of losing the star athlete to a commercial venture, for Helen was considering all options. Helen intentionally got lost, she later said, in the subway crowd, slipping from Dee's grasp at the end of their shopping spree. She felt that Dee did not understand or appreciate her predicament—her love life at home was in shambles because of "the sex thing"; her mother (not seeing sports as a career) was telling her not to worry, just to come back home and finish school. Helen didn't like or want Dee speaking for her to newsmen and making decisions for her. And if the sex thing had messed up everything, including school, what could she do? She had to consider every offer. With her temper spewing, she told Dee she did not need her to manage her life. As for sports, Coach Moore had taught her more than Dee ever could.

Angrily, Helen stormed off but then remembered their appointment, got a cab, and headed for the AAU office where Dee was waiting, cooling her heels.

Helen arrived loaded down with her new swimsuit, raincoat, and souvenirs for herself and friends. There, encircled by the men who ruled every aspect of amateur athletics in the country, she listened as they explained that if she accepted any contracts, she would jeopardize her amateur status and her chance for the 1940 Olympics. Dee presented the concerns she and Helen had hashed through, remarking on Helen's mother's desire that Helen finish college and on Helen's wish to benefit from Coach Moore's enthusiasm for her talent. Dee assured them that there wasn't a thread of truth in the claim made by the women's Polish coach: Helen's qualifying entrance physical and recent disembarkation exam would dispel that rumor. Dee offered to do anything they wanted her to do to avoid scandal and asked about legal counsel. Would the AAU provide assistance, if needed? On that score, they said let's wait and see.

SEPTEMBER 2: DAY FIFTY, NEW YORK CITY

Another day in New York. . . . busy running about hither & yon. Eddie was about as usual. Went to see picture of our team's arrival & saw & heard myself. Took Olympic diplomas to Duke for picture. Met some wealthy guys who took us to the Hollywood Restaurant. Saw a fair show there & Carson Thompson picked the beauty. We were introduced there. Later we went about ferreting out celebrities. "You should have stood in bed."

Tales told by a tourist—this day's entry carried no reference to anything important, except for the fact that she allowed someone named Duke to take publicity photos of her Olympic certificates. Dee was referenced in the collective "we," and it was apparent that if Eddie could manage it, he would monopolize as much of Helen's time as he could. She had become unreceptive to his ideas. People he was to introduce her to didn't materialize. Charming and lively though he was, Helen grew tired of Eddie; hence her wisecrack about staying in bed.

SEPTEMBER 3: DAY FIFTY-ONE, NEW YORK CITY

Arose quite early in order to go to dock to meet the Manhattan with the returning athletes. Met the athletes and "Celebs." Went on boat & ship. The parade of the athletes started at 12 o'clock from docks. There were many cops on motorcycles & much noise. Jesse Owens led in first car & I was in the second with Com. Fowley. Great thrill as we passed down Broadway, Park Ave., Harlem, etc.

They had endured unusually wet weather in Europe; back in the United States, they suffered oppressive dust-bowl heat. Everyone, not only farmers, was aggrieved by the widespread, record-breaking drought—the worst ever known. The bright New York noonday sun moved temperatures into the high nineties. Even so, well-wishers crammed together as a blizzard of confetti endlessly drifted down upon them. Handheld American flags waved riotously; others streamed from both sides of Park Avenue in large metal holders bolted to storefronts. Helen rode in an open limousine driven by Commissioner Fowley, following the car carrying Owens and his track mates. Helen, Alice Arden, Harriet Bland, and Betty Robinson perched on the ridge of the backseat; low in the front seat were Anne O'Brien, Nurse Riche, Dee Boeckmann, and Gertrude Wilhelmsen. All wore Olympic dress uniforms: dark blue jackets, white hats, white skirts, and white shoes.

Afterward, she wrote: *Went to Randall's Island for luncheon. Met Mayor LaGuardia. Marched to Stadium & presented to crowd & radio & given medals. Rode home with Mayor. Dinner at French Casino. Drinks at Poo's. Train for C. at 12:45.*

One might speculate that Poo, given *this* reference, owned a bar or a restaurant. Though not noted, Dee and her relayers stepped onto the podium for commendations from the mayor of New York. LaGuardia gave Helen the key to the city and a commemorative medal. Helen posed with Glen Hardin and Jesse Owens and others for the award picture. In one-inch heels, she stood a full head taller than the mayor and several inches taller than Owens and Hardin. The mayor's reception for the athletes followed; then she hopped a late-night train to Toronto, where she was to give an exhibition in the 100- and 220-yard races and a 4 x 100-meter relay. Annette Rogers probably arrived in New York with the others returning on the SS *Manhattan*, but for whatever reason, she did not ride in the limo with her teammates.

SEPTEMBER 4: DAY FIFTY-TWO, TORONTO, CANADA

Got up for grand breakfast. Discovered I had left some money at New Yorker Hotel. Felt awful. . . . [Arrived] *in Toronto about 11 o'clock. Interviews at station by Phyllis Griffith & later in King Edward Hotel. . . . Mr. Frye took us out to Exhibition. . . . saw two automobiles crash. . . . were presented to the audience. Had dinner on grounds & ate heartily after the tea we had had—Dee, Nettie & I. Saw the play "Mystic Mois" at Stadium. . . . were interviewed by Alex Gibbs & she brought us home. Received several letters.*

Someone tossed $5,000 in a brown paper bag into Owens' hands while he paraded down Park Avenue. Helen wasn't so lucky. For safekeeping, she had stuffed what remained of her funds (about $400 in cash) in an envelope and put it on top of the bathroom mirror cabinet in her room. Rather than leave money in the hotel safe as Dee had advised, Helen thought it would be safer to keep it with her. That day, she was log-headed from drinking too much and being out too late the night before. She hastily bathed, dressed, brushed her hair, applied makeup, grabbed her purse and luggage, and flew out of the room, and she forgot to take the envelope with her. When she remembered it, with a sudden sickness in her stomach, she told Dee what she had done. Dee told her to phone the hotel desk clerk to report the loss, which she did, and later that night from Canada, she called the hotel again. Maids had cleaned her room, the manager said; no envelope had been turned in, but if it were found, he personally would hold it for her until she returned in four days.

September 5: Day Fifty-three, Toronto, Canada

Got up about noon. Dee, Nettie & I went shopping & I bought sweater. . . . Charlie took us out to Fair for Track Meet. About 25,000 there & a fine day. I won 100 yds in 10.3—new record. Wind. Our relay team won the relay easily—without effort. I won 220 yd special with 12 yd handicap in 23.3. Four Vi-tones. Spoke over radio at field & was introduced to the audience several times. I refused to run Metcalfe & Wycoff. Betty & I appeared on radio program with Phyllis at 7 PM. Group of us went to fair & took in several thrilling rides. Came back—bar—Mr. Foster—Bland's room—.

Dee loaned Helen money for the sweater and miscellaneous needs. An AAU official, Charles J. Gevecker, timed her race at the Canadian Carnival and was involved in the event's broadcast. Helen ran the 100-yard race—her speed was wind assisted—clocking in at three-tenths of a second under the established American mark. Running anchor in the relay race, Helen teamed up as before with Nettie, Betty, and Harriet. They easily beat Canada's team, as Helen recorded it. She won the 100-yard race, clocking a speedy 10.3 and emerging as a starring individual winner. Consequently, her three teammates slipped into the background as Helen received most of the publicity and attention. None of the three other women runners received challenges to race against male athletes. Might Helen Stephens eventually run as fast as a man? That was the question of the day. Eddie had almost set up a match for her against Frank Wycoff and Ralph Metcalfe, in a money-making deal enlisting James Hoey of the Caledonia Club, touting a man-versus-woman exhibition race. Helen flatly refused—fearing, perhaps, the loss of her amateur status.

In the hub of Toronto's bar scene, Helen quaffed nightcaps and then, per invitation, knocked at Harriet's door and soon was unhappily ensnarled in a shouting match over sharing the glory that came with anchoring and also winning an individual medal. Tactlessly, Harriet carried on, demanding that Helen ask Dee to let her anchor the next exhibition race. When it dawned on her that she wouldn't get what she wanted, the also-ran-Bland threw a pot-shot—saying that it wouldn't hurt Miss Big-head to let her have the last leg now. Circumspectly firm, Helen said she wouldn't, even if she wanted to, spur Dee into doing anything.

SEPTEMBER 6: DAY FIFTY-FOUR, LAKE ONTARIO, U.S.A.;
LAKE ONTARIO, TORONTO

Arose about noon for dinner. Dee & I were taken to harbor by Mr. Duthie & put on Lake Steamer "Northumberland" bound for Niagara Falls. We enjoyed the captain's horn play on bridge on way over. Another ocean—so it seemed. Took train or streetcar to Falls. Arrived about 6 PM. Looked at Falls & went over into U.S. & then back. Ate on Canadian side. 5th time I have crossed into Canada. Took car for boat at 8:11 PM. Fun. Enjoyed a cool lake ride to Toronto. Arrived about 12 o'clock after eating enough for tomorrow. Grabbed cab for home very quickly.

SEPTEMBER 7: DAY FIFTY-FIVE, TORONTO, CANADA

After a refreshing sleep I awoke to find it had rained somewhat. . . . [ate] breakfast & lunch in one. . . . relay squad & Dee took cab to grounds of the Fair. Won the 100 yds. in 10.9 & the 220 yds. In a shuttle relay Betty & Annette fumbled the pass & we lost. Got medal & sweater set & prize will follow. Met Mayor & President. Was presented upon stage. . . . dinner with weight lifters. Ray Pitcher took us to see French chef & champagne. Never saw gang before leaving. Bland, Dee & I docked chair in for fun. Some fun! Hot pin! Good-bye Toronto! Stay over in Buffalo. Not much sleep.

Her pace did not seem to be lagging much due to excess food and drink, little concern for diet, little sleep, and no workouts. On the contrary, her 100-yard sprint time improved (to 10.3) a day or so earlier and was not wind aided. Since one meter equals about one yard three inches, Helen's 11.5-meter time four short weeks earlier was minutely faster than what she had clocked this day. Having won, she recorded the numbers. But she did not note the 220-yard time, because she wasn't as proud of it. The relayers fell from grace, losing the victory to the Canadians with an unforgiving and familiar error. In the third leg, the baton slipped from Annette Rogers' hand; now the girls knew how the German team felt when Doerffeldt fumbled the stick. Luckily, as an individual event runner, Helen had the face-saving grace of winning another individual medal and was honored with more prizes.

By now, she was comfortable with the concept of brunch. The three women invented a shuffleboard game with deck chairs, competing for the greatest distance; while knocking each other's chairs off the target mark, one flew into the air and over the railing.

SEPTEMBER 8: DAY FIFTY-SIX, NEW YORK CITY

Arrived in New York about 11 AM. Bland got off at Albany for Boston. Ate in station & called Eddie. Dee & I went to Eddie's office. No money!! Met the office gang & Eddie took us to Hotel Lexington. Cleaned up & we had lunch at the Silver Grill. Dee went to Long Island to get doc [illegible]. Eddie & I went to M.

Johnsons (P) & she later picked me up. Saw Columbia pictures. Saw Duke at Trans-Lux. Came back to Columbia. Stopped at Eddie's brother-in-law. Saw Johnson again & "Oh, Sweet Adeline." Coffee in room. No Dee! Eddie & I went to "Leon's & Eddie's" night club. Eddie introduced us & worked me into his program. Got in & cleaned up clothes. And a good bed.

Eddie, Eddie, Eddie. He had clamped onto her and wouldn't let go. Eddie's brother-in-law came into the picture by working Helen the star Olympian into a nightclub show. Harriet was in Boston and out of Helen's hair, and now, without a chaperone for the present, Helen had to rely on Eddie. The hotel manager said no one had found her envelope of money. Promised advances from various deals Eddie had cooked up hadn't come through. But he paid for lunch and dinner. Eddie was with her when Mrs. George P. Johnson, of Fulton, visited. Mrs. Johnson had been to Berlin and had sent a congratulatory postcard to Helen after she had won the 100 meters. Helen told her about the newsreel and that Columbia Pictures was considering her as a possible subject for a motion picture feature.

Dee set out to find a physician attending a meeting in Long Island, a Dr. Joel W. Hardesty, who practiced medicine in Hannibal, Missouri, not more than an hour's drive from St. Louis. Dee was checking out an option for Helen, who was saying that she wanted to look into the possibility of a sex change operation. In God's name, why? Dee demanded. Helen confided that from the earliest days on, she had felt out of joint as a girl. Now she was famous and in the public eye, with some people thinking and some people saying she wasn't fully a woman. And it wasn't only Stella or Stella's coach. Well, maybe it was true. Few boys had ever shown interest in her as a girlfriend. She had never been interested in boys or men, except for Coach Moore. In high school, some girls had had major crushes on her, and it felt right. In Berlin, with Ruth hugging and kissing her, it felt good. Girls were throwing themselves at her now, partly because of her celebrity and partly for other reasons. A certain look in their eyes would catch her eye, subtle flirtations and a romantic impetuousness that seemed imperceptible to "normal" people.

But, Dee asked, why take such a drastic step now, at the very beginning of a career? Because, Helen told her, a certain girl she was in love with at William Woods had backed out. The publicity had been too much for her. If she changed into a man, maybe that would make their love okay.

Dee didn't return until late. Helen spent another evening with Eddie, forgetting her woes in a nightclub.

SEPTEMBER 9: DAY FIFTY-SEVEN, NEW YORK CITY

We like our balcony & suite of rooms. Eddie & I had breakfast in coffee shop & went to see Cohen about picture. Got my bracelet. Came back to Lexington Hotel

& Dee & I had our picture taken for the "Coronet." Lunch in the Silver Grill. . . .
Eddie & I went to Chrysler building & back to Columbia studios. Drew up deal
& saw some pictures. . . . back to hotel finally. Saw girl I had met at WWC in
morning. Dinner in Grill. And Grandpa & Marion!!? The blond across the way.
FDR, Jr. gone. Went to Fr. night club. Met [blank line] *. . . went by several the-*
atres & then home.

Columbia Pictures wanted her exclusive appearance in

> a one reel motion picture sports reel . . . "The News World of Sports."
> Such appearance . . . shall consist of your acting, posing, talking and
> rendering sound effects, particularly your performance in various sports
> and athletic contests which we may desire for this production. We . . .
> [agree] to pay for your transportation and lower berth from Fulton . . .
> to New York City . . . and your reasonable actual living expenses during
> your stay in New York City . . . while your appearance is required. . . . We
> are to pay you nothing further than such transportation and living ex-
> penses for our right so to photograph and record and give publicity to
> your . . . appearance. . . . You agree not to act or appear for your own
> benefit or for any others in or in connection with any other motion pic-
> ture . . . [for] twelve months from . . . first general release of . . . photoplay.
> . . . We shall always own all rights of every kind and character now or
> hereafter . . . including copyright and its renewal.[3]

Eighteen-year-old Helen was by law a minor whose signature on a contract
would not be binding. Authorization signatures of her parents were required. She
could accept small gifts, like the commemorative bracelet given her, but she
couldn't accept any larger offer without parental consent. Eddie told her to sign
it anyway, to show good faith. If she signed, she wanted to know, would she lose
her amateur status? Compared with today's offers made to rising star athletes,
this contract shows an exacting degree of exploitation typical of the era. But it
impressed Helen because it offered glimmers of fame. Her diary notes were becoming more blatantly encoded; she left blank one full line and referred to a bur-
lesque show as *Fr.* (meaning a French nightclub). Dee's association with Eleanor
Roosevelt, the honorary chair of fund-raising for the Olympic team, brought a
young member of the Roosevelt family temporarily into their entourage.

SEPTEMBER 10: DAY FIFTY-EIGHT, NEW YORK, TRENTON, PHILADELPHIA,
BALTIMORE, AND WASHINGTON, D.C.

Dee & I were accompanied out of NY by Eddie quite early. Saw Anna Roosevelt,
Boe Higer before leaving in regard to meeting President. Enjoyed the drive, cities,
scenery on way to Washington. German at station. Had lunch at station. Got into
Wash. & drove to Capitol & circled the circles trying to find Shoreham Hotel. Swell

hotel—pool, etc. . . . Interviewed by several reporters. Wrote several letters . . . more than glad to get some rest after our mad rush.

The previous day, she had been in the company of Franklin Roosevelt Jr. Today, she met the Roosevelt's eldest child and only daughter, Anna—recently divorced from Curt Dall and newly married to John R. Boettiger, who was affiliated with the *Chicago Tribune*. Expecting a brief introduction to the First Lady, Helen had bought a newspaper at Shoreham Hotel, especially to read Mrs. Roosevelt's newly syndicated column, "My Day." Dee tried to set up a meeting with the First Lady through her Washington, D.C., Olympic contacts. But it was not to be.

SEPTEMBER 11: DAY FIFTY-NINE, WASHINGTON, D.C.

Arose about 9. Met by Roy & "Yank" Roberts. . . . photos taken in hotel lobby. Sneaked into breakfast & "Yank" came in & posed for picture. Went for inspection tour. Went into Capitol—dome, etc., hall of fame, sound room. Went to House of Rep., Senate, Library of Congress—Cons't in original form, Supreme Court, & Department of Justice. Toured Department & was a great treat. Met J. Edgar Hoover who is head G Man, & pictures. Went to dinner at Occidental Hotel. Broadcasted over WMAL. Came to hotel & got calls, wires & headaches as regards receptions. Didrikson & Helen Dettweiler took us for swim.

Tourist attractions were swell and duly noted, but it was the Babe's company that Helen remembered.[4] The Great Babe Didrikson, Helen's childhood idol. Just months after winning two Olympic events, the AAU had pulled Babe's amateur status because her name was used in an automobile advertisement. Babe quit a pitching stint for the House of David Baseball Team, quit basketball barnstorming, and was concentrating all her skill on the golf green. By 1936, she had become the best woman long driver in the country, and golf was her game.

At age twenty-two, Babe stood five feet seven inches and weighed about 135 pounds. She had taken up the sport of the elite three years earlier under a young instructor named Stanley Kertes, at Pico, California. She had yet to meet the man she would marry, George Zaharias, the golf addict known as the Crying Greek from Cripple Creek. Using "us" with no explanation, Helen wrote that Babe and her friend "took us for a swim." She said she was fooling around at the piano in an empty ballroom at the Shoreham when Didrikson and her golfing buddy, Helen Dettweiler, sauntered in. Helen was both startled and pleased. By Helen's account, the Texas tomboy (Didrikson) grabbed her hand, shook it enthusiastically, and asked for an explanation of what had happened in Helen's discus event. Helen began to explain, but Babe busted in, asking why she hadn't gone for the javelin, anyhow? Helen tried to answer, but Didrikson jabbered right past her. Why not the hurdles? Shiley would help her, she assured

Helen. (Mrs. Jean Shiley Reps was Dee Boeckmann's Olympic colleague and friend.) Helen said she thought she might do all right with the javelin but wasn't interested in hurdle jumping. She said she hoped to try her luck with the javelin next time. Babe offered to show her a thing or two about pitching it and suggested they go to the hotel pool, where she could show Helen some throwing techniques, using life preservers.

It was an Olympic-size pool, and they swam a few laps and took turns diving off the board. Babe dragged four kapok life preservers to one end of the pool and yelled to Helen to get out and join her. Helen obeyed and felt Babe's eyes watching her. Dettweiler was to referee. Babe took the first toss, instructing Helen as she went along, stressing footing and then form. She let fly a hefty swing, and Helen watched it skip across the pool. Babe picked up a second preserver, wound up, and threw again. "Get it?" she said. Helen said she thought so, and without a practice swing or fanfare, tossed one. It hit close to where Babe's ring had landed, about a foot or so poolside.

Didrikson remarked something like, "Not bad. Not bad at all. 'Course, I wasn't tryin' when I showed you. Okay now, try again. Go ahead. Try again, then I'll try."

Helen picked up another life preserver and reared back, sensing Babe watching her. She held the ring far back, swung it forward a couple of times, then let go. The ring flew the length of the pool, hit the farthest wall, bounced, and plopped down. "Your turn," Helen said.

"You don't need no help from me, kid," Didrikson said. "Come on, Dett, let's go."

SEPTEMBER 12: DAY SIXTY, WASHINGTON, D.C.

Arose in spite of myself. . . . Dee & I went to beauty parlor across street to get fixed up. Boys came by at one o'clock & took us to Central Park for meet. Met Fultonians & Missourians. Burt's telegram. Won 220 or 200 meters in 25 [seconds] *against 40 or 50 yd handicap. Hoover presented me with leather bag. Mrs. Pi—* [spelling illegible] *took us down to the George Washington U. football training camp after we straightened up the NY & home wires. Mr. Pi— had fine dinner for us. Autograph for football players. Missed "Yank" as we came back too late.*

J. Edgar Hoover was honorary referee of the third interdepartmental track meet in which Helen ran her races that day; he gifted Helen with a monogrammed valise, *HHS* embossed in gold. Helen notes other essentials. Coach Moore sent her a telegram; and she won an unusual distance race of "220" (probably 220 yards). The practice of using both Anglo-American measurement (yards) and the metric system (meters), especially in the popular sprint distances, caused confusion, especially when an error in reportage mixed up these distances in print. Helen's own record of these races show the variations.

Moore's telegram, like a forerunner, conveyed the excitement that awaited her at home. Unnamed Missourians and Fultonians visiting Washington, D.C., were merely noted and remain unidentified.

September 13: Day Sixty-one, Washington, D.C., Mt. Vernon

Dee got some more money from "Yank." . . . drove about city, visited Lincoln's Memorial & passed Washington Monument. Went down to Mt. Vernon—a lovely ride. Admitted, as special favor, to grounds & saw home, building, & tomb . . . a very lovely & inspiring place. . . . commands respect. . . . went back to Washington & started West. . . . dinner in Frederick, Md. . . . passed through . . . beautiful country & gorgeous mountains. Ate supper in Clayside, West Va. Arrived in Wheeling, W. Va. about 9 o'clock. Put up at McTure Hotel—what a place. Did some laundry & dropped off.

Dee drove Helen and Harriet to St. Louis, via Washington, D.C., through Mount Vernon. The trunk and backseat were crammed with suitcases, new hats and clothes, gifts and souvenirs, awards and medals, and newspapers; everything the three women had taken or bought on their trip. Helen was resupplied with funds from "Yank" Roberts, possibly a promoter who hoped to lasso and tie the great Helen Stephens into his stable of stars, or maybe he was affiliated with, and therefore a source of funds from, the Olympic or AAU committees. Helen never could recall who Yank was in the scheme of things.

September 14: Day Sixty-two, Wheeling, West Virginia

I arose about 11 o'clock. . . . refreshments across the street & . . . back to hotel for interview. Took watch to the jeweler & our hats to cleaner. Enjoyed lunch at Walgreens. Walked about town & gave autographs in dime store. Went to doctor's & then went on ride with him to see patients, etc. Dee got her car greased. Dr. Bickel took us to the Country Club for dinner along with another couple. Then we all went to the Moss home. Came to hotel. Talk with Dr. Bickel. Harriet came in from Boston but lost our bag.

Helen took the wristwatch she had "bathed" to the jeweler and stopped for lunch at a new, large department store, Walgreens, where people crowded around her seeking her autograph. Dee was getting her car checked for the trip home to St. Louis; the engine had an odd noise and was losing oil. Harriet, who joined them at this juncture, had left a shared luggage in the taxicab—on the floor in the backseat. This particular piece of luggage contained Helen's Olympic shoes and some memorabilia. The side trip to the doctor was Dee's doing, preparation for the lawsuit that Dee, Gertrude Webb, and AAU officials thought might be necessary to stop the gender assaults. In retrospect, Helen said she could not recall much about Dr. Bickel's speciality or his patients. Dee apparently did not accompany Helen to the doctor's office but joined the girls for dinner and at the chamber of commerce, and they talked about it later at the hotel.

SEPTEMBER 15: DAY SIXTY-THREE, WHEELING, COLUMBUS,
INDIANAPOLIS, TERRE HAUTE, AND ST. LOUIS

Harriet, Dee & I settled up & checked out of the hotel. And was our car packed! We left about 9:30. . . . a beautiful day & we enjoyed the trip except we were a little sleepy. We had some car trouble. We ate along the road at our stop, etc. We grew very, very sleepy before we got to St. L. but got there about 2:30. Mr. Lyle, Mr. Carr, & Mr. Sam Wilson from Fulton were there to meet me. Mr. Bullock of St. L. Chamber of Commerce put us up at Jefferson. Letter from Someone. Finally got to rest after hard day.

Helen and Harriet squeezed into the car and braced themselves for a full day's drive. Though the mechanic had given their rental car a once-over, three hours out of Wheeling, West Virginia, engine trouble delayed them. It was about two in the morning when they arrived at the downtown St. Louis Jefferson Hotel. A small welcoming party was still waiting for them in the bar—family, friends, and city officials P. W. Bullock, vice president of the St. Louis Chamber of Commerce, and Sam Wilson, of the Fulton Chamber of Commerce, and others. The desk clerk handed the weary travelers a pile of mail. A Western Union night letter from James Hoey of the Caledonia Club briefly informed Helen that Jesse Owens had been denied reinstatement of his amateur status, and their meet was canceled.[5] However, a more important piece of mail for Helen was the letter from "Someone." She tore it open quickly: S wanted to see her; wanted to know what time she would arrive in Fulton; and where they might see each other privately.

SEPTEMBER 16: DAY SIXTY-FOUR, ST. LOUIS AND FULTON, MISSOURI

One month ago today the Olympics ended. Word of cancellation of NY engagements. Reporters & friends in St. Louis. Greetings by St. Louis people in hotel. Ride in decorated cars to City Hall & welcome there. . . . parade through streets of St. Louis. Welcome & presentation of scrolls of honor at luncheon. Radio talk. Cancellation of flight & departure for Fulton with Mr. Lyle. Police escort out of city & police out of Mexico [Missouri] into Fulton. Welcome home. Parade up Court St. to WWC. Speeches of welcome & every crazy response. Presentation of watch. Someone absent. Went to Gramma's for night. Call. Home at last!!!

Helen had been away from home approximately ten weeks, and she wanted to see friends and family again. As the single most celebrated female athlete that Missouri had ever known, she had all the hoopla focused upon her, surpassing the attention given to her coach and teammate, both native-born St. Louisans who had lesser or past accomplishments. While Dee Boeckmann and Harriet

Bland waited in the wings, Helen was interviewed in the hotel lobby by KMOS radio commentator Harry Flannery. Afterward, the three traveled by motorcade to city hall for the official welcome. Threatening clouds darkened the sky as the parade slipped through downtown St. Louis, and rain began to fall.

At the banquet at the Jefferson Hotel, city and state figures and the acting mayor of St. Louis, William Mason, presented the athletes with commemorative scrolls and awards. Helen was first at the podium, according to reporter Bob Burnes. She acknowledged the help of both her coaches, and the support various people had given her. She thanked them, the press corps, and the St. Louisans who had adopted her as their own. She told the luncheon audience that she was proud of them for their effort in supporting the women's team. She spoke of her greatest thrill, "beating Stella Walsh. It was a grand race and Miss Walsh is a great runner. We had a wonderful time, and I think Dee Boeckmann deserves a lot of credit [for holding] our team together when it looked as if we wouldn't have a representative squad, and when she did get it going she trained us in splendid style."[6]

Harriet Bland giggled nervously and said she had loved every minute of the experience, especially when training rules were relaxed. She confessed to gaining fifteen pounds and said the whole trip was one grand thrill. Without naming anyone, she thanked everyone who had helped her. Dee Boeckmann appeared somber and dignified. Yes, it had been a grand trip, she told the audience, and she was proud of all the girls. But, she said, Americans were fighting a losing battle; other teams received substantial aid from their governments and were showing exceptional progress. She reportedly said that "unless we get the same kind of assistance I'm afraid we are not going to do so well in 1940." Her comments were received by some as too serious and dampening for the occasion. She came off as being haughty and too intense and was criticized in print for it. Congressman Thomas C. Hennings concluded the program. "It's easy to be a winner," he said, but "real heroes and heroines are those who carry their honors modestly, as you girls have. It's a spirit that Missourians are proud of—it's a spirit that was first exemplified by one of our adopted sons—Charles A. Lindbergh." For the girls' sake, he could have better referenced a Missouri girl, Amelia Earhart of Kansas City.

Helen was set to fly from the St. Louis airport and land in a field in Fulton that afternoon, and she looked forward to another airplane ride. She hoped to spot her parent's farm from the air, but bad weather caused the flight to be canceled. Helen and Dee hurried from the luncheon to the celebrations in Fulton, set for about three o'clock in the afternoon. St. Louis police escorted the entourage to St. Charles. A Missouri highway patrol motorcade picked up the group from there, racing at high speeds to be on time. One report noted the speed queen passed Warrenton on Highway 40 traveling one hundred miles an hour.[7]

It stormed in Fulton most of the day, but by the time Helen arrived, at 3:15, the rain had stopped. Governor and Mrs. Guy B. Park greeted them downtown and caravaned behind the patriotically decorated car, provided by J. B. Fenley, carrying Helen and Coaches Burt Moore and Dee Boeckmann. Other cars provided by the chamber of commerce transported state and city officials. Helen sat between her two coaches as their driver, "Dude" Fenley, headed for William Woods College. Court Street was festooned with flags that were whipped by a strong wind; at the front of the parade, a two-band delegation of senior and junior high school students played music all the way. The Mexico (Missouri) Junior Chamber of Commerce Band brought up the end of the parade, providing music for a long line of Girl Scouts waving oak leaves of victory, followed by some of Helen's high school and college teachers and various others.

Policemen from Jefferson City, Mexico, and Columbia joined Fulton's own force to handle the crowd. The mass of Fultonians lining Court Street stirred Helen's soul as they shouted and screamed her name. Most of her old high school pep squad buddies called out, "Hey, Popeye! Popeye!" Betty, Martha, Ralph, Bonnie, Bob, Sara, Julia, Leona, Ophelia, Elizabeth, Gladys, Louise, Arthelia—all were there, as were her many Woodsie friends, all screaming and cheering her on. "Steve. Over here, Steve!"

Helen looked around, hoping to catch a glimpse of her particular Someone.

An outdoor platform had been built for the occasion, but they were prepared to relocate to the college auditorium if bad weather prevailed. The stage was festively draped in bunting. Boyd's Fulton Band poised in a semicircle on the lawn, waiting for a cue. The afternoon sky brightened, and by 3:30, everyone was in place. Proudly, Mr. and Mrs. Stephens and Helen's little brother sat in folding chairs, up front, near the platform. Dr. Franc L. McCluer, the president of Westminster College, began by presenting the speakers. Fulton's Mayor Hensley was first; he welcomed Helen home and presented a congratulatory resolution, signed by city council officials and bearing the city's seal. He then presented her with a gold wristwatch, a gift from the citizens of Fulton.

On the long list of speakers were ninth district congressman Clarence Cannon and the Democratic nominee for governor, Mayor Lloyd Stark of Louisiana, Missouri; Coaches Moore and Boeckmann, P. W. Bullock, J. W. McIntire (Fulton's oldest citizen), and William Woods president Harmon. Harmon gave an apology from Governor Park, who quickly had to leave just after Helen arrived. Harmon read congratulatory telegrams received at the school in Helen's behalf, among them one from Senator Harry Truman, one from Senator Bennett Champ Clark, and one from Jesse W. Barrett, the Republican candidate for governor. Finally, Harmon added his own accolades, proclaiming to the three thousand people gathered there (an impressively high percentage of the county population) that Helen had been a fine example of her generation, had met friends graciously, and had accepted success modestly. He called Mr. and Mrs. Stephens to the stage to give a few words; briefly, modestly, Frank Stephens expressed their thanks to everyone for all they had done for their daughter. When her parents relinquished the platform, tears were trickling from Helen's eyes.

It was now her turn to speak. Minus the aplomb displayed in St. Louis, Helen felt a little shaky, facing so many familiar faces in the crowd. She couldn't say much, but spoke simply: "My arrival in Berlin brought me no greater thrill than my arrival here today. I feel lost for words to express my appreciation to you, but I want to thank you for your support and moral encouragement." Then she stepped back, fighting back more tears. There was nothing more to say. Everyone on the stage stood up and clapped, and the rest followed. The band picked up its coda. The program was over, and as the applause died out, Helen stepped down. People gathered around her, but the one face Helen felt sure would be there among the crowd was missing. Her special someone, whom she thought would be waiting just for her, hadn't come. Briefly, it crossed her mind that their love could not withstand the test. In the letter Helen had composed in the purser's office on August 24 (only days after the slanderous accusations got into the press), she had tried to prepare S for possible legal action and the publicity it would generate. Helen knew that things could go badly if their romance were uncovered in the process. She had written that she was going to see a specialist to get some medical guidance, that Dee was helping, and that AOC officials wanted Dee to help. She had told her lover everything. Dee had contacted the doctor in Hannibal, initially phoning him on September 8, amid New York's celebration.[8]

In her first letter, S had asked, "Why haven't you written. Mother says you've forgotten us now that you've become a celebrity. Just a word or three from you, dear heart, is all I need. I know your days must be filled with a whirlwind of excitement, but have you forgotten about me? Oh Steve, I miss you so." She wrote "I love you" over and over again. In her last post, S warned Helen that her letters were being intercepted because her parents opposed their relationship, "wrong as it is." Mrs. "Someone" was hammering away at her daughter, disclaiming all probability of her finding happiness or friendship with someone like Helen who, she said, had dubious character. All the words were there: "Father won't have it! No daughter of mine will be involved in scandal with this unnatural athlete." S was being sent away, and wherever that was, her mother didn't want Helen to find out.

A landslide of international fame had changed their relationship. It took S away from Helen and pushed Helen away from her in more than just geographical ways. Though she was home and on campus, Helen seemed to others to live in the lofty realm of Mount Olympus. Even so, a general delivery post to "William Woods Track Star Helen Stephens" brought cancellation to her stardom. The Columbia Pictures deal offered on September 9 was withdrawn. Had that, too, caved in because of the possibility of scandal? Reading that letter brought a chilling moment, but she didn't let it last long. Her family was gathering for its own celebration of Helen's homecoming at Grandmother Herring's house. Once there, Helen telephoned S. Rural phones at that time were party lines, so one can imagine that the transfer operator and others, hearing the Herrings' call-out bell, might have listened in while Helen tried to patch up things with her girlfriend.

The next day, the papers reported that Harriet Bland's competitive running days were over. There was practically no advantage in running professionally, she said. For three years, she had turned down jobs such as a girls' athletic instructress at a playground and a salesgirl in a sporting goods store. She was going to work and "forget all about being an amateur and get the kind of job I am best suited for—something that deals with athletics. I don't like to bar myself from amateur ranks and the thrill of running in races, but I've passed up so many good jobs to protect my amateur standing that I think I owe it to myself to start earning some money now."[9]

"Miss Stephens," the article noted, would run in competition races during the winter, but for now, she was with friends in Fulton, resting a few days before classes resumed. Few people knew that she was worrying over what to do or how sad she was.

9

Steve Goes Pro

The latest star to turn a pro is Helen Stephens of Fulton, Mo. She says "one cannot live on medals."
—L. C. Davis, "Sports Salad," *St. Louis Post-Dispatch,* 1937

*T*he truth about going professional was that Helen was scouted for commercial gain while she was still a wet-behind-the-ears high school kid. Only days after she had eclipsed the world sprint star, Stella Walsh, in 1935, C. M. Olson had pushed his way into Helen's face with a contract in his hand. Coming from the little berg of Cassville, Missouri, Olson tried to recruit her away from high school. "Just call me Ole," he told Helen, coming on like a carnival barker. "I own the all-girl All-American Red Heads Basketball Team. We tour throughout the U.S. of A. and Canada!"

Ole also owned and operated, largely with his wife's help, a chain of seven beauty salons. Mrs. Olson applied an "authentic" Egyptian henna tint (commonly a mud pack) on each girl's head to create a full team of redheaded basketball players. It was Olson's version of the multiples gimmick, as eye-catching as "Ham" Olive's full-whiskered House of Davidites that Helen had seen swinging the bat in Fulton's newly lit ball park. Olson badly wanted to sign on the star sprinter and high-scoring captain of her church basketball team. Selling his latest venture to America's new speed queen, he entreated her to envision the banner headline: HELEN STEPHENS—STAR RED HEAD!

The blonde Amazon, then under Coach Moore's wing, had dodged Olson's bullet. With their sights set on the Olympics, they turned Olson down flat. After Berlin, Olson reemerged in Helen's life and again played his hand, this time by telegram on October 17, 1936:

> Helen Stevens [*sic*] WIRE ME immediately if you are interested
> in playing basketball this season with Olson's Red Heads
> representing chain of Olson Beauty Salons. Will travel thru
> US and Canada . . . extensively.
>
> —C M Olson, Terrible Swedes World Champions[1]

Olson claimed that his Red Heads, just beginning a third season, were world champs!

The fall 1936–spring 1937 school year was a cruel year for Helen, beginning with an abrupt twist of fate. Her sweetheart's parents refused to let their daughter return to finish her studies at the Woods, and in less than four months, Helen's Olympic honeymoon was over. However, by December 1936, Helen had a replacement love, one who was much more intellectually matched to the quick-witted Helen and more steadfast. And she was resourceful; she wrote to her favorite aunt, a nurse, and to her grandfather, a physician, about Helen's problem. This girlfriend's family accepted and supported Helen.

Like many afflicted by the Great Depression, Helen was caught in an economic quandary. She felt a strong sense of responsibility; she wanted to venture forth to make something of herself and help her parents. Her father had moved the family again, a third time in four years, to a community known as Little Dixie, seven miles southwest of Fulton, and he was struggling heroically to earn a living. With Helen in college and often away, Frank had only one farmhand, his fourteen-year-old son, Bob, helping him tame the savage land and the seasons of Callaway County's calamities—a record drought and fifty-one days with temperatures of 100° or more.

The Associated Press had polled hundreds of sportswriters across the nation before naming Helen Stephens America's most outstanding woman athlete of 1936, calling her a champion of champions. Tallying 97 points, she had soared from dull obscurity to national acclaim in less than two years—beating out tennis champ Alice Marble (78 points), golfer Pamela Barton (56 points), and tennis player Helen Jacobs (30 points), as well as golf star Patty Berg, swim champ Eleanor Holm Jarrett, diver Marjorie Gestring, skating starlet Sonja Henie, and tennis tycoon Helen Wills Moody. In a special reprint from the *St. Louis Globe Democrat*, the local paper presented a personal look at Helen, as told by her high school teacher Miss Georgia Richardson. She said that Helen was not "a man-hater. . . . As to love affairs, Miss Stephens admits she has never had any serious ones."[2] Richardson had stayed at the Stephens farm a few days the previous summer and assessed that the Olympic aspirant was a high-minded girl who loved art, music, and fine books. Helen, she said, was one of her most interesting and lovable girls.

But the truth was that Helen was not happy.

Within minutes of stepping off the *President Roosevelt* (a lesser ship than the *Manhattan*, which could be viewed as an omen of the ambush that lay ahead), contracts were thrust into her hands. Dee Boeckmann opined, "None of them seemed good and I warned her not to sign."[3] Within weeks, the contracts fell through without explanation. Promoters initially had vied to align themselves with the newest human racehorse, wanting to ride her as far as they could to make fast money. Agent Eddie Mayo had been the most persistent. Helen too quickly relied on Eddie, and a curious attraction had developed between them. Above all others, Mayo is mentioned in her diary, though nothing substantial ever resulted from her association with him. He, too, brought disappointment.

The Ozark Amateur Athletic Union claimed authority early on, bestowing travel permits and authorizations for displays of her medals, trophies, and certificates. National newspaper and magazine writers hotly pursued her. Some sought interviews through Helen's parents, some contacted her through Dee Boeckmann, and others reached her through Coach Moore. Not counting personal correspondence, and beginning in the fall of 1936, Helen responded to over ninety letters and telegrams from interested parties and fans. Some people phoned the college administration offices; some got themselves connected through the switchboard to Reid Hall via the dormitory hostess, Mrs. Fannie Longmire. Dorm telephones were switchboard-directed party lines, so many folks got word of who was trying to reach her and what was being offered even before Helen knew.

In October 1936, when Helen's Olympic oak tree arrived in Fulton with a clean bill of health from the Agriculture Department's Bureau of Entomology and Plant Quarantine, the president of the college saw an opportunity for school promotion and publicity. Dr. Harmon invited Helen to plant her tree on campus, and she agreed. During the planting ceremony, he focused on the fact that, although she was still receiving scholarship offers elsewhere, this young lady valued the education that William Woods provided modern young women and would be completing her second and final year at her hometown institution. In a drizzling rain, Harmon expounded upon Helen's generosity and exemplary character. He shook her hand while cameras flashed. He also had the college newsletter carry a full page on the athletic prowess of his student, decked in the green-and-white college colors, wearing a lettered sweat suit. The cutline claimed this star pupil was expected to earn greater glory in Japan at the 1940 Olympics. She certainly *looked* happy in that picture, standing proudly erect with both arms folded across her chest.

A less flattering photo soon began to circulate among the community, and by then, she was fighting to finish the last half of a seriously agitating senior year. By late February 1937, Helen was entangled in scandal and litigation, and her life was roaring up and down in roller coaster fashion. The scholastic rug

William Woods had swiftly thrust under her feet *before Berlin* just as quickly was pulled out from under her. She was working odd jobs on and off campus in order to pay for the remaining year of college. Her spirit was dampened by the turn of events and twists of fate, but she felt optimistic about her future. There would be no more thoughts about changing her Popeye self; she had no money for it, and anyhow, her new girlfriend professed to love "Steve" just the way she was.

First-year student Shannon Chenoweth later recalled that Helen was never without a smile on her face, and most everyone liked her because she was a very pleasant person.[4] At that time, Helen had one of the jobs reserved for needy students. She waited tables in the Jones Hall dining room, and when she came toward you, Chenoweth said, it always was with a smile. Helen seemed to go out of her way to be nice. Shannon, at age fifteen, was the youngest girl on campus; she was the only child of a country doctor in Pulaski County. She lived in Jones Hall; famed Helen had the tower room of the adjacent Edwards Dormitory. Many girls had a habit of running barefoot up and down the hall in their underslips. When their fathers visited them or when a man's voice was heard in the halls, the girls scuttled for their rooms. Sometimes it dawned on them that it was just Helen coming through.

Shannon said she wasn't sure why she was called into the dean's office one day, or what Ruth Keith (a former dean of students) was trying to get at, even after several minutes of respectful listening to the dear lady, who was nearing sixty, if not past it. She said that Dean Keith nervously fiddled with a pencil and said there was something she had to discuss but didn't know how to begin. "I'm sure you're aware that there are two sexes," she said, gulping a time or two. "Well, you know there are some that are not truly male or female." Shannon said that the former dean didn't put a name to what she meant, but in those days, such things were not talked about openly. She told Shannon that she wanted her to know that Helen Stephens was one of *those*, and she named another girl. She said something to the effect of "Don't let them touch you or get near you. Be sure not to let them in your room." This perplexed Shannon, she said, because in those days, girls put their arms around each other, held hands, kissed in public, and displayed affection in ways that would be interpreted much differently today. Finally, the poor woman said, "I just hope I made myself clear." She hadn't. All the while, Shannon was thinking, "What is the matter with her? What is she trying to say?"

Afterward, she didn't delay in calling her father. And he said, "So you've run into that already. That's nothing for you to worry about. We'll talk when you come home this weekend." Dr. Chenoweth was a matter-of-fact, straight-talking man who raised his only child without much quibble, going about his functions as a physician, tending to all manner of human conditions. Shannon had followed after him and, of necessity, was often treated as if she were blind, deaf, and dumb. Thus, she had already gained much education before entering William Woods.

Dean Keith had not directly confronted the situation, and Shannon decided that neither would she. All the teachers took that stance, according to Shannon. Shannon said their history teacher, Miss Lessie Lanham, had chaperoned Helen in Germany and treated her like the Queen of Sheba in class and out, and that when speaking of the trip, Lanham made no reference whatsoever to Helen's "difference." Shannon said that Lanham inspired students to learn more European history and other subjects on their own. Lanham claimed she could teach them only so much in five hours a week, and that war was imminent.

As a senior, Helen challenged, foiled, and out-parried the college's top fencer, winning the college tournament, but Helen's achievement in this arena was not much touted by the administration. Fear of overdoing a good thing may have constrained Harmon from capitalizing on this feat, or something may have forged a change of heart in him toward his world-famous athlete, making him reticent. Details of this are sketchy, but Helen wrote about this achievement to Dee Boeckmann, herself a champion fencer. Dee's reply noted that her own oak tree bestowed by the relay team was planted in Forest Park (St. Louis). Dee was now the women's division deputy marshal-of-arms of the Fencers Federation of New Orleans. Dee had slated Helen to run a 100-yard exhibition during halftime at the Sugar Bowl, December 27, and arranged lodging at a convent affiliated with Ursuline Academy, where she was employed.

An editor of a new magazine called *Look* (with offices in Iowa) learned that Helen was visiting Drake University in Des Moines during Christmas break, December 15 through January 6, and was staying with the family of a classmate (Helen's new girlfriend). The editor arranged for a photographer to take action shots of Helen on the university track field. Also during the break, Helen was to be in New York. A hotelier, speculating that her celebrity status would be a drawing card for his business, asked "the Great Helen Stephens to please accept a train ticket" to Gotham, New York, to be his hotel guest, and to let him introduce her to his friends and business associates, where she might enjoy nightclub entertainment on the town and consider future employment in one of his glamorous hotels. He claimed to have Olympian Glen Hardin as a hotel poolside attendant and thought she might fit in somehow. He said that Eddie Mayo had told him she was looking for work.

For local folks, the invitation might as well have been to Sodom and Gomorrah. Dee advised Helen to look into the opportunity but to be cautious and not accept any offer outright. In her letter of March 1, 1937, after all hell had broken loose, Dee explained:

I guess you are wondering what happened. Well, I am too. I have sent air mail specials, and wired and have heard nothing. I think because of the church revolution, they are all in jail.

Helen may have told Dee (in a phone conversation) about the instructions and the advice she was beginning to get in letters and calls from religious fundamentalists in Fulton and elsewhere. Dee's letter continued:

As you know, Mexico has a President about every other year. And, each man empties the treasury, and they have very little money to spend on bringing people in.

So, when you write Eddie, you can tell him that he will not be able to get a lot of expense money from any of those countries for an amateur. You should have had a clause in your contract giving you a month's leave of absence, so in case you get bids from foreign countries, you can take the trips.

If you get a room at the New York Hotel, have them put twin beds in the room so that when your guests come to town, they can be with you. Let me know if you have any bids for any track meets in the near future. I will keep working on the Mexican trip. And also some southern countries.

Did Eddie tie you up for business and athletics? If he did that will leave out your track trips. I have been working very hard but have been unable to write. I received your letter this morning and was glad to hear that St. Louis will have the women's track meet some time in April.

Without escort, Helen departed Union Station and met her host in Grand Central Station. He called the Associated Press to his hotel, where photographers posed her in a white serving jacket behind a bar, smiling, hoisting a cocktail shaker. Then, as the saying goes, they ran with the story. "From Cider to Cocktails" supposedly told all: Helen was moving to New York to take a job as a nightclub hostess. She was going to be a Gothamite! When folks in Fulton see the photo, they won't believe their eyes, the reporter claimed, for the "flying farmeress" was to play "the Lullaby of Broadway with a cocktail shaker." Scotty Reston revealed personal details even Helen didn't know. His article "Fulton Sprint Star to Live in Gotham Starting January" stated that she had come to town to see how much hay Radio City Hall would hold.[5] Reportedly, she had said, "Quite a pile!" and presumably would be a cocktail waitress at the Broadway Hotel and live there "after January." She supposedly was quitting college because she liked nightlife and wanted to live in the Big Apple. "Miss Stephens said it was not absolutely necessary that she earn her own living." When asked if she drank alcoholic beverages (prohibition had just been repealed a few years earlier), she fibbed: "Well, no, I don't, but I think it's fine that other people do"—an impious stance to the minds of the men occupying the board of the church-backed college Helen attended. And several things were bothering her; grades, for instance. Also, she had fallen off her training schedule during the Thanksgiving holiday and had gained several pounds beyond her best running weight of 155, as evidenced at the Olympics. Dee had noted the excess weight during their December event in Louisiana and told Helen to get back on the track and take training more seriously.

Helen thought she *might* work as a hostess in Gotham but had no intention of giving up her amateur status. In fact, she had told Reston she planned to concentrate on the discus and shot put for the 1940 Olympics. He wrote that she was interested in tap-dancing and playing harmonica on a vaudeville tour. He stretched truth and spread the rumor that she was getting married but would not divulge the name of her fiancé. Fultonians who had listened in on her party line and heard Mayo's voice and name might have wondered whether he was the one. Reston wrote that he saw embarrassment in her eyes during the interview. The *Missouri Ruralist* picked up the story: Helen with the "flashing smile, lovely eyes, [and] poise" would become a hotel hostess in New York in February but "expected to retain her amateur standing and compete in the Olympics in Japan."[6] The writer construed that, by 1940, a twenty-two-year-old Helen would be earning a salary in excess of $10,000.

Looking back on this much later, Helen explained her predicament simply: "I wanted my folks to have a better farm, and after all, in those days a woman couldn't actually endorse cigarettes or beer or whiskey and for that matter, there weren't even deodorants to endorse."[7] Helen had received an offer in April from the United Brewers Industrial Foundation asking her, ostensibly because of her "interest in foods and food values . . . to send any recipe or any other data on beer" she might have. No cash consideration was made. Another endorsement offer came from a gym-equipment manufacturer, Narragansett Machine Company, without payment or remuneration. Apparently, Helen was to lend her name and image but receive nothing for it.

Fultonians who saw the photo of Helen the Olympic champion depicted as a cocktail waitress thought they knew best what she shouldn't do. One woman acquainted with Helen's high school nemesis Isham condemned Helen vehemently in a letter. That Helen should be a barmaid and that "drinking should be the order of the day shocked and disappointed most of the good people in Fulton." She wrote, "get your bible and read Proverbs 23:20–21 and Habakkuk 2:15. You have chosen the applause of the world." Helen's former classmate, by contrast, had become the Reverend Isham Holland of the Reform Holiness Church.[8]

Yet to emerge, but far more scandalous, was the premier issue of *Look* magazine, showing Helen in her stride, wearing William Woods letters across her flat chest.[9] The designed-to-perplex caption, "Is This a Man or a Woman?" caused people to whisper things deeply disturbing to Helen. None of the Drake University photos were used; instead, an unflattering picture of Helen surfaced to appear along with photos of other "muscle molls." Propelled by the European press, this "scourge" had swiftly torpedoed across the Atlantic and flapped its way throughout the sports world and into the popular media. Rural Fulton was not yet a market for this new magazine, but metropolitan St. Louis was. Gertrude Webb (then with the Missouri Athletic Club) sent the heartbreaking news to Helen as soon as she saw it.

Helen claimed she was unperturbed by the cocktail waitress flack, having discussed everything with her mother; but neither women were aware of advance copies of *Look* magazine sold in January from metropolitan newsstands. After semester break, Mrs. Stephens had driven her daughter back to school in the Model A Ford that her brother Otis had relinquished for a fair price. Her husband Frank was farming a new place, a better place than the last. With Helen's help, and if this and next year's crops held, they might be able to act on the option to buy it. And though her daughter fretted over not making the honor roll, the important thing, Mrs. Stephens said, was to graduate. Bertie told her daughter that medals might open doors for her, but an education would keep them open. In just five months, Helen's parents and brother Robert Lee, Uncle Thomas and Aunt Laura, and all their relatives would be attending her commencement. And she said that they—mother and daughter—would be alumnae sisters! Waving good-bye, Mrs. Stephens wished her daughter well and headed back to New Bloomfield.

Helen picked up her mail at the campus office and headed toward Reid Hall, the new dorm assigned to her. One envelop bore her uncle's return business address: T. G. Nichols Company, Kansas City. Since his marriage to her aunt Laura M. Stephens in 1909, Thomas George Nichols had held a variety of jobs. He taught college and became a friend of Superintendent J. Tandy Bush. He had been a publishing house sales manager before starting his own company, when Helen was five years old. In the past year, Helen had written a term paper about him that told of his slaveholding ancestors who came to Callaway County in 1823 and about the street in Fulton named after his grandfather George, whose soul rested in the cemetery near Westminster College. All his family had once known poverty, he wrote to Helen, so his advice about her New York offer was, "Cash in now, take no less than $500 per month; you can have as decent life in a saloon as in a mansion—it's all up to the individual."[10]

Another piece of mail came from Gertrude Webb. Inside was the cover of *Look* magazine, torn away, and folded with it was the offending page, on which Gertrude had penned, "Don't let anyone else see this but yourself!!" Helen knew she must call Coach Boeckmann as soon as possible. She coiled the papers into her hand and stuffed both letters into her travel bag that she kept under her bed. Just as she was about to change clothes for lunch, her roommate, Judy Galt, a Washington University transfer student, poked her head into their room and, according to Helen, said something like, "Looks like trouble, Steve—Longmire's huffin' down the hall." Judy vanished, leaving the door ajar. To which Helen shouted back, "Sure, sure." She closed the vanity drawer, turned, and braced herself for whatever came next. Mrs. Fannie Longmire, the senior dormitory hostess, famous for surprise curfew checks, darkly materialized like a phantom from nowhere. She was a widow, wiry as a clothes hanger, and wore short permanent waves plastered against her forehead like a wig. Her thin, gold-rimmed glasses encircled, as Helen judged, "small beadlike eyes incapable of smiles."

Helen later said that their conversation and the story went something like this:

"Dr. Harmon wishes to see you. Immediately," Longmire began. "I suggest you stop what you are doing right this minute and come with me. Right now." There would be no waiting for a change of clothes. In tandem behind Mrs. Longmire, Helen clipped across campus toward the administration building.

"I cannot say what this is about," Longmire edged Helen out right away, making it clear there would be no conversation between them as they walked. Captured like a mouse by the sanctimonious matron, Helen found herself dropped at the threshold of the president's office. "You asked to see me, sir?" she said, flashing a friendly, apprehensive smile. In spite of her predilection for trousers, she felt strangely uncomfortable and awkward wearing khaki jodhpurs, riding boots, and a polo shirt. It crossed her mind that she should have worn something proper. Suddenly, she felt awkward about her size, too, standing roughly half a foot taller than Harmon.

"Sit down, Miss Stephens," he said, pointing to a leather chair near his desk. Heavy brown and green brocade curtains blocked out the gray overcast of light; a rug swirled in shades of dark greens and weighty magentas, Helen remembered. In his middle years, Dr. Harmon stood as if planted to his desk, his left hand curled and bent like a twig on the surface. His dark eyes peered through wire-rimmed eyeglasses. Helen noticed a flash of disturbance when he swooped up the newspaper from his desk. He squinted. It seemed to be a nervous tic.

He wasted no time on cordiality. "Of course, you know why I have asked you here." But she didn't; at least, she wasn't sure. "We disapprove," he proceeded, "of the distasteful publicity that one of our girls has brought upon us." He paused to let the silence work for him, then said, "*You* have embarrassed us." Now he targeted her directly: "That a William Woods girl should be publicized in a cocktail lounge, of all places! Well, the impression it gives is something that will not pass without reprimand. Celebrated though you may be, Miss Stephens, in some circles, with your footrace to fame," he said, and Helen fixed on those last words, "I am compelled to remove the scholarship we bestowed upon you last year.

The damaging impression this and other such speculations you may be contemplating, Miss Stephens, have caused the college grave concerns and disgrace!"

He went on and on, punctuating his speech by waving the newspaper in front of her, a pointer assisting the lesson he was teaching. When he put it down temporarily, Helen saw it was January's *Missouri Ruralist*, opened to the article about her, which was circled with a pencil marking. He then caught her short, stepping briskly before her and thrusting it toward her at eye level: "Word has also come to us that you have had visitors in your room long past curfew. And we know that you have broken other rules, visiting past curfew yourself, in a dorm other than your own. What do you have to say for yourself?" He paused again, waiting for her reaction.

"Well," she started, but he shushed her immediately.

"There can be no explanation for your behavior. We have revoked your scholarship. There will be no appeal of our decision. We are sorry, but I think you fully understand." Helen's mouth opened in shock. He didn't wait long enough for her to say anything. "If you expect to finish your studies here, you will have to make other financial arrangements, you understand, Miss Stephens?" Helen assessed his remark the way it was meant, as declarative, not interrogative. She rose up and stepped away from the chair as if hit by a fist blow to her stomach, her long arms hanging by her side, shoulders slumping, eyes half closed. Defeated, Helen's chin dropped to her chest.

"You may go now," he said, pointing. She nodded acceptance. Dismissed without the opportunity for self-defense, she turned to the door.

She closed the door behind her quietly but in the hallway fell into a frenzy of despair and rage. She broke into a run, sped the length of the hall in an emotional flurry, leaped down the building's side stairs, and tore into Reid Hall. There, she packed her things, talking to herself: I didn't agree to take the job. I've no intention of taking that job. I didn't know what kind of job Mister What's-his-name had in mind. Besides, I'm not about to ruin my, what was it he said? My footrace to fame.

She stuffed shoes and boots, books and hats, together, cramming in dresses and trousers and toiletries; she pulled newspaper clippings and photos from her dresser mirror, tossed them on top, and slammed close the locker lid. Everything she had brought there, she boxed or forced into the luggage and locker. This, she felt, had to be that snitch Longmire's doing! She lugged these things out of her room and deposited them at the end of the hall, near the main entrance. Then, composing herself with somber deliberation, she knocked on Longmire's door and asked to use her private phone, offering no greeting, no explanation, no please, no thank-you. Feeling sad, angry, wounded, enraged, she called home and asked her mother to come for her right away.

Here's Helen's version of what happened next.

Her mother stopped the car at the steps of Reid Hall where Helen sat waiting. By the time Mrs. Stephens had put on the break and opened the car door to get out, Helen had opened the back door and shoved in some of her things. Her mother asked what was going on, to which Helen replied she would rather talk about it at home. But her mother persisted until finally Helen told her what happened. Mrs. Stephens decided that they would talk to Dr. Harmon together and somehow find a way for Helen to graduate with her class. If Helen did nothing else, her mother told her, she was going to finish college, and somehow they would find a way to pay for it.

In a few days, Helen and her mother were waiting outside Harmon's office; it seemed a long wait to Helen. His secretary finally ushered them into his office, and once there, her mother began by thanking him for taking time to see them. She spoke of the unusual weather for January, then launched herself to the task. She told Harmon that Helen would do whatever it took to finish her studies at William Woods and suggested that Helen might take on additional campus work. She told him that Helen was willing to earn money for tuition and campus room and board. She expressed gratitude for any concession the college might make and reminded him that she herself was a Woods graduate with a sense of school loyalty. She said she hoped that her son might attend Westminster, and that everyone in the family placed a high value on education. She reminded him that other schools had wanted Helen to enroll, but they chose William Woods over all others. Mrs. Stephens told him that Helen was not going to New York and there was no truth in what he had been reading in the papers. She informed him that her brother-in-law in Kansas City was counseling and advising them at this time. She said she did not approve of alcoholic drinks, that members of her family did not drink, and that she and Helen's father would not allow Helen to accept employment in a business that encouraged drinking.

While listening to all of this, Helen recalled, Harmon puffed away on his pipe and said nothing. When at last he replied, Harmon presented what he called a reasonable compromise. He could not reinstate the scholarship, he said, because board members had voted on that decision; he thought he could find work for Helen on campus, but she would need to room in town. Helen could work at Dulany Library as a librarian's assistant, he said, and continue as a server in the dining hall during breakfast hours; but there must be no more bad publicity. And also, he said, if she intended to graduate with her class, she must catch up by taking twenty-five hours of classes that semester. He told her that was more than any other Woods student had ever carried.

Helen wondered whether or not he really wanted her to graduate. He did not seem to be the same man who paraded and displayed her around town like a prized bull. The one who had touted and used her to generate revenue for

William Woods in as many ways as he could think of. Now, as she neared the finish line, he treated her like a poor relative, a wayward stepchild who had trampled upon the good name of her benefactress. As his office doors closed behind them, Helen said later, she realized it was "a lot of hooey over nothing!" She would graduate in the spring of 1937 with her classmates, no matter what.

Though Harmon had pulled the academic rug out from under her feet, Helen's Booster Club supporters showed their gratitude at the annual Kingdom of Callaway Supper. They chose Helen as the honoree to receive the McCubbin Cup—given to an outstanding Callawegian who had brought the most recognition to the county in the preceding year. Harmon was the presenter of this award on January 18.

Now Helen was verifiably overtaxed, arising at 5 AM to serve breakfast, training with Coach Moore when weather permitted, attending classes, studying, and working in the library. Free time seemed nonexistent. She felt unfairly treated but "knuckled under," to use her father's words. To earn enough money, she also worked as a campus rep for Niedergertke Truck Lines, picking up and delivering baggage and steamer trunks. "They're as big as a heavy old icebox," she told her brother, whom she now called "Squirt." She worked as a campus courier for McGregor's clothes cleaning business, also.

Around that time, Helen received letters from Dean Shafer and W. Ed Jameson, the president of the State Eleemosynary Institution.[11] Jameson said he was "much gratified" when Harmon told him that she had decided to complete her studies at William Woods: "I think it would be a fine thing if you complete your education . . . preparatory to a useful life in your wonderful profession. After a while your joints might get stiff like the rest of us old people and then you can fall back upon a good teaching position." The philosophical Dean Shafer wrote: "You live on campus two short years, but you remain part of WWC forever. Like a family. This will pass and all will be forgiven." Others were not so kind.

Some community members agreed that the issue was hooey; some were intrigued, Helen said. Some helped her however they could behind the scenes. The owners of McIntire's Log Cabin Flower Shop and of Blattner's Clothing Store, a person at the campus bookstore, a beautician at Boren Beauty Shop, and a salesman at Brown Shoe Company continued to provide free services and products to Helen.

Much more went on in Helen's private life than what Harmon, the dean, and even Helen's parents knew about. Helen was observed on January 12 visiting with a friend late at night. Voted the "most adaptable girl on campus," Helen's new friend "K" was a bright student who typed Helen's term papers. All the spicy ins and outs were recorded on paper, for K kept a log of their every happy or unhappy hour, inclusive of their late-night visits. K's "Ode to Chemistry" prophetically closes with, "surely problems and equations will follow" the days of their life together. They were in history class together. They shared a passion for swimming, rowing, and movies. They saw *Two Fisted Gentleman, Charlie Chan at the Race Track, Charlie Chan at the Opera, The Man I Marry, One in a Million, Anthony Adverse,* and others. They went to church together, ate Sunday dinner together, went to town, and took weekend day trips. K's artsy friends became Helen's friends. Whenever a pal had a part or a performance or a recital, the two were in the audience enjoying the chorus, the Campus Players, or the Brushes Club. Among this circle of friends were Drum and Bugle Club members Thelma Egbert, Selma Cooperman, Marion Schweer, Virginia Williams, Vera Bedell, Margaret Stalder, Dorothy Bierman, and Virginia Sherman.

Of course, Helen was up late studying, too.

February had started perfectly fine, according to K, for Helen's roommate, Judy, threw a birthday party for Helen, and later that night, Helen serenaded K on the harmonica. Helen and K exchanged heart cards on Valentine's Day. Helen also received a valentine from Eddie Mayo. But on February 26, K logged, "Fight with Longmire." Helen and K had been "romping around." In March, at the Highlanders costume party, Helen dressed up as a pirate; K had "two talks with Longmire," one in the company of Helen. The word "piddled" was what K used to describe their romantic time together. When Dean Shafer showed up one Sunday morning in K's room "checking for church attendance," K hid in the closet and Helen in the bathroom. April 11 brought "Heaven, almost" and "Threats from Devil Pussy." K accompanied Helen to Squirt's ninth-grade graduation and her family on a day trip to Bagnell Dam. On April 17, Helen and K, who was a Brushes Club member, went to see the new mural in the state capitol and to hear the artist, Thomas Hart Benton, lecture on his work. Three days later, K wrote, "Washed your hair. Longmire caught us. Cried." This led to "Called to the Dean's Office. May move you. Walked, cried." But evidently, Dean Shafer looked the other way, for it was noted on April 26 that Helen was "Not to be moved!"

As to the treatment the school meted out, Helen was pragmatically mature for a person of her age: "I felt betrayed but I felt I could rise above it, that *my* heart was in the right place, even if theirs weren't, even though some people running the school were extremely closed minded." Like the time she wore jodhpurs to the dining hall for Sunday's formal luncheon. People gossiped as if the walls had caved in, she said, such as, "Did you hear what Helen's done now? Wearing trousers in the dining room, and she wore them to Miss Booth's tea, oh my!"

Now, when anything went wrong or astray on campus, Helen Stephens *probably* was behind it. Who was the phantom midnight trumpet player who climbed Jones Tower and blasted taps, announcing the first day of the last semester of class? It was Helen. Had to be Helen. Ruth Small swore she herself was the guilty party, but who believed her? 'Twas daredevil Helen! The twenty-five-foot tower built in 1892 was a hazard, swaying in high winds as much as fifteen inches. The *Fulton Daily Gazette* reported a February winter storm toppled the wobbly steeple only weeks after someone had performed the high-level horn music.

Helen's father still wanted her to work in town at the shoe factory for a salary of $10 a week plus a lunchtime meal. The job offered "all a person could eat." Squirt said, with her appetite, the factory would lose on that deal. Frank, however, would have a much-needed hired hand. Helen had seen crop failures year after year. She had seen the poverty in city streets and alleys, had seen people peddling whatever they could and ragmen pushing carts, collecting scrap cloth, bottles, metal, any item that could be recycled. She had seen long soup lines and heard Woody Guthrie singing mournfully about the Hoover Dam, social *in-securities*, and New Deals. The Farm Recovery Act, the Industrial Recovery Act, and the Works Progress Administration were in all the newspapers. And people all around her worried that Germany's warmongering would bring America into war. Come spring, she knew she had to get a job that would not meddle with her amateur standing yet earn enough money to help her parents. She wanted to help with her brother's high school and college needs, too.

In March, an Alabama paper quoted Dee Boeckmann as saying that Helen was a better competitor than Babe Didrikson, that Helen had not yet reached her prime, that the sports world should brace itself for more from her in the next four years, because Helen possessed powerful "legs . . . her timing is per-fect . . . a great runner . . . [with] smashing triumphs in her events. Unlike Babe Didrikson who barely won her events . . . Stephens has completely outdistanced her field. Babe was a more colorful performer and finished in sensational style but . . . lacks the natural ability of Helen."[12]

In her second national AAU competition last spring in St. Louis, Helen had set three national records and heaped more glory and attention on herself, her hometown, and of course, her school, for she was wearing William Woods colors.

During spring break (March 24–31), Helen flew to New York to meet with *Look* representatives. One of *Look*'s lawyers took her out for dinner. He bought a bottle of wine with the meal, ordered afterdinner drinks, and in the course of the evening became amorous. Helen told her friend Gertrude Webb, "I had a sense he was trying to find something. So this ole country girl let him roam around awhile 'til he found what he was lookin' for. I just wanted to settle it then and there!"[13]

Webb had advised Helen that the only solution to end such rumors was a head-on attack, and she supplied her lawyer, Henry A. Freytag, of St. Louis, who

accepted Helen as a client. Freytag suggested that they sue for $50,000. Afflu-
ent, bilingual, well-connected, well-educated, and well-traveled, Webb agreed
to serve as Helen's spokesperson, for Helen was a minor at that time. *Look*
offered a four-year scholarship to Drake University and a Ford convertible of
Helen's choosing. Freytag told her not to accept, and Helen obeyed. *Look*'s
attorneys decided to not contest the suit. Acknowledging fault to Circuit Judge
Harry F. Russell, the defendant (Look, Incorporated, a subsidiary of the Des
Moines Register and Tribune Company, Alco-Gravure Division of the Publication Corporation and American News Company) requested an out of court
settlement. Helen agreed.

On April 11, the *St. Louis Globe-Democrat* reported that Helen had won a
$5,500 legal suit.[14] Her lawyer's fee was $550, so her cash amount tallied at
$4,950. That was a lot of money in 1937. Dee, who had urged Helen *not* to sue
because of the bad publicity it would bring, now told Helen to put as much of
the money in the bank as possible and urged her to get a job as quickly as
possible. She recommended Helen for a job as a stenographer for Curlee
Clothiers—to begin in June. Helen would be working on the seventh floor at
Tenth and Washington in downtown St. Louis, in the heart of the Midwest's
major dry goods and garment industry, long established and well supported
by many freight lines and low shipping rates. It was a stable business that offered steady employment.

Helen said she would think about it.

According to K's log, on May 6, the day Helen gave a talk at a school in
Trenton, Missouri, K was in a hospital having undisclosed surgery on her face.
Helen gave an exhibition race during the outdoor "colored" state track meet
on May 8 at Lincoln University, in Jefferson City. Olympian Tidye Pickett and
John Brooks were also there. Her event was set early in the afternoon so she
could also go to the "white" meet held that same day in Columbia. On May 14,
she was in Cape Girardeau for another exhibition. The day before Mother's Day,
according to K's log, they "Shopped for my ring." A few days later, K drove Helen
to Jefferson City, where they stayed overnight. K highlighted the date with
asterisks: "13—Senior Day—got ring. Central Hotel in Jefferson City—bridge
ceremony. To Bed. Serenade." Evidently, Helen had packed her harmonica. K
ended the list of their commencement day activities together, noting that dozens of letters had traveled between them. She had begun her log on December
1, 1936, and ended it on May 26, 1937, with, "I ask you—how have we done—
darling, darling, darling? I love you, love you, love you."

It is easy to imagine the two young girls, standing in an embrace on the two-
lane Missouri River Bridge, exchanging vows and rings and pledging themselves
to each other for eternity. Though the two might be living in different states, they
believed they could find a way, thinking that their love affair would never end.

Helen moved to St. Louis to work for $25 a week, a pretty good salary at the time. She would play on Curlee Clothiers's softball team. Her amateur status would remain intact. K went to Des Moines, Iowa, to pursue a bachelor's degree. Shortly thereafter, and newly fitted with eyeglasses, Helen got dolled up with a new perm and visited her. The newspapers there reported that the Olympic star was eying Drake University and might accept an offer in the fall to train with the National College Athletic Association president, Coach Franklin "Pitch" Johnson.

In August 1937, Harriet Bland competed against Helen in Chicago in the Irish-American Exhibition. Helen visited Dee Boeckmann and Chicago-based Betty Robinson and Annette Rogers, and while there, Dee talked to Helen about her future. During this trip, Helen lost her Olympic running shoes and trowel, her new Olympic running suit made for her by Curlee Clothiers, and her prized *HHS*-monogrammed athletic bag that J. Edgar Hoover had given her. What happened was that Helen thought Harriet had grabbed their gear as they exited a taxicab in downtown Chicago; Harriet assumed Helen had gathered her own things. Helen called the cab company and the hotel where they had stayed in an attempt to recover these mementos, but they were lost to her forever. Harriet told her that losing those things was a sign that she would not be needing her track shoes anymore.

Helen lost a lot of things that year. In Mayfield, Kentucky, she left behind a leather horse whip in room 463 of the Hall Hotel. According to an August 13 correspondence that supports this little detail, shortly after Helen checked out of the hotel a person "in the Curlee party, a Miss Laura Scatizzi, reported the whip to the desk clerk and suggested that they would take the whip along with them and return it to you."

Helen also lost her amateur status. Almost exactly one year after the Olympics, Helen startled the sports world by announcing that she was dropping out of the game. Headlines blared: "Helen Stephens Goes Professional." She signed a contract on August 18 with one-time Chicago sportswriter Byron Schoemann, whose main claim to fame was as the agent for a star billiard player. Helen, Annette, and Betty had signed on as professional athletes, to be represented by Schoemann. Within a few days, however, forceful outcries from key AAU members influenced Betty and Annette to renege. Helen stayed firm, out and alone on a limb. Schoemann promised endorsements, radio appearances, and exhibition events, which would cull an impressive income for her. He borrowed some of her Olympic souvenirs, pictures, scrapbook, awards, Olympic posters, certificates of victory, and other memorabilia for promotional purposes and then headed out to parts unknown to make a few deals.

The contract was short lived; the only things Helen got from it were two endorsements amounting to $100 cash "plus 40/60 arrangement of any $500 draw," which proved nonexistent, and a year's supply of Quaker Oats and Huskies cereal.[15] The last anyone had heard of Schoemann, he had moved into a paltry little rooming house in New Orleans, leaving behind a suitcase of Helen's things as security with his landlady. In this way, Helen lost more of her treasured Olympic keepsakes and a bit of faith in her fellow human beings.

When Helen finally caught up with Schoemann, he was back in Chicago, and she had a more lucrative deal caging for the All-American Red Heads. Schoemann claimed he had tried to reach her by phone, telegraph, and letter. But Ole Olson—who now caged the golden goose at a price of $1,500 per season, plus expenses, meals, and room—said he never got any communications for Helen from her former agent. At the outset, aware of the fragility of her amateur status, Olson advised, "Be careful how you handle these payments."[16] He told her to destroy all his letters pertaining to her salary. But she didn't.

Dee Boeckmann drew the ire for Helen's decision to go pro. Dee's name was typed on the first page of Schoemann's contract but was marked through. Blame was put on Dee via a newsman who was goaded into running the story by key members in the AAU's inner circle. Rankled by the advances women were achieving, the secretary of the executive committee of the Ozark AAU, Alfred Fleischman, fired a letter off to the national secretary, Daniel Ferris, in New York, to protest Dee's appointment to the distant 1940 Olympic track committee. As Helen later explained it, the "Republican" *St. Louis Globe-Democrat* reporter Bob Burnes never liked Dee anyway. Burnes thought that Dee was uppity and too aggressive, and he was happy to report what these two AAU men fed him. Speaking in behalf of his committee, Fleischman said, "The opinion prevails here that Miss Boeckmann as a constant companion and advisor of Helen Stephens had much to do with her becoming professionalized."[17] He said that Dee—the former Loretto Academy physical education instructor and superintendent of recreation in St. Louis, now with the Penn Hall School for Girls and the chair of the Ozark AAU records and ladies' track and swimming committees—was not entitled to be in charge of any sports committee. He claimed Dee had capitalized on her association with Helen and had not prevailed upon Helen to take other steps, and thus her appointment was inconsistent with the AAU's stand taken against Ohio State coach Larry Snyder, the manager of Jesse Owens, who turned pro in 1936. He asserted that Dee's professional relationship to Helen set a bad precedent for Olympic coaches.

"Petty jealousy," retorted Dee, from Chambersburg, Pennsylvania. Of her long association with the Ozark AAU, she said, "I am quite disappointed in St. Louis because I have been one of the pioneers in the field of women's sports."

Ferris declined comment, viewing it as a private fight by officials at national headquarters. But he pointed out that Dee had been a pro for several years and that her Olympic committee appointment was in the nature of a reward for the effective work she had done as coach of the Olympic track squad. Unidentified newspaper sources claimed that though Dee was an Olympic committee member, her appointment did not necessarily mean she would be named the coach of the 1940 women's track squad.

The "Democratic" *St. Louis Post-Dispatch* presented Dee's point of view. Dee said she and Betty Robinson had made preliminary arrangements with a Chicago promoter to make a motion picture sports short.[18] Offers came as soon as they stepped off the boat; Helen was handed dozens of contracts. "I warned her not to sign. . . . Nobody offered her a job, no one helped her in any way. I told her to come to St. Louis and got her a good job with a company here that sponsored a softball team and a basketball team. She played on the softball team. But she still was restless, too restless to be punching a time clock." She said Helen threatened to do "this and that . . . had quite a few movie offers. They asked me if I would supervise the making of a film."

Dee told reporters that Helen's father had lost his farm in 1933, her brother was in high school, and she wanted him to go to college rather than become a farmer because he had possibilities as an athlete. She told how Helen's family sacrificed to send her through college; that Helen wanted to help her folks; that little of the settlement money was left, and Helen needed to save it for the future when she could start a small business of her own; and that last Friday in Chicago, Helen had signed a "contract which made her professional."

Having been in amateur sports for fifteen years, Dee did not favor amateurs turning professional. She knew the life of a professional athlete was hard—harder for women even than for men. But Dee believed that going pro was the only thing Helen could do. She said Helen had lost incentives, having reached the top, and there was nothing left for her to do. She predicted that Helen would never run faster unless given "the strictest training." Then she might reach 11.2 in the 100 meters. Why? In the Olympic trials, with a very slight favoring wind, she had clocked 11.4 even after breaking her stride at 75 yards, a point that got lost in the news, she said.

But what was done, was done, she said. Professionals know that they don't have to do their best to collect gate receipts. It's different with amateurs, she said; if they don't win first place, they're nothing. Dee was as emphatic as she could be. Helen wouldn't go to the 1940 Olympics, Dee said, for she was drifting away from sports, she had no competition and nothing to strive for. Dee's own plans were to organize an exhibition tour, of a dozen or so Olympic girls, and take the girls to Mexico, South America, Australia, and Europe, where they could compete, meaning *train*. "If I go with them I may give fencing exhibitions with Joanna DeTuscon of Detroit, American Olympic competitor," Dee said.

Coach Moore stirred Helen by telling her what happened to Jim Thorpe. In less than a year after his victories, Thorpe's Olympic medals were stripped from him amid the amateur/pro debate. Moore told the press he thought Helen had made a big mistake. Her decision surprised most sports followers in St. Louis. Columnist Maurice Shevlin was concern that "a great many of the Simon-pures are being lured away by professional offers." A week after Helen quit her job with Curlee Clothiers to go pro, Ozark AAU president Charles Gevecker said there was "no reason why the Fulton girl had chosen to leave the amateur ranks ... [and] no question of her amateur eligibility being damaged by her playing softball."[19]

But Helen wasn't sure. That was not what she heard. The newspapers reported that Owens wasn't doing too badly after hanging up his amateur track shoes. His reason for quitting? "There's no one to run against."[20]

And Helen was in the same boat.

10
Olympic Caging

When you come to a fork in the road, take it.

—Yogi Berra

A cast of characters vied for a piece of "La Stephens professionale." The earliest was her manager of sorts, C. M. Olson, "the Swede" of Cassville; then came agent Byron Schoemann, of parts unknown, who was to secure radio spots and endorsements, handle other deals for her, and report to her through her manager. A year later, when she set up her own team, she hired a booker, John "Buster" Connors, out of Springfield, Illinois. He was replaced by a little dynamo from Chicago, Abe Saperstein, of Harlem Globetrotters fame.

Helen first signed on with Olson, complete with the stipulation that she color her tresses a crimson shade. Ole agreed to pay her $1,500 a season plus expenses and a cut of the gate tallies. This salary might far exceed her uncle's "holdout" figure. The 1937–38 Red Heads season featured Helen Stephens—billed as "the World's Fastest Woman!" At halftime, she showed off her sprinting and jump shot skills. Switching from playing women's rules to men's rules was not a problem for her.

Prior to the basketball season, the soon-to-be star "cager" accepted a nine-to-five desk job. Clerking for Curlee Clothiers in St. Louis, she played softball at night in an "electrified" field for the company's regional championship team. She had no experience with this sport, she told reporters: "It's all new to me!" The lights befuddled her a little, but she loved the game. She liked to get on base and have a pitcher try to throw her out: "I'd hit a ball, let it touch ground and bounce about twenty feet high, and dash to first base. With a pitch to the next batter, I'd steal second; then with another pitch, I'd make it to third.

And then, watch out! I'd be comin' in home, kickin' up a lot of dust."[1] Helen (with a batting average of .358) and star pitcher Marie Wadlow made news with each game.

Buster Connors, working out of the Empire Hotel in Springfield, hooked up with Helen via Dee Boeckmann. He booked her as an added attraction during baseball seventh-inning stretches and football halftimes. Buster hawked Helen as if she were a carnival sideshow and had her running against men, horses, automobiles, and airplanes: "The World's Fastest Woman, Appearing in Person! Runs 100 Meters against Men! And Throws the Disc and Shot Put!!!" At the Illinois State Fair, in August 1938, her speed remained the attraction, and it was announced that three world champs would race at the fairground. Helen was matched against Greyhound, a champion trotting horse, and Floyd Roberts, the 1938 Indianapolis Speedway winner.[2] Both horse and man lost. That year, Helen was billed as a sports entertainer with the Harlem Globetrotters and with African dancer and anthropologist Katherine Dunham.

Buster said he could set up Helen at pep rallies, at state fairs, and on radio programs, where she could tell her story and talk about track. He propelled himself forward with a persuasive sales pitch in person, in print, and on the phone. He sold Helen to sports programmers with the cocksure clatter of a name-dropper. His references were reputable enough but only regional and mostly Illinois based: E. Whlie (the Decatur Ball Club president), E. E. Irwin (the Illinois State Fair manager), Pop Boyer (the Bloomington Ball Club secretary), and John Mac Wherter (the Springfield Baseball Club president). Buster worked his underage minor client via her parents, through letters and phone calls, thus bypassing Olson.

The son of a known, retired, but testy boxer, Buster himself was an old basketball Hall-of-Famer. He was a "has-was," according to Helen. At present, his right-hand man was a woman: Isabelle Payne, of Green City, Missouri. "Issy" had quit Ole Olson to manage Buster's Empire Hotel and Coffee Shop, among other things. Before that, she had helped Ole establish and manage the first Red Heads team and was the team captain. Buster said he had gotten Issy a pretty good endorsement deal with Wheaties, "the Breakfast of Champions." In the 1920s, Buster had represented the famous baseball player Grover Cleveland Alexander of St. Louis. Buster still had Grover, now in his cups, working in the hotel bar as a greeter and general helper. Backroom crap games and other gambling kept Buster's place lively. The Grover Alexander Stars of the World billed Grover as manager, but Buster put Helen in charge of scheduling and promotions. Though she got free lodging and a lot of education at the Empire Hotel and on the road, ate a lot of free breakfast steaks and plate dinners there, and got occasional packages of one-hundred-pound crates of Washington apples, Idaho potatoes and onions, and California oranges, Helen soon caught on that Buster's hard-cash percentage and hers would never square. She was getting an education of another kind.

And as for Schoemann, other than the monster-size cartons of Quaker Oats and Huskies (payoff negotiated for Helen's endorsements) and other "loot" arriving at the Stephens farmhouse (much to brother R. Lee's delight), and having her picture taken with baseball great Dizzy Dean in Sportsman's Park, St. Louis, her contract with Schoemann fell flat. Even after she ended the contract, "Schoemann-the-shyster," as she called him, continued to promote Helen as his client.

Olson's other star cager was Ruth "Casey" Osburn, the 1932 Olympics silver medalist in the discus throw. In January 1938, the Red Heads were in Hollywood as guests of Bing Crosby Studios. They played in the Los Angeles Coliseum to a crowd of 1,500, beating the Warner Brothers Studio men's team 43 to 27. They met Bing and Larry Crosby, Pat O'Brien, and Caesar Romero but only spotted Marlene Dietrich, Constance Bennett, Douglas Fairbanks Sr. and Jr. and their wives, Fred Astaire, Ida Lupino, Edward G. Robinson, and Dick Powell. Metro Goldwyn Mayer, Fox Movie Tone, and Warner Brothers filmed shorts of the Red Heads for release as newsreels in February. The cagers had the media's attention, and Olson raked in the money.[3] Schoemann wrote to and cabled Helen in care of Olson, but the energetic little Swede wanted her all to himself. He never gave her any of Schoemann's messages.

Helen now weighed 175 pounds. Her formerly trim sprinter's image appeared on cereal boxes, and her *Ladies Home Journal* endorsement put many veteran and freshmen reporters on her doorstep, seeking interviews. Reporter Alene Rasmussen asked her whether girls would ever run as fast as boys. Sitting on the edge of her bed in her room at the Strand Hotel, swinging her legs back and forth, Helen was slow to answer: "Girls are comin' forward all the time, but I don't think they'll ever equal the boys." Rasmussen assessed that Helen was lonely, set apart from her companions, and wondered whether this was because of the honors she had won. She wrote of Helen's husky drawl, noting that she was nursing a cold and muttering between vigorous rubs of a washcloth across her face. Rasmussen asked about competitive sports for girls. "Oh, it's just the natural thing for people to do. We all like to play." But she said she wasn't sure what she would do when her season with the All-American Red Heads ended. "Maybe go on a softball tour."[4]

Another reporter wrote that Helen, having traveled 35,000 miles, was suffering with "mosquito poisoning, a bad case of tonsillitis and scarlet fever after a six-months' barnstorming . . . over 30 states."[5] By April, Helen was clearly ill—she had gotten pneumonia somewhere between California and the Dakotas and hadn't played the last few games. Traveling all over the country while most folks enjoyed holidays and family weekends was not as glamorous as she figured it would be.

At season's end, twenty-year-old Helen was running faster than ever, despite her weight, and Olson tried to sign her for another season. Helen was reluctant. She had made comparatively little money, while Olson had made a bundle of cash riding on her fame. In her first year as a taxpayer, her income via Olson, Connors, and Schoemann was much less than she had expected. Helen headed home to recuperate and to think about what to do next.

The circulation manager of the *St. Louis Star-Times*, Ray Robinson, owned and farmed some property about a half mile from Helen's parents, but he lived in St. Louis on weekdays with his wife. Helen was home on the weekend that he was helping her brother start a little business of his own. Fifteen-year-old R. Lee was to supply and supervise thirty-five peanut vending machines Ray had set up around town in gasoline stations, restaurants, and elsewhere. R. Lee got 80 percent of sales after buying (at nine cents a pound) and packaging (weighing and putting into paper sacks) salted red peanuts. R. Lee made about two dollars a week. When interviewed in the 1990s, he said that most of his money came from the dispensers in "colored town." Whites often jimmied the machines and didn't pay, he said. He also borrowed Ray's mower to make a few more nickels mowing lawns in town. That spring, Ray and Helen became "sort of smitten by each other," she said, and her relationship with K got lost in the scramble.

During the off season early that summer, Helen dragged her heels back to Curlee Clothiers. But within a couple of weeks, she quit again. She had convinced Issy that they should start a basketball business together, with Helen's capital and Issy's know-how. Helen used part of her lawsuit settlement and launched herself then and there, making her the first female sports entertainment entrepreneur—if not the first female pro basketball team owner—in the world. She contracted with Curlee Clothiers to design and manufacture the team's uniforms, and though she didn't know how to drive, she bought a touring car.

A driver she would find later. For now, Issy ("who *went* both ways sexually," according to Helen) got behind the wheel. The two women swung into Chicago hoping to interest Abe Saperstein, the owner and manager of the razzle-dazzle, "all-Negro" (the term used in promotional materials) Harlem Globetrotters who, for ten years now, had thrilled audiences. Abe liked the idea of an all-girl team playing men's rules against men's teams. He saw it as pure show biz, glitz, and glamour—plus athletic prowess. A battle of the sexes on the hardwood court. "Tag your name," Saperstein said, "call your girls 'The Helen Stephens something-or-other.'" Saperstein, a short, chunky little man, put them in touch with his Springfield client, Emory "Hambone" Olive, a former handler of Grover Cleveland Alexander's ball club. "Ham" himself was an outfielder, having once played baseball in the American League for Kansas City; he had once booked Saperstein's House of David baseball team (which Helen had seen play in 1935 in Fulton) and after a season or two extended his business hand and ran a new team, the House of David*ites*. Hambone sported bold-striped zoot suits, puffed on fat cigars, and occasionally managed gambling ventures. Issy "smit" Ham when first he laid eyes on her, said Helen. He became the team's driver and gatekeeper/watch dog. Helen and Issy's "take" would be 60 percent, and his 40. He would be their male representative when a man's presence was needed. And sometimes it was. Fights and funny business could often break out after a game.

Their team uniform had a snappy, All-American look: white gym shoes, white satin shorts, and pullovers with an Olympic All-American chevron and red-white-and-blue trim. Warm-up jackets were red satin with the Olympic emblem. She bought face and knee guards and basketballs imprinted with the team's name. With college zeal, she versified the Helen Stephens Olympic Co-Eds theme song, sung to the simple, popular tune of "Glow Worm."

> We are the Olympic Co-Eds, Co-Eds
> We never, never see a bed
> We never know where we'll be next
> Maybe we will end up in Tex.
>
> What's the difference, as we go, go-oh
> Just so we can give a show
> So if you like to see us play
> We'll be back another day.

Helen recruited Helen "Onse" Onson (from Wisconsin), Fern "Simmie" Simmons (from Shelbina, Missouri), Victoria "Vic" Cook (from Chicago), "Torchy" Blair (a sure shot-putter from Chicago), and little but speedy "Chief" Riley (from Oklahoma). The Helen Stephens Olympic Co-Eds basketball team included an aviatrix, a ski star, a female wrestler, a baseball star who held the women's world record for projecting a baseball through the ozone, and an expert "horsewoman" (equestrienne). The *Puyallup (Wash.) Press* ran a chiding but funny story in January 1939 about Chick Hogan's team competing against a tough bunch of girls.[6] Days earlier, the Vancouver newspaper had reported that Saperstein once upon a time only talked about his Harlem Globetrotters, but now he had

> a new heart interest. And it's a gal, too; purely platonic, y' understand, but Mr. Saperstein is definitely enthralled, completely sold on the "AA" (athletic appeal) of his latest sports attraction, Helen Stephens, U.S. and Olympic sprint champion.

"There's a girl who's so full of color she makes my Trotters look like Albinos by comparison," says Abe. "She's bigger than the average man— and faster, ever so much faster. On the track, I mean, of course. She's not a bit 'fast' otherwise. Doesn't care for boys or night life or anything like that. In fact her only ambition is to pile up enough money barnstorming with her basketball team and running in exhibition events, so she can retire to the 325 acre farm she just bought near her home in Fulton, Mo. . . . She's close to six feet tall and weighs better than 185 pounds. Imagine the picture we made when we walked down the street in Chicago, just after I signed her up. I tried my dangest to stretch my five-foot-four frame and walk on my toes, but Helen just completely over-shadowed me."

One of the strange things about Helen and her band of Amazons is that they draw more women customers than men. Helen really arouses the curiosity of the fair sex. The girls like to play against top-notch boys' teams and beat a lot of them. They don't need bodyguards either. In a recent game, Helen thought one of the players was too fresh and up and bopped him one. The boy hit the deck, out cold. . . . Helen seldom wears dresses, preferring riding habits, or slacks. And her feet are big, even bigger than La Garbo's. . . . One time, Abe relates, when Helen was jumping rather indifferently at Yakima, one of the customers spoke up and advised her to remove the boxes from her feet. Helen thereupon opened up and jumped better than a foot over the world's record. "Thaat guy just gawt me maad," she drawled.[7]

In Augsburg, Saperstein double-billed them with his Globetrotters. He also had Helen giving exhibitions with his House of David baseball club. In the spring of 1939, Leni Riefenstahl was showing an English-language version of her film *Olympiad* in Chicago. Saperstein took Helen to a viewing in the home of Riefenstahl's guest, Avery Brundage.

Helen now claimed that she would rather compete against men than women and that team sports were more fun than individual events.[8] Crowds loved the high jinks that the gals put into the game. They shouted at opponents, "Naughty, naught!" Or picked out someone, as if choosing a date: "Hey, the cute one's mine," or "I get the short one!" At the microphone, Helen joked, "pinching is a personal foul." Amid laughter, someone might let out wolf whistles or yell, "Beat the broads!" Helen said that "It was swell fun" and only occasionally marred by an injury, antagonism, or sneers from the fans of a losing team.

Though bumped and bruised by occasional jeering, Helen's morale remained intact. The Co-Eds logged some 42,000 miles by the end of the 1938–39 season. Said Helen, "Sometimes Saperstein paid us off with jewelry, and he was especially fond of Simmie. We ran into a few snags." Helen was also fond of Simmie.

Co-Ed "Onse" Onson recalled that "Steve was our drawing power, no doubt about it." She spoke of an incident in Nebraska where some guy mouthed off during breakfast. Helen had heard enough and nodded toward the door. Onse got up, opened it, and then "Steve" grabbed him by the collar and tossed him out. The girls gathered their stuff and left, saying how bad the water tasted— "It was so bad it'd give me a hatchet face if I drank another glass." Onse told of another time, when they were en route to Vancouver Island late at night, high in the mountains: "We were starved, so we stopped at an iffy-looking place to eat. Steve ended up in a fisticuff with a man who was drinking too much." He was harassing Helen, who was dressed in a man's shirt, tie, and trousers, and yelled for her to take off her wig and be a man, and then grabbed her hair. "Steve slugged him as hard as any man could," and the girls cleared out, leaving their hamburgers frying on the grill.[9] Of herself, Onse said,

> I am not an old maid. I am unclaimed treasure and this staying single business hasn't been easy. . . . Simmie was a fast number with an itchy foot as far as men were concerned. Her father was a minister, so she said. I would say she was dangerous around men. Always tried to date the ref before the ball was tossed. You never knew just what she had in mind. Rather attractive, but got to drinking too much in later years. Simmie could put any of them under the table. We enjoyed her singing on those late night drives, as she sang in the choir. Now Chief was a native American, fast on the floor and the smallest, next to me. She was quiet, didn't talk much. Vic, also attractive, wasn't well liked by some of the team. She was Polish and had a short fuse. . . . [She] hated Issy and Ham.

Onse said the nicest gal on the squad was "Little Mary Schierbaum, six feet three inches, from O'Fallon, [Missouri,] an industrial nurse with Western Cartridge Company, and rather strange in her own quiet way." Onse herself left the team in 1940 to play for the Ozark Hill Billies, a farm team for the All-American Red Heads, which Ruth Osburn was then managing.

Columnist John Wray, steadfastly interested in Helen's athleticism, wrote, "it now appears the Olympic Games of 1940 are washed out by war which, incidentally, vindicated Helen's adventure in pro circles."[10] When Congress voted to reinstitute selective service in 1940, Wray declared that Helen had made the right choice because she had not "sacrificed three, lucrative years in vain . . . [but] made good money, helped her folks and gained independence." However, her rival, Stella Walsh, at the age of twenty-nine (older than Helen by seven years) had kept her amateur standing and held a new, 1940 women's 60-yard record. Wray speculated that had Helen remained an amateur, there was little doubt she would have "shattered all world sprint records up to and perhaps beyond 200 meters. . . . Her marvelous stride, almost masculine, guaranteed tremendous speed and power. . . . Too bad '*economic necessity*' forced her to retire from the amateur field before she had reached her peak."[11]

With the death of the Father of the Modern Olympics (Pierre de Courbertin), many expected a demise of his amateur ideals. He wanted to make the Olympics a vehicle of understanding, goodwill, and peace among nations. But his first three modern Olympics (Athens in 1896, Paris in 1900, and St. Louis in 1904) lacked international scale. After the 1908 London games, a wave of Olympians deserted into professionalism—action that was greatly abhorrent to Courbertin. His 1924 Paris games were marred by intense partisanship; his 1936 Berlin games were rent with Nazi propaganda and international bickering. The 1940 AAU secretary-treasurer, Daniel J. Ferris (Brundage's 1912 Olympic teammate), lashed out against accusations that his organization had used Kansas miler Wes Santee to fatten its coffers but then suspended him on the grounds of his taking a couple of thousand dollars for expense money. "We don't receive a penny from . . . invitation track meets," said Ferris. "They are promoted privately. Our only connection with them is to see that the competitors meet amateur regulations. The lone exception is the AAU championship meet itself, such as the one we had . . . at Madison Square Garden. That's our project. If we are able to do so, we make . . . money on it. But our outdoor championships usually just break even."[12] Ferris (a 1909–14 sprinter from Pawling, New York) also supported the removal from amateur status of his and Brundage's teammate, Jim Thorpe. Thorpe was the 1912 gold-winning decathlon and pentathlon athlete.

In the years 1939 through 1941, Helen-the-pro handled promotions throughout North America for Ham's bewhiskered baseball team spin-off, the House of Davidites. In her track exhibitions during seventh-inning stretches, she challenged and stomped the fastest men in each town in 100-yard sprints. She vanquished all male contenders routinely at the Illinois State Fair and elsewhere. She had moved to Sparta, Illinois; still restless in the midst of this activity, she took up the game of golf. When she returned to St. Louis, she took seasonal work at Curlee Clothiers and signed up for bowling lessons.

Babe Didrikson (now Mrs. George Zaharias) was among the crowd at a Co-Eds game in Texas. Helen asked her about the prospects of professional golfing. There was no *real* money in it, Babe told her. When she started out, Babe had grossed about $50 per appearance and was starving to death, living in cold-water tourist cabins and driving an old, beat-up, secondhand car.[13] Helen "felt tempted to listen" to Babe's advice but investigated it anyway. Sam Snead offered her golf lessons, but she would have had to pay for them.[14] With little or no income likely from golf and substantial lost-opportunity costs factored in, Helen accepted Didrikson's advice at face value.

Helen decided to golf for fun and to bowl in earnest. She soon bowled an average of more than 170 and won local, city, state, and national awards. At age twenty-two, she became the president of the Powder Puff Bowling League in Berkeley, a St. Louis suburb. Her amateur status was still secure, she thought, as bowling was not under AAU jurisdiction. Before changing residency from Illinois to Missouri, Helen enlisted Louise Towns to notarize a document that she signed June 14, 1940: "One Dollar, receipt of which . . . transfers of all right, title and interest in the 1937 seven passenger Imperial Chrysler automobile, being financed through the Majestic Finance Company, Springfield, Illinois, to Isabelle Payne. All remaining payments to said finance company are to be made by Isabelle Payne."

After three years as a hoopster, manager, and owner, she was calling it quits. The *Knoxville Journal* sympathized yet editorialized against the "vulgarity and poor taste" of women matching strength one-on-one with men: "It is regrettable that an athlete of Miss Stephens' stature finds it necessary to knock around the country playing one-night stands . . . [given her] great track record and the dubious excitement of seeing females scuffling with males in so-called athletic combat. In fairness to the Co-Eds . . . their performances are aesthetic jewels as compared with wrestling bouts between women. We came away from our first and last ladies' grunting shindig convinced that the proper place for some women is in the kitchen with the shades down."[15]

Fletcher Sweet lined up the Co-Eds for a picture and asked Helen whether marriage were part of her future plans.[16] "Marriage plans? Phooey, forget it." Even if she were interested, when did she have time for it? She had traveled in all but five New England states; accepted charity benefit events sponsored by schools, clubs, towns, and organizations; toured, competed, gave exhibition and benefit races, and trekked throughout the country in buses, trains, and cars; and lived out of suitcases in hotels, motels, and friends' flats and homes. She had played eighty-seven basketball games. Consumed by all of it, she fashioned a business card out of a luggage tag, which she showed to friends and newsmen who asked when they might phone or see her. One side read, "Calling Card of Helen Herring Stephens (Over)"; the reverse side identified her hours: "At home every nite except Monday, Tuesday, Wednesday, Thursday, Friday, Saturday, and Sunday." Her business venture tested friendships and romances, of which there were plenty, most of them fast and facile.

The wedding bells were Issy's. Helen sold her touring car to Issy because Issy was becoming Mrs. Ham Olive, and those two lovebirds were starting a business of their own.

Helen returned home in May. The Fulton paper stated that Helen was home for a needed rest, but fans could see her "pit her speed against a Ford automobile" come Sunday at the Jefferson City airport.[17] The president of the Women's Amateur Athletic Association of Canada, Edith McKinsey, wrote to her about the disbanding in June of the world-champion Edmonton Girls basketball team. Helen scrawled her view on this news at the bottom of the letter: "Dan Ferris just got through suspending them!!!" She was well aware that a great measure of power passed to Dan Ferris when the baron-founder of the modern games died and Brundage moved up the AAU rung.

Helen met a June exhibition obligation in Nebraska with the House of David team and by a wide margin defeated two runners with the Fremont Merchants. Reporters there got wind of her prospective retirement; she told them she was planning the last Co-Eds season. In the fall, Helen recruited a few replacement players. The 1940–41 baseball year was riddled with forty days and forty nights of rain, cancellations, and poor gate receipts. The substantial cutback in exhibition income and rumors of war sealed Helen's fate and further validated her decision to call it quits.

The 1941 Selective Service Act served to add a line of wool uniforms for Curlee Clothiers. Its managers welcomed Helen back and put her to work as a stenographer and manager of the company basketball team and other athletic events. Various news media carried the news: "Miss Stephens, who traveled some four thousand miles in 17 days this summer with the House of David baseball team, giving exhibitions of her track and field prowess, said she had had enough of traveling for a while."[18] One story quoted Helen as saying that interest in girls' track was on the wane; but this was to be remedied by various state physical education boards. About Walsh's new 60-yard dash record, Helen said, "I'd sure love to meet that girl again. Why I could beat her runnin' barefoot—no foolin'."[19]

She solicited business as an independent a month later, using Curlee Clothiers letterhead and adding her own Mulberry exchange telephone number. As the present Olympic champion runner, well known to sports fans, Helen pitched herself, offering track and field exhibitions:

> I run the fastest men in town for 100 yards or less, circle the bases against opposition or time, throw the discus and heave the shot. If a man is not available to run, I often sprint a 100 yard dash against a stock automobile. I did this . . . at the Midget Auto Races at Walsh Stadium. . . . This show takes about 15 minutes and can be placed into the program at any time. I have appeared in hundreds of ball parks throughout the United States and Canada. . . . I furnish newspaper material and mat for pregame publicity. . . . this summer, I was appearing in baseball parks with the House of David club. At the present . . . [I am] available for bookings in surrounding towns on week nights and on week-ends.
>
> The price for . . . exhibition varies . . . dependent upon the size of the town, the drawing power of the local teams, [and] the distance from St. Louis. . . . admission price . . . [is usually set] somewhere around $25 and $50.

Helen now had her own place in St. Louis, at 6300 Dardanella Avenue, and a job, though she didn't like being a timekeeper. But seasonal employment suited her; she worked at Curlee Clothiers from July 1940 to November 1941. She liked the girls on W. J. Kuhl's division bowling team: Helen Wood, Margaret Edwards, Thelma James, and Hellene O'Connell. *Curlee News* reported their comings and goings: In May, Helen was a high-score bowler; in June, she and "special friend" Hellene were fudge judges; in July, they pledged never to pick blackberries again, having exposed themselves to poison ivy during the company's Owl Hill picnic. One of the Curlee "big-wigs" (Helen's term) sent her to night classes in bookkeeping at the St. Louis Comptometer School. Afterward, Helen asked the store management to buy a modern piece of equipment—a comptroller's adding machine.

At age twenty-three, Helen still didn't know how to drive; Hellene, about five years older, offered to teach her. For $375, Helen bought a dark green, 1937 Plymouth coup, equipped with pig iron fenders and, oddly enough, a set of golf clubs and shoes in the trunk. She paid $0.25 for a license (Missouri didn't require a driver's exam until 1951) and gave the golf clubs to Hellene. They were too short for Helen, who now drove a golf ball almost 300 yards. The golf shoes also were too small for Helen but fit Hellene. They enjoyed plays at the American Theater, movies, and bars downtown, and they jitterbugged on the hardwood floors of Casaloma Ballroom. Within a month of knowing each other, they were lovers. Two can live as cheaply as one, Hellene had said, when she asked Helen to move in with her. They spoke of sharing expenses and beginning a life together as a couple, in Hellene's cozy, two-room efficiency. Helen said yes and moved to 1309-A Monroe Street, into a neighborhood inhabited mainly by factory workers.

In May 1941, they attended a rally at Kiel Auditorium to hear the famous flying ace Charles Lindbergh; 15,000 people showed up to see "Lucky Lindy," a man Helen admired. She told Hellene that she had first seen him in the stands at the Olympics; and that she had been a kid when she saw her first airplane circling and landing in a field near Westminster College. Lindbergh had made quite a stir when he met with Hitler and toured Germany's aviation plant. Now aligned (as was Avery Brundage) with the "America First" peace stance, Lindbergh told the crowd that, no matter how many planes America built and sent to England, the British Isles could not be made stronger than Germany's military force.

About that time, Helen applied for a job that paid three times the money she was making at Curlee Clothiers. She joined the accounting office of the Curtiss-Wright Corporation, a major airplane producer, in July and was put in charge of managing and playing on the company softball team. She also played center for the company's basketball Flyerettes. Both teams had won several industrial-league city championships.

A few months later, while listening to the radio, Helen and Hellene heard President Roosevelt's shocking announcement: "December 7, 1941—a date which will live in infamy." Japan had bombed Pearl Harbor, and America declared war.

Helen stayed at Curtiss-Wright for several years during the war. She and other women took jobs that men vacated as they left to join the military. About a year and a half into the war, on June 17, 1943 (just two months after his twentieth birthday), Helen's brother enlisted in the air force. He was sent to Cape Roberts, California, for basic training. When 40,000 men were transferred into the Seventieth Division Ground Corps, U.S. Air Force private R. L. Stephens was one of them. Betty Dotson, a civil service secretary at Fort Leonard Wood, Missouri, accepted his proposal of marriage before he left for special training at Montana State University. He was sent to Camp Adair, Oregon, for air-ground force training and then home to await an assignment to France or Germany.

Opinions about women's roles during wartime were discussed in newspapers, factory newsletters, and on radio. Women's Olympic potential was viewed by some as a measure of their ability to compete with men. The *St. Louis Post-Dispatch* headlined one piece "Will Women Ever Be Man's Equal in Sport?" Dee Boeckmann, then the superintendent of public recreation in St. Louis, gave her two cents' worth, again. John Wray wrote that Dee, always a live wire, now had outlined a plan so that women could beat Johnny in sports when he returned from the war. Dee wanted to advance the athletic development of American women so that women athletes could meet men on equal terms. Wray rebutted that women had engaged in track and field for about three decades, "but the fastest woman runner, Helen Stephens, still was a second or more slower than the top rank men."[20] He did not point out that Helen's training opportunities were nil due to a lack of programs for girls; and unlike most young women, she was lucky because a fledgling coach had taken her under his wing.

References to Helen and speculations about her provoked a miff between brother and sister. R. Lee, home on furlough, thought his sister's claim to fame, now six years old, was ancient history. He, who never could beat his sister in a race, though he was good at high school baseball, lashed out at her. Asserting masculine superiority, he snickered, "You went to Germany on a lark, to run a footrace. I'm being sent to keep America safe!" Helen elevated snideness to a new plateau: "You're so jealous, Ollie, you can't even think straight." They fumed at each other for the rest of the visit.

Back on Monroe Street, Helen ranted to Hellene about it, and Hellene said, "Once you calm down, you're going to regret it." Helen snapped, "What do you know?" But Hellene was right. On Christmas Day, 1944, Private Stephens was trampling through mud on the front lines in the Battle of the Bulge, and Helen was frazzled with worry, fearful that R. Lee might not return.

People hoped the war would end quickly, and many thought the Olympics would resume in 1944. Walter Byers of the *St. Louis Star-Times* wrote that Helen wanted a comeback and was "investigating a belief" that the AAU would take professionals "back into the fold after five years of inactivity."[21] But the ongoing war canceled the 1944 Olympics.

Helen's old rival, Stella Walsh, had tied her 100-meter record during the national AAU women's championships in Cleveland. For Stella, then thirty-two years old, this was a major achievement. Runners of her vintage usually rested on past laurels. But not Stella. And evidently not Helen. Stella reportedly said she could beat Helen (then twenty-five) "any time, any place, with my arms tied behind me." Helen contended that Stella hadn't made good on her boasts in races when her arms swung freely in St. Louis, at the Olympics, and three times in Europe. Helen realized Stella would stay an amateur as long as she could and certainly would run—for Poland—in the next Olympics. Since she was financially supported by her family, Stella could stay amateur forever.

Helen, however, had to earn a living for herself, and one way was in exhibition races. In the 1940s, Helen's friend Ray Robinson arranged exhibition competitions between her and America's top male sprinter, Jesse Owens. Touted as America's fastest woman in the world, Helen ran five exhibition races against him. On Sunday, June 4, 1944, she ran against Owens in a 10-yard handicap race at Wrigley Field, Chicago—midway into a Kansas City Monarchs' doubleheader against the Chicago Brown Bombers and the Chicago Firemen. The program was set up by the "Negro major league baseball teams [with] Leroy 'Satchel' Paige . . . the highest-paid pitcher, white or Negro."[22] Noted for his famous "trouble ball," Paige pitched a ten-inning game, winning 4–3 for the Monarchs.

Helen lost to Owens, running 90 yards in 10 seconds flat. Columnist Wray explained that she had not matched the 100-yard record of 11 seconds but "undoubtedly, with intensive training for a month . . . could crack all the records up to 440 yards held by women. . . . Had she finished out her 100 yards in her 90-yard Chicago handicap run against Owens . . . she might have bettered the record then . . . [because] to run 100 yards in 11 requires 27.2 feet per second. At the finish line . . . any athlete was faster than the average per second for the whole distance."[23]

Even among Olympians, Helen was exceptional. When would she reach her peak? For now, in exhibitions, her speed varied; frequently, she clocked in several seconds faster than those officially recorded. Her races against Owens were always close. Once, officials announced over the public-address system a tie—a dead heat; but afterward, Helen told Wray, she was surprised to learn "that Owens had won by various degrees of measurement." She said her finger got broken in that race:

Naturally, I was driving full steam ahead near the finish and as Owens came up, it seemed that we were very close together, although well-spaced at the start. In some manner, the little finger of my right hand was severely jammed and X-rays have revealed a chipped bone in the first joint and a badly sprained finger. Spectators told me that I must have hit him at the finish line, but it was done so quickly that even we didn't realize it, and who ever heard of breaking a finger while running?

Considering Owens' time of 10 seconds for the full 100 yards, I estimate that I would have been running better than the world record had I run the full distance. And this on grass, too, as the race was run from near center field toward the infield, finishing between second and third bases!

In fact, I personally was very much pleased with my own condition, not having donned a pair of track shoes in four years and having had only two week's training under the supervision of Mr. F. N. Moseley ... counselor/former coach at Salem (Missouri) High School. Although Owens is employed in the personnel division of Ford in Detroit, he devotes his Sundays to exhibitions.

Frankly, I still believe I can beat Owens in a match race of similar type. And if it were my old friend Stella Walsh—she wouldn't even be in the picture at the finish! And I wouldn't be asking her for a handicap, either! I hope that I will meet Owens again, and particularly here in St. Louis.

In another exhibition that day, Helen threw the eight-pound shot put 46 feet 10 inches—a distance far better than the existing women's record of 42 feet 3 inches held by Rena McDonald, of Chicago. She also threw a baseball 275 feet. Reporters said that Helen sought to better the world sprint record and to set world women's records in shot put and baseball throws. *Allsports* magazine touted her as one of the most powerful women athletes in history, for she still held both world and Olympic sprint records.[24]

On Sunday, July 16, she raced Owens again in a 10-yard handicap at Red Bird Stadium, in Columbus, Ohio, in the seventh-inning stretch between the Detroit CIO Cubs (managed by Jimmy Wilson, once captain of the Indianapolis Clowns) and the Brown Bombers (managed by Bingo DeMoss). Anthropologist/dancer Katherine Dunham threw out the first ball to start the game.

Weighing 190 pounds in 1944, Helen threw the shot put nearly 46 feet (and unofficially tossed it 54 feet) and had a standing broad jump mark of 9 feet 1 inch. In various competitions, she was consistently running the 100-yard dash at 10.4 and the 100 meters in 11.5, sometimes clocking as fast as 10.0 and 11.1, respectively. She threw the discus 133 feet 6½ inches.

Allsports asked her in 1945 to write about Dee Boeckmann, for $50 pay. She wrote this news to her brother, stationed at Fort Leonard Wood, and told him she had signed up for business and typewriting courses at St. Louis Compto-meter School, but after a few weeks and with little time for completing assign-ments, she had quit. School director Miss Leonor Kretzer (later Congresswoman Sullivan) scolded her, "You'll never amount to amount to much if you don't stick with this!" She had gotten what she wanted from the course work, she told R. Lee. Mrs. Stephens learned about this and wrote to her with a mother's patience, advising her to above all be mindful of employment security.

Helen still sought work that suited her. While writing the Boeckmann ar-ticle, she asked Dee for help in getting a job with the American Red Cross as an athletics-recreation assistant. Dee gave her a letter of recommendation, and Helen pursued this position at the local level and pushed her application as far as the Red Cross office in Washington, D.C. There, her file died. The Red Cross rejected her sports know-how in favor of persons with musical, craft, social recreational skills.

By then, Helen had shared Hellene O'Connell's two-room efficiency for close to five years, and their relationship had turned sour. Hellene objected to Helen's weekday-through-weekend athletic schedule and accused her of infidelity. She told Helen to move out.

Helen was looking for a place to stay when she heard that America had bombed Hiroshima and Nagasaki. Her own personal turmoil, plus her brother's rebuke that women had it easy while men risked their lives for their county, led Helen to a quick decision. She enlisted into military service in June 1945. Helen H. Stephens, soon to be recruit number 773605, marched into the federal building and signed onto the Women's Reserve of the U.S. Marine Corps. She listed her home as Rural Route 2, New Bloomfield, Missouri, and requested an overseas assignment. She was told she would have six weeks of boot camp at Le Jeune, North Carolina, but for the moment would be on inactive duty. She was given a things-to-pack list, bus tickets, and a fistful of papers and ordered to go home to wait for a call.

Within four months of her enlistment, the war ended, and Helen's foreign assignment was canceled on October 31. When R. Lee came home, five months and two weeks later, Helen showed him her honorary discharge papers. Irritated about this, he pointed out that, as of April 14, 1946, he had served a total of thirty-four months. Like Helen, he had returned home to live with their parents in New Bloomfield, but he would move out when he married in February. For now, both brother and sister helped work the farm. To Helen, "Bob" seemed different, more querulous than ever; and the two got on each other's nerves easily.

Helen began scouting for work in the recreation programs of Caterpillar Tractor Company in Illinois and other large companies and with the USO. She put in a plea for help from her state senator, Michael Kinney (Democrat from St. Louis) and finally entered federal service at the Rural Electric Administration as a clerk-typist in November 1945. But in January 1946, the REA closed its St. Louis office and opened a new one in Washington, D.C.; and though she was asked, Helen chose not to relocate there. On February 20, she found what she thought would be a secure job as a comptroller for the General Accounting Office in downtown St. Louis. She rented a small place in Maplewood, Missouri, and talked her parents into letting her help "electrify" the family farm. The GAO's in-house publication announced Helen's appointment to the board of directors of the Welfare and Recreational Association, her chairmanship of the Athletic Committee, and her presidency of the Women's Bowling League; soon, she was the leading slugger on the White Swan softball team, playing center field at North Side Park.[25] And the word was out that the Ozark AAU committee was processing Helen's bid for eligibility in the Olympics; she expected a decision from the national AAU in December.

She was poised once again at a crossroads. Barely into this new job, she learned that the GAO was moving its offices. She could go to either Indianapolis or Denver or look for work elsewhere. She scanned office bulletins and classifieds, and on a Monday morning, as a walk-in, she interviewed for a job with Curtiss-Wright's Aeronautical Chart plant, later known as the Defense Mapping Agency Aerospace Center (DMAAC). Personnel officer Clare Horn told her to see Colonel Alfred H. Burton. The colonel, a British career-military type, liked Helen instantly. He assigned her to the adjutant officer as a clerk-typist. From there, she was promoted and transferred to the Technical Library as a reference librarian, in May 1950. The name of her supervisor, Charles Guenther, rang a bell. Smiling ear-to-ear that first day on the job, she reminded him that they had met before. If he was the younger brother of college classmate Hilda Ann Guenther, then they had met when he was fifteen, visiting his sister on campus. And indeed he was.

"Dear old Charles," Helen said, "was a bit of a recluse, a sensitive type who just could not let himself go, make man-talk, etc." But she granted that he could write and that he taught her a thing or two. Of a different sort was Coach Fred N. Moseley, who worked in the airplane division and lived, as she did, in nearby Maplewood. They struck up a friendship, and he encouraged her to reorganize her Co-Eds team. He even offered to help her.

Within the year, Helen was in love with someone who supported her Olympic ambitions and served as her booking agent. This time, using her own letterhead, a picture of herself in Olympic duds, and a list of her official track and field records, Helen solicited business. She used the nebulous salutation "Gentlemen" and signed the names of both herself and her booker/lover Mabel Robbe, replete with their Parkview exchange phone number. Their solicitation offered a moneymaking opportunity to organizations, athletic funds, and charities and offered communities a chance to see the world's most famous woman athlete in action. . . . Helen Stephens' internationally famous Olympic Co-Eds . . . [has been] reactivated and revitalized and are ready to hit the road for their sixth "big-time" season. Miss Stephens has again brought together some of the most brilliant and talented girl basketball players in the Mid-west and welded them into a powerful court-wise aggregation.

Previous to the war, the Olympic Co-Eds traveled all over the United States; played engagements in Canada and Mexico. Every place that they appeared, they packed the gymnasiums and never failed to please the enormous crowds with their basketball wizardry. Helen Stephens, Olympic and World Champion, will give an exciting track exhibition between halves of the game. Added interest is created by selecting a local male opponent to race her across the gymnasium. Broad jumping and shot putting are on her program if mats are available. She will also throw the basketball for distance in the larger gyms. In addition, she plays and is captain of the clever Co-Eds. Miss Stephens averaged 18 points per game last season for a total of 1565 points.

The Co-Eds play straight men's rules and play men's teams only and ask no favors. They are booking independent teams, veteran's teams, civic clubs and private organizations from November 1948 to April 1949. Posters, mats and cuts are furnished free to you; copy material for your newspapers is also forwarded to you prior to the game.

Write, wire or call should you want this crowd-pleasing attraction. . . . Tell us the seating capacity of your gym, admission prices, available dates and your best proposition. The Co-Eds prefer a straight 60–40 arrangement, the girls receiving 60 per cent of the gross after essential taxes. However, we will consider a sizable guarantee. We suggest again this year a minimum admission price of $.65 for adults and $.35 for children. . . . Towns located about 150 miles from St. Louis are requested to offer Saturday and Sunday dates whenever possible. A game time of 8:30 PM is preferred for most games to allow the team ample traveling time. Help us to arrange our schedule and be assured of a date by contacting us at once.

Helen had fallen in love with yet another older woman; she was happily engaged in a serious relationship with her GAO section supervisor, Mrs. F. J. (Mabel) Robbe. They moved into a house together, in Ferguson, Missouri, and were hell-bent on revivifying the Helen Stephens Olympic Co-Eds. Helen felt she finally had found someone to spend the rest of her life with.

Without corporate backing and in a social climate hostile to women who undertook self-promotion, athletic or otherwise, they lurched boldly ahead. With Mabel behind her, Helen was doggedly set on taking charge of her destiny. She took a one-month, $300 contract to set up an employee recreational program and social club for Dorsa Dresses, a manufacturer of women's apparel in St. Louis, Cape Girardeau, and Jackson, Missouri. Its management capitalized on the publicity that *Olympic*-Helen spawned for its business, and she for hers.

Helen now settled in as a reference librarian at DMAAC. Her boss had begun his service on New Year's Day, 1942. Charles Guenther was a quiet, soft-spoken, introspective man, fond of writing poetry. He spoke five languages; his translations of the poetic works of the modernists were published in literary magazines in the United States and abroad. His own creative work received commendable notice from members of the world's most noted literati, including Ezra Pound, among others. His literary talent drew international acclaim, but his accomplishments meant little to Helen. According to her then, he was a writer of limericks and sing-song verse, and she thought Guenther lacked administrative talent. Gregarious by nature, or perhaps bent that way by fame, Helen assessed her boss as inept at managing people; his gift was with the pen, not personnel, she said. From day one, it was oil against water—fast moving water (Helen) forced to blend with deep, rolling oil (Guenther).

Guenther's talents as an interpreter put him in a delicate position, for which she lacked appreciation. As chief of the research department, he translated confidential government material (geographical documents and treatises), a task demanding a sober mien. Guenther also held the classified position of command historian. His newest charge, colorful, common, and comfortably centered in the public limelight, drew notice wherever she went. It was something he seemingly couldn't bear. But Helen, unflappable, loved to infuse laughter and move into the epicenter of attention. Working together in close facilities, the urbane-tempered, well-mannered poet rarely cut loose; he retreated from the raucous celebrity female jock.

But she wouldn't leave it at that; she had to go after him with his own foil. She gave her supervisor a nom de plume, just as she had renamed other co-workers, whether she liked them or not. In this case, sensing his discomfort, ruthlessly she penned him "Poor Chicken Charlie." She wrote doggerel and illustrated it with caricatures of herself and her coworkers in and about the workplace. Scrawny-legged Chicken Charlie scratched and scattered across her penciled artwork, which she posted on the bulletin board in her work cube. The colonel himself tripped in to see Helen's almost daily editions. She kept "the doozies" inside her middle desk drawer, which she pulled open for favored pals Suzie Garrison and Eleanor Sikorsky for a quick look-see. Like a flasher on a side street, Helen meant to shock, and no one was spared, especially not the boss. In her attempt to entertain, no office event or occasion went by without her whimsical scrutiny. She sketched office squabbles and critiqued arcane military procedures and civil *servant* protocol, which her supervisor fought, often in vain, to uphold. How did she get away with "dissing" her supervisor with her little morale boosters that trampled his officialdom? Colonel Burton himself copied some of her art, using the office duplicating machine! The colonel liked her spirit and enjoyed her celebrity. His presence buffered any flack that rose up between the versifier-flasher and the administrator-poet. Over time, the inspired, prolific athlete/librarian filled a three-inch binder with office art.

Helen's mother hoped and prayed she would settle down in this federal agency, which was aligned in some way with McDonnell Aircraft Corporation, where R. Lee was employed. However, the Co-Eds always were foremost in Helen's mind. When the heads of state came to Fulton for Winston Churchill's Iron Curtain speech, she scheduled the Co-Eds to play a game at Westminster College. At some point during the event, Helen supposedly shook hands with the president and the prime minister, and this "happenstance" was reported in *Airscoop*, the employee newsletter. Supposedly, both Truman and Churchill expressed regrets at not being able to stay and watch her play basketball.[26] This was the kind of heady thing that made a certain DMAAC supervisor frown, Helen said, but she didn't care. Her Co-Eds were double-billed with the Harlem Globetrotters and en route to Oklahoma!

One workplace incident ruffled her supervisor even more. In the pit of her usual prosaic boredom, Helen had lit up a cigarette and retrieved an ashtray from her desk drawer. "C. C." was nowhere in sight. Minutes passed. Absent-mindedly, she lit up another one. Something or someone caught her attention, and she left her post, with one cigarette cocked in the corner of her mouth. Guenther dashed like a flash from his office, sniffing the air: Smoke meant fire somewhere in his section. Someone who smoked cigarettes had thrown a lit butt into a wastebasket. He pulled the CO_2 extinguisher from the wall and snuffed out the hazard. More troublesome to him, he let it be known to Helen, was the paperwork to requisition, per government regulations, a replacement extinguisher.[27] Perfect scenario for a sketch! thought Helen: Summoned to action, Big Chief Charlie puts out fire! Her sketch depicted the artist (herself) as a hapless civil servant sitting at her tidy desk—Old Helen Stephens, the librarian, with thick, dark-rimmed glasses—busily working. I DIDN'T DO IT! read the balloon floating over her curly head.

However feisty, the towering Helen was a team player with a devilish streak, though short on clemency when it came to Charles Guenther, but she learned a lot from him. "I dared anyone to improve on his writing, his letter composition. Writing bureaucratic government language was tough!" As months passed into years, in spite of their differences of temperament, they developed respect for each other. Helen was, like Charles, diligent, reliable, and hardworking. Her work, like his, was flawless 98 percent of the time. They mended fences. When Charles retired, he recommended Helen as the interim supervisor. She took his place for several months, but women weren't considered for top jobs back then, so she served as an interim only and until a man was hired for that position.

In the fall of 1946, Helen was invited to the Olympic association's semi-centennial dinner in New York. The December 23 occasion celebrated the fiftieth anniversary of the revival of the ancient games and was a fund-raiser. It provided the forum that initiated plans for the 1948 games—the first since war had canceled those set for Japan in 1940 and London in 1944. The event was limited to competitors, committeemen, officials, managers of the U.S. teams from the various Olympiads from 1896 onward, and the wives, daughters, and sons of the Olympic family. In other words, anybody who would purchase a $5 ticket. Asa Bushnell acknowledged Helen's letter regretfully declining the invitation; full-time work and her Co-Eds schedule precluded a trip to the Big Apple. Bushnell thanked her for her cash contribution and told her that over six hundred people were expected for the Monday night event. Looking back on it, Helen thought that if she had gone she might have been able to cement her amateur status then and there, on the word of one particular person, namely the USOC president, Avery Brundage, who always had liked her, she thought. Brundage presided over a program of speeches by John McGovern, Asa Bushnell, Dan Ferris, Gustavus Kirby, and Charles Ornstein—all important decision makers. (In the 1940s, the AOC had undergone a name change to United States Olympic Committee.)

The *St. Louis Post-Dispatch* identified the St. Louis contingency: Dee Boeckmann, the number one Olympic sports personage in the country; Joe Forshaw, a 1908 Olympic team member; Artie Eilers, a Missouri Valley Conference commissioner; and Charles Gevecker, the former president of the Ozark AAU. One topic under discussion was Olympic transportation, whether it should be by air, in cargo planes carrying one hundred people each, or by water (as before) but using the navy's flattop vessels.[28] The time-saving advantage of air transport would allow a longer training period in London and undoubtedly would cost less, supporters said. An eight-day sea junket offered limited facilities to keep athletes in condition. Only $110,000 had been raised so far. It had cost $350,000 for ocean travel alone in 1936.

Predictably, Dee Boeckmann shifted the focus; it was "time for Miss America to wake up to her deplorable weakness in track and field." The United States, she predicted, would lose to China, India, and Europe. She said that America's best were "Tuskegee (Negro) college girls, headed by Alice Coachman, present champion sprinter. American girls from California, the Northwest and . . . Southwest were not represented at our national championships. St. Louis hasn't any women [athletes] . . . that I know of and this once live center of women's track activity is as dead as others I could name."

In her travels with the Red Cross, Dee had seen the progress other countries had made. England's championship events for women were held right along with the men's. She thought the AAU should adopt this plan so that American women would have opportunities to develop, and she hoped the United States would send a sizable and strong women's track and field team. Under Dee's influence, Helen wrote to the president of the USOC to urge planners to establish a budget for girls who had ability but not the backing of all members of the committee. After the 1936 games, she pointed out, Louise Stokes had simply slipped away and out of sight, and so had Tidye Pickett. Helen won no friends or points on that maneuver.

But Helen had problems of her own regarding the games. An athlete with a booking agent, who owned a basketball team, officials said, could not be considered an amateur and could not participate in the Olympics. Some said she was still an amateur runner because her business and booking agency were for basketball—an Olympic sport unavailable to women in the 1940s—and she, of course, wanted to compete in track and field; coaching possibly offered the only truly professional route she might have taken with track and field.[29] Coaching jobs for women (or for blacks such as Owens, for that matter) in the 1940s were, Helen said, "as rare as a Rocky Mountain hen's tooth."

Early in 1947, Helen wrote John Wray because he had reported on the U.S. team from Berlin. Her words were an indirect request for guidance or help. She told him that Stella Walsh, writing to her from Krakow, had recounted her recent athletic feats in her homeland, and that it appeared that Stella was still going strong. "I . . . defeated her five times, at all distances from 50 to 200 meters. . . . Naturally I would like to meet her once more, after getting into tip-top condition."[30] In the summer, she wrote to the Special Committee on Eligibility for Ozark AAU membership, the governing body for her region of residence. Chairman Frederick Armstrong told her to reapply for registration, and he helped compose the following statement:[31]

> I, Helen Stephens, wish to submit the following for your consideration:
>
> 1. In the fall of 1937, while under the age of 21, my father, as my guardian, signed an agreement with a Mr. Byron Schoemann of Chicago, Ill., giving him the authority to make arrangements for personal appearances and exhibitions. There was no money involved in this transaction. The obligations of this agreement were not fulfilled and this said agreement was disaffirmed by me before I reached the age of 21 years.
>
> 2. Several appearances and exhibitions were made by me where I received expenses only—equal to and not more than I was

permitted to receive as a top amateur athlete under the AAU regulations.

Typical appearances:
A. Springfield, Ill. against an auto
B. St. Louis, Mo. against men and a car
C. Chicago, Ill. against a man

3. Inasmuch as there has been no activity in women's track and field events for the past 10 years in the local Ozark AAU, I have had no incentive to re-apply for membership in the local body. At no time have I received any official work or written statement from the local or national body of the AAU informing me of my status disbarring me as an amateur athlete. Therefore, I have played with and competed against various and innumerable amateur teams in both softball and basketball during the past 10 years.

4. For the past 7 years, I have been a local resident of St. Louis, Mo., active in amateur sports and helping to win two Muny basketball titles while at a local war plant.

5. At no time did I ever compete or make an appearance for a cash award or prize for any personal athletic activity.

6. At all times, I have endeavored to encourage women's participation in amateur sports of all kinds and have sincerely tried to live up to the ideals of good sportsmanship in every manner, act and deed.

7. Letters from known people can be secured to testify to my amateur activity the past five years that may be attached to my application for membership in the AAU if necessary.

Respectfully submitted this 11th day of June, 1947

Helen recomposed this information in petition form for the board of governors of the national AAU. In that June 21, 1947, document, she requested "full amateur status and eligibility to compete as an amateur in the sports and exercises over which the AAU of the U.S. has jurisdiction." Newsmen jumped on it, using the IOC handbook definition of an amateur: "One who participates and always has participated in sport solely for pleasure and for the physical, mental or social benefits he derives therefrom, and to whom participation in sport is nothing more than recreation without material gain direct or indirect and in accordance with the rules of the International Federation concern." Helen, now twenty-nine years old, was a full-time army ordnance plant accountant. Accord-

ing to one newspaper report, she had competed in amateur basketball and softball for several years but had not been active in track competition since 1940. It
stated that her professional "fling was anything but a financial success and she
claims that at no time from 1937 to 1940 did she earn more money than she
might receive from expenses as an amateur."[32] President Henry Kemper said the
AAU would decide on Helen's petition at its next regular meeting.

Helen pled her case in person before the Ozark officials at a meeting in the
DeSoto Hotel. She said later that the officials seemed only interested in a young
and pretty new track star on the Olympic horizon. They asked Helen about the
runners in the women's June 13, 1947, event at the public school stadium in
St. Louis. As a volunteer, she had helped Ozark track chairman Artie Rilers with
the 50-yard race, the 440-yard relay, and the shot put and discus events.[33] She
had worked diligently with several track hopefuls at that year's Ozark championships, where St. Louisans seemed to have found another wonder girl in
Barbara Mewes.

The June 22 newspapers had earlier headlined that this "17-year Old St.
Louis Girl of Many Talents Is Being Groomed for Olympics." Mewes excelled
in sprinting and shot put. One reporter conveyed the prevalent masculine
concern: "On the more feminine side, she is a comely and talented dancer." Dee
Boeckmann groomed Mewes at Washington University's Francis Field and had
clocked her in the 50-yard dash in excellent time, 6.3 seconds. Dee told the press
that this speed had been accomplished within a short time of training, and she
was taking Mewes to the nationals in San Antonio, June 27–28, "with an eye
on the 1948 Olympics."

In August 1947, Chairman Armstrong asked Helen to send a notarized copy
of her letter to the Ozark AAU. He said, "The only purpose is that of atmosphere.
It [notarization] does have a beneficial effect on many persons untrained in the
use of similar matters." She sent it off, crossed her fingers, and waited.

A surprising turn of events occurred that year. The consummate amateur,
Stella Walsh, decided that she was not going to the games as a Polish runner. She
wanted a change of citizenship in order to compete as an American; the thirty-
six-year-old Walsh was also awaiting a decision that would determine her fate.

Over the last few years, Helen had become a leading female softball hitter
in the St. Louis area. Even so, the strongest undercurrent of her psyche was her
track and field ambition. She felt she had been born to compete in track, born
to run. But a second Olympic peak was not in the cards for her. Officials determined in early 1948 that amateur status for the once-great Helen Stephens
was "unthinkable." Unhappy, Helen said later, "Regardless of circumstances, if
you even smelled like you had taken a nickel, Brundage wouldn't budge."

A year later, Dee and Helen co-coached two St. Louisans who showed Olympic potential.[34] Dee's prospect this time was seventeen-year-old Evelyn Tullis.

Helen's Olympic hopeful was a twenty-year-old University of Missouri graduate from Ferguson, Darline Hilker. Helen had spotted Hilker at the AAU meet in Cape Girardeau, where she had won the discus throw and third place in the shot put event. Dee had found her protégée there also. But neither one had the stuff that the Fulton Flash had displayed.

Lamenting the lost of "La Stephens amateur," columnists were gloomy in their outlook for an American girls' track team. Could nothing be gleaned from those competing in the July 12 Rhode Island tryouts? Though not connected with the Olympic team in any official way, Dee called Wray weeks before the team set off to London and told him that American women didn't have a chance of winning. Why? Because "Our girls simply haven't gone in for track and field sports in a major way."[35] She doubted that many contestants would make it past the qualifiers, other than the girls from the coeducational Tuskegee Institute. "They have won the championships year after year . . . [and] are likely to do so again. . . . They have a fine coach and they train by competing against the men. . . . Their competitive spirit is fine."

Dee was right. Four Olympic track women's titles were taken at Wembley Stadium: Alice Coachman took the only gold for America, winning the high jump event with 5 feet 6⅛ inches. A Dutch housewife and mother, Francina (Fanny) Blankers-Koen, with a time of 11.9 won a gold medal in the 100-meter sprint but didn't come close to Helen's record, though she won the 80-meter hurdles with 11.0 seconds and helped win the 440-yard relay (47.4). Fanny also won the gold in the 200-meter race in 24.4. In the field events, European girls made a grand sweep: A French girl won the shot put; a Hungarian won the long jump; and an Austrian won the javelin. Though people didn't want to hear her message, Dee's assessments were right on target.

Helen might have easily beaten those marks, but the rules of amateurism prohibited her from trying. The Fulton newspaper lamented, "All we needed at London was Helen Stephens, who last performed as an amateur 12 years ago."[36] She hadn't been training nor was she being coached, but at her recent Wisconsin shot put exhibition, she had thrown the iron ball almost 8 feet farther than the world record (47 feet) and 9 feet farther than the distance that won the Olympic gold (45 feet 2 inches), and she had tossed the discus 133 feet 6 inches, a bit shy of the throw by Micheline Ostermeyer that won the gold for France at 137 feet 6½ inches.

Helen's Rhineland, Wisconsin, exhibition came at the request of her old friend and first-string Olympic Co-Ed, "Onse" Onson. Upon learning that her reinstatement had been denied, Helen had moped around for months. What she needed, Mabel Robbe said, was a distraction. So, in early August, just as the Olympics were beginning, Helen and Mabel set out to visit Mabel's relatives in Mount Carroll, Illinois, and Helen's friend Onse. Onse was now the recreation director for the Rhineland park board and asked Helen to give an exhibition during the Rhineland-Merrill baseball game. "Steve and Robbe" (as Onse called them) stopped at a newspaper office in Mount Carroll to let the local press in on the itinerary. The small-town paper carried the news in the guests and visitors column, which was picked up by several other papers.[37] Now weighing about 200 pounds, Helen leaped a distance of 8 feet 10½ inches in the standing broad jump and ran the 75-yard dash in 9.0. She stirred Olympic fans by heaving the shot put to eclipse the Olympic mark by 9 feet.

When Helen took up swimming in 1949 and placed third in a backstroke competition and eighth in the 40-yard freestyle, the *St. Louis Post-Dispatch* unglowingly reported that the Fulton Flash, "former world champion among women runners is no great shakes as a swimmer."[38] R. Lee clipped the column for her. He had bought a house in a new subdivision and wanted Helen to move there, too. She and Mabel purchased a modest little brick house several blocks from R. Lee and Betty in Ferguson.

In spring 1952, Helen folded her Olympic Co-Eds once and for all. Since being revived in 1945 and counting the three prewar seasons, the Co-Eds had known a decade of barnstorming. Helen had made a little money, though not much. That year, the Swedish press took a swat at Brundage for his stance on amateurism, calling him the apostle of hypocrisy on broken-time pay (the continuation of wages for needy athletes when absent from their jobs during competition): "Despite his holy amateur idea, Brundage comes from a country where a top tennis player doesn't go to a tournament for less than $500 to $800 and their university sports is the world's biggest amateur fraud."[39]

Brundage's five-man commission had made recommendations to the IOC, but any changes they might agree on would come far too late for the Fulton Flash.

11

The Flash Fires Back

Our girls can't be blamed too much. . . . they haven't gone powderpuff exactly. . . . Our girls' schools do not promote women's athletics enough. . . . There is no system of school competition extensive enough to develop our girls, such as exists in Europe, Japan, and Australia.

—Coach Dee Boeckmann, quoted in
St. Louis Post-Dispatch, October 14, 1953

*W*ith Japan and Germany excluded from the 1948 Olympic Games, America's track men won nine gold medals; her track women, one. Francina Blankers-Koen of Holland came in with 11.9 seconds in the 100 meters to win the gold. Her time was considerably shy of what Helen's had been. Great Britain's Dorothy Manley took the silver, and Australia's Shirley Strickland took the bronze. The only American women medalists were Alice Coachman (gold in high jump at 5 feet 6 inches) and Audrey Patterson (bronze in the newly added 200 meters at 25.2). American women lost out completely in the 80-meter hurdles, 400-meter relay, long jump, shot put, discus, and javelin throws.

The inveterate woman-watcher of Olympic sports, John Wray, told why: "Lack of interest and organized development among the girls in track and field events explains our Olympic backwardness."[1] Wray surmised that organizers might add events for women in 1952, a 400-kilometer marathon, for example, but few took the idea seriously. It was rumored that Avery Brundage aspired to head the International Olympic Committee and was likely to succeed the retiring President Edstrom of Sweden. Wray spoke of growing opposition to Brundage's insistence on amateur purity. Wray foresaw huge battles over paying amateurs for time lost when employers failed to give leave or absence pay. This would lead to backsliding since a "cash-on-the-barrel spirit has swept over our college and amateur institutions in recent years. . . . if this wave is not halted, it will sweep the Olympic Games into semi-pro or real professional class. . . . It is not difficult to forecast the finality. . . . You can correct an incident. . . . But you can't halt a trend."

Americans watching the Olympic results bemoaned their country's plight, and some asked: *Where was the Fulton Flash now that we needed her?* What a disappointment it must have been for Helen.

Stella Walsh, in tune with the predicament, was aware that the Flash was out of the picture. Counting on approval of her citizenship application, Stella had meant to fill the void by competing as an American. She thought her affiliation switch would be accomplished by 1948, for after all, she had been a resident of Cleveland since childhood. But the games came and went without her; her application was still being processed as the 1952 games approached. She waited for the wheel of naturalization to turn in her favor, yet continued to run exhibition races and still compete for Poland in amateur meets, setting new records in existing and newly added events. This did not suit the U.S. Olympic Committee, and it rankled Helen to see her senior nemesis prevail like a cat with nine lives. Old Stella kept running as if powered by an industrial strength, replenishable battery.

Retaining the native-born American's amateur athletic status was a horse of a different breed. Helen's bid for reclaiming amateur rank having been denied, she, too, had played a waiting game in vain. Irretrievably classified as a professional, Helen fell into a deep depression that was compounded by passing her thirtieth birthday.

Mabel Robbe watched Helen's mood drop and her morale dip. She worried as Helen moped off and on for several years, and Mabel could see that Helen's mind was in need of jarring. "There's more to life than Olympic competition," she carped, but Helen seemed unable to ease herself past the AAU's decision. Over time, Mabel's patience was pushed too far. She finally said, "Life begins at forty, remember? For God's sake! It doesn't end at thirty! Stop feeling sorry for yourself." She told Helen, "Time out! It's time for a time-out, Helen!" Her voice carried a force by then that Helen knew she couldn't match, a timbre that meant Mabel wasn't going to let up or be swayed. Mabel threw a travel flyer into Helen's lap and told her they were taking a two-week vacation. In search of peace of mind, Helen put aside her baggage of disappointment, and they drove through Missouri's foothills that led to the then-placid Lake of the Ozarks.

While the Flash vacationed, America's hopes for Olympic victories in Helsinki in 1952 shattered into pieces like a dropped mirror. Once again, American women returned home without much gold. On new track surfaces and with new running gear, Australia's Marjorie Jackson matched (with the aid of the wind) but did not beat Helen's speed; she also won the gold in the 200 meters at 23.7 seconds. The United States won one gold medal, the 400-meter relay, with the team of Mae Faggs, Barbara Jones, Janet Moreau, and Catherine Hardy, but lost out completely in the 200-meter sprint, the 80-meter hurdles, shot put, high jump, long jump, discus, and javelin. Helen wrote to Jackson, wishing her good-luck and offering to exchange photos and autographs, graciously saluting the Olympian: "I am proud to hold the Olympic record jointly with you and . . . Blankers-Koen . . . whom I remember . . . in 1936 when we were both 18 and she went unnoticed, developing her prowess much later. It is one of those rare phenomena that women should develop, attain, and maintain their athletic ability at a much later age than most men. Stella Walsh is another good example."[2]

Communist women and women of color had taken the lead. Australia's Shirley Strickland won the gold in the hurdles; Czechoslovakia got the gold in the javelin; the U.S.S.R. took home two golds—shot put (50 feet 1¾ inches) and discus (168 feet 8 inches).

Americans were sorely disappointed in Uncle Sam's girls that year. Dee Boeckmann, visiting St. Louis in August a year later, rang up "Mister" Wray, who indulged the testy, one-time-and-one-time-only Olympic track coach who had seen a lot during her stint with the Red Cross and the Army Special Services in Indochina, Japan, India, Hong Kong, and other Eastern countries. She said, "The Far East is taking an amazing interest in athletics and all sports, especially for women. . . . the Communists . . . are becoming sports-minded."[3]

Helen was still a technical librarian for the air force's Aeronautical Chart and Information Center of the Defense Mapping Agency Aerospace Center, and though comfortably settled down in her home in Ferguson, her high ambitions and relentless energy had not diminished in any noticeable way. She needed diversions, physical outlets. Her brother, Bob, and his wife, Betty, made her an aunt in 1949, and a second niece arrived in 1954. Helen enjoyed the girls as preschoolers but did not like infants much and never understood all the fuss women made over babies—they made messes with food, had stinky diapers, couldn't talk, slept all day, cried all night. But once "the kids" could walk and get into things, they had more of Aunt Helen's and Aunt Mabel's attention.

For Helen, real excitement came one day in the summer of 1953 when a telegram and an embossed invitation arrived from the White House. President Eisenhower was hosting a luncheon for some forty athletes prior to the congressional baseball game, an annual benefit game to raise funds for a summer camp for kids. The sponsor, a Washington, D.C., newspaper, sent out invitations to boxer Rocky Marciano, golfer Gene Sarazen, tennis champ Helen Jacobs, sprinter Art Bragg, baseball slugger Joe DiMaggio, and others. Helen was told that Eisenhower had personally put her name on the list. The invitation came May 29, and Mabel had answered the door. She singled out the small, expensive envelope and called Helen.

Helen didn't think she could get time off to go. But Mabel urged her to reconsider, said there were many reasons she should go, and offered to put together the required dossier. Helen phoned to tell Bob, who responded with indifference and hurt her feelings, implying that it was strange that she, a *former Olympian*, was getting such special attention.

Mabel, on the other end, headed for the basement to search through what she called "the old gladiator's stuff." The old Co-Eds typewriter sat on an oak desk, near the clothes washer and sink and a rope line of winter clothing awaiting its season. Never one to throw anything away, be it binding string from her morning paper or Christmas cards from friends and family, Helen had stacked boxes of newspaper and magazine clippings, photos, business and personal letters, autograph requests, trophies, awards, souvenirs, and scrapbooks. There were score books, score ledgers, promotional letters, bills, and advertisements for her Olympic Co-Eds basketball team, her bowling league records, her softball and golf tally sheets, the programs of baseball and football games she had attended, speeches she had drafted, and other memorabilia saved over the years.

In addition, Helen—the mistress of this domain—was a compulsive entrant of the Irish Sweepstakes and various other lotteries, like the long-running Publisher's Clearinghouse drawing. Always a soon-to-be-winner of contests and games of chance, she collected a multitude of offers that shuffled into her mailbox. Helen didn't pass up any chance to win a jackpot, an all-expenses-paid vacation, a condo in Key West, and so on. Proof of all of this was there, too.

Mabel was familiar with the corridors of this collection. She understood that this was Helen's own monument to herself, a testimony to the great spirit of her sports career. She, herself, had put some of the papers and things into boxes, arranged and built these stacks that seemed to reach, on average, about four feet high. She pulled the string of the naked light bulb that hung over the columns leaning against the back wall and went to work.

Much later, Mabel emerged victorious, having distilled from the dross the records that supported Helen's claim to fame. She had lived with Helen for over a decade and knew her way around their—or was it Helen's?—basement. She had found a résumé and clippings on Helen's most impressive athletic achievements to send to Eisenhower's press secretary. She also had selected photos she thought appropriate. Upstairs, where her order reigned, Mabel phoned Eastern Airlines for tickets. Helen would go to a White House luncheon, and R. Lee could turn green.

The *Evening Star*'s Howard Bailey via telegram wanted to know as soon as possible the time of Helen's arrival in Washington, D.C. He wanted to meet her at the airport and needed to know how many tickets to provide for the congressional baseball game on June 5. From her office, Helen called to accept all invitations. Having committed herself, the first order of business was to ask the powers that be at DMAAC to sprint through the proper red tape to obtain her travel release.

Of course, she ran into a bit of a sag. It seemed to Helen that Supervisor Guenther actually lacked enthusiasm for processing her leave of absence request. On the other hand, her pal, Colonel Burton (Guenther's supervisor), saw the promise in her venture as a semiofficial emissary when, just to be safe, she asked for his help. He approved her civilian travel at government expense and had Captain Harold Edwards, Colonel J. E. Morrison, and Colonel Thomas Finnie hastily apply their signatures to a document authorizing her for "access to classified material up to and including: ***SECRET*** for the period and purpose shown above under Items 8 and 10." Item eight licensed her to enter the Research and Liaison Office in Washington, D.C., for four days for the purpose (item ten) of orientation "on Technical Library activities . . . and to assist procedures for foreign geographic and aeronautical publications." The undeclared Korean war, begun June 25, 1950, was about to end (July 27, 1953). The United States was testing hydrogen bombs; Operation Bikini was the code name, and it was relevant to one of DMAAC's projects.[4] Helen's official mission was to acquire and return with related data, map literature, and other information pertinent to DMAAC's projects.

On May 25, Bailey sent Helen the admission card and details regarding her gratis hotel accommodations for June 5–7 at the Willard Hotel in Washington, D.C. Helen replied that she would arrive either by commercial or military aircraft and be in the nation's capital on government business connected with the Washington branch office. Around seven in the morning at St. Louis's Lambert Airport, she bought a $5,000 flight insurance policy from Fidelity and Casualty Company of New York and mailed it to her 225 Henquin Drive address, naming Mabel Robbe as beneficiary, and off she flew.

"What's Ike like?" a reporter later asked her. She liked Ike. She had voted for Ike. She thought he had a good sense of humor and the sort of direct candor and midwestern wit she expected. "The President is a gracious and interesting host," she said. "It was certainly an honor to be a guest with so many notable persons. . . . We also enjoyed a tour of the White House personally conducted by the President."[5] She was introduced as "Helen Stephens, Olympic champion sprinter, Fulton, Missouri," and the president reportedly said he had heard of Fulton and its Winston Churchill Memorial. Their chitchat centered mostly on sports. He asked Helen about her basketball team and its upcoming season. "Well, we played our final and last season this spring, beating a strong men's team 61 to 30. I think that's good enough to retire on," she grinned. Helen, afterward, collected autographs of visiting athletes and political figures. There was talk of telecasting the 1956 Olympics; twenty years had passed since the Olympics had first been filmed. Television, some said, hurt spectator sports. Reporters asked Helen to explain why American girls didn't measure up to the foreign competition. She had answers ready for them: "Girls' athletics . . . seldom received the specialized attention they needed. . . . coaches don't take enough interest. . . . Better organization and support from the schools and colleges would do a lot." She spoke the truth. Communist countries were making headway in sports. The Olympic results played out as obvious indicators that America's claim to superiority was doubtful.

Before the ball game began, Bailey announced Helen's presence at Griffith Stadium: "The Fulton Flash is here! Star cager, manager, and captain of the Olympic Co-Eds! Let's welcome Helen Stephens!" The crowd rose, giving a standing ovation. The Democrats won the game, three runs to the Republicans' two. It was reported that Senator Joseph R. McCarthy, a Democrat-turned-Republican from Wisconsin (1947–57), hit the hardest ball of the night.[6] McCarthy played political hardball, too. With help from FBI director J. Edgar Hoover, McCarthy's Permanent Subcommittee on Investigations overshadowed the House Committee on Un-American Activities and ruined the lives and careers of many Hollywood artists and sports celebrities alike. Among those under surveillance were fly-boy hero Charles Lindbergh, the Olympic committee's Avery Brundage, *and* Helen Stephens. Helen, however, claimed to know nothing about it.

Helen was promoted in September 1955 to chief librarian of the Technical Library of the Air Force's Aeronautical Chart and Information Center. The ACIC displayed her sports memorabilia when another appointment of sorts catapulted her into America's Athletic Hall of Fame. Mabel flew with Helen to Los Angeles for this ceremony, sponsored by the Helms Foundation. Helen was singled out as Missouri's most outstanding woman athlete of all time; other honored inductees were Babe Didrikson, Alice Coachman, Lillian Copeland, Dorothy Dodson, Frances Kaszubski, Dorothy Poynton Hill, and her old nemesis, Stella Walsh. When they returned to St. Louis, Helen appeared on *Federal Agencies*, a television show moderated by AAU chair Shirley Zeman and the ACIC's Mel Kramer, and she told all about it.

Dee Boeckmann came into town in October. Still associated with the American Red Cross and Army Special Services, she took a month's leave to visit her brother Ed, his wife Rose, and friends. She had spent five years in Japan, Singapore, Hong Kong, and other Far Eastern ports and continued to harp on women's athletic programs in these countries. When she got together with Helen, naturally, she talked about Olympic hopefuls, and she phoned news reporters to give her views: "Our girls' schools do not promote women's athletics enough. . . . There is no system of school competition extensive enough to develop our girls, such as exists in Europe, Japan, and Australia. If our girls haven't wakened to the importance of physical development perhaps it's because we haven't encouraged it."[7] Few other women had the nerve or the depth of knowledge to discuss this issue publicly.

At year's end, Helen took a leave of absence, again approved by the air force upper echelon, and flew to Chicago as Abe Saperstein's guest to appear on Jack Brickhouse's WGN television program, which was a *This Is Your Life*–type show for Abe. It included Helen, Jesse Owens, Satchel Paige, and others.[8] The program aired January 21, 1954, the same day that the United States launched its first atomic submarine, the USS *Nautilus*. In March, Puerto Rican nationalists shot five U.S. Congressmen on the House floor; April 22 brought McCarthy's Waterloo—the *Army v. McCarthy* hearings lasted into mid-June. Also that year, the Supreme Court unanimously banned racial segregation in public schools, in *Brown v. Board of Education of Topeka*, and demanded equality in the public educational system. This meant that physical education programs also would see improvements.

All this led Helen to become more politically active than she had ever been. She joined Dee in being a women's sports advocate. Helen threw herself into the middle of it in May, trying to effect needed changes by opposing the National Education Association's sidestep actions. The NEA's proposed solution to correct "certain abuses" in the schools was to underpin school sports programs with the tired, old, once-tried play days and sports days for girls. Helen never doubted that abuses (meaning, inequalities) existed; she had seen them, the segregated shipboard quarters for her teammates and segregated elementary and secondary schools in Fulton. Because she believed in the value of *competitive* sports, she added her voice to a "strong cry of protest . . . mounting against the NEA's policy commission." In Helen's opinion, the NEA's move was retrogressive, patronizing, and very much like the bad old days. The NEA's recommendation that competitive sports be eliminated in the lower grades of all schools and that high school sports activities be curtailed was, in her view, wrongheaded. As it turned out, such thinking rankled a majority of people. Metro Goldwyn Mayer director Roy Rowland said that the idea of substituting mass exercise for school athletics smacked of state dictatorship. He asserted that America's "wars and . . . civic, industrial and spiritual vitality are won on the ball diamonds, gridirons, basketball courts and tracks of the nation's schools."[9]

Jo Hindman, a freelance writer from California, asked Helen for her thoughts. She said, "On the surface, it appeared that NEA would weaken our nation by undermining the very moral fiber of our youth." She said she had won her first three titles in a regional competition, which was her first opportunity, wearing a pair of shoes and a warm-up suit loaned her by someone on the boys' track team. Not everyone would have done that, she said, "but I had faith in myself—all I wanted was a chance to prove myself."[10] Wanting a chance to compete is as natural as wanting a hamburger and a Coke after a game, she said. Most everyone, she said, chooses an

> "ideal" baseball player, football player or track star and tries to imitate his hero[;] and many of our stars started out this way. I did. I thought . . . Didrikson was wonderful when I was in my early teens—and still do! We must give our youth a well-balanced program and encourage them to take part. I believe most of your schools do, have and will continue despite the NEA policy. Sports are here to stay in our schools, the NEA not withstanding. In fact, it is my considered opinion and I know other sports authorities will agree that the school sports program should work in cooperation with the National Amateur Athletic Union and help develop interest in our youth, particularly the girls, in sports on the Olympic programs of the future. Our Olympic women's track and field teams have been weak because little or no encouragement was offered in schools where future stars may start development. Encouragement should be offered and facilities furnished to remedy this unfortunate situation.

She spoke of the value of competitive sports with considerable insight. Competition teaches young people how "to take it," she said, and though everyone doesn't become a sports champion,

> properly supervised sports programs can be of immense value to the young in building their . . . bodies into strong, healthy and vital young Americans with the well-balanced mental attitude and high moral characteristics so vitally needed today to fit them for life—in business, our Armed Forces and the challenge of this Atomic Age. I believe all young children should participate in a school program of athletics but not too strenuous for their age and growth, not forced by superiors for glory of school or club—but keeping the welfare and development of the child in mind at all times.

With conviction and clarity, Helen told what sports programs had meant to her. Among other things, she had learned how to get along in all kinds of circumstances, good or bad, learned not to be a quitter—to see things through to the bitter end, "just as you do not quit in a game because you may be losing or the score is against you and the going is rough and the effort does not seem worth while." As if confessing, she told of a strong desire to raise herself "head and shoulders, above the mob in sports," but most of all, though one might become a sports star "with many friends and well-wishers, prepare yourself mentally for the day when someone else takes your place and you are forgotten by the new generation. I believe this is where the coach and the gym teacher can play an important role. High school sports helped me to develop a strong body, mind and character." Helen had become a visible women's sports activist by January 1956. At the U.S. Olympian reunion in Chicago, she spoke of problems still facing women athletes. Past Olympics had produced a large group of *former* Olympians, and she hoped they would do something collectively. "Grandma Herring used to say I'd be riddled with arthritis in my middle years, if I kept at it. Even now, this kind of thinking is trying to impose itself on the present," she said.

Many people still believed that strenuous track and field events made women infertile. Helen's own 1936 relay team dispelled that idea. Harriet Bland (now Mrs. William Green) had given birth to a son after hanging up her track shoes. Annette Rogers (Mrs. Peter J. Kelly, a high school physical education teacher) had two sons and a daughter; Betty Robinson (Mrs. Richard S. Schwartz) had a son and daughter. Flat-chested and square-hipped, Helen alone had remained single. She said she didn't want children and was probably one of those women who couldn't have kids anyway.

During the reunion conference, Helen was appalled by the pessimism about the upcoming games in Melbourne and the sports politics of the Communists. It made her "old" Olympian blood boil. Frank Walsh, an influential West Coast promoter, said that Americans should reconcile themselves to the fact that Russia would win and keep on winning future games.[11] One editor claimed, "Officially, no country wins the Olympics; only individuals or teams receive awards . . . [but the] Soviets well know the propaganda value of beating our athletes in particular and the rest of the world's in general." Jess Gorkin ignited readers with a plea for help, alerting Americans to what he called a little-known fact: That even in sports, "Russia wants to conquer the world. Our athletes are not ready to give up Olympic supremacy to Russia. But they need money—for equipment and transportation, food, housing. Unlike Soviet athletes, ours get no government subsidy. They must appeal to the public . . . for funds."[12]

About $1 million was needed, plus sponsorships, according to the USOC. For the first time in history, the Olympics were to be televised worldwide. Contributions were to be sent to the USOC in care of the Biltmore Hotel, New York. The conferees were informed of how the U.S.S.R. did things. Russia's first-year athletes were trained in one of thirteen Institutes of Physical Culture and were paid $70 a month for twelve months, although they attended school only nine months a year; fourth-year athletes got $100 a month, room and board, and expenses. Athletes had class six days a week, spent twenty to twenty-four hours per week in class and twelve to eighteen hours on the field. Some athletes were culled from the institutes and others from the army and sports clubs and from factory and farm teams. The purpose of the institutes was to create Olympians and to develop coaches and instructors. One such institute had 79 teachers and 520 students—about 100 of them women, who were trained just like the men and got the same pay. And there was a large number of masculine-looking Russian women throwing the shot put, discus, and javelin.

Helen's position was reinforced when she heard about discus thrower Nina Bonomareva (the twenty-five-year-old mother of a two-year-old), who said it was ridiculous to think a mother couldn't be a successful Olympian. Many agreed, however, that the excessive musculature of the Soviet Union's nineteen-year-old javelin thrower Nadia Konyieeva was something American women would not want to emulate. A sports promoter and AAU official who had seen their program for himself said the Soviet women would be victorious; he reminded the conferees that in 1952 American men only barely edged out the Soviets. He and others, in Helen's view, held a misguided interpretation of Dee Boeckmann's perspective: "America's Olympic future looks dark, for this year as well as for 1960, unless we can erase the apathy of our women toward sports."[13]

Whose apathy was he talking about?

Avery Brundage (the new International Olympic Committee president) took the podium and projected the Soviet Union's international successes as "phenomenal and destined." The next speaker was bravely optimistic. Jesse Owens, now an officer of the Illinois Athletics Commission, operated an insurance agency and owned a drive-in clothes cleaning business. He offered encouragement. He said it was time to quit spreading gloom about America's chances.[14] While it was true the Soviets were setting new records, he said, the "Russians put their pants on one leg at a time, like we do, and they can get only so many men in each Olympic event. When that gun goes off, you're not trying to make the stop watch do any tricks. You're just trying to beat those other guys. . . . That's when we do our best . . . when the pressure is terrific. I have great faith in our coaches and coaching methods in colleges and high schools." Owens understood the value of competition. Helen was elated.

She discussed all this with Brundage as she sat at his banquet table. His wife, the former Elizabeth Dunlap, sat on one side and Helen and Mabel on the other. Brundage spoke of his own Olympic experience in Stockholm in 1912, in the pentathlon. He ranked sixth among seven contestants, and his events were those everyone seemed focused on. Records show "DNF" for his 1,500-meter event, meaning he did not finish the race, but his time for the 200 meters was 24.2 (not fast enough to touch Jim Thorpe's time), his discus and javelin distances were 24.72 and 42.85 meters, respectively, and his long jump measured 6.58 meters.

Brundage said that Jesse's point was well taken, athletes shouldn't feel defeated mentally. If they expected to win, they had to think positively and have confidence that they could win.

"And that's where coaching comes in," Helen offered.

No one had directly addressed what the media and everyone else was concerned about and euphemistically referred to as "the muscle molls" in track and field. The topic was spawned by Brundage, who posed a question to her.

By the mid-1950s, Brundage had the most power ever amassed by any American in the sports world. Helen had known him since 1936, of course, and corresponded with him over the years. In 1937, he had asked her to help Herbert Bocher, a prominent, 1920s German athlete-turned-journalist. Bocher was writing a book about Olympic champions, and Brundage had urged Helen to cooperate with him. Now, here Helen was, sitting beside him—the former president of the AAU (1928–33), president of the AOC/USOC (1929–53), vice president of the IOC (1945–52), and since 1952, in his highest Olympic role of all, the IOC president.

Bespectacled, balding, and, according to his foes, belligerent and bullheaded, Brundage was a man of astounding Olympic education and experience. As a child, he was abandoned by his father and reared by his aunt and uncle; he worked his way though the University of Illinois and managed the track team there, where he had become a star performer—winning an intercollegiate discus championship, playing basketball, and editing the school magazine. After finishing the engineering program in three years, he studied philosophy and literature during his fourth. In a few decades of effort, his Cook County construction company—in spite of the Depression—made this man of great determination into a millionaire.

Helen recalled his subtle conversation—hedging into an issue she had squarely faced (and he knew about) thirty years earlier. He began by saying "we've" always had a heck of a lot of challenges with each and every game. But, he said, he would be darned if he knew how to tackle that other one. She followed along, asking what one that was, and he blurted out, finally getting to the point: "Men-women! What do *you* think can be done, Helen?" She seized it: "Examine 'em!" Mrs. Brundage, who sat quietly by as her husband led Helen down the primrose path, gave a soft little laugh, feigning shock. Mrs. Brundage said she couldn't imagine the embarrassment that might cause!

Contrary to what they might think, Helen knew it was a problem one had to face. She knew the problems that *that* kind of thing created, especially for track women. She replied, "Doesn't matter! You can't ignore it." Ratcheting up her voice over the clatter, she told him, "You're the IOC! It's your ball game, your responsibility." In the long run, it was the only thing to do, she said, to control, if not curb, the controversy. Brundage seemed to not know how to reply, she said; he stirred his food with his knife and surveyed the crowd. But from their hotel room that night, watching television coverage of the event, Helen and Mabel saw Brundage, bigger than life, say that Helen Stephens thinks that all female athletes should be given physical exams before being allowed to compete in Olympic events.

"A lot of flack came my way because of that telecast," Helen said. "My position didn't win me any friends. In fact, I lost a few because of it." Brundage had the highest office that amateur athletics afforded, but he wouldn't stick his neck out for that one. Without nomination or vote, he virtually promoted Helen into the spotlight, putting her in a spokesperson position for all female athletes. He himself had skirted it and had used her as his buffer.

Helen's main concern at that time, however, was the failure of American track women—the business of training girls for Olympic competition. According to Helen, she really got going in early 1956 after reading an extensive screed of sports gloom and doom in her local paper. Helen told this story: She and Mabel and Puss-Diddle ("our old feline partial to the hum and heat of the refrigerator") were in the kitchen. Helen sat at the breakfast table with coffee in hand, flying through the Sunday news, reading much of what they had heard at the reunion. Helen read the paper aloud, "Americans might as well be reconciled to the fact of Russians going to win in Australia this time—and keep on winning in future games. . . . Soviets well know the propaganda value of beating our athletes in particular."[15] Mabel, just returned from church, had not yet finished her first cup of coffee when Helen went silent, thumbing through the seven-page feature. The report claimed with great detail that the Russians were making a huge effort to select and train athletes for the Olympics. As Helen read through it, she became more and more upset.

Mabel continued to read her favorite section, the travel pages, saying nothing. Helen rose to her feet and spread the papers on the table. According to Helen, the rattling disturbed the cat, who rose up onto her wiry paws and meowed. Puss-Diddle (sometimes "Pussy" for short) had shown up on their doorstep in 1947, got herself adopted, and according to Helen, from day one assumed the role of arbitrator.

And while Helen's irritation may have bothered their cat, nothing ruffled Mabel. Every hair stayed in place, whether at work, at church, at home, or at play. In that regard, Mabel was just like Helen's mother. Both were always neat as a pin, their nylon hose without snags, and seams always in straight lines. Perfumed and powdered, she would appear in a crisp linen or cotton dress that was starched and pressed as though laundered by a professional. Lavender- or rose-scented, she always presented an outward appearance that reflected a steel continence. She remained calm before a gathering storm. Mabel watched Helen working up a dark cloud.

Helen read on, aloud, spotting-in what she thought important. It was everything they had heard in Chicago. The pet, now up and underfoot, let out another, louder "meow." "Are you going to read the *entire* article, Helen?" Mabel interrupted. "Puss wants to know." Mabel moved some of the paper aside to uncover the plate holding her toast. Helen proceeded, a twinge of misplaced glee in her voice: "Girls trained just like men." She waved in Mabel's face a photo of Nina Bonomareva heaving the discus and then skimmed a companion story titled "The Future? It's Up to Our Girls." Helen said, "Walsh again . . . as told to Jim Scott." She paused. Silence. Exasperated sighs. Again she read to Mabel," Dark. Dark in 1960 unless America erases its apathy toward women in sports." Then she roared, "They've given up without even tryin'. Damn!"

Helen said that when Mabel rose from the table, she took Helen's cup, put it in the sink, and quietly raised a challenge. "Well, what can be done? What do you think can be done about it, Helen?" Of course, Helen had to do something. She rang up Harriet Bland, now settled in Webster Groves, Missouri. Harriet hadn't read Sunday's news, but she rifled through the pages while Helen talked. Harriet told her it was too late for 1956. But relentless Helen persuaded her to get a group together and to try to put some Olympic fever into some coaches and Phys-Ed teachers. Harriet agreed that they needed to start immediately for 1960. She agreed to call a P.E. teacher she knew, Shirley Theodore, and Helen would call Wanda Wejzgrowicz, an Olympic hopeful she knew who was a member of the St. Louis Polish Falcons track and field team.

By March 11, 1956, the four women had aroused interest in women's track and field in the St. Louis area. They elicited the help of coaches Henry Schemmer of University City, Fred Moseley of Maplewood-Richmond Heights High, and George Beltz of Webster Groves. The *St. Louis Globe* carried the news: "Former Olympic Woman Star to Set Up Clinics."[16] Track clinic organizers fostered "several entries for the 1960 Olympics," with two clinics taking place at Maplewood-Richmond High School on March 24 and 31. They set up train- ing-teams by region, with weekday evenings for extra training. At the outset of fieldwork, each instructor gave informative talks in a classroom. Helen told how athletes achieved a berth on the Olympic team and showed the film of herself and Harriet in the 1936 Olympic relay.

The women got the Ozark AAU to cosponsor; they planned a track meet and fund-raiser for June. In three months' time, they uncovered new Olympic tal- ent. Helen and Harriet knew it was a long shot for 1956, but their odds would be better by 1960.

The old competitive spirit between Helen and Harriet rekindled when the relay teams were named after both Olympic coaches. The Helen Stephens Team—Shelly Miller, Rosemary Cooper, Marge Lane, and Jacqueline Mueller— took first place in the relay, beating the Harriet Bland Team. Helen's protégée, Shelly, of St. Francis de Sales High School, took division honors, winning the 50-yard (in 6.5) and the 75-yard (in 9.4) competitions. Helen's student Marjorie Lane won the standing broad jump, and her discus protégée, Dorothy Clayton, of Decatur, Illinois, won the discus throw. Harriet kidded Helen about also taking first place in media attention. Reporters still found Helen the more newsworthy of the two Olympians. Harriet said she didn't mind, since she was retired from athletics and more interested in raising her family.

In the 1956 Melbourne Olympics, Betty Cuthbert became the second Australian in a row to take the gold for the 100-meter race; she was the second woman to tie Helen's 1936 world record. It was beginning to seem as though women had reached their peak speed for this event, set at 11.5 by the Fulton Flash twenty years earlier. The Americans won one gold (high jumper Mildred McDaniel), a silver (long jumper Willye White), and a bronze (relayers Mae Faggs, Margaret Matthews, Isabelle Daniels, and Wilma Rudolph).

A year later, the four women organized clinics again. Harriet and Helen continued to rouse girl athletes from their apathy, as the press put it. Focused on the 1960 Olympics, Helen was pictured in the foreground with student Ellie Wolf.[17] Helen was proceeding like a career athlete—in mind and spirit. After her own Olympic experience, she had maintained high visibility in various sports arenas—in basketball, softball, bowling, and now coaching, though without pay. She kept close watch on most athletic events—for men and for women—near and far. She lived and talked sports to members of her Midwest Olympic chapter and to friends, relatives, and anyone at all interested.

She and Mabel attended Chicago's Pan-American Games in August 1959, getting into the thick of things once again.[18] Dee Boeckmann was officiating in the opening day parade and invited her to attend the fund-raiser reception for former Olympians and to be in the parade, along with Harriet, Betty Robinson, and Annette Rogers. Dee wanted all members of her 1936 relay team to host some of the ceremonies. Betty agreed, but Harriet and Annette couldn't make it. Helen had ex officio responsibility as the chapter secretary and, as such, kept up correspondence between the midwestern members. Helen loved being part of the Pan-American ceremonies. The three charter representatives of the Midwest Chapter of the American Division of the IOC—Dee, Betty, and Helen—marched arm-in-arm on the field. Situated in Chicago, the Midwest Chapter, of course, was well represented. Shirley Theodore and her husband (a coach) drove up from St. Louis. Helen's friend and former Co-Ed teammate Fern "Simmie" Simmons (now Mrs. Fern Wilson) was there also. Newcomer athlete and friend Wanda Wejzgrowicz won a medal in the discus. At the national competitions in Washington in 1956, Wanda broke the women's indoor record for the shot put, but her distance did not win in 1956. Helen was glad that Wanda had placed in these games, thus making her public bid for the 1960 Olympics. Helen did everything she could to help get her there. She had coached Wanda for several years via the St. Louis clinics.

Now Helen felt purposeful and rejuvenated. She had new stories to tell, and she seemed happy once again. Four years of track clinics helped as she passed her forty-year marker in 1958. With the 1960 Olympics before her, as well as clinics, bowling, and a new basketball season, her spirits rose. The gardener of the house, the gardener of her life, Mabel, busily planted bulbs—tulip, daffodil, gladiolus—bringing color into their spacious yard. Helen began accepting the fact of being forty. On Columbus Day, 1959, her career adjustments seemed complete. She and Mabel drove to New Bloomfield in high spirits, bringing tulip bulbs to Mrs. Stephens. An early frost was expected, according to *The Farmer's Almanac*; old-timers said that woolly worms were a sign of a long, hard winter coming. Because canning chores took precedent over planting flowers, Mrs. Stephens delayed putting in the bulbs. She planted them in early November on a damp and cold day. Within a few weeks, R. Lee called his sister with the news that their mother had pneumonia and was in Callaway Hospital. Helen expected to visit her on the weekend, but a few days later, he called again to tell her that their mother had died.

Bertie Mae Stephens died November 18, 1959. She had seen her family doctor, R. Lee said, to be treated for what she thought was a bad, unshakeable chest cold. The doctor diagnosed influenza and prescribed some medication, which didn't seem to help. So Bertie saw another doctor in Fulton, who prescribed a another medication, but she didn't tell the second doctor she had taken medicine prescribed by her family physician. Helen speculated that what may have caused her death was the interaction of the drugs and her prolonged respiratory ailment, which had not been treated soon enough or properly. Ultimately, Helen blamed herself. It was the tulip bulbs. If only she hadn't given her mother the bulbs. Now, her mother was gone, and the loss was tinged with a sense of guilt. Remembering her mother, Helen said, "I think of her every day. Not a day goes by that I don't."

But the old gladiator carried on. Fortunately, "Coach" Mabel was there to support her through this loss and the professional loss that came in the summer of 1960, the loss of her world sprint record. At least, she said, it was taken by an American. Wilma Rudolph set a new 100-meter time at 11.0 *wind-aided* seconds; she was now the fastest woman in the world. Rudolph also won the 200 meters (24.0) and took a third gold in the 400-meter relay with Martha Hudson, Lucinda Williams, and Barbara Jones. America's Earlene Brown won the bronze in the shot put. Helen bemoaned the victories by Soviet women— Iryna Press won the 80-meter hurdles, and her sister, Tamara Press, set a new Olympic shot put record at 56 feet 10 inches—and the loss of her own shot put hope, Wanda Wejzgrowicz, who didn't even make the top six.

In 1961, at the Sherman Recreation Center sports clinic and at Francis Field, Helen and Harriet carried on their volunteer work, giving encouragement and pointers to aspiring Olympic track and field athletes. Helen encouraged Wanda to focus on the discus. Wanda's 129-foot discus tosses came within 5 inches of Helen's mark set twenty-five years earlier. Helen's sprinter Dolores Hall broke her own Ozark AAU record of 11.5 in the 100-yard dash.[19]

Stella, too, was coaching, in Cleveland. Olympic officials were adding two events for women: the 400- and 800-meter individual races. Maybe, Helen hoped, one of her girls would beat one of Stella's girls. Both Olympians knew that American girls needed coaches, facilities, and programs. In a few, short years, there would be another Olympic opportunity and time enough for Helen to get her girls ready for it. She felt she had to carry on, sensing with certainty that her mother would have supported her in this.

12

The Old Gladiator

In the self-centered world of men, it is sometimes difficult to
understand the intensity of a woman's commitment to athletics.
—Jake McCarthy, *St. Louis Post-Dispatch,* March 17, 1978

*H*elen Stephens didn't march on Washington with civil rights activists. She wasn't a women's libber, never burned her bras, never joined the National Organization for Women. But when women's basketball rules were eliminated, she cheered. In the decade known by some as the "sexy sixties," she subscribed to *Playboy* magazine and read the gossipy *National Inquirer.* From time to time, stories about masculine women appeared in these publications, as did articles on performance enhancing drugs that some athletes used. These things intrigued her.

Miss (not *Ms*) Stephens supported the IOC's Midwest Chapter of Olympians. As one of sixty-seven members, having helped with its founding, she enjoyed the rights and privileges of lifetime membership. Mrs. Betty Robinson Schwartz was elected chapter vice president in 1959–60 and president in 1962. The 1936 Olympic swimmer Dorothy Schiller served as secretary-treasurer. Helen emerged as a kind of self-appointed correspondent.

On the twenty-fifth anniversary of her graduation from William Woods College, Helen was asked by alumnae secretary Myldred Fox Fairchild to chair the class reunion festivities. With Mabel Robbe by her side, Helen renewed friendships with an apparent all-is-forgiven attitude toward the school that had withdrawn its scholarship from her. Here, old "Steve" looked for particular faces, past friends. She saw among them half of the Bluhm twins (Evelyn, now

Mrs. Basenger; and Eleanor, now Mrs. Tuepker). Helen scanned the 1936 year-book and pointed to one particular entry: "I never want to see another ship!"—a hint at her catastrophic history with her former girlfriend known only as "Someone," or "S." Absent also was "K," bright, witty, full of zeal K, the last Woodsie who got close to Helen's heart, distinguishing herself, according to the yearbook, by adaptability and by artistic and musical talents. Helen still had (somewhere in her basement) every letter and card K had sent to her. From the mouths of her college ivy-chain sisters, she heard that K was in a rocky marriage.

The next year, Helen was asked to address the graduating class of 1963. Armed with fifteen pages of handwritten notes, she tossed out statistics on women in the workforce, using facts on back pay from a sex-discrimination case in the Lake Mills School District in Wisconsin, where female coaches received considerably less pay than male coaches. The source of information came from her old Co-Eds buddy Helen Onson, now living in Rhinelander, Wisconsin.

Helen put the alumnae reunions on her calendar each following year, feeling more kindly toward her alumnae sisters and alma mater. "Robbe" was accepted as Helen's special friend and treated as cordially as the husbands of married alumnae. There, on these occasions, Helen's outgoing and witty personality won new friends and cemented old allegiances, but she was unable to discover K's whereabouts and renew their acquaintance.

On June 10, 1963, three and a half years after her mother's death, Helen's father died. Frank Stephens had complained for a week about chest pains but did not see a doctor. Neighbors found him near a shed; apparently, he was sharpening the blades of a push mower, having mowed the grass around the farmhouse. He was seventy-four. A few years later, Helen and her brother sold the farm, and shortly thereafter, she honored her parents' memory by establishing the Bertie Mae and Frank E. Stephens Endowment Scholarship at William Woods College. Her reunion activity and financial support led the board of William Woods to honor Helen with its Alumna of Distinction Award in 1965. Within a few years, she set up another fund, the Helen Stephens Athletic Scholarship Award for Excellence in Physical Education (established in 1967) and bestowed this award in person. Helen may have created this scholarship in part to help defray enrollment fees to this private all-girls school for her niece, who enrolled there that year. (Helen and Mabel attended the niece's graduation ceremony in 1971.)

In 1964, in St. Louis, ever-active Helen was a starter official at the Ozark AAU meet at Washington University and, with Mabel, rooted for the St. Louis Cardinals during the World Series there, and watched the Olympic games in Tokyo via Telstar. Also that year, Helen was the guest speaker at a track "letterman's" banquet in St. Louis. Here, she told boys *and* girls, coaches and parents, that sports benefited girls and boys alike and contributed to a healthy, wholesome outlook on life. She asked the audience, "What is sportsmanship?" And then answered her own question:

> We read about it in the newspapers. We read of famous athletes receiving recognition for it. But Webster defines it, thusly: Sportsmanship— conduct becoming to a sportsman and involving fair honest rivalry, courteous relations, and a graceful acceptance of results. Sportsman—one who in sports is fair and generous, one who in any connection has recourse to nothing illegitimate, a person who is a good loser and a graceful winner. Sportswoman—a female sportsman. So, as one of our favorite radio announcers used to say: If you must be a sport, be a good one.[1]

Now posturing as an "Old Olympic Gladiator," she affirmed that, win or lose, all athletes must be good sports. Attuned to the times, she used a feminist term, *sportswoman,* and encouraged everyone, girls and boys, black and white, to pursue their interests. Olympians in Germany, Russia, and China excel athletically, she said, but "I don't think this country wants to be second to any nation in the field. All of us may not be an Olympic champion, but *all* of us can be good sports, good athletes, good Americans, and that's what's most important after all."

The year was professionally renewing for Helen. Editors from the two major St. Louis newspapers chose her as one of the all-time greats and put her picture in the Gallery of Great St. Louis Athletes. A nationwide Associated Press poll of sportswriters and broadcasters put her in the number ten spot of outstanding women athletes of the first half of the century. They put Babe Didrikson in first place, and then Helen Wills Moody, Stella Walsh, Fanny Blankers-Koen, Gertrude Ederle, Suzanne Lenglin, Alice Marble, Ann Curtis, and Sonja Henie.

This acclaim, plus the women's movement, probably nudged the Missouri Sports Hall of Fame electors to admit her as the first woman into its ranks. Helen's induction in October brought its number of Hall of Famers to twenty.[2] She took the occasion to acknowledge and recognize other deserving women athletes. Man after man had entered this and other halls of fame—a fact that Helen did not overlook. Missouri's sports hall, inaugurated in 1951 at the state fair, chose baseballer Carl Hubbel as its first and only inductee that year. Two were honored the next year—baseball great Casey Stengel and basketball coach Forrest "Phog" Allen. Twelve years after its founding, this hall finally opened its doors to Missouri's only Olympian (a double gold Olympian, at that) and tenth-ranking female athlete in the nation. Also inducted that year were footballer Jim Conzelman and golfer Horton Smith.

Now, as an insider, Helen lobbied for other worthy Missouri women. A second woman, golfer Opal Hill (who gave Didrikson some nervous moments on the green) was admitted a few years later. In 1969, a third, trapshooter Leah Hall Frank, was honored. Each year, Helen had nominated her Olympic coach Dee Boeckmann and relay teammate Harriet Bland. Helen's charm and persistent, subtle prodding were long required before these women were given this distinction. The Old Gladiator advanced untold phone calls, letters of inquiry, and support before successfully winning their nominations. As the news of her awards and honors became known, Helen was drawn more and more onto speakers' platforms.

In 1966, Helen and Mabel sold their little house of seventeen years in Ferguson and bought a larger home in Florissant, Missouri, on Thackery Court, a pink brick, three-bedroom ranch with an attached garage and a patio extending the length of the house. The finished half of its basement offered a recreation room with a wet bar and abundant shelves to hold Helen's immense memorabilia collection and her many trophies; the other half was used for laundry appliances and storage. Its colossal backyard promised ample space for Helen's new pastime, spawned by Mabel's devotion to it: gladiolus. Always the competitor, Helen leaped headlong into the Gladiolus Society, entering annual flower shows with minimum effort on her part, heroic care on Mabel's, and won blue ribbons. And she joined the St. Louis Women's Bowling Association and became president of, and a key player on, the Powder Puff League's Wishing Well team. Once Mabel retired, the two became tourists, flying to New York to see the world's fair and visiting friends and relatives in various states.

The year 1968 was a surreal nightmare: two assassinations—Martin Luther King's in Memphis, and presidential candidate Bobby Kennedy's in Los Angeles; riots in Chicago (Brundage's hometown) at the Democratic convention; a bank robbery and kidnapping of Patty Hearst by the Palestinian Symbionese Liberation Army. In Ohio, the National Guard shot and killed free speech demonstrators (four students) at Kent State University who were protesting America's role in an undeclared war in Vietnam; and there were Black Power race riots in Watts, Newark, Detroit, and in Helen's town, St. Louis—all very dismaying.

Even so, at the podium, she stayed focused on athletics. She was elated about the Equal Rights Amendment and sports advances for women: Enriqueta Basilio becoming the first woman to light the Olympic flame, and America's Madeline Manning winning the 800-meter race in Mexico City. The proposed Title IX education reform would insure that no one in America could be excluded from participating in, or denied the benefits of, educational programs, which included intercollegiate athletics. Prohibiting discrimination against women on the basis of their sex, Helen felt, was one change long overdue.

Title IX mandated that school athletic programs supported by federal funds were to be equally accessible to male and female students alike. But, as in the days when she set foot on the track, strong resistance was marshaled against sharing gym facilities and programs. Female sportswriters were ridiculed when they interviewed men in the sacrosanct male domain of the locker room; opponents spoke of unreasonable costs and the supposed harm to a girl's health and, as in Helen's day, they impugned the femininity of sports-minded girls. One youthful basketball player (the daughter of a sports columnist Helen knew) asserted it was both wrong and unfair to call girl athletes names such as "dyke." She (Jody McCarthy) pointed out that the coordination and grace so necessary in sports had always been feminine attributes.[3] Many voices sang long litanies of the difficulties facing schools. St. Louis University's athletic director, Dick McDonald, publicly disagreed with the law, appalled by the havoc that he thought would be brought about by governmental policy changes.[4]

In February 1971, Helen had her say as the principal speaker at a banquet for the Ozark AAU, where young girls were honored for athletic achievements. Track official Bob Hyten asked her to tell how attitudes toward female athletes had changed. Comparing circumstances, then and now, she started off by using the humor she seemed born with and made her point with jokes and one-liners. She claimed she was so poor she couldn't afford shoes, so "I just laced up my feet. Russians have become real track stars . . . because the starters use real bullets in their starting guns. Bowling is the second most popular indoor sport. Some of those German girls in the 1936 Olympics were so flat chested that nurses in the compound gave them first aid everyday—two band aids."[5] To disarm with lighthearted appeal was her method; to stimulate thought about worrisome financial matters, Soviet dominance, and the gender issue. At age fifty-two, Helen still played her own cards close to her chest. She meant to convey, to those who would listen, the message that a sense of humor had carried her a long way and could do the same for them. Undoubtedly, she admired the courage behind the June 1969 Stonewall Rebellion, but she herself would not "foolheartedly come out of the closet" and risk losing her job.

By then, she had amassed twenty-five years as a civil servant and was thinking about retiring. Dee Boeckmann had retired to Sun City, Arizona, and told Helen that she had contributed her Olympic sweater for a 1977 auction to support tennis ace Billy Jean King's All-Star Salute to Women's Sports. It brought $200. Dee now enjoyed adult education courses and tennis, and their former thick-or-thin friend Gertrude Webb, also retired in Sun City, was likewise active in sports. Retiree Charles Guenther (whose favorite sport was baseball) sent Helen a note with a copy of the title poem of his new book, a line of which, "I'm handsome as a 100-meter runner," suggests that Helen had had a certain influence on her boss's psyche. A capstone to Guenther's literary career was his Pulitzer Prize–nominated book.[6] "I'd heard that he, in his retirement years, was writing away like mad," Helen said. She was the interim supervisor at work only until, she told Dee, "a 'new man' could be found for the job. . . . I knew I wasn't going to get this position, because I was a woman." Though she did not get Guenther's position, her employee suggestions were used in operations, and her other contributions were recognized. In April 1973, she received the DMAAC Employee Award.

Helen was throwing "strikes" in the Women's International Bowling Congress (WIBC), giving credit to her instructor (national winner Myrtle Schulte) for starting off her bowling career on the right foot. In Texas, Illinois, Louisiana, and elsewhere, Mabel traveled with Helen to bowling tournaments. In November 1974, in St. Louis, Helen bowled her highest game thus far (269) at Bowl-Ero, throwing eight strikes, with spares in the first and seventh frames, and taking home another trophy. She had a 157 average going into the 559 series (of three games).[7] (She achieved membership in the St. Louis 600 Club in 1970, participated annually in the WIBC championships throughout the United States, and entered the St. Louis Bowling Hall of Fame in 1977.)

Devotedly, Helen watched the 1972 Olympics in Munich on television and followed these events in sports magazines and newspapers. She felt dismay when, once again, America's team failed to distinguish itself: East Germany got the gold in the 1,600-meter relay (3:23.0); Monika Zehrt set a record for the 400-meter race (51.08); Renate Stecher won the 100 meters (10.07) and 200 meters (22.4); and Annelie Ehrhardt won the 100-meter hurdles (12.59). West Germany took the 4 x 100-meter relay (42.81); Hildegard Felck won the 800-meter race (1:58.6). The U.S.S.R.'s Ludmila Bragina won the 1,500 meters (4:01.2). European women still reigned in track and field, setting records in the longer footraces (400, 800, and 1,500 meters) as well as in shorter "standards."

Helen was stupefied, not just because Americans were less winning than their foreign counterparts, but because she was captured, mind, body, and soul, as political horrors literally invaded the Olympic village. Israeli athletes were taken hostage by terrorists demanding the release of two hundred Palestinian prisoners from Israeli jails, and a policeman, a wrestling coach, and thirteen others were killed before it ended. The media showed the bloodbath over and over and over. Bietar, a Zionist youth organization, demanded intervention by the United Nations. Rhodesia was "forced to leave the games by black athletes. . . . the stage was set for an escalation of political warfare at the Games."[8] Discus thrower Olga Fikotova-Connolly distributed antiwar, antiviolence petitions. Unlike the luckless Stella Walsh, Connolly was blessed with dual citizenship; she had won the gold for Czechoslovakia in 1956 but had won nothing while representing the United States in 1960 and 1968, and this year, she was America's flag bearer. The games were suspended for thirty-four hours, and a memorial service was held in the stadium. IOC president Brundage opposed stopping the games. Terrorists, he said, should not be allowed to abort the international cooperation and goodwill that the Olympics represent. The games must go on, he said. Later that year, Brundage resigned from his office.

On June 14, 1975, the National Track and Field Hall of Fame, in Charleston, West Virginia, admitted Helen into its fold. Mabel, in travel-agent mode, readied them for the trip. They invited niece Cindy to go along. In Helen's opinion, Cindy had natural athletic talent; she was interested in sports and would enjoy meeting sports figures. The NTFHF's twenty-six charter inductees included Brundage, Daniel Ferris, Brutus Hamilton, Glenn Cunningham, Jesse Owens, and two lone women, Babe Didrikson and Wilma Rudolph. Many charter members attended this second awards program, which enshrined thirteen champions, among them Helen, Ralph Metcalfe (now an Illinois state representative), the incomparable Jim Thorpe (inducted posthumously), the stellar Alice Coachman Davis, and the lofty and, of late, married Stella Walsh-Olson.

The event had its moments, said Helen. As she and Mabel and Cindy headed for their hotel room, she spotted Stella in the hallway, arm-in-arm with her driver and a girlfriend. This was the first time since 1936 that the two Olympians had seen each other. Said Helen, "Stella was just a few yards in front of me. The *only* time in history! I yelled her name, 'STEL-LA! Stella WALSH!' and startled her, hoping to scare the hell out of her. Of course, I succeeded. She jumped as if the devil himself had poked her, flinching and swirling around."[9] Stella replied with something like, "I'd know that voice anywhere." As fate would have it, Helen learned that the room assigned to Stella and her companions was next to Helen and Mabel's room. What they heard through thin hotel walls, Helen said, finally put two-and-two together for her.

In addition to the induction banquet, the Hall of Fame Classic attracted some of America's promising runners and various dignitaries, the new Mrs. Avery Brundage and the NTFHF founder and president, Dr. Donald Cohen, among them. Avery Brundage had died a month earlier; his first wife had died in 1971. In 1973, at the age of eighty-five, he married an East German princess whom he had met at the Munich games. Helen understood why old men wed young women, but why did the royal pedigreed, thirty-seven-year-young Princess Mariann Reuss marry him? "Title *and* money?" Mabel guessed. The princess presented her husband's portrait for the new Olympic House. Brundage's successor, Irish patrician Michael Morris Lord Killanin said Brundage had been "an idealist to whom Olympism was a religion."[10] Killanin supported athletes' need for financial help if it did not jeopardize their amateur status, and he believed, he said, that the Olympics were "Olympian." The new facility was supported by $1.7 million in state funds. With plans for permanence and growth, Director Jack Rose said he was certain that the history these athletes had made would never be forgotten. Grace and Richard Thorpe expressed hope that their father's 1912 gold medals, won in the decathlon and the pentathlon (the year and event that Brundage placed sixth in) would be returned to the family. Of the country's racial disharmony, Owens stated that athletics transcend all prejudice. Various inductees announced what they would contribute to the hall's exhibition. Burt Moore, now of Ames, Iowa, introduced Helen to the audience; she donated her Olympic track sweater and a pair of track shoes.

Two months later, Helen nominated Dee Boeckmann in her August letter to selection committee member Nell Jackson, setting the stage for Betty Robinson's entry. She wrote to Betty: "Why don't you fly down to Charleston . . . for the induction ceremonies June 11–12. . . . I'm sure Dee would be tickled to death to see you there. It might help your chances of getting into the Hall next year, too!" Dee and Mae Faggs Starr (1952 gold and 1956 bronze medalist) were inducted in 1976. Helen was glad that hurdler Forrest Towns (1936 gold medalist) was enshrined and was happy to introduce Dee for induction. Betty gained entry in 1977. Due mostly to Helen's initiative, Olympic women began networking.

Helen and Mabel attended NTFHF functions regularly. As Mabel's health began to fail, Helen decided it was time to retire from the Defense Mapping Agency. In the summer of 1976, about a week after retiring, Helen flew to the Montreal games, alone. Mabel was not feeling well enough to make the trip. Her doctor told her to quit cigarettes, and Mabel was trying to, but without much luck, especially since Helen smoked, too.

Helen explained to sportswriters that she was going to Montreal alone; Mabel would watch the event on television with an eye out for her, since National Educational Television had the broadcast rights to the film of the 1936 Olympics and would show footage of the women's 4 x 100-meter relay. (Parts of Riefenstahl's *Olympiad* had aired during the Olympic years 1968, 1972, and 1976.) Showings of the film triggered new autograph and photo requests from Helen's fans, students, and journalists; some sent questionnaires and letters. Mabel helped when she could, by stamping and addressing envelopes and stuffing signature cards, notes, and letters. Helen answered letters personally and filed carbon copies. The following reply exemplifies her diligence:[11]

> Sorry I have not replied sooner to your inquiry of June 21st but I am in the process of winding down my career in the Govt. . . . I retire Friday, July 16. Also, there have been a lot of other distractions, interviews, stories, TV appearances, planning of trips, including one to Montreal shortly.
>
> I will try to quickly answer the questions posed in your letter. . . . I do not think Stella could quite bring herself to forgive me back in our "heyday" for beating her in my first race at 50 meters in the Nat. AAU championships in St. Louis in 1935 when I was a 17-year old high school senior and she was the reigning Olympic champion. She would never meet me in any races until the 1936 Olympics where I again "showed her my heels" in the 100 meters. I went on to defeat her two more times in the

100 meters and also the 200 meters in post-Olympic meets in Germany. So . . . I raced Stella 5 times and beat her 5 times! Naturally, I suppose it was a blow to her pride as she was a fierce competitor. Last year at our National Track and Field Hall of Fame inductions (we were both put into the Hall at the same time) in Charleston . . . Walsh told me and was quoted in the papers as saying, "Helen ran the legs off me!" But she also told me that it was for her "like a business back in our running days" but now she could relax about all of it. Stella was one of the great woman runners of all time! . . .

Women's participation in the Olympics has come a long way since 1936 or in the last 40 years! Many more women on a world-wide basis are taking part, competition for the elusive gold is keener, the general acceptance by the general public of women taking part in sports has improved 100%, and, of course, many more events and several sports have been added to the Olympic program. I am glad to see some of the old taboos have fallen by the wayside, such as, people are no longer shocked to see the girls perform in scanty costumes that permit them more freedom of movement, and just because a girl sets a new record in running, throwing, jumping or whatnot . . . she is not immediately jumped upon in the press as "probably shaving twice a day" or even more insulting, disgusting, and derogatory reading insinuations that she is "probably a man!" Yes, women have come a long way, Baby! And perhaps we still have a ways to go yet!!

Using the vernacular of the day, she was telling it like it was, then and now, and dealing straight on with the issue of masculine women.

Her ardor for women's Olympic track events was boosted when she saw Germany's Annegret Richter fly in the 100-meter race in 11.08. Very few women had beaten Helen's "historic" speed. Though disappointed over the outcome in the 200-, 400-, 800-, and 1,500-meter races, all taken by Europeans, Helen eyed these events with keen interest. She had hoped that the American sprinters would win the 4 x 100-meter relay. But that race, too, was lost to European athletes.

Several nostalgically joyful events happened in 1976, her year of retirement. The Kingdom of Callaway County Chamber of Commerce honored her with its prized recognition award. Mabel felt well enough to attend the occasion. Helen also was surprised when notified by phone that she was a 1977 candidate for the U.S. Track and Field Hall of Fame. She bellowed, "I'm already in it!" This *national* Hall of Fame was based in Angola, Indiana, but its ceremonies were to be held in the nation's capital. She and Annette Rogers Kelly were nominees. Yes, she said, she'd be honored to be honored again. So, on October 14, Helen and Mabel went to Washington for the induction ceremony.

Helen and Stella Walsh-Olson had stayed in touch with each other by mail. Stella's Christmas card to Helen one year shows a cartoon of herself in spiked shoes and running suit, pulling Santa's sleigh lettered with Polish season's greetings: *Wesotych Swiat*. Cordiality prevailed, but Helen's letter to Stella shows that she was still rubbing it in. Noting the postal date of Stella's card, she wrote:

it was some 42 years ago on March 22, 1935 that I first met you in a 50 meter dash here in St. Louis at the Arena. . . . how ironic?

Thanks very much for the Christmas card and greetings.

No, I did not go out to Charleston, West Va. for the ground breaking ceremony last November; however, Dee Boeckmann, our 1936 Olympic coach . . . who I was instrumental in getting into the Hall of Fame last June, was on hand and she tells me they had a great week-end on that occasion. If you get the *Olympian* magazine, you will see an article on the event in the February 1977 issue.

I suppose you noted in the sports pages last week that nine more had been selected for the Hall of Fame this year but only one woman—Betty Robinson-Schwartz of Chicago area (Northbrook, Ill.). I was particularly pleased at her selection because I strongly recommended her as my nominee for honors last year along with Annette Rogers-Kelly of Chicago area also (Niles, Ill.). But as you know, women are lucky to get more than one recognized at one time. I am sure that you will remember these athletes. Hopefully, I will be on hand to see Betty receive her honors this year if they hold the affair in June but just hope it is not on June 18 as that is the date that my niece, Cindy, whom you met in Charleston, is to be married.

Sally Hale, a longtime friend of mine from St. Louis and now of California who will be going soon to Washington, DC to serve on the President's Council on Physical Fitness, is writing a book on Olympic women of the 1920–30 era. She asked me for information on myself and others that I could recommend to her that were outstanding during that period. She is also going to include some swimmers that she knows personally. I recommended Dee Boeckmann, Betty Robinson, Annette Rogers, and *you*. She has my material; both Dee and Betty have forwarded information; I must check with Annette again; she called me last week from Calif. and asked me to write you (as I know you) and ask that you send some information on your athletic career. She promises to return all materials and pictures. (I think she hopes to have the book approved for distribution in schools and colleges by the President's Council and if this is obtained, it would be good publicity for those of us from the past.)

So, Stella, would you consider getting some information together on your past athletic achievements, records, etc. . . ? She would like a picture or so of your choosing (an athletic type). Any comments from you will be appreciated too, especially how you got started, your view of today's athletes and records as opposed to those of the past, and just about anything you would like to say. (I have passed along some favorable comments on you as one of the greatest track & field woman athletes of all time!) If you could get this information to her sometime in April it would be fine as she plans to stop in St. Louis in early May and get together with me on some of it as she is not too familiar with track & field herself. So, please drop me a line and let me know if you will be able to do this, Stella. Send materials to: Ms. Sally Hale, Box 433, Moraga, California 94556.

Formerly an Olympic Co-Ed, single, and living in St. Louis in the 1940s, Mrs. Sally Ray Clark Hale was then known as LaVeryn Hempen. She was good at tennis, golf, badminton, field hockey, softball, and the art of exaggeration, in Helen's assessment. Sally was yet another healthy athletic ghost from Helen's past. Sally asked Helen's help with an article, as the letter explains; she also wanted Helen's help in setting up her American Sports Camp for Girls, in Pacific Grove, California. Helen offered people contacts; she wrote to Stella, Betty, and others to promote the concern. She also signed a contract to give a clinic at Asilomar, with accommodations at Cypress Shores, but it fell through. A lot of long distance phone calls and cards from various exotic places came at Helen like a hurricane, all at once, en masse, and then, silence. In time, Helen discerned that many things Sally-LaVeryn said were going to happen wouldn't. Helen declined other ventures that she sallied forth and put less stock in what Betty all along had called "little LaVeryn's big ideas."

In reviewing Stella's career, Helen saw that she was still pursuing her glory on and off the track. Helen's files show that Stella had more than once publicly stated she *probably* would retire from track. Being barred from the games in 1948 provoked her first retirement announcement. At the end of the war, Poland's newly resettled borders had made her an athlete without a country. The USOC had dangled Stella's fate in its hands for awhile and then rejected her. Some said the American officials harbored a grudge against her for competing for Poland in previous games—for withdrawing her naturalization application in 1932 when Polish officials asked her to represent her native land.[12] A 1943 shoplifting charge against Stella may also have damaged her case. When American officials pointedly pronounced the Clevelandite resident ineligible, Stella only momentarily speculated on retirement.

In her psuedo swan song of 1949, the thirty-eight-year-old with twenty years of amateur mud on her racing shoes praised Helen as the only American who ever gave her serious competition. "I've beaten Koen [the 1948 Olympic sensation] every time I have run against her—about four times," she said.[13] What Stella didn't say was that she lost every race she ran against Helen, and that Helen's Olympic record remained unbroken at that time.

At the 1949 National Women's Senior AAU meet in Odessa, Texas, Stella again had vowed to quit track *once* she had taken three victories there. She proposed to duplicate the successes of the first year of her career. But she failed to do it. Nell Jackson of Tuskegee overtook Stella in the 200-meter dash with a time of 24.2. Stella leaped third in the broad jump and lobbed behind in fifth place in the 100 meters. Not what she had hoped. So then, Stella said she planned on writing a book about her world travels and her sixty-four world and national titles picked up along the way. She also expressed interest in a career in teaching physical education.

Again, Walsh's last race was announced, this time to be in Washington in January 1956, at the women's national indoor meet. Prior to the event, forty-five-year-old Stella flew to Las Vegas to marry Harry Olson, thirty-three, of Northridge, California. Marriage to an American citizen secured her citizenship and Olympic eligibility, but it made no difference.[14] On August 25, she couldn't run fast enough in her 220-meter trial heat; Lucinda Williams of Tennessee State took it from her, in 25.5. Asked if she would compete in any of the other Olympic events, she replied, "Why should I?"[15] But she didn't quit. Though Stella was eligible for the U.S. Olympic squad, that same month at American University, she finished third in a 200-meter heat and failed to make the team. Tearfully, the aging sprinter cried, "This is the end."

Twelve years after Helen entered Missouri's Hall of Fame, she finally succeeded in getting Dee Boeckmann through its door in 1978. She nominated Harriet Bland in 1983. Harriet had suffered a stroke a few years earlier and arrived in a wheelchair. Throughout the 1970s, the Old Gladiator successfully brought other women the acclaim that male counterparts were enjoying. In 1977, Annette Rogers Kelly thanked Helen for nominating her for the U.S. Track and Field Hall of Fame. Backing Helen's nomination of Annette was their mutual friend, Betty Robinson Schwartz.

Correspondence with friends "of old" brought news of various deaths. Helen's "In Orbit" file (obituaries she clipped or those friends sent) was growing fat. She competed in the Women's International Bowling Congress tournament in Houston and at one in Illinois, where she learned of Mary Schierbaum's death. The six-foot-three nurse and star player for the reorganized Helen Stephens Olympic Co-Eds basketball team died in June 1974. Three years later, Helen clipped the obituary of longtime USOC official (and nemesis) Dan Ferris.

Other news from Helen's basketball past came from Issy Payne, also known as Mrs. Emory "Ham" Olive. Issy wrote from Wisconsin, where, she said, she had heard from Co-Ed Helen Onson. Issy told Helen that she and Ham had celebrated their fiftieth wedding anniversary on March 15. How well Helen remembered. March was the month, but the year was 1940, when she, Issy, and Ham had parted ways.

Celeste Roehrig Morris, a college friend, sent her congratulations on the Hall of Fame inductions. Congratulations also came from Charles Guenther and his sister Hilda. Guenther asked if it was true that Helen would be coaching track for her alma mater. It was true. After the excitement of her fortieth class reunion died down, Helen had written a long and purposeful letter to college president Randall Cutlip, thanking him for the safe return of her medals exhibited on campus, for the Centennial Fellow Award that the college had bestowed on her, and for her membership in the President's Society. The latter resulted from her steady flow of monetary contributions to the college. She thanked him for all those honors and mentioned that, at the Florissant Valley Junior College AAU track meet, she had talked with Westminster's athletic director, Ken Morris, who was also an organizer of the Missouri Hall of Fame. And, she said, she had met a William Woods student, Lane Buder, a runner in the 200-meter race, who had asked her if she coached at William Woods!

Full of subtle name-dropping, Helen impressed Cutlip with the news that she had talked with *former* Westminster coach Burt Moore—a recent inductee of the Ames Bowling Hall of Fame. And at the request of "the Colonel" (a former boss), she had served as the starter for her past employer's annual one-and-a-half-mile run. *And* in West Virginia, at the request of the NTFHF's Don Cohen, she had welcomed the Olympian Betty Robinson into that Hall of Fame. She had learned recently, she went on, that she needed six quarters of employment to flesh-out her Social Security benefits. After this grand buildup, she asked whether he had any idea of how she could be of additional service to William Woods?

Cutlip replied promptly: Would she accept a 1977 fall-term coaching position and help develop a track program at William Woods? It would be part-time work, but it could be fun. Yes, she would, she replied. And so she became Assistant Coach Stephens. She had been a clerk, a library assistant, a librarian, and an acting section supervisor. Now, she would be a coach. She accepted Cutlip's offer and readied herself for a part-time coaching job with her alma mater.

Helen also joined the National Association of Retired Federal Employees (NARFE) and attended its meetings for social reasons and for the watch-dog aspects of the organization. In the summer of 1977, Mabel's illness was diagnosed as emphysema. Both women had begun smoking cigarettes in their late teens; neither one wanted to quit. Mabel's doctor said that for Mabel's sake, Helen should quit smoking, or at least not do it around Mabel. But that was not possible. Instead, Helen bought a large electric gadget called a "smoke-eater," put it on a TV tray in the kitchen, and installed overhead fans in the kitchen and in the TV room.

That fall, Helen coached six students in track and field. Within the year, the school had a track and field team of sixteen. No doubt, Helen's reputation as a double gold Olympian was a recruitment draw. Initially, Helen worked three to four days each week, lining up events and establishing and monitoring workout schedules at Westminster College's Priest Field, coordinating it all with head coaches Ken Morris and Dick Alt. Nothing had changed in Fulton in that respect; men were in charge of their "sister school" programs; track and field girls scheduled field facilities when the boys weren't using them. They held practices and events accordingly.

Helen glad-handed the maintenance man into opening buildings and gates and accessing vehicles. She adopted a record-keeping system, handled the book work for entry fees, did correspondence, wrote publicity releases, and called coaching aide Carl Meinke when her girls needed prescription care for injuries. William Woods was getting its money's worth. Helen was getting what she needed, staying active in athletics and tabbing up her Social Security benefits. In April, the sixty-year-old assistant coach bore an injury. She canceled a trip to Miami, where she had expected to compete in a national women's bowling tournament. She sent regrets to Coach Morris regarding a campus party hosted by one of her star sprinters, Lane Buder. She wrote, "With two front teeth knocked out, I resemble Leon Spinks [1978 world heavyweight boxing champ] and can only bite soup!" She also reported the results of her first year on the coaching team.

From March 22 to May 27, 1978, Helen's girls engaged in a dozen events and traveled to Springfield, St. Louis, Warrensburg (twice), Florissant, Joplin, Jefferson City, and Fayetteville, Missouri; Emporia and Wichita, Kansas; and Knoxville, Tennessee. Nine of Coach Stephens' girls qualified for the regional championships. At Florissant Valley Community College in St. Louis, they made a strong showing: seven first places in thirteen events. Ella Cole won the shot put, Jennifer Mueller the long jump, Lane Buder the 440-yard dash, Jane Alves the 3,000-meter race, and Johanna Faust the high jump and the 880-yard race. William Woods College also won the one-mile relay.[16] They won their divisional race, hosted by Washington University, beating Lincoln University's much larger team. Other runners to watch, according to Coach Stephens, were Mary Underbrink, a distance runner, and Bridget Siefner, a hurdler. Formidable in its first year of competition, Helen's team excelled in the long distance races that were forbidden to women athletes years earlier. In the Association of Intercollegiate Athletics Region 6 meet held at Emporia State University, May 12–13, her team placed twelfth among forty-two small colleges. One of Helen's girls won second place in the 3,000-meter race, clocking in at 10:56.74. According to Coach Sallie Beard, the meet sponsored by the Missouri Association of Intercollegiate Athletics for Women was "the biggest meet ever!" William Woods took fifth place among eleven colleges, large and small.

Fulton's newspaper widely covered Johanna Faust's win—the first state championship recorded for a Fulton girl since Helen's victory forty-two years earlier. Faust clocked in at 2:17.6 in the 800 meters, helping win fifth place for the college, close behind four sizable state universities. "Records speak for themselves," Helen wrote in her report to Coach Morris, but it was Helen who was the prime motivator in getting the school's first track program off on the right foot.

Mabel was proud of Coach Helen. She understood the Old Gladiator, whose heart beat wildly as she tabulated the score book and watched her girls compete. On the field, now in her senior years, she showed her girls how to win. She threw the javelin ten feet farther than any of her girls. They challenged her in footraces, but Helen declined. "These girls would love to be able to tell their grandkids some day that they beat the Fulton Flash," she chuckled. By then, she had given up sprinting in favor of jogging.

In August 1978, Westminster's board of regents announced its decision to go coeducational, and the brother-sister relationship between the two private schools fell into a state of limbo. William Woods initiated a lawsuit to change the two schools' previous arrangement of shared facilities, coordinated school calendars, fund-raising, and cross-enrollment. The lawsuit sought to restrict Westminster from admitting more than forty women in its first year of coeducation, fifty in its second, and fifty-five in its third, with no restrictions thereafter. Sports facilities and coaching assignments were reshuffled; Head Coach Ken Morris resigned. The athletic program and Helen's status seemed "iffy." William Woods' only other woman coach (tennis, basketball, and volleyball), Sue Neal, had at times worked with Helen and her track girls, but both women lost out for the head coaching position to Richard Theibert. Though Helen and Sue had coached winning teams, they took a backseat to the men at a women's college, even at the end of a decade touting equal rights for women. As far as Helen was concerned, the women's movement didn't exist in Fulton.

That fall before classes resumed, Helen and Mabel took a vacation to New Orleans. When they got back, stacks of mail besieged Helen—from autograph hounds and from people making requests for speaking appearances and interviews. An editor of a new magazine, *Women Coaches and Athletes*, wanted to feature Helen in a January 1979 issue. Helen replied in the affirmative to everyone.

In March, she flew to Omaha as a paid consultant for the Midwest Sex Desegregation Assistance Center conference. She spoke about her own experiences with sex discrimination in sports and in the workplace. She related that she had her first contact with discrimination when she was a child and realized that her father wanted a son to help with the farmwork. To gain his favor, she became a tomboy. She said that when she was five years old, "my brother came along and was really the apple of his eye."[17] She told of her one-room country school—only three or four girls ever attended at one time, and the rest of her classmates were boys, the oldest sixteen or seventeen—and of walking or running to school along with six or seven boys. At an early age, she said, she was a sex object

> in the eyes of the older boys. . . . my best defense [was] to be either a good offense or [make] a hasty retreat. . . . they came to respect me after first wanting no girls to play on their various team games, because I could outrun, out jump and out hit most of them. . . . about this time I became curious as to why the black men who came to work in the fields were not allowed to eat with the family or to sit in the living room. The answer? It is not done; it isn't proper; they are not good enough, etc. Some black children attended no school. I asked, Why? Still no answer. I really wanted to get away from the farm and my mother said education was the road. My father said that I should go to work in the shoe factory in Fulton when I finished grade school. But, I had a dream. At the age of 8, I had gone to sleep one day on a hillside . . . [where I] dreamed . . . I was the fastest runner in the world and thousands cheered as I went up to receive a trophy. . . . at that time I had never heard of the Olympics and women were not permitted on the program in track and field until 1928.

She spoke of another kind of discrimination, too, of sharing boarding rooms with other farm girls in high school and doing light housekeeping for room and board:

> Those of us from the country were no doubt discriminated against by the town kids but there were so many of us we didn't care (or know any better). Of course, we didn't have store-bought clothes, drive a big car, or go to the local drug store for lunch (we brown bagged it). But we learned to compete in the classroom for that was where the action was. And of course our sports program for girls was limited to volleyball, softball, and soccer. No scheduled competition and no gym. The boys had track and football.

She spoke of her Olympic years, when women had only six track events while men had nineteen. She talked about *women's work* at Curlee Clothiers: being a payroll clerk, a pattern dispenser, a cloth layer, and pattern layer. "I quit," she said, "because there was no future. . . . women were not considered for men's jobs. . . . when single girls got married, they were supposed to quit."[18]

She spoke of government work in the General Accounting Office's mapping agency. She told of her war years as a forklift operator, a spray painter, and a manager of an airplane-parts station. She said that racial and sexual discrimination prevailed, though supervisors denied it. The 1970s supposedly ended discrimination. Most people got a fair shake, but back then, she said, if she had been a man, she would have gone much higher in government service.

> I was sitting in a job as chief of our library but denied promotion to it. I had fought a running battle for five years with U.S. Civil Service Commission before obtaining rating as a Librarian, GS-11 in 1966 and was a bit tired of the old ball game. I had my 30-plus years and decided I still had time to do something else. . . . I believe Virginia Slims cigarettes had an ad directed to women, "You've come a long way, Baby!" [Maybe so, but] I don't think women are home free yet. . . . I think one of the greatest enemies of women are women. Women should hang together or be hanged separately, as one historical person once said. Women have won the right to enter gyms . . . have their own sports teams, but there's still a keep-em-in-the-kitchen mentality involved in handing out athletic scholarships.

Women had no opportunities in distances longer than 1,500 meters in the Olympics, she said. She continued:

> The question of spending the same amount of money for the men's and women's sports in the colleges and universities is not settled. Women reporters have gained access to the men's locker room of pro sports teams, to serve in the armed forces, to serve as sports broadcasters and umpires, and to even compete with the men. We read often of some girl bringing a lawsuit to force some school to allow her to compete on the boy's wrestling, baseball, basketball team, etc. . . . I've been on the athletic scene over 40 years and I have yet to see a girl or woman who could sustain a competitive status with a conditioned male in any sport. Career women often devastate everyone in their path to the top. Men are intimidated by this and only the strong, successful man who is completely sure of himself can handle this. Even though there is a whole new ball game out in the business world, secretly the most successful woman still likes to be treated like a woman!

Being polite, lighthearted, and humorous in the Defense Mapping Aerospace Agency had worked for her to some extent. Much of the joking was done in harmless fun, she said. Her own doggerel and cartoon sketches showed regard for current ethnic and sexist issues.

When her Olympic tree died (planted forty-three years earlier on the William Woods campus), various people asked for a piece of it to use for plaques, clocks, and novelty items. A specialist in forest diseases and insects working for the Missouri Department of Conservation attempted to propagate healthy seedlings from it.[19] The planting of this and other Olympians' "Hitler Oaks" drew attention once again to the Fulton Flash.[20]

At age sixty-one, her daybook was as full as it ever was. It seemed every aspect of her career was worthy of an article. In October 1979, Helen flew to Dallas where the USOC gave tributes to her and twenty-four other Olympians. In November, she joined local sportswriter June Wuest Becht to discuss "Women in the Early Olympics" and "The Olympics: Past and Present."[21] She planned to spend Christmas with her brother, who had retired on lakeside property near a golf course in Hot Springs, Arkansas. Helen, too, was thinking about retiring from coaching. Bob advised Helen and Mabel to move to Hot Springs Village, to settle back, go fishing, and enjoy the good life, as he envisioned it.

She wondered if this would be how an old athletic gladiator like herself would finally end up, calling it quits on a golf course, before finally flying into orbit.

13

Show-Me Senior Jock

We've gotten the attention of the Russians . . . but I doubt it will have
any effect on the politics of the leaders or their designs on other
countries anymore than our participation or non-participation would
have deterred Hitler in his desire for world domination.

—Helen Stephens, unpublished notes, 1980

On March 17, 1980, on the opening day of the amateur women's national indoor track championships in Columbia, Missouri, Helen spoke of women's
track and field history. The Amateur Intercollegiate Athletics for Women
(AIAW) president, Christine Grant, introduced Helen, noting the relationship
between Title IX and the phenomenal growth in women's intercollegiate programs: 970 U.S. institutions and over 100,000 athletes in the 1970s. The new
Hearnes Sports Center was proof of the progress Grant spoke of, for forty-five
years earlier, almost to the day, Helen acknowledged, things were a lot different. It was men's turf when she competed in her first indoor championship.
Now, the opportunities and conditions at Hearnes were a far cry from her
experience at the old Brewer Field House. Athletics (i.e., track and field) had
advanced tremendously, she said, due to "interest and participation by our
young women today. With many new methods of training and conditioning,
coaching techniques, and a better knowledge of the human body itself, the
future of this popular sport appears very bright."[1]

Changes had occurred for American women, but forces still worked against
feminine athleticism. The pain and anguish she had known still stalked women
who dared to be amateur or professional athletes. True, the opportunity for an
Olympic experience for American hopefuls, for either girls *or* boys, was dim

that year. It seemed that in each decade of her life, in some part of the globe, warfare had pushed its way into the Olympic arena. When the Soviet Union invaded Afghanistan, President Carter proposed to boycott Moscow's games. Reporters noted that in ancient Greece rulers stopped wars to accommodate the games; warring states observed a truce during Olympiads because they considered those periods of time to be sacred.[2] Jesse Owens, who was seriously ill that year, said he would rather not see the games canceled, but he supported the president's decision and hoped others would, too.

One reporter seeking Helen's opinion on the boycott made the mistake of referring to her as a "former Olympian." "Former Olympian?" she challenged. "Once Olympian, always Olympian." Helen recalled the boycott of 1936, when one vote swung the decision to send a team to Berlin. She said that any boycott or postponement would hurt individual athletes but that allegiance to one's country should come first.[3] "I don't blame him [President Carter] for using every trump in the deck. . . . if we pull out I hope enough other countries pull out [so] that it won't be worthwhile for the Russians. . . . Saudi Arabia had the guts to pull out first. If we pull out alone, we could look worse than anything," she said.

She said that the Russians' words of peace and goodwill were hollow and that Russia should not have been allowed in the games in the first place, that Roosevelt did not publicly support a boycott (in 1936) but worked behind the scenes and had divorced himself from it. Finally, she said, "We were aware that nazi Germany was up to something but they hadn't proven themselves like Russia has. . . . [The Soviets] can't be trusted, they're evil." Helen told how Olympians had received cables urging them to boycott: "Young and tender in those days [they] had no idea until they reached Germany or the Olympics had ended that there was talk of a boycott." In the February 1980 photo taken for a newspaper story, Helen was leaning against her bicycle. This year, "a boycott might be a valid idea," she said. She wrote to President Carter and enclosed articles that showed her support:

> As a winner of two gold medals on the USA team . . . my opinion has been requested by members of the media since the announcement of your call for a boycott. . . . I wish to inform you that I support your stand although I have great sympathy for our athletes and have been active in various fund raising for support of our U.S. Olympic team. I am still hopeful that there still may be a way out for all concerned. . . . I've been interviewed and quoted by a number of major newspapers in the country, been on several TV programs, and made my feelings known to Mr. Bob Paul of the U.S. Olympic Committee. I have great sympathy for the athletes, having been one under similar conditions in 1936. I have been and will continue to engage in various fund raising events to support the U.S.

Olympic program. I believe in the Olympic Games. But, as a citizen of the U.S., I believe I must bow to the will of the President and of the Congress. The IOC should never have awarded the Games to the USSR in the first place."[4]

She also wrote that same month to her congressman who had sponsored the legislation to increase funding for the Olympics, Richard Gephardt. His office wrote back on March 24 and then phoned to ask for her endorsement of a bill allowing taxpayers to designate a dollar of their federal income tax to the U.S. Olympic Fund. Gephardt wrote that if 30 percent of those filing federal taxes earmarked money for the fund, some $28 million a year would be generated for the Olympic committee's use. The USOC's 1976–80 budget was $52 million; this was his answer to the decreased funds that the boycott threatened. Before Helen replied to Gephardt, she wrote to C. Robert Paul Jr., the USOC director of communications, asking for the USOC's official stance on this bill and guidance in answering Gephardt's question on how the funds should be used. Helen ended her letter with a somber note, for Jesse Owens had died that month of lung cancer at age sixty-five: "I am very saddened to hear of the death of Jesse Owens. The media kept me busy yesterday commenting on him (copies of my remarks will be forwarded later) and I was on a local (KSD) radio program last evening that paid tribute to him." After hearing from Paul, she wrote to Gephardt on April 14, regarding his check-off method on federal tax forms:

> I support it fully and am sure it has the support of the USOC as a means of fund raising in their behalf during these troubled times for the Olympic Games.
>
> It is my opinion and understanding that any funds . . . generated by your legislation would probably be used mainly for the support of the "grass roots" sports federations (such as AAU) for the youth of the country . . . [for] purchase of much needed sports equipment, in support of their several sports medicine programs . . . to improve or better equip physical plants of their two sports training centers at both Colorado Springs and at Squaw Valley. Such funds would not be used for general operating expenses by the USOC.
>
> I hope my comments may be of some help to you, and thanks for writing to me. . . . I think the Olympic experience is one of the highlights in the life of anyone privileged to represent their country in the Olympic Games.

Other thoughts (below) came later, roughed out in penmanship, clarifying her stance on this sad turn of events. Tormented by a reporter's careless assessment—of being a *former* Olympian, she relented—her facile mind had not yet formed the image of herself as a *pioneer* Olympian. She was distressed by the boycott. At first, she thought it was only a threat to get the Soviet Union's attention, that in the absence of an outright confrontation with the Soviets, the United States would send a team:

> As a citizen, a former federal employee, a member of the women's Marine Corps in World War II, and as a former Olympic gold medal winner, I publicly stated my support of the President and the Congress on their stand while expressing great sympathy for our young athletes and the plight of the USOC. There has been much said by everyone on all sides and the question still remains up in the air.
>
> I am beginning to question if the boycott idea may have been conceived in haste as a weapon rather than an act that is of benefit to us and affects us adversely. I think we have gotten the attention of the Russians on the matter, but I don't think it will have any effect on the politics of the leaders or their designs on other countries anymore than our participation or non-participation would have deterred Hitler in his desire for world domination. I hate to see this internal controversy in the country over this question. It may have been better to let our athletes go, take part, and win.

National security was an overriding factor in the president's decision. Bill Lucas called from Washington, D.C., pressing Helen for more comments.[5] Echoing Owens's "American first, Olympian second," she backed Carter's boycott, confident that Olympic ideals would survive, that Americans would gain a sense of unity and national purpose as a result of it. She wrote: "If the major nations, or 50 as reported, decide to boycott, the IOC should cancel the games, or they would be a sham!"

Helen had chatted with Owens about five months before he died, in November 1979, during the USOC fund-raiser in Dallas. Owens spoke of being short-winded then and about smoking his first cigarette prior to the 1936 Olympics. Helen told him she began smoking cigarettes in college, that girls were allowed to smoke in their dorms. She wouldn't give them up, either. Helen told Neal Russo of the *St. Louis Post-Dispatch* that Owens began smoking about the same time she had. "He was Mr. Track and Field, Mr. Sports, Mr. Olympics. . . . a great help to the Olympic Committee."[6] She told of their races against each other, in Chicago, Louisville, Toledo, Columbus, and Muskegon; with an 8-yard handicap in the 100-yard dash at Wrigley Field, Owens had edged her out in a photo-finish win: "Jesse's arm flew up at the finish line, banged and broke my little finger. Even in our prime, I doubt if Jesse and I could qualify for some of the races today. But he was such a superb athlete. . . . Lord knows how much better his times might have been had he had the advantages of better training and coaching techniques . . . not to mention using starting blocks." She recalled the election year when hotheaded Father Coughlin and Alf Landon opposed Franklin Roosevelt, when Hitler favored Charles Lindbergh for president, and when one guy had written that if Jesse were white, he could have been president. "We've lost a national hero," Helen said.

Before Christmas 1980, shocking news broke on the front page of the sports section—another America-First patriot, world champion, and Olympic medalist was dead. Stella Walsh died in Cleveland on December 4, killed by a robber's crossfire. She had been shopping in a discount store, buying ribbons to hold the medals for the Polish women's basketball team scheduled to play at Kent State University. She died in the parking lot, a tragic death, a friend said. Her life had been tragic, filled with shame and ridicule.[7] Because Stella did not die from a natural cause, an autopsy was required, revealing what some people had suspected for years. The city editor of the *Cleveland Plain Dealer* said his sources claimed "she had the sex organs of a male, some say she had both, others swear she was a woman. We've been reluctant to say what she is before we know what she is."

Stella's death forced a dilemma upon the sports world. Gender testing under the auspices of the USOC only had emerged thirteen years earlier when the buccal smear test was used to resolve "perplexing vagaries." However, physicians had been troubled for many years when anyone, adult or newborn, presented ambiguous genitalia. Gender *assignments* were not fully understood by members of the general medical community, the press, or society at large.

Casimir Bielen defended his friend, saying that Stella had been examined hundreds of times and was declared eligible to compete in women's events. He told newsmen that she grew up several blocks from where he lived, that neighborhood children knew about her physical deformities and ridiculed her. Bielen said it was commonly known that Stella was born a hermaphrodite, that she wasn't 100 percent female. He said she was a low-key, self-conscious woman, acclaimed throughout the world, who had difficulty making a living. "She lived with her bedridden mother . . . in a modest house . . . on Social Security. I got her a job. She started at $10,000. She told me that was the highest she'd ever been paid. . . . she was happy that she earned it for something she loved to do."

Ten years after Stanislawa Walasiewicz arrived in the United States, she had equaled the American women's 50-yard dash record but had failed to qualify for the 1928 United States Olympic team. After she won the women's all-around high-scoring title at an international meet, Polish officials invited her to represent Poland, and the Polish consulate in New York employed her. She then began a winning streak, amazing everyone. In 1932, she won the 100-meter race in 11.9 seconds and an Olympic gold medal for her native land. When Helen still hoped to compete against her in the 1948 Olympics, Stella tried to shift her sports allegiance to the country of her residence and sought U.S. citizenship. However, the authorities decided that the Polish-born Clevelandite was ineligible to represent America. Her athletic career seemed over in 1955, but by marrying an American, she automatically gained American citizenship. By the unlikely age of forty-three, she had thirty years of experience in amateur competitions and over a thousand awards and had won her fifth U.S. pentathlon. Though marriage assured her eligibility for the Olympics, the American Polish Flyer finished third in a 200-meter race and failed to qualify for the games in Melbourne. From her new home in Southern California, she organized women's track meets and was instrumental in developing women's track in the 1950s.[8] It was there that Stella discovered an amazing shot put and discus thrower. Her protégée, Earlene "Ma" Brown (a housewife, mother, and beautician), became America's first Olympic shot put medalist, winning the bronze in 1960.

Stella's petty shoplifting escapades in her youth seemed inconsequential compared to the scandal that erupted over her gender. One of Stella's rivals, now a coach, saw this as an opportunity to strip Stella of all her titles, awards, and medals; thus, one of her own girls could gain an elevated status.

Helen composed her thoughts in a letter, made a list of those to send it to, and photocopied newspaper accounts that told the story. Dee Boeckmann and Burton Moore were on her list, as were C. Robert Paul, Annette Rogers Kelly, Betty Robinson Schwartz, June Becht, Fern Wilson, Helen Onson, Dot Herbst, Sue Neal, Julie Ward, R. O. Leary, and Hermon Phillips. Dee lamented that Stella had not died of old age—it was terrible that she had been shot.[9] She wrote that Switzerland's Olympic committee was looking into Stella's life: "If they revoked her medals, then Annette Rogers would get a medal. I saw Gertrude [Webb], had a long talk, she said she got a long letter from you." It seems Gertrude and Dee were again closing ranks against a problem that could harm women athletes.

Helen told the IOC representative to Greece, Jack Rose, of an experience she once had with Stella, a revelation she hadn't shared with newsmen:

> It will be of interest to learn of the final decision if a "cover-up" is not in effect . . . .
>
> Personally, I never did think that "all was kosher" with Stella; however, I assumed that she probably had had a sex operation of some kind along the way to qualify her as a female for purposes of athletic competition. This *theory* received a *jolt* in *1975* when both of us were in Charleston, West Va., for induction in the Hall of Fame. As you know, Stella came down from Cleveland with two girls—one who drove her down. Stella & company occupied a room adjacent to mine and there was much hollering and tossing about of the furniture for several days/nights. Stella seemed to be drinking quite a bit. The little blonde Sicilian girl who drove Stella down, came to me on several occasions and informed me that al-

though she had known Stella for only about a week, she agreed to drive Stella and her girl friend to Charleston. She said I wouldn't believe what was going on in that room! That Stella was having *sex* with the other girl day & night, and Stella had male sex organs. She said she told them she was going to the police and Stella knocked her down for her trouble & told her if she did that then Stella would "get her" when they returned to Cleveland.

I do know that you or Don Cohen had a session with this group at midnight & sent them packing back to Cleveland; however, I don't know if the sex thing even came up at that time. But, I recall you were pretty disgusted at the turn of events.

Promoting herself a bit, Helen also asked Rose if he wanted a slice of her Olympic tree to exhibit in his Hall of Fame and filled him in on her current activities: "I will be into my 4th and last year with the college track program at William Woods—March, April, May will be busy months. I am also into our 2nd Mo. Senior Olympics Program on a state & local level. Our St. Louis program will be May 25–28 & I may defend my gold medals in the dashes."

Helen also sent a note and clippings to the Helms Athletic Foundation Hall of Fame director, Bill Schroeder, who considered Stella one of the great women athletes of all time. With the recent turn of events, Helen suggested that he might be forced to reconsider his evaluation. "In any case," she wrote, "Stella may have been packing 'a little something extra' that gave her a bit of an edge in athletic competition." Schroeder was deeply sorrowed by the tragedy that befell Stella, whom he had come to know when she lived in Southern California. "What a pity," he wrote. "We always liked Stella so much. She was a good person . . . constantly thoughtful of others. . . . It is really too bad, and I know that you will agree that the sex matter should [never] have been brought up. . . . Nevertheless, I guess that this is the way of life." As the months passed, the controversy died down, and the IOC's revocation of Stella's status seemed unlikely.

Helen gave more talks and sent hundreds of signatures to autograph seekers all over the world. She served on committees and competed in an impressive number of track and field events offered to women of her age in the newly established Senior Olympics. William Woods College acknowledged Helen's faithful (annual) financial contributions and affirmed the prestige she had earned in her lifetime by bestowing upon her an honorary doctorate during alumnae weekend, in May 1980. Alumnae secretary Myldred Fairchild enthused that "most well-known William Woodsies fade away after a few years—but not our Helen!"

Helen won medals and set records in her age bracket in the Senior Olympics, preferring competitions rather than the boardroom activity that most "former" Olympians were satisfied doing. Former boss Charles Guenther commented on her achievements in a May 1981 letter, dubbing her "the

Florissant Flash." He wrote, "What a great performance—or should I say performances! Congratulations, a half dozen times! My uncle John called my attention to your front-page photo with Stan Musial, and I've been following your performances since then, this past week: your shot put (and photo), the discus and running broad jump, and the three dashes. You certainly keep, as you've always kept, the stuff of champions."

Though officially retired, Guenther taught English at the University of Missouri-St. Louis and wrote and translated poetry. He, too, had gained national attention—winning the 1979 Witter Bynner Poetry Translation Award of the Poetry Society of America, the James Joyce Award, the Missouri Library Association Award, the Order of Merit from the Italian Republic, and the French-American Bicentennial Medal—and he had received an honorary doctorate from Southern Illinois University, Edwardsville. That May, as National Association of Retired Federal Employees (NARFE) members, he and Helen lobbied Congressman Volkmer and Senators Danforth and Eagleton, opposing the elimination of the twice-yearly cost of living adjustments for federal service retirees. They urged support of President Reagan's Economic Recovery Tax Act, the all-savers bill; and they opposed the Tax Equity and Fiscal Responsibility Act that withheld 10 percent interest and dividend income.

By June 1981, the Florissant Flash was in the thick of Ageless Olympics activity sponsored by Delmar Gardens West, St. Louis. She carried the torch in the opening ceremony for the Explorer Olympics held at the Country Day School. Reporters said that she ran in the best Olympic tradition, covering half the track's distance effortlessly.[10]

A "Faces in the Crowd" item on the Flash appeared in a 1982 issue of *Sports Illustrated*. Shortly thereafter, her alma mater gave her its Award of Merit trophy and set up an exhibit of her sports memorabilia in its administration building. In July, Helen participated in the Hazelwood Parent-Teacher Association Council's scholarship run-or-walk event.[11] And she solicited businesses for attendance prizes for the sixty-third Women's International Bowling Congress championship and the sixteenth national 600 Bowling Club tournaments, in which she competed that April and June.

In 1984, the Soviet Union retaliated with its own Olympic boycott. The focal point for the IOC's Medical Commission was twelve athletes who tested positive for drug use: stimulants, sedatives, steroids, and hormones. Though vindicated and lauded beyond her dreams, by then, Helen felt compelled to mollify the "related" Stella Walsh issue—which still hovered like a dark specter over women athletes. "I trust I didn't shock 'em at the conclusion of my little skit," she wrote Myldred Fairchild about the talk she gave on alumnae weekend:

> I noted the President [Bartholomy] beat a hasty exit! It is all part of
> Olympic history now—books & articles are being & have been written

plus it has been discussed on TV—recently on the "David Letterman Late Night Show," but I have not discussed my own feelings about the false Polish charges back in '36 & subsequent exposure of Stella Walsh's sexual identity plus one of the gals(?) from the German '36 Olympics surfaced in Holland as a man (married & the father of 2 children). . . . in those days Germany & Poland were willing to do anything to win & to avoid any suspicion of their own athletes; the Poles decided to speculate in the press that I might not be running with a full tank! It took me 44 years to fully understand what the ruckus was all about—upon Stella's death!

Incidentally, a number of those big Russian women, who were breaking records like crazy, dropped out of sight & were never heard from again upon the initiation of the sex tests for women in the Olympics & international competition. So, in a way, I may have made a big contribution to women's athletics by sparking the idea to bring one & all to heal & "examine 'em"!!

In 1982, Helen signed a contract offered by Herbert B. Leonard of Playboy Productions. She was to be paid $250 for an interview. He had similar contracts with Eleanor Holm, Marty Glickman, Marjorie Gestring, Mac Robinson, and a half dozen other athletes of 1936 Olympic vintage.[12] His assistant, Chris Sorge, asked if he could film her recollections about the 1936 games. But the famed Olympian sports filmmaker Bud Greenspan already had claimed that privilege. Greenspan had offered Helen a small honorarium to participate in an on-site film that would include her thoughts and remembrances about the 4 x 100-meter relay. Greenspan said Helen had written "some very nice comments about my book, *Play It Again, Bud.* . . . in particular the story concerning the dropped baton of the German women's relay team." Greenspan expected to finish his film in time for the fiftieth anniversary of those games.

Late in April 1984, Helen flew to Germany. Mabel took care of their cats, and their friends took care of Mabel. Helen stayed at the Bristol Hotel in Kempinski, compliments of Cappy Productions, and over dinner, she learned about the shoot and the subjects that might be addressed on film; for example, the 1983 story of the popularly accepted but doubtful episode of Hitler's snubbing of Jesse Owens that appeared in a black newspaper in St. Louis.[13]

During the shoot, Helen got reacquainted with Emmy Albus, Germany's lead-off relay runner. With cameras rolling, Helen walked down the track and paused, recalling her moment of high drama. "It happened right about here," she said, pointing out the exact spot where Emmy's teammate Ilse Doerffeldt dropped the baton in the last leg of the race. Afterward, Helen dined with IOC president Juan Antonio Samaranch, Berlin's mayor Eberhard Diepgen, Emmy Albus, and others. It was an event that seemed to bring full circle Helen's long career, the end of which, even now, did not seem to be in sight.

Greenspan's *America at the Olympics* aired in Los Angeles on the evening of July 4 (Channel 2), on the eve of the games. Reviewers felt it conveyed a sense of patriotism with a generous helping of nostalgia. It offered fairly predictable testimonials to the thrill of Olympic competition from those who emerged as champions.[14]

During the 1984 Missouri Sports Hall of Fame induction luncheon held in St. Louis, Helen visited with Dee Boeckmann. They had known each other for over forty years and had been members of the Midwest Chapter of Olympians since it was established. Helen had resigned from it, she said, when militant Black Power confrontations took place within the organization: "I have not been to a meeting in Chicago since 1968." Helen encouraged Dee to participate in the Senior Olympics, which she did. Dee competed in her age group in the softball toss and several other events.

During the national Senior Olympics, held in St. Louis in 1986, wearing entrant number 1198, Helen waited on the mark. At sixty-eight years of age, she was celebrating the fiftieth anniversary of her 100-meter Olympic victory. Her runner's tag in Berlin in 1936 had been number 1199, one digit higher than that assigned to her. Not to let the anniversary slip by uneventfully, Helen strove to make it something special "for nostalgic reasons." She broke the tape four-hundredths of a second faster than her previous (and the existing) Senior Olympic record for women between the ages of sixty-five and sixty-nine. Coming in at 16.4, Helen ran the 100 meters only five seconds slower than the wind-aided mark she had set as an eighteen-year-old girl! Afterward, she compared herself to an old racehorse, saying, "There's the bugle. There's the distance. . . . [The horse] starts panting, ready to go."[15]

Publicity generated publicity in the years that followed. One reporter took a look at Helen as a competitor in the Senior Olympics and focused less on her 1936 Olympic heights and more on her athletic longevity: "Over the years the glory has paled, the step has slowed, and the regimen has softened, but Helen Stephens still keeps in shape."[16]

Still a cigarette smoker, Helen trained earnestly for six weeks that spring. As a youngster, her standard quip about cigarette smoking was, "It's cigars that get you," but later in life, the senior Olympian admitted to having "one bad habit—smoking. But, I don't inhale. That's probably why I'm able to keep going." Quizzed about diet, exercise, work, and sleep habits, Helen said she had never counted calories but tried to eat a balanced diet, and that from early on, she had had a healthy appetite. Pictures show how heavy she had become. For most of her adult years, her weight teetered between 170 and 175 pounds, but "when I ballooned to 225, I just started pushing myself back from the table and got my weight back down to what it had been." As a youth, she gravitated toward macaroni and spaghetti. Her favorite meal? Steak, salad, and a baked potato. It was Coach Moore, she said, who taught her the value of a good night's rest: "I need about eight hours of sleep." And to stay in shape? Besides the chores of lawn mowing and shoveling snow, she said, a daily walk, frequent swimming, an occasional golf game, and bowling weekly for some forty years, all were good substitutes for running the track, and "In the morning I do a few exercises to get the blood circulating."[17]

School kids routinely asked for information for their term papers. One breath-of-fresh-air question put to her was, "What is an Olympic gold medal?" Masterfully, Helen nailed it: "It is solid silver dusted with a certain percentage of gold. They are not for sale; they must be earned. They personify the highest award an amateur athlete can achieve in sports—excellence! They are stolen, lost, given to family, girl friends, boy friends, worn, stored away, displayed in museums and Halls of Fame."[18]

Throughout the 1980s, Helen earned more honors, accepted more speaking engagements, and did more Olympic committee work, and the number of newspaper and journal stories about her mounted. In one month in 1983, Laura Herren's story on Helen appeared in *Rural Missouri*, and an African American paper, the *St. Louis Evening Whirl*, printed the ubiquitous Hitler-and-Helen photo with a poem by an anonymous poet whose verse perpetuated the notion that Hitler had slighted Owens. And Helen was selected by *Runner's World* as a member of America's Olympic Dream Team of outstanding athletes. In August, she was noted for raising funds for Pike's Peak American Olympic Champion monument. Then, a street in the new sports park in Sedalia, Missouri, was named after her. In October, the Missouri legislature adopted Resolution 3220, recognizing her place in sports history. And much to her surprise, Councilman Gene McNary proclaimed the date of November 5, 1983, as Helen Stephens Day in St. Louis County.

From her first Senior Olympics event onward, Helen tallied a decade of outstanding athletic accomplishments for her age bracket in each event she entered. Now tagged "the Florissant Flash" in print, she established new records for herself, sometimes clocking speeds and distances longer and stronger than women in younger categories. One regular competitor kvetched that there was no need to try for a gold medal if Helen Stephens showed up on the track. Apparently, she was right. The *1980–92 Best Times and Distances Records of the St. Louis Senior Olympics* show Helen as *the* unbeatable competitor—a present-day, senior-age Olympian of track and field in each of her age brackets:

Age 60–64: discus, 82 feet 1 inch (beating 55–59 Charmaine Sobkowski's 73 feet 3½ inches); shot put, 36 feet 9½ inches (beating her 55–59 friend Wanda Wejzgrowicz's 30 feet 4¾ inches); 50-meter dash, 8.58 seconds; 200-meter dash, 35.45 seconds

Age 65–69: football throw, 77 feet 2 inches; discus, 73 feet 6 inches; javelin, 72 feet 10 inches; shot put, 35 feet ¼ inch; standing long jump, 7 feet 4¼ inches (beating 55–59 Carol Taylor's 6 feet ½ inch and 60–64 Helen Darnall's 6 feet 1¼ inches)

Age 70–74: discus, 59 feet 9¾ inches; softball throw, 95 feet 5 inches; shot put, 28 feet 4½ inches; standing long jump, 6 feet 3 inches; javelin, 67 feet 8 inches (beating 55–59 Betty Adams's 61 feet 8 inches)

Laurels kept coming. President Reagan greeted Helen and other outstanding sports women in New York in the fall of 1984. Along with track star Mary Decker, tennis champ Martina Navratilova, and other younger "women jocks," Helen was chosen by the Women's Sports Foundation for special recognition and inducted into the National Women's Sports Hall of Fame. She was singled out and honored as a major athlete in the "pioneer" category.

That year, Helen appeared on a television program taped in California. In late January 1984, though Mabel was not well, the two flew to Los Angeles for the taping. They met prominent women athletes during the filming of "Women and the Olympics," a segment of the *Woman-to-Woman* television show, among them Wilma Rudolph, Penny Johnson, Hilda Gurrey, Ella Svirsky, Mary Lou Kauder, Dara Torres, Pam Spencer, Rosaly Bryant, Julianne McNamara, Tai Babilonia, Cheryl Miller, Jo Jo Starbuck, and Ward Grant. This show aired in July in the middle of Olympic fever. While there, Helen tried to get a couple of tickets for several Olympic track events. They were expensive and in limited supply, even for someone like herself, whose past work as a member of the Midwest Chapter of Olympians had helped raise funds for the games, but she got two. Also that year, the St. Louis Sports Hall of Fame added her name to its list of honorees. She now had entered six Halls of Fame.

In March 1985, Mabel spent a week in the hospital to have a growth removed from her bladder. The doctor told her the tumor was cancerous. "All you can do is hope," Helen wrote to alumnae secretary Myldred Fairchild on April 5. "I have gotten her out to the beauty shop and back this week. Mabel is a fighter and tough but she sometimes says, What's the use? Her mother & two sisters were brought down by cancer—it seems to run in the family." Helen sent a check for the alumnae house fund and one for alumnae weekend, for Mabel urged her to go with one of their friends, telling her, "It's too late in the fourth quarter for me." Helen wrote Fairchild:

Bernie and I plan to drive down . . . May 3. . . . I got to see my aunt in nursing home & look up friend Julie Spearman regarding 50th high school class reunion on June 22 as I hear I am to m.c. the affair. Every time I get to Fulton, I am short of time to look in on different folks. . . . It's getting late in the 4th quarter, as my coach Moore used to say, and a person has to start distributing personal things before it is too late. I think I have a lot of things that should be on permanent display at William Woods College. I hope you still have my WWC track suit, shoes & Olympic parade hat for this collection. I hope you are still on board to set it up, if & when.

Yesterday Bernie (you met her at your house last fall) helped me take some things down to the St. Louis Sports Hall of Fame located in Busch Stadium.

Incidentally, June and I will drive up to Fulton on April 16 to be at City Hall, per call from Ron Moody . . . to go out to city park (Veterans?) for dedication of a street named for me by Fulton Board of Parks & Recreation last fall.

Classmate Ovid Bell, of Ovid Bell Publishers, was the co-master of ceremonies of the reunion, held at The Stables restaurant. Among familiar faces were Martha Sue Faucett, Julia Spearman, Bonnie Lammers, and other girlhood friends.

That year, an offshoot of the annual St. Louis Senior Games evolved in Poplar Bluff, Missouri, calling itself the Mid-South Senior Olympics. Helen carried the torch for opening ceremonies, and as a contestant in the 65–69 age bracket, she walked away with first-place awards in the Frisbee, softball, and football tosses, discus, shot put, and javelin tosses, and the standing broad jump events.

In December, Bob Paul, now the special assistant to the secretary general of the USOC, wrote to tell Helen that the use of the word *Olympics* was restricted:

Apparently no one at Olympic House is concerned about the . . . Senior Olympics . . . in St. Louis. . . . For 20 years we have not taken any real action to shutdown the impostors conducting these events at a state level. . . . But now that plans have been made for the National Senior Olympics one of these days we will move into action, probably seeking a temporary restraining order . . . at the 11th hour. In short, the amateur Sports Act of 1978 precludes the use of the term "Olympics" without permission of the USOC. Two years ago after many appearances in court, The Gay Olympics in San Francisco (featuring many Olympians) were forced to cease and desist using the word . . . in their title. The organizers . . . got socked with a large judgment for thumming [*sic*] their nose at the court.

Paul said he had discussed the matter of Hitler's *not* snubbing Owens with the producer of the Jesse Owens movie before shooting began and had told him that "There were many factual errors . . . some of which they corrected." Though not speaking of it directly, Paul alluded to drug testing and the ongoing concern of twenty years earlier; the IOC's February 1968 newsletter informed readers that "Female athletes may be subjected to medical proof." That issue was now coming to the foreground. Paul wrote that the IOC would opt to allow each of the thirty international federations to adopt their own eligibility regulations. He wrote: "I used to give a speech 'Let's Take the Mystery Out of Olympic Eligibility.' With what appears to be the resolution [that] will definitely take the mystery out of eligibility, but it won't necessarily be the best solution."

Helen's response to Paul (February 1986) was at first placating and then angry. She mentioned that when she attended the national board meeting of the U.S. Olympians organization in New York in November, a heated discussion over the use of the word *Olympics* "in our name" had ensued. The senior Olympian defended it:

> Senior Olympic groups using the word 'Olympics' in their title, I had always assumed that someone had been granted permission by the USOC as a disclaimer of any connections/applications with the USOC is always printed on their literature, at least in the St. Louis area. If I recall rightly, these type games for seniors were originally started at the suggestion/ recommendation/support of the President's Council on Physical Fitness. As for me, I sincerely believe in them and the good things that have been done for our senior athletes and have been involved in them on a local and state level since 1980. I hope and trust that some of the "young blood" out to make a name for themselves do not create a national ruckus about this use of the word "Olympics."
>
> … one of your … staff wrote a letter to the group suggesting the name be changed to: "Alum of U.S. Olympic Teams" or something like that. I know we had the name long before the Amateur Sports Act of 1978. There was no indication at the meeting of anyone wanting to change the name. A man from New York area on USOC spoke to us and indicated he might be able to smooth things over to make everyone happy.
>
> Another matter that came up was that most all Olympians from pre-1984 teams still felt very much disgusted and had little desire to support the USOC due to lack of recognition and support by both LAOC [Los Angeles Olympic Committee] and the USOC regarding the disaster in 1984 when all previous Olympians (gold medalists, I believe) were to be flown to Las Vegas along with spouses or a friend and during the closing ceremonies the Olympians only were to be flown to LA and marched into the stadium and introduced. Several representatives of U.S. Olympian chapters reported some of their members were still so bitter that they wanted nothing to do with USOC or the Olympic movement. I, personally, feel that we were short-changed!

In fact, the Senior Olympics began in Los Angeles in 1970 when Warren Blaney and his son Worth established an organization called Senior Sports

International. Starting with swimming and track and field events, participants over the age of forty were eligible (but women could compete only in swimming events).[19] Athletic games for men and women fifty-five and older began in 1980 in St. Louis, with the sponsorship of the Jewish Community Center Association to commemorate the group's one hundredth anniversary. Helen met among the first competitors a woman seven years older than herself, Marie Uedel, who also won gold track medals that year; like Helen, Marie returned every year.

The Gay Olympics (later Gay Games) founded by Olympic decathlete Dr. Tom Waddell were first held in San Francisco in 1982. The Gay Games occurred there again in 1986 and in Vancouver, British Columbia, in 1990, where they doubled in size and included a cultural festival. In the summer of 1993, St. Louis area Gay Games athletes visited with Helen in her home and asked her to participate in the 1994 games slated for New York, but she declined. Helen opted to play safe; was still unwilling to risk being visible amidst a group seeking validation of the life she long had lived in the closet. She spent her energies instead on equal rights for women athletes, the Senior Olympics, and the new Missouri Show-Me State Games. Here, she felt comfortably safe; here, she carried the opening ceremony torch, competed, and won numerous events.

As the original Olympics approached, *16 Days of Glory* premiered in Los Angeles as a benefit for the USOC. It showed in Richmond Heights, a suburb of St. Louis, at the Esquire on April 16, 1987. Helen and Mabel attended the event, and both were pleased with the film.

By the spring of 1986, Missouri historian Bob Priddy was sketching the story of Helen's Olympic victories for his new book, *Across the Wide Missouri*, and noting them on his radio show during the Olympic year. Also that spring, a horticulturist had established seedlings from several vintage Olympic oak trees. Olympic tree preservationists provided Helen with a seedling replacement that was to be planted on the front lawn of the new alumnae house at William Woods College during alumnae weekend, April 1986. College president Dr. Bartholomy had arranged to have Helen's portrait put in the administration building alongside exhibit cases of her sports memorabilia. But by that time, Mabel's emphysema was provoking emergency trips to the hospital, and though unable to make the tree-planting trip on alumnae weekend, she knew Helen had to go. She insisted that Helen take one of their friends.

Then, in May, along with thirty 1936 U.S. Olympians, Helen attended a fifty-year Olympic reunion in Columbus, Ohio. Helen visited with Annette Rogers Kelly, track star Glenn Cunningham, and muscle builder John Grimek. The *Columbus Dispatch* photographer snapped their photo for the Sunday sports page.

In the fall of 1986, Helen's longtime companion Mabel Robbe died. She was seventy-eight. According to Mabel's wishes, Helen released the body for scientific research. Helen wrote and placed the obituary in the papers: "Mabel Olive Robbe (nee Wires) Tues. Oct. 28, 1986, formerly of Mt. Carroll, IL, former wife of the late Frank J. Robbe, preceded in death by mother, father, 5 sisters, 1 brother. Longtime friend of Helen Stephens, dear aunt, great-aunt, cousin. . . . Member two local NARFE chapters."

Mabel's last six years had been hard for both women. Neither one had quit smoking. In those years, Robbe's cheerful personality was tested by poor health, by the loss of parents, aunts, uncles, and every sibling she had. She had been a dietitian at Schirmer College in Illinois for twenty-seven years and then worked in federal agencies in Chicago and in St. Louis, where she and Helen had paired. On November 2, standing before those gathered at Ferguson United Methodist Church for the memorial service, Helen eulogized her mate:

> It is difficult to put into mere words the true feeling I had and have for this fine lady. Fortunately, I met her as my supervisor at the General Accounting Office, St. Louis, in 1946—40 years ago. We became good friends, wielded a lasting and rewarding relationship, shared two homes together the past 38 years in Ferguson and Florissant. Her family became mine and mine hers as did our many friends. She was a loving, caring, kind, understanding, and generous woman. She had many and varied interests but enjoyed the simple things of life—birds, wild animals, the seasons, and she greeted each day of her life with a smile. Her interests became mine and mine became hers. She gloried in my many sports awards, especially those received at William Woods College.
>
> She believed in sharing with others and her baking and distributing of thousands of Xmas cookies to many people became legendary. She possessed a great sense of humor and was a good judge of character but always found good qualities in everyone. She loved older people, young people, and, especially, little children. She had a large family living in several states and she maintained contact with all of them and their interests.
>
> Although she was in ill health the past six years, she never complained. I did my utmost to care for her needs and probably fell short. She was a great Christian lady that I truly admired, respected as a devoted friend and companion and loved very much. I will never forget her guiding influence and the impact she had on my own life for the better.[20]

Mabel had been a wonderful friend and companion for Helen.

Helen thought she was prepared for the void Mabel's death would cause, having cared for her ailing friend over the years and watching the illness advance and her body decline. But how empty life felt without her. Mabel's doctor had forewarned her that only a few years remained to them, but now, confronted with their empty house, Helen felt profoundly lost. Soon to turn seventy, she felt life's door had closed to her, also. A strong urge to cancel all engagements and withdraw invaded her mind. Left alone, she knew depression could completely overtake her. Thinking about Thanksgiving and Christmas left her feeling sorely dejected, but her friends refused to let her be alone.

Nor would her public. Commitments she previously made, inked in on her calendar, entreated her to follow through. Under this pressure, she realized, "Mabel would really let me have it, if I quit. . . . she'd reproach me from the grave if I benched myself, if I took myself out of the game."[21]

Reluctantly, Helen went on. Several friends drove to Jefferson City with her for the Missouri Sports Hall of Fame induction ceremony. It was the year football coach Pete Adkins and basketball figure Andy McDonald were honored. "I went," Helen said, "but I was in a haze of depression."

When the new year rolled in, Helen was the guest of honor at the eighty-second Kingdom of Callaway Supper, January 20, 1987. The high school kid who loaned his track shoes so she could compete in her first track meet, T. J. Neukomm, presided. He had called to urge Helen to follow through on the arrangement made months before Mabel's death. Helen acquiesced; she wouldn't let down an old classmate. In spite of the snow and ice, the audience gathered for the occasion that night was huge. Among the crowd was her biographer-to-be. Her pal T. J. in his introduction recounted the story of the smart, funny, big old country girl he once knew who was so poor she couldn't afford her own track shoes, but who ran faster than anyone he had ever seen. When Helen rose to speak, she wove a part of the full story, which had yet to be written, she said. With a lot of help and encouragement from townsfolk, some of whom sat before her, she had lived the American dream. Back then, she said, she was a tomboy, a poor kid reaching for an Olympic dream. "I had a lot of help," she said, paused, nodded to T. J., and then carried on:

> Many folks around here encouraged and helped me live my dream—for which I am forever grateful. . . . I had to go on from there, though . . . the Depression hung on into the forties. I found both sports opportunities and desk work. . . . the barnstorming redheads, the industrial leagues . . . that was a long long time ago. . . . now there's the Senior Games . . . fishing from a pier in an Arkansian resort. Rocking in a chair on the porch? There's time enough for that . . . but for now, why, I will stay in the field as long as these old bones and muscles hold up! It wasn't just being a winner, though that was a big part of it. But the social aspect of it . . . is equally important. . . . and it's fun![22]

In June, she spoke on aging healthfully at a leadership conference on sport chaired by Glenn Clark, again elaborating on its social benefits.

When I was a young person, anyone 50 years old was referred to as an old person. People were expected to die of *natural causes* (whatever the reason) in their 60s. Often it was said they just *worked* themselves to death. Back then, there was little being done for the aging. Their families either took care of them or they were sent to the *poor house* or the *state asylum*—loss of memory or a few blank spots was enough to qualify.

Today, Senior Citizens are a big part of our population. We play an important role in today's society. We are people! Seniors today usually are in better financial shape than those of yesteryear. You see us doing many things—we are in the news, we are discussed on TV talk shows. The . . . press write articles about us (some in wonderment), the business world wants our money. . . . we are often asked for advice on our former area of expertise, we volunteer to aid many causes, etc. Even politicians want a piece of our action.

Keeping active and involved is the key to our mental health and well being. Maybe we don't always recall everything that happened yesterday but have total recall about things last year and before! To remain active and involved, we need to maintain our good health. There are different strokes for different folks. A certain amount of movement of our body parts is a must. Some call it exercise. Exercise, per se, is unpleasant to many but can take many forms (housework, working in the flower garden, or mowing grass). Others may embark on some type of group exercise program. . . . Group exercise is more fun!

We read . . . all types of articles by so-called experts or self-styled authorities on types of exercise. . . . there is little agreement on type of exercise. From the wide variety of types available, we have a choice of doing something that makes us feel good and happy. . . .

The main point I want to express is: Keep the body moving, don't sit on your duff. . . . Do something, whatever it may be. I advise a check-up with your doctor before starting any exercise program. As an old gladiator on the field of sport for over 50 years, I highly recommend walking and swimming as exercises that are easier on your body parts. Simple exercise (calisthenics) in your home done to Richard Simmons [exercise tapes] is very popular. Stretch is important. Our muscles need work—the heart and circulation improve and we not only think better, we feel better. For myself, I remain very busy and active in a lot of things—home (house and yard), meetings (NARFE & AARP), public appearances, Senior Olympics events, bowling. . . . Personally, I don't exercise a lot or even work-out and yet I managed to pick up some 15 medals (including 12 gold) this past month. I will be out at the first national Senior Olympics next week and will open our Show-Me State Games in Columbia on August 7.[23]

At age sixty-nine, the glimmer of a champion was evident still. Helen kept her commitment to again run the last leg of the Show-Me State Games, carrying the torch. It was her third consecutive competition and the third time that officials had asked her to be the opening ceremonies torchbearer. She also accepted the nomination to be a delegate to NARFE's convention in Arkansas in 1988. It was an opportunity to visit her brother and sister-in-law, retirees living "the life of Riley" in Hot Springs Village, Arkansas. She also went along to New York with an NARFE member and friend, Bernie, who would, in the midst of funeral proceedings for Helen, convince Bob and Betty to let her be the administrator of Helen's estate.

14

Sportswomen: Pandora's Box

I was dreaming of the past
And my heart was beating fast.

—John Lennon, "Jealous Guy"

*I*f she had lived a typical life most women know in this country, she might have slipped into a comfortable grandkid-doting grandmother mode. But circumstances and decisions made long ago precluded that. If, indeed, the exercise of her talent, her athletic passion, had not directed and influenced her choices, Mother Nature might have averted her (as it did many women prior to birth control pills) and her life might have followed that path.[1]

If she were the kind of person—woman or man—who naturally sought all the comforts of her status, having left but not forgotten the battles of a dirt-poor childhood, Helen might have settled for luncheons, family reunions, church functions, bingo, and other venues of easement. And if she had been able to close the breach between herself and sibling—end their sister-brother quarrels that (minus the blows) so mimicked father-daughter clashes of old—there might have been a chance that Helen would have retired to Arkansas to be near Bob and sister-in-law Betty. But, returning home from Thanksgiving and Christmas family gatherings, Helen invariably felt relief. She was put off by Bob's materialism, his talking about his boat, his cars, his pool table, his fishing rods, and the good deals he got for them. She reasoned, "It's second nature for some of us who've been through the Great Depression to be like that [to be materialistic]."[2] Helen herself felt more at ease and comfortable among less acquisitive friends and felt more safely accepted.

And she was the kind of person bent on doing, not getting—unless winning gold, silver, and bronze medals can be considered materialistic.

Helen still attended National Association of Retired Federal Employees (NARFE) dinner meetings regularly, something that she and Mabel had enjoyed doing together, mostly for the social aspect, but now she arrived in the company of other women. Both the statewide Show-Me State Games and the national Senior Olympics were in their fifth year when news of her latest sports achievements appeared in NARFE's November 1988 issue of *Retirement Life.* By competing in and volunteering to help with the first and succeeding athletic events for people fifty-five years and older, she developed ties with the Jewish Community Center Association Senior Olympics. When the first nationwide Senior Olympic Games took place in St. Louis in 1986, Helen was clearly and totally in her element.

About that time, Helen spoke to a group of young athletes at the Missouri Military Academy in Boonville and was interviewed by Jo Ann Mason Beecher for the *Mexico (Mo.) Ledger.* As she neared the fiftieth anniversary of the 1936 Olympics, Helen said she was determined to make her mark again.

On the far end of the Senior Olympic 65–69 age bracket (to repeat, for the sake of summary here), Helen had signed up for ten events (one more than the previous year) and trained for weeks prior to these games, which was not her habit. Usually she just showed up and let go. But for this anniversary year, Helen was hell-bent on besting the fastest time she had clocked in Senior Olympic competition. Now, she wanted to best all of her age-group's 100-meter records: her 100-meter gold-winning time of 17.37 of 1982; her slower but still gold-winning 19.2 of 1983, and her faster run of 17.1 of 1985. She intended to crack her personal best of the decade, which she had set two years earlier—her fantastic 16.8! Helen, in her late sixties, was still an incredible athlete. But was she seeking the impossible? Not at all. In her anniversary year, she took medals in all ten events. She ran her all-time-record-Senior speed of 16.4 in the 100 meters— which was just about five seconds more than her wind-aided speed in Berlin. The gold was hers. She won the 50-meter race, the discus, the javelin (throwing her best, 72 feet 10 inches), the shot put, and the standing broad jump events. She won two silver medals (in the 200 meters and the football distance throw) and two bronzes (in the softball throw and for bowling 531).

In the few years after this event, she harbored the thought that all would go downhill after 1986. Still, a number of events brought the Fulton Flash again into public view. There was a lengthy feature story about her in *Missouri Life* magazine, and she was the much-applauded guest speaker at the Kingdom of Callaway Supper in January 1988. Happily, Helen would attain her anniversary athletic goals prior to Mabel's death and before her Olympic coach and longtime friend Dee Boeckmann died (June 1989). The St. Louis reporter who often had equivocated with Boeckmann wrote a generous tribute to her, lauding Dee for having battled for women's equal status in the man's world of sports.[3] Sadly, Helen added Dee's obituary to her "In Orbit" file.

Though Helen took some of her own advice, the aging process itself taught its own lessons. On December 19, 1988, she broke her ankle by slipping on a patch of ice as she hurriedly scuttled across Thackery Court en route to her neighbor's house. During holidays and vacation times, they always looked after each other's place, picking up the mail, shoveling snow, and so on. Helen said, "the freaky accident caught me during mid-bowling season. I was having a bad season anyway."[4] The injury meant wearing a plastic air cast, which laid up Helen for awhile. The cast would be off February 25, but she was chomping at the bit from the beginning, disappointed at being unable to go to the Kingdom of Callaway Supper in January 1989. She feared this injury meant an end to her athletic days, but her sauntering onto the field that summer again discouraged those in her age bracket who hoped to win a gold.

She told the press, "I'm sorta like an old fire horse whose pace picks up each time the fire bell rings." The Show-Me athlete hoofed onto the field and won more gold, silver, and bronze. She quipped, tossing out the moniker she now preferred, her broad smile widening her face, "I'm an Old Gladiator. I'll keep running on the field as long as these ole legs'll get me there." Helen was recovering from her ankle injury when I interviewed her for *Show Me Missouri Women: Selected Biographies*, a project of the American Association of University Women. In 1990, she and I attended a book signing at Boone Regional Library in Columbia, and though she had just met most of the people there, she turned to the page where her bio-sketch appeared and inscribed a few words in the book with a fine and cordial friendliness. It was then that Helen told me that a journalist friend once had tried to write her full biography as an as-told-to story but had quit after writing about four pages.

In April 1990, I visited Helen in her home to discuss the possibility of trying again. She led me to the basement where, among her other career papers, she produced the 1937 "Is This a Man or a Woman" *Look* magazine article (testing, I think, my fiber and nerve). Stacks and stacks of what she called her "stuff," collected over sixty years, held the story of Helen's life, loves, sports ambitions, and legend. I agreed to write her authorized biography with the condition of having full access and first publishing right to these materials. We wrote up a contract, and I began what turned out to be my own long-distance run.

That summer, Helen carried the torch during the Show-Me State Games opening ceremonies, and in competitions, she wowed spectators again, and I was there to see it. On August 5, she began to enjoy the attention that came with being interviewed on a regular basis, and I began excavating the documents previously lying fallow in her basement. In November 1990, Helen reviewed the first draft of the first chapter, and we spoke with an archivist about what to do with her treasure trove of sports history.[5] She no longer wanted to store these things in her home, plus her housekeeper was threatening to put it all into big plastic bags and throw it away as trash, she said. The librarian in her saw no logic in going through this information piece by piece without organizing it at the same time, for future researchers. Nor did I.

During one of our interview sessions, I asked if there was anyone, new friend or old, whom she might invite into her home to live with her. No, she said. Her friends had their own lives, and there wasn't one among them she wanted, as she had wanted Mabel, to be near her twenty-four hours a day. Having her biography written seemed to bolster Helen. Whereas friends and family members had grown tired of hearing her retell her past and present glories, the likelihood of having her story written down, once and for all, pleased her. It also, from time to time, unsettled her. Every few weeks, after lunching together, we would sit at her kitchen table, and she would answer questions and discuss topics I had asked her to think about.

"Make something up!" she once blurted in exasperation and reached for another cigarette. Her pack of Marlboros was always on the formica table, and nearby, turned up to the highest setting, a giant smoke-eating machine crackled audibly. Some of the finer details, she said, she just couldn't remember. "That was a long, long time ago."

And some of those memories weren't happy ones.

She knew that what lay ahead was literally and figuratively a Pandora's Box. For among her scrapbooks and assorted ephemera—career clippings, score books, posters, photographs, passport, Olympic Co-Eds letterhead and correspondence, bills, program flyers, table-place tabs, membership cards, letters received and carbons of letters she had written, and more—was (she claimed) every letter any of her girlfriends had ever written to her. She had safely kept bundles of some very special letters in a red-and-tan, boot-size box. Designed to look like a chest, with fake lock and ornamental filigree, it bore the name of the brand of footwear: Pandora's Box.

She had stumbled upon the box while digging through a four-drawer file cabinet. She had forgotten about those letters. She would need to burn them, she said. But she couldn't do it. She handed them over, saying, "Read them, if you want to, but they're not for the biography." She said she wanted them destroyed once I was finished with them. "Don't you want them back, at least for the collectible stamps?" I asked. "No. Don't bring that stuff back here," she said. She later allowed some use—if I would agree to keep the anonymity of some.

For several weeks after that, Helen's destiny sailed uneasily. Once the contents were espied, her personal life would, in some minds, tarnish her professionally. Would people understand her better if her full story were told? Would people understand and accept?

"Not in my lifetime," she said. Even though there were Gay Pride marches, Gay Games, gay rights legislation and organizations, it would probably be another hundred years or so, if it happened at all, she said.

"Perhaps in mine," I said.

Once her Pandora's Box was reopened, she felt unmoored, without anchor (Mabel was long gone), and with no other harbor to go to (Dee was not there to advise). She admitted to having some halting weeks—worried whether she had put her trust in a trustworthy person. She wanted to protect her friends; those still living would not want their lesbianism published or announced in a book about her. But she openly discussed the issue and expressed her views.

"Homosexuality won't be accepted in my lifetime," she said, restating her opinion grounded in her own personal experience.

Unlike most of us, Helen lived her dreams, reached her goals, and sprinted far, far ahead of her competitors, gay or straight. She slooped basketballs through innumerable hoops, the crack of her bat struck hundreds of home runs, the smack of her golf club almost always meant a long ball that easily outdistanced all others. But the one thing she couldn't do was step out of the closet in Olympic fashion and declare her private self.

We discussed homophobia several times, talked about what people thought of homosexuals in her era, and how homosexuality is viewed today in the United States; how the connotations of terminology have changed, thanks to the women's movement "taking back the night" and the "queer nation" infusing positive values. Name-calling terms, for example, once used to belittle gays, lesbians, bisexual, and transgendered people are now used by activists as mantles of pride (such as *I'm here and I'm queer*).

Even today, Helen countered, lesbians fear that their sexual "deviance" or lifestyle (a word Helen and many others used in the 1990s) might be discovered, and they could lose their jobs. Attitudes in Helen's time, however, more strongly influenced and kept her and thousands of others secreted in closets of various fashion.

"Labels are limiting," she said. "*Lesbian* is a scare word. It can be very hurtful if applied incorrectly to young girls who are athletic. There are troops of self-righteous people who snoop and hound maliciously." She knew what she was talking about. In the years when J. Edgar Hoover ran what Helen called the "Federal Bureau of Infestation," dossiers were created on anyone suspected of homosexuality—male or female, youth or elder. In 1995, replying to my inquiry via the Freedom of Information Act, the FBI reported that there was, indeed, a file on Helen Stephens, and it would be provided to me within a few years, after processing my request. In 1999, the FBI notified me that the file on

Helen Stephens had been destroyed. I realized then, as I neared completion of Helen's story, that some trails of substantiating history, for whatever reasons, are forever lost to plastic trash-bag purgings, bonfires, and shredders.

The task of organizing Helen's stuff and deciding where to put it so that future researchers could benefit from it suggested the need for a professional archivist, but the idea of paying someone to do this was not in Helen's view of things. I had agreed to be, as a matter of fact, her authorized biographer on speculation (meaning no pay) and then offered to put order to her papers while I researched through them, not realizing the magnitude of the task.

We approached her alma mater, William Woods College, where various objects of her sports memorabilia were exhibited (then, in the hall of the Administration Building), and inquired whether the college was interested in having Helen's "papers." But at that time, the college had no space or available file cabinets or staff to properly preserve and protect such a huge collection, and the staff suggested that if we raised funds for it, they would be able to accept it. For a short while, we sought funds for the file cabinets and boxes and file materials needed to begin. Much to his credit, Helen's old coach and longtime friend W. Burton Moore gave his financial support, just as he had when Helen was in the beginning stages of her career.

When raising enough money proved futile, we talked with Ann Morris, the director of the University of Missouri's Historical Manuscript Collections, a repository with professional archiving staff and facilities in St. Louis. Morris was very interested in these historical materials and offered to receive the collection without any cost to Helen, but she suggested that we hire one of her student assistants to help do the archival work.[6] Helen held firm on not paying for these services, so I solicited (and Helen accepted) the volunteer help of Pam Miner, a professional archivist employed by the Missouri State Archives in Jefferson City.

Pam was a graduate of William Woods College (luckily, a scholarship student with interest in track and history) and thus Helen's alumnae sister. I knew Pam as a result of being a member of the Missouri Historical Records Advisory Board and through my volunteer work as a board member for the Missouri State Library's Missouri Center for the Book. Pam readily agreed to show me how to organize and prepare archival material for repositing and suggested that a finder's guide to the collection would be necessary.[7] Our work began in July 1991. Pam donated several weeks of her time and was delighted to help and to meet Helen Stephens. Following her advice, Helen selected and paid for archival boxes, folders, and paper for duplicating the fragile, brittle, and yellowing papers, and she had these items shipped to me in Jefferson City.

Both writing the biography and archiving the material proceeded slowly, and Helen's impatience grew. She wanted to see the book finished in her lifetime. Her fame, it seemed, now rested in my hands.

Some research included driving Helen around Callaway County. We walked the grounds of her parents' grave site. We visited Middle River School—its well was still in the front yard, its big Sycamore still offered a tree swing. We meandered through Veterans Park, and she stopped for a photo opportunity on Helen Stephens Lane. We went to William Woods College and discussed certain items in her sports memorabilia exhibited there and visited the new sports complex bearing her name. She remarked that the exterior block letters that spell her name seemed less permanent than those carved into the Berlin stadium monoliths: "I bet they [the letters on the Helen Stephens Sports Complex] can come down easier than they were put up," she told me. Perhaps she feared that her school might once again pull the rug out from under her, once she flew into orbit, or when certain aspects of her personal life became public with the publication of her biography. Revisiting her childhood home further disturbed her. We traveled the narrow path that crossed Middle River in Callaway County and paused for a moment among wild overgrowth. Down along the worn little road where potholes everywhere made the going difficult, we stopped near the Stephens farm house, now falling down, uninhabited; we slowly drove through land once tilled by her father. It was beautiful, rich, and flat, but her father couldn't afford a tractor, she said; he walked behind mules, guiding a handheld plow, as she had done. She told me, "We had two neighbors nearby, farmers with tractors; we all helped each other from time to time." One place recalled for her the bag of kittens that her father made her drown there: "He said we had too many cats on the farm, but I loved kittens."

The blues and greens made it seem cool in the quiet, yellow glow of the late afternoon sun. It was peaceful there, that day. But afterward, Helen admitted that visiting the old place had depressed her, though she had not revealed her feelings, either outwardly or with words, that day.[8]

During the two weeks of June 15–27, 1991, I drove Helen to Arkansas to visit Bob and Betty Stephens. En route, we stopped at Sedalia's Sports Park, and I photographed her standing near the street sign named for her, Stephens Drive. This trip was Helen's chance to mend ties with her brother, who was recovering from a heart attack. But they were quarreling by the second day, tempers flaring over a game of pool that Helen won. At my suggestion, we watched Helen's videotape of the *Woman-to-Woman* television show in which she was featured. Bob snapped that she was always living in the past. To this, Helen announced that she was leaving and stomped upstairs to her room. Her parting shots drifted across the family room: "That's the last of it. I never want to bother with you again!" Betty said to me, "Oh, they always spat, it doesn't mean much." Upstairs, Helen furiously packed and swore to herself. I told her that I would drive her back to St. Louis, if that's what she really wanted. I asked her to think before deciding, because this might be the last time she would see her brother.

Betty said she watched Helen walk toward the dock where Bob had retreated. Helen stayed there, fishing from the pier with him for over an hour. They came back, his short and fleshy arm holding onto her long and lanky one, all the rancor seemingly forgotten. No one asked who caught the most or the biggest. We stayed on into another and better day. At the driving range, they got into a distance contest. But everyone was cordial for the rest of the visit. Bob talked about his years in Europe during World War II and related some family information that he thought would be useful for the biography.

But by the spring of 1993, family friction again erupted, this time between Helen and her niece during a phone conversation. Helen had asked her about her infant child, saying "How's the kid?" The word choice, for some reason, hurt her niece's feelings, and when Grandmother Betty learned of it, "they gave me the silent treatment," Helen said. But it was Bob this time who made the first overture to smooth things over. Helen said she had lost enthusiasm for family gatherings at the niece's house during the last two Christmases because of "screamin', noisy, whinny kids!" Relatives faulted her for not being much of an aunt; she faulted them for "givin' those kids anything and everything they wanted."[9] Helen simply did not feel comfortable around infants or preschoolers. She much preferred the holiday time she spent with the group of women she bowled with or once worked with. These friends went out to eat together, exchanged gifts, attended each other's house parties, and though some had kids and grandkids of their own, Helen said, she felt more at home among these women.

Helen said she was sensitive to criticism from family and others, though she hid it better than most. An intimate friend from the 1940s, to whom Helen had sent a career-update letter around 1986, complained that Helen had gotten the big head. Helen licked the wound of that accusation into the last year of her life, and perhaps to lessen the hurt, she explained to me that this woman had only jabbed at her because the lady had "fallen off the wagon" again.

Helen hated what she called "busybody activity," games requiring no talent, no skill or mental activity. Bingo, for example, "a game engaging only the butt and optic muscles," was far too sedentary for Helen. In the last six months of her life, she bad-mouthed bingo frequently; she saw it as an unworthy competitor that repeatedly won a friend away from her. Every Wednesday and Saturday night, this friend sat at the bingo boards, hoping to hit a jackpot; sometimes, she would win a hundred dollars or more.[10] What was the lure? Helen didn't know. She had little patience for her friend's bingo interest, but they stayed friends.

Was it vanity that compelled Helen to have the raspberry birthmark she carried on her forehead all her life finally removed? Was it strictly a cosmetic concern, or did this mark carry a symbolic meaning for her? Was she trying to remove the fearful blemish of superstition imprinted on her when she was a child? It is puzzling why she did this, but she finally did, in 1990.

In 1991, controversy again fell into Helen's lap. It was the same thing that ensued in 1936, in the 1960s, and in the 1980s. As the 1992 Olympics neared, a growing concern about women athletes emerged that focused on performance enhancing drugs. Steroids were a primary worry for all athletes, but now the IOC had a policy that required physical exams to verify gender. Attorneys pursuing the matter said that gynecological checks, or inspections (which were abandoned more than twenty years earlier in favor of the more discreet buccal smear test), would not only catch impostors (as if there were any), it would deter *women* from entering sports. (*Inspection* was the code word Helen had used in her Berlin diary.) According to the news, male athletes would not be required to undergo such inspections. One story coming from Toronto referenced Helen and rehashed the sad story of Stella Walsh: "Physical inspection was carried out sporadically in the early days of track and field. At the 1936 Berlin Olympics, a Polish journalist claimed U.S. sprinter Helen Stephens, a native of Fulton, Mo., who won a gold medal that year, was really a man. German officials issued a statement that she had been checked and was a woman. Ironically, years later, an autopsy of Stephens' chief rival, Poland's Stanislawa Walasiewicznova, renamed Stella Walsh, revealed that she had the genitals of a male."[11]

Six months before the games were to begin, a woman dead for twelve years was making *good copy*. And Helen once again was pulled into the fray. This time, it was initiated by a 1936 Canadian Olympic team member (a hurdler) who seemed determined to strip Stella Walsh of her claim to fame.

"She ran like a man," said Roxanne Atkins Anderson.[12]

"Roxy," Helen said, "is just being a sore loser." Roxanne had petitioned the Athletics Congress (TAC), a 105-member governing board for track and field in the United States, to strip Stella of all her world records, her ribbons, and her medals, including her 1936 Olympic silver medal for the 100-meter race in which Stella competed against Helen. Interestingly enough, "Roxy" had coached Mildred Fizzell, who had placed second to Stella in a disputed 50-yard dash in 1954. Almost a half century later, Roxy was bringing up what she thought was unfinished business. She told Karen Rosen, a staff writer for the *Atlanta Journal*, "You have to be a coach to understand that you fight for your kids every time something is unfair." Rosen rang up Helen to ask what she thought about the possibility that the TAC might strip Stella of all her accomplishments on the record books.

"THAT would be a dastardly thing to do," said Helen. Rosen related what Roxy had told her about Stella's five-o'clock shadow, and Helen replied, "I know a lot of women, strictly feminine, who have that problem. . . . maybe Stella Walsh had a birth defect. . . . it wasn't her fault in any case. . . . Well, I don't think she was a man, that's just my opinion. . . . Let bygones be bygones. Let the woman rest!" The decision to admit Stella Walsh to women's events, when physical exams were given, had been made by previous officials. The chair of the TAC's committee agreed with Helen who asked, "Why are we bringing this up?"

This issue had always involved Helen and now stalked her in her senior years. The almost maniacal, delinquent focus on sex delineations never let up, never let her be.

As is true with prepubescent children and infants, sex distinctions and gender differentiations are also sometimes difficult to discern at a distance in the elderly. I had read this somewhere and pointed it out to Helen then, when we talked about Stella Walsh. Helen was quizzed on the topic by another person, athlete/author Mariah Burton Nelson. Aware of Dr. John Money's biological continuum studies and the IOC's concern to prevent impostors like "Dora" Ratjen from competing, Nelson asked Helen's opinion on sex testing, which she wanted to use in her new book. Helen complied: "I guess they have to do something to keep men out."[13] She also said she thought Stella's was "an unfortunate case of birth defects."

That fall, Helen attended her Middle River School reunion and again competed in the Senior Games and the Show-Me State Games, again saying this would be her swan song competition. She carried the torch and again won gold, silver, and bronze medals. That year, her Olympic Co-Eds and All-American Red Heads team member and friend Ruth "Casey" Osburn was inducted into Missouri's Basketball Hall of Fame, in Springfield. Helen expressed an interest in also being inducted into this Hall of Fame. I nominated her, and several key people endorsed her nomination, among them an "old-timer basketball buddy" from Fulton, Tyke Yates. Ample documentation came from her now partially archived collection to qualify her for that honor. One piece of ephemera used was an original 1938 four-color, double-bill poster announcing an evening of basketball: MGM vs. RKO, and the All-American Red Heads vs. the Warner Brothers Studio Team. Helen's name appeared in large display caps, with the subtext "Star of 1936 Olympics, Fastest Human Female on Earth." The events took place at the Pan Pacific Auditorium, with "good seats 40¢, children 25¢, box seats $1.10."

About the same time, *USA Today* ran a story on the National Women's Hall of Fame, in Seneca Falls, New York, and someone suggested that Helen try to get inducted into it. I requested the forms and composed a letter of nomination and sent it off in a hurry, while Helen went on about her business. The odds of getting into both halls in the same year were improbable, she said, and if given her druthers, if it had to be one or the other, her heart was most set on the basketball fame.

Helen's final year proved to be a whirlwind one for her. In July 1993, she competed in the Show-Me Games, which had grown so large that events were held in two cities, Jefferson City and Columbia. In August, much to her delight, the famed Red Heads/Co-Eds basketball star was granted her wish and was admitted into Missouri's Basketball Hall of Fame. As I drove Helen to this induction event, she talked a good deal about her basketball years. Although Helen had owned and managed, coached as well as played, basketball for over ten years with her own team, she was admitted to this hall in the *player* category. I think she was happy with that. During that same week, Helen and a freelance sportswriter friend drove to St. Joseph to participate in a women-in-sports conference. In September, surprised and ecstatically happy, Helen flew to New York, where she was inducted into the National Women's Hall of Fame, along with Rosa Parks, Betty Friedan, Chief Wilma Mankiller, and many other famous American women. In November, she drove to Jefferson City for the opening of the Missouri Sports Hall of Fame, where a suite of plaques was installed in the secretary of state's new Information Building, and also she learned that her basketball career would be part of a forthcoming book, *The Lure and the Lore of Basketball in Missouri.*[14] In December, the BBC and Boston's WGBH television crew appeared on her doorstep to film her for a segment of *The People's Century: Sporting Fever.*

Unfortunately, she did not live to see it aired. During Christmas week of 1993, she had a mild stroke and experienced numbness in her right (writing) hand. The last thing Helen asked me to do for her was to write to Coach Moore, to tell him that she was unable to write and that she was scheduled to have surgery in mid-January. She died several weeks later, January 17, 1994, just hours after surgery for blocked carotid arteries. She had drafted the beginnings of a will, but it never materialized. Her estate fell to probate court. Her brother Bob got Helen's 1936 autograph book and Olympic gold medals and household items, but the Western Historical Manuscript Collection would receive her Olympic diary and her archived collection, once her biography was published. Her housekeeper held a yard sale in March 1994; her home on Thackery Court sold within the year.

The news of her death broke into the early morning hours of Monday, January 17. The Old Gladiator was dead. The Fulton Flash was dead. The once-quick, lifelong athlete slipped away to rest on the blue-white slopes of Mount Olympus. The state flag flew at half-mast; the governor and both houses of the state legislature issued proclamations to recognize and honor a native daughter whose stunning athlete achievements would live on. Her devotion and work as an officer of the Midwest Chapter of Olympians were mentioned in the documents that lauded her as Missouri's most captivating goodwill ambassador, who tackled any pressing need with diplomacy and speed. Her wit, generosity, and kindnesses were far-reaching, never conspicuous, and never buoyed by arrogance.

She was America's last great athlete-soloist to rise up without agent-managed mega-promotions, commercial backing, professional handlers, or any of the trappings of today's sports celebrities—yet looming forward historically, she stands grandly among them all.

The *New York Times* carried a lengthy obituary with an Olympic photo of Helen in full stride.[15] And the *St. Louis Post-Dispatch* paid homage in a retrospective of their adopted daughter,[16] but it was her hometown paper that brought human interest and tears to those who knew her.[17]

Two funeral homes—one in St. Louis County and one in Callaway County—handled the matter of her burial, and hundreds of people came to show their respect and love for her: For Popeye the Great. The Fulton Flash. The Florissant Flash. The Show-Me Senior. The Old Gladiator. The Senior Olympian.

Home in Fulton on January 20, she lay dressed in a bright red jacket; a black stone ring was on her left-hand "betrothed" finger. Olympian Francis Johnson put one of his Senior Olympic gold medals in her pocket. Fragrance from a plethora of flowers filled the room at Debo Funeral Parlor. Alone, in contrast, among a bank of color was a small basket of white gladiolus and white roses—for remembrance.

At Callaway Memorial Gardens, an old friend, Olympic runner Oscar Hartmann, appeared in the distance on a gentle slope, holding high a ceremonial torch and sprinting unhurriedly toward Helen's burial site. It was the torch she had carried in times past. The weather that day turned bitter, cold, and gusty. It was just below freezing, but the sun shone intermittently, according to her old friend Julia Spearman. And as the mourners began leaving, sleet fell differentially, conciliatingly, slowly forming a smooth and brilliant blanket of ice upon her grave.

Notes

Notes

1. Childhood of a Champion

1. "The City of Fulton," *Fulton Gazette*, September 3, 1935, reprinted for 125th anniversary commemorative edition in *Kingdom Daily Sun Gazette*, October 13, 1984, 1. Also Stanley J. Kunitz and Vineta Colby, *European Authors, 1000–1900* (H. W. Wilson, 1957), 974.

2. "The City of Fulton," 4.

3. "Going After Idlers," *Fulton Gazette*, reprinted in *Kingdom Daily Sun Gazette* commemorative edition, 6A.

4. "Community Meeting," *Fulton Gazette*, reprinted in ibid., 5A.

5. "Abolish Use of German," *Fulton Gazette*, August 22, 1918, reprinted in ibid., 6A.

6. "August Anniversary of Two Lynchings," *Fulton Gazette*, August 22, 1918, reprinted in ibid., 6A.

7. Margaret Maunders, "Fulton, Mo., Prepares for Churchill Visit," *St. Louis Globe-Democrat*, January 27, 1946, 1.

8. Quoted in Gordon Campbell, *Famous American Athletes of Today* (L. C. Page, 1972), 343–44.

9. Author interviews with Helen Stephens (hereafter, HS), August and November 1991. Quotes and paraphrasing throughout from HS and from correspondence with W. Burton Moore, Helen's coach, in HS archives.

10. "Citation: Legum Doctor," William Woods College, 1980, in HS archives. Information on Frank E. Stephens is probably from the Fulton paper obituary, unidentified newspaper clipping in HS archives. It lists no parents' names, identifies Frank as the seventy-four-year-old father of Olympian Helen Stephens and Robert Stephens, and names his surviving siblings.

11. Author interview with HS and Julia Spearman, August 1991.

12. Author interview with HS, October 1991.

13. Script of Harry Flannery interview with HS, *Views on News*, KMOS radio, St. Louis, September 21, 1936.

14. Author phone interview with Thomas Thornton Meloy, October 1991. Also see "Where Are They Now? 1936 Olympic Champion Helen Stephens," *Olympian,* August 1978, 13–15.

15. HS to Brenda Chiles, Fulton, Mo., April 16, 1979, in HS archives.

16. Author interview with HS, October 1991. Population and segregation information from G. A. Hamlin, *Community and Its Schools* (Fulton Public Schools, 1984); a 1920 photo identifies North Elementary School, built 1882, as Fulton's first school for black children and their teacher as Arthur White.

17. Quoted in Carol Herkstroeter, "The Fulton Flash Isn't Finished Yet," unidentified newspaper clipping, in HS archives.

2. Popeye Becomes the Fulton Flash

1. Whitney Martin, untitled AP news item in unidentified newspaper clipping dated November 10, 1935, in HS archives; Flannery interview with HS, September 21, 1936.

2. Leroy Atkinson, *Famous American Athletes of Today* (Ayer, 1977), 342.

3. Author phone conversations and correspondence with Burton Moore, 1991.

4. "Polish Star Will Compete against Betty Robinson: Seventy-five Women Athletes to Try for Trials in Track and Field: Gertrude Webb and Harriet Bland Are St. Louis' Leading Entrants in Meet," unidentified newspaper clipping dated March 22, 1935, in HS archives.

5. "Did She Beat the Gun?" *St. Louis Post-Dispatch,* March, 24, 1935. The caption reads: "After her defeat in the 50-meter dash in the national title meet here Friday night, Stella Walsh of Olympic fame declared Miss Helen Stephens . . . had beaten the gun. This photo shows the contestants almost in line, after having taken a few steps. . . . five of the runners took the first stride with the right foot. Miss Walsh alone started on the left foot."

6. "Stella Walsh and Helen Stephens Will Likely Meet Again"; "After the Race Was Over," *St. Louis Globe-Democrat,* March 25, 1935. Also see *Fulton High School Hi-Life,* October 9, 1936, 1.

7. *St. Louis Post-Dispatch,* October 9, 1936.

8. Helen Stephens, "Notes on Athletic Career of Helen Stephens," typescript, c. 1954, 1, in HS archives.

9. "Fulton Dash Star's Coach Confident of New Records," unidentified newspaper clipping from one of HS's scrapbooks.

10. W. H. James, "St. Louis Columnist Has Comment, Reflections from the Sideline," *St. Louis Globe-Democrat,* March 28, 1935; L. C. Davis, "Sports Salad," *St. Louis Post-Dispatch,* March 27, 1935.

11. "Fulton Girl Becomes Famous Overnight," *Fulton Daily Sun-Gazette,* March 23, 1935; "Helen Stephens Day at the High School—Excitement over Feats of Fulton Girl Athlete Make Study Impossible: Applause and Thrills—Coach Moore Tells of St. Louis Trip, Helen Speaks of Thrills," *Fulton Daily Sun-Gazette,* March 25, 1935.

12. Virginia Irwin, "From Farm to Fame on the Cinder Track," *Fulton Daily Sun-Gazette*, April 4, 1935.

13. *Fulton High School Lo-Life*, April 1935; and *Fulton High School Hi-Life*, April 19, 1935. Also see "Fulton High School Lauds Miss Stephens," undated clipping from unidentified newspaper, HS scrapbook.

14. *Fulton High School Hi-Life*, May 23, 1935.

15. Horace Carr, "St. Louis Hopes to Get Helen Stephens, President of Athletic Club of That City Here Again to See Coach Moore: Fulton Indifferent, Nothing Done for Track Star: Rathert Talks of Miss Stella Walsh," *Fulton Daily Sun-Gazette*, May 23, 1935.

16. Author interview with John C. Harris Sr., chairman of the board, Callaway County Bank, Fulton, Mo., February 14, 1995.

17. Quoted in O. K. Armstrong, "Dashing Young Lady," *St. Louis Globe-Democrat This Week Magazine*, July 26, 1936.

3. Stella Who and Who Else?

1. Quoted in Whitney Martin, untitled AP news item in unidentified newspaper clipping dated November 10, 1936, in HS archives.

2. Quoted in unidentified clipping from *Fulton Daily Sun-Gazette*, May 8, 1935.

3. "Fulton and Wright City High School Girls to Run Exhibition Dash, Annual Indoor Meet: Helen Stephens Will Be Opposed in Race," *Fulton Sun Gazette*, April 6, 1935; author interview with Martha Faucett Pearre, February 1995.

4. "Stella Walsh and Helen Stephens Will Likely Meet Again," undated, unidentified newspaper clipping, HS 1935–36 scrapbook; "Polish Star Will Compete against Betty Robinson: 75 Women Athletes Try for Titles in Track and Field: Five High School Events: Gertrude Webb and Harriet Bland Are St. Louis' Leading Entrants in Meet," unidentified newspaper clipping dated March 22, 1935, HS scrapbook.

5. "Flash: Farm Girl's Olympic Dream," *Columbia Missourian*, May 2, 1991, 1B.

6. "Helen Stephens in Limelight Again," *Fulton Daily Sun-Gazette*, May 6, 1935.

7. Quoted in Campbell, *Famous American Athletes of Today*, 343.

8. Campbell, *Famous American Athletes of Today*, 343–44.

9. Quoted in Whitney Martin, AP news item, November 10, 1936.

10. "What Ever Happened to . . . ?" *St. Louis Globe- Democrat*, July 23–24, 1977; author interview with HS, February 5, 1993.

11. Quoted in "Stephens Back from Canadian Expedition," undated, unidentified newspaper clipping, HS scrapbook.

12. Quoted in Robert Morrison, "Fulton, Mo Turns Out for Helen Stephens Day: Helen Cracks the World Record Again," *St. Louis Post-Dispatch*, June 12, 1936.

13. "She's a Track Team . . . A New Didrikson," unidentified Rhode Island newspaper clipping, July 4, 1936, HS scrapbook.

14. Quoted in Robert Burnes, "Cheated Out of Berth on Team Twice, She Charges,"

St. Louis Globe-Democrat, July 6, 1936. Also see Robert Burnes, "Forgotten Champion," *St. Louis Globe-Democrat,* February 28, 1978.

15. Maurice O. Shevlin, "The Sporting Mill," *St. Louis Globe-Democrat,* July 8, 1936.

16. John E. Wray, "Injured Tendons May Hurt Helen Stephens' Chances in Olympics," *St. Louis Post-Dispatch,* July 27, 1936.

17. *Fulton Sun,* reprinted in *Fulton Daily Sun,* July 12, 1961.

18. O. K. Armstrong, "Dashing Young Lady," *St. Louis Globe-Democrat This Week Magazine,* July 26, 1936.

4. From Fulton to Berlin

1. HS kept her diary of her trip abroad, July 15–September 16, 1936, in *My Trip Abroad* (Holyoke, Mass.: National Blank Book, 1930). All diary entries appear in italics.

2. HS's 1936 passport, no. 10444, in HS archives.

3. Author interviews with HS, 1989 and 1991. Also see Sandy Danisky, "For Olympic Hopefuls, Boycott Is No Game," *Baltimore Sun,* January 20, 1980.

4. "A Significant Step," *Amateur Athlete,* October 1935, in HS archives. The 1936 foil gold medalist was Ilona Elek (Hungary), the bronze went to Karen Lachmann (Denmark), and the silver went to Helene Mayer—who gave the Nazi salute from the winners platform. Without the tie-breaking rules that are used today, the 1936 high jump event played out with a three-way tie at 1.60 meters among Ibolya Csak (Hungary), Dorothy Odam (Great Britain), and Elfriede Kaun (Germany), although Csak cleared it at 1.62 in a jump-off. The German "Dora" (aka Herman) Ratjen jumped 1.58 for fourth place; Marguerite Nicolas (France) cleared 1.56 meters; and Francina Blankers-Koen (Holland), Doris Carter (Australia); and Annette Rogers (U.S.A.) all marked in at 1.55 meters.

5. Alan Gould, "U.S. Best Ever Team, Avery Brundage Says," AP news item in unidentified newspaper clipping dated July 21, 1936, in HS archives. Also see Irving Settel, *A Pictorial History of Radio* (New York: Grosset and Dunlap, 1967), 99–100.

6. Quoted in Will Grimsley, "Champagne Girl of 1936 Recalls Fun and Games," AP news item, *Herald-Star,* June 8, 1978, 15.

7. Bruce Hackmann, "Nazi Put On Propaganda Show at 1936 Games," *Fulton Sun Gazette,* February 12, 1980; author interviews with HS, 1993.

8. "First the Liberation of Innocent German Political Prisoners—Then to the Olympic Games in Berlin!" A. S. Houwink, Schielbaanlaan 74b, Rotterdam (Holland), no date. HS received the manifesto at Olympic village, July 24, 1936. It is commonly referred to as the "Anti-Hitler Manifesto."

9. *The Story of the Olympic Games,* chap. 12: "Berlin, 1936," pp. 178–79 (photocopied), in HS archives.

10. Campbell, *Famous American Athletes of Today,* 352–53.

11. Quoted in Campbell, *Famous American Athletes of Today,* 357.

12. Quoted in Campbell, *Famous American Athletes of Today,* 357.

13. Quoted in "Mrs. Jarrett Remains in Germany as a Reporter," *St. Louis Post-Dispatch*, July 27, 1936, 3B. Also see Sally Guard, "Still Very Much in the Swim," *Sports Illustrated*, June 1992.

14. Campbell, *Famous American Athletes of Today*, 355.

15. Quoted in Campbell, *Famous American Athletes of Today*, 355.

16. John E. Wray, "Helen Stephens, after Unimpressive Workout, Confident She'll Win," *St. Louis-Post Dispatch*, July 31, 1936. Also see Campbell, *Famous American Athletes of Today*, 357.

5. Winners and Losers

1. This account of the opening day ceremonies is taken from three undated, unidentified clippings in HS archives: James Simms, "The Opening Ceremonies"; "The Olympic Village"; and "Olympic Sports Facilities."

2. Richard Mandell, *The Nazi Olympics* (New York: Macmillan, 1971), 173. After World War II, Germany's Dora Ratjen was identified as Herman Ratjen; he claimed that Hitler youth organization leaders pressed him into transvestite service for Germany.

3. Bruce Hackmann, "Nazis Put On Propaganda Show at 1936 Games," *Fulton Sun Gazette*, February 12, 1980.

4. David Hinton, *The Films of Leni Riefenstahl* (Metuchen, N.J.: Scarecrow, 1978), 139, 141; Leni Riefenstahl, *Leni Riefenstahl: A Memoir* (New York: St. Martin's, 1992), 169–77, 199–200. Also see author's 1978 correspondence and 1981 interview with Horst Kettner and Leni Riefenstahl in Pössenhoffen, West Germany.

5. Quoted in *Sportscan*, November–December 1986, in HS archives.

6. HS's notes, "The Thrill of Winning a Gold Medal," speech delivered to Amateur Softball Association, July 1985, in HS archives.

7. Quoted in Mary Sennewald, "The Fulton Flash," *Missouri Life*, March–April 1979. Also see June Wuest Becht, "America's Olympic Oaks," *American Forests*, August 1986; and "Fulton Flash Recalls Tensions of '36 Olympics," *St. Louis Journal*, July 2, 1976.

8. Jesse Owens with Paul Neimark, *Jesse: The Man Who Outran Hitler* (New York: Faucett, 1978); Dave Dorr, "Jesse Ran Hitler's Racial Theories Out of Stadium," *St. Louis Post-Dispatch*, March 1, 1972; Max Seibel, "A Lifetime on the Track," *Phoenix Gazette*, August 16, 1978; Hackmann, "Nazis Put On Propaganda Show"; Sally Guard, "Still Very Much in the Swim," *Sports Illustrated*, June 1992.

9. Author interviews with HS, 1992, 1993. Also see David Wallechinsky, *Summer Olympics 1996* (New York: Little, Brown, 1996), 189.

6. In the High Callaway Style

1. Quoted in Dave Lipman, "Helen Stephens Was a Model for Women Sprinters," *St. Louis Post-Dispatch*, February 2, 1964. Also see Robert Burnes, "Odds and Ends," *St. Louis Globe-Democrat*, January 28, 1980.

2. Sharon Kinney Hanson, "Propaganda, Documentation, Art?" *Sheba Review Literary Magazine for the Arts* 1:2 (Fall–Winter 1978): 4–5; author interview with Horst Kettner and Leni Riefenstahl, Pössenhoffen, West Germany, March 1981.

3. Author interview with HS, October 2, 1991.

4. Ibid.

5. William Shirer, *The Rise and Fall of the Third Reich: A History of Nazi Germany* (New York: Simon and Schuster, 1960), 146.

6. Mary Sennewald, *Missouri Life*, March 1975; "Missouri Girl at Olympics," *St. Louis Globe-Democrat*, undated clipping in HS archives.

7. Paul Gallico, *A Farewell to Sport* (New York: Knopf, 1941), 233–34.

8. *New York Mirror*, newspaper clipping from August 1936, in HS archives.

9. Obituary from an Aurora, Illinois, newspaper clipping dated November 17, 1986, in HS archives. The notice mentions that after the 1936 Olympics, Tidye Anne Pickett Phillips became a school principal in East Chicago Heights.

10. See Robert Burnes, "Forgotten Champion," *St. Louis Globe-Democrat*, February 28, 1978.

11. Author interview with HS, October 2, 1991.

12. June Wuest Becht, *St. Louis Post-Dispatch*, June 3, 1985.

13. June Wuest Becht, "The Duchess Enters Sports Hall of Fame," *St. Louis Globe-Democrat*, May 21, 1978.

14. *The Story of the Olympic Games,* chap. 12: "Berlin, 1936," pp. 178–79 (photocopied), in HS archives.

15. Quoted in Becht, "Duchess Enters Sports Hall of Fame."

7. Running the Continent

1. Author interviews with HS, 1991, 1992.

2. *My Trip Abroad* (Holyoke, Mass.: National Blank Book, 1930). Page 7 gives German Reichmark/U.S. cent exchange rate (1:23.8); page 14 details the ship's structure.

3. Ibid., 19.

8. Victor's Return

1. Quoted in Robert Burnes, "Royal Reception Given Missouri Olympians," *St. Louis Globe-Democrat*, September 16, 1936.

2. Quoted in Louis Effrat, "199 U.S. Athletes Back from Berlin Overjoyed to be Home Again: Olympians Find New York Eager to Entertain Them: Venzke in Bitter Attack Charges American Officials with Being Aloof, Unfair," *New York Times-Mirror*, August 29, 1936.

3. Columbia Pictures contract, September 9, 1936, in HS archives.

4. Author interviews with HS, 1992. Also see Will Grimsley, *Golf: Its History, People, and Events* (Englewood Cliffs, N.J. Prentice-Hall, 1966).

5. Robert Burnes, undated clipping from *St. Louis Globe-Democrat*, HS scrapbook;

Western Union Night Letter, from James A. Hoey, Caledonia Club, NA 1069 11 4, New York 15 11:31P, to HS, Jefferson Hotel, St. Louis, Room 472A, in HS archives.

6. Quoted in Robert Burnes, *St. Louis Globe-Democrat*, September 16, 1936.

7. "Stephens Back from Canadian Expedition," undated clipping from *St. Louis Globe-Democrat*, HS scrapbook; Campbell, *Famous Athletes of America Today*, 363.

8. Joel Hardesty, M.D., 100 North 6th, Hannibal, Mo., to HS, c/o 1143 Pratt, Chicago, Ill., October 6, 1937. The author returned the original letter to HS in 1992.

9. Quoted in "Harriet Bland Home from Olympic Games in Berlin, Says Her Days as a Competitive Runner Are Over," unidentified newspaper clipping dated September 17, 1936, HS scrapbook.

9. Steve Goes Pro

1. Western Union 19AWC 32 DL 2 Extra, Cassville, Mo., 11:15AM, Oct. 17, 1936, to Helen Stevens [*sic*] Girl Athlete, Fulton, Mo., in HS archives.

2. Quoted in "Success of Helen Stephens Didn't Detract from Handiness on Farm," undated clipping from *Fulton Sun*, HS scrapbook.

3. Quoted in Robert Morrison, "Helen Stephens Too Restless to Punch a Time Clock So She Joined Pros—Dee Boeckmann," *St. Louis Post-Dispatch*, September 11, 1937.

4. Author phone interviews and correspondence with Shannon Chenoweth Graham, spring 1997 and May 1, 1998.

5. Scotty Reston, "From Cider to Cocktails," undated clipping from *Fulton Sun*, and "Fulton Sprint Star to Live in Gotham Starting in January," unidentified clipping from New York newspaper dated December 11, 1936, in HS archives.

6. John F. Case, "Most Outstanding Woman Athlete Is Missouri's Helen Stephens," *Missouri Ruralist*, January 9, 1937.

7. Quoted in Bob Broeg, *St. Louis Post-Dispatch*, July 26, 1976.

8. Letter dated January 12, 1937, correspondence file, in HS archives. The two passages referred to are as follows: "Be not among winebibers; among riotous eaters of flesh: For the drunkard and the glutton shall come to poverty; and drowsiness shall clothe a man with rags" (Proverbs 23:20–21). "Woe unto him that giveth his neighbor drink, that puttest thy bottle to him, and makest him drunken also, that thou mayest look on their nakedness" (Habakkuk 2:15). Three other moralistic letters (antidrinking, antismoking) arrived during the period December 1936 to February 1937.

9. "What Do You Think? Is This a Man or a Woman?" *Look*, February 1937, 37–40.

10. Thomas G. Nichols, Kansas City, to HS, correspondence file, in HS archives.

11. Marie Gragg Shafer, to HS, and W. Ed Jameson, to HS, January 29, 1937, correspondence file, in HS archives.

12. Quoted in "Boeckmann Says Stephens Better than Didrikson," *Mobile Alabama Register*, March 25, 1937.

13. Author interview with HS, April 14, 1993.

14. Author interview with HS, summer 1993. Also see *St. Louis Globe-Democrat*, April 11, 1937, and 1937 correspondence file, in HS archives.

15. Author interview with HS, April 14, 1993.

16. C. M. Olson to HS, December 4, 1937, correspondence file, in HS archives.

17. Quoted in "Appointment of Dee Boeckmann Draws Protest," unidentified newspaper clipping, ca. 1938, including February 8 AP reports from Chambersburg, Pa., and New York City, in HS archives.

18. Robert Morrison, "Miss Stephens Chafed at Holding Down Job: Fulton Flash Too Nervous to Push Time Clock Says Miss Boeckman [*sic*]—Saw Interest Wane—Olympic Champ Had Reached Top and Nothing Else to Strive For," undated clipping from *St. Louis Post-Dispatch*, in HS archives; author interviews, 1993.

19. Quoted in Maurice Shevlin, "Surprises St. Louisians," *Fulton Daily Sun-Gazette*, September 8, 1937.

20. Quoted in James S. Nutter, "Medals vs. Money: Jesse Owens Holds Ten World Records but Realizes They Won't Buy Groceries," *Sunday Oregonian*, February 6, 1938. Also see Jesse Owens with Paul Neimark, *Jesse: The Man Who Outran Hitler* (New York: Faucett, 1978), 71–89.

10. Olympic Caging

1. Author interview with HS, fall 1992. Also see video rushes of Kathy Corley interview with HS, July 16, 1984, *Turn About*, Ch. 2 TV, St. Louis (broadcast August 5, 1984).

2. *Illinois State Register*, August 19, 1938. One cartoonist depicted Helen outrunning the famed racehorse Seabiscuit.

3. "Olson's Red Heads Making Big Hit on Pacific Coast: Entertained by Bing Crosby," *Cassville Republican*, January 20, 1938.

4. Alene Rasmussen interview with HS, "Olympic Athlete Tells of Career," unidentified newspaper clipping in HS archives.

5. "Helen Stephens Here for a Month's Visit: Fulton Girl Athlete Recuperating from Recent Spell of Illness," undated clipping from *Fulton Daily Sun-Gazette*, ca. 1938, in HS archives.

6. "Totems to Play Helen Stephens' Team Saturday," *Puyallup (Wash.) Press*, January 26, 1939.

7. Bill Forst, "In This Corner," *Vancouver Daily Province*, January 21, 1939.

8. Eugene Fitzgerald, "Helen Stephens US Olympic Sprinter, Human; She Prefers Fencing to Running," unidentified newspaper clipping dated December 23, 1938, in HS archives.

9. Author correspondence with Helen Onson in author's archives.

10. John E. Wray, "Lucky Break for Girl Who Turned Pro," *St. Louis Post-Dispatch*, February 9, 1940.

11. John E. Wray, "Famous Woman Runner Returns," undated clipping from *St. Louis Post-Dispatch*, ca. 1940, in HS archives.

12. Ferris quoted in Tom Anderson, "From Close Up," *Knoxville Journal*, March 9, 1940; "AAU Received 50 Cents a Year from Santee," unidentified AP news story clipping from New York, dated March 1 (no year), in HS archives. Also see "Daniel J. Ferris, Longtime Leader in Amateur Athletics, Is Dead at 87," *New York Times*, May 3, 1977.

13. Author interview with HS, fall 1992.

14. Author phone interview with Sam Snead, summer 1996.

15. Fletcher Sweet, "Helen Stephens Holder of 14 Track Records, Recalls Races with Walsh," *Knoxville Journal*, March 7, 1940.

16. Fletcher Sweet, *Fulton Daily Gazette*, May 8, 1940, in HS archives.

17. "Helen Stephens to Race with an Auto," *Fulton Daily Gazette*, May 11, 1940.

18. "Helen Stephens Plans to Hang Up Shoes, Outclasses Two Local Speedsters," Fremont, Neb., dated June 5, 1940, in HS archives.

19. Quoted in "Helen Stephens, Travel Weary, Gets Job Here," *St. Louis Post-Dispatch*, July 3, 1940. Also see "Helen Stephens Ready to Quit Barnstorming and Seek Regular Job," *St. Louis Post-Dispatch*, June 17, 1940.

20. John E. Wray, "Will Women Ever Be Man's Equal in Sport?" *St. Louis Post-Dispatch*, December 30, 1942.

21. Walter Byers, "Helen Stephens, 1936 Olympic Champ, Eager for Comeback Match Race with Stella Walsh," *St. Louis Star-Times*, August 24, 1943; Walter Byers, "Helen Stephens Fanning Feud with Stella Walsh," *St. Louis Star-Times*, August 20, 1943.

22. John E. Wray, "Fastest Man and Woman Meet in Race," *St. Louis Post-Dispatch*, June 4, 1944; souvenir program, June, 4, 1944, in HS archives.

23. John E. Wray, "When Helen Went to Berlin, She Went to Town," *St. Louis Post-Dispatch*, June 11, 1944.

24. *AllSports* (November–December 1944), 13; C. Norman Fry, director, Creative Dept., R. L. Polk & Co., Detroit, Mich., to HS, June 12, 1940, re: Boeckmann article.

25. "New President GAO Welfare and Recreational Association," *Pointer* 1:1 (July 1947): 1.

26. *Airscoop* (employee newsletter of McDonnell Aircraft Corp.), October 18, 1946, 4.

27. Author interviews in person and by phone with Charles J. Guenther, 1991, 1993; correspondence and notes in author's archives.

28. John E. Wray, "Plane or Flattop for Olympic Team?" *St. Louis Post-Dispatch*, November 26, 1946.

29. Jimmy Conzelman, "There's No Pot of Gold at the Rainbow's End for Professional Sprinters: Helen Now Back at Work as Stenographer: Jesse Owens Olympic Star Found This Out," *St. Louis Post-Dispatch*, July 5, 1940.

30. Quoted in John E. Wray, "And Never the Twain Shall Meet," *St. Louis Post-Dispatch*, January 10, 1947.

31. HS to Frederick Armstrong, Ozark AAU membership chair, June 11, 1947, in HS archives.

32. "Helen Stephens Wants to Run in Olympics Again," unidentified newspaper clipping dated June 10, 1947.

33. "112 Athletes to Seek Honors in Ozark AAU Meet," *St. Louis Post-Dispatch*, June 13, 1947. The Ozark track chairman is identified in this source as "Rilers," although the same paper had given his name as "Eilers" the year before.

34. "Headed for the Olympics?" *St. Louis Post-Dispatch*, June 27, 1948.

35. Quoted in John E. Wray, "Just a Nice Joy-Ride for the Girls," *St. Louis Post-Dispatch*, June 30, 1948.

36. John E. Wray, "We Had Many Firsts and Plenty Worsts," *St. Louis Post-Dispatch*, August 16, 1948. Also see "Columnist Says the U.S. Needed Her in the London Olympics," *Fulton Sun Gazette*, August 17, 1948.

37. "Helen Stephens Olympic Champ Is Visitor Here," *Mt. Carroll (Ill.) Mirror-Democrat*, August 5, 1948. Also see "Miss Stephens Sets Shot Put Mark Here," unidentified newspaper clipping from Rhinelander, Wisc., dated August 9, 1948, in HS archives; "Sets World's Shot Put Record," *Milwaukee Sentinel*, August 10, 1948.

38. "HS an Also Ran—But in Swimming Meet," *St. Louis Post-Dispatch*, August 26, 1949; author interview with HS, summer 1993.

39. "Brundage Target of Swedish Criticism on Amateur Stand," AP news item from Stockholm in unidentified newspaper clipping dated June 14, 1952, in HS archives.

11. The Flash Fires Back

1. John E. Wray, "Living Up to Advance Notices," *St. Louis Post-Dispatch*, August 8, 1948.

2. HS to Marjorie Jackson, undated letter from 1956, correspondence file, in HS archives.

3. Quoted in John E. Wray's column, *St. Louis Post-Dispatch*, June 11, 1953.

4. Author interview with C. J. Guenther, summer 1991, author's archives.

5. "Helen Stephens Tells of Her Visit with Eisenhower at White House," unidentified newspaper clipping, ca. June 1953, in HS archives.

6. "Democrats Win Congressional Ball Game 3 to 2," *Times Herald*, June 6, 1953.

7. Quoted in John E. Wray, "Miss Asia Awakens as Miss America Slumbers," *St. Louis Post-Dispatch*, October 14, 1953.

8. "Sports Scrapbook," *Chicago Daily Tribune*, January 21, 1954.

9. Quoted in "Ban on School Sports Competition Hit," *Los Angeles Evening Herald Express*, May 3, 1954.

10. Jo Hindman's questionnaire to HS (1954), and HS to Jo Hindman, 8920 Second Ave., Inglewood, Calif., June 20, 1955, in HS archives.

11. Frank Walsh, as told to Jim Scott, "The Future? It's Up to Our Girls," *St. Louis Post-Dispatch Parade Magazine*, January 22, 1956, 14.

12. Jess Gorkin, "Warning—and a Plea for Help," *St. Louis Post-Dispatch Parade Magazine*, January 22, 1956; "Why Russia Expects to Win the 1956 Olympics," ibid.

13. "Why Russia Expects to Win the 1956 Olympics," 8.

14. "Mr. Speed of the '30s," AP-Chicago news item, *St. Louis Post-Dispatch*, December 2, 1955.

15. Gorkin, "Warning—and a Plea for Help," 9.

16. "Former Olympic Woman Star to Set Up Clinics," *St. Louis Globe-Democrat*, March 11, 1956; "40 Girls Take in Track Clinic of Ozark AAU," *St. Louis Globe-Democrat*, March 25, 1956; "Track Meet for Girls Planned Here April 14," undated clipping from *St. Louis Post-Dispatch* in HS archives; "Sports Scrapbook," *Chicago Daily Tribune*, January 21, 1954.

17. Untitled clipping from *St. Louis Globe-Democrat*, March 26, 1957, in HS archives.

18. "Helen Stephens in Pan-American Parade," *St. Louis Globe-Democrat*, August 23, 1959; author interview with HS, June 1993.

19. Untitled clipping from *St. Louis Post-Dispatch*, June 11, 1961, in HS archives.

12. The Old Gladiator

1. HS's speech notes for lettermen's banquet, June 4, 1962, Cleveland High School, St. Louis, in HS archives.

2. "Helen Stephens on the Run Trying to Catch Up with Fleet Fame," *Fulton Sun Gazette*, October 23, 1964. Also see "Helen Stephens Still Plays Active Role in Sports World," *Orienter*, April 30, 1965.

3. Jake McCarthy, "Women in Athletics," *St. Louis Post-Dispatch*, March 17, 1978.

4. Bill Beck, "Tiptoeing around Pitfalls of Title IX," *St. Louis Post-Dispatch*, February, 11, 1979.

5. "Helen Stephens Exhorts Athletes," *Orienter*, February 26, 1971, 3; HS to Myldred Fox Fairchild, May 10, 1965, in HS archives.

6. Peter Simpson, "Perception-Distillation," *St. Louis Post-Dispatch*, January 24, 1991; line of verse from Charles J. Guenther, *Phrase/Paraphrase* (Iowa City: Prairie, 1970).

7. "Helen Stephens Gold Medal Winner Wins MIBN Trophy," *Missouri-Illinois Bowling News*, October 18, 1974.

8. "Olympic Politics Led to Terror," *St. Louis Post Dispatch*, September 6, 1972.

9. Author interview with HS, April 27, 1993.

10. Quoted in "Olympian Avery Brundage: The Last Amateur," UPI news item, *St. Louis Post-Dispatch*, May 12, 1975; author interview with HS, April 27, 1993.

11. HS to Pat Miller, Lansdale, Pa., July 14, 1976, in HS archives.

12. "Women's AAU Track Meet a Walk-Away for Stella Walsh," *St. Louis Star-Times*, July 7, 1948; "Miss Stella Walsh Gets Continuance: Her Trial in Indiana on Shoplifting Charge Now Booked for June 14," unidentified newspaper clipping dated May 5, 1943; "Stella Walsh to Get Hearing Soon," *Fulton Daily Sun-Gazette*, November 12, 1942.

13. Quoted in "Stella Walsh Retires at 38," *Chicago Herald-American*, August 15, 1949, 19.

14. "Stella Walsh, 44, in 'Last' Race Saturday," *St. Louis Post-Dispatch*, January 18, 1956.

15. Quoted in "Stella Walsh Reaches End of Line, Fails in U.S. Trials," UPI-Washington news item from unidentified newspaper dated August 25, 1956, in HS archives.

16. Julie Ward, "Ex-Olympian Helen Stephens Still Loves Her Track, Women in Sports," *St. Louis Globe-Democrat*, May 13–14, 1978. Also see "Florissant Valley Invitational Women's Result," unidentified newspaper clipping dated April 8, 1978, in HS archives; "Johanna Faust State Champion in Track," *Fulton Sun Gazette*, May 1, 1978.

17. HS's notes for 1979 conference of the Midwest Sex Desegregation Assistance Center, Omaha, Neb., in HS archives.

18. Author interview with HS, fall 1993.

19. Joel Vance, "Lonesome Oak," *Missouri Conservationist*, February 1975.

20. Mary Sennewald, "The Fulton Flash," *Missouri Life*, March–April 1979.

21. "Presentation on the Olympics," *St. Louis Journal*, November 14, 1979.

13. Show-Me Senior Jock

1. Program, AIAW National Indoor Track and Field Championships, Columbia, Mo., March 8–9, 1980.

2. Sandy Banisky, "For Olympic Hopefuls, Boycott Decision Is No Game," and David M. Ettlin, "Olympians Recall Politics That Marred Past Games," *Baltimore Sun*, January 20, 1980.

3. Quoted in "Olympic Boycott May Be Valid Idea," *Fulton Sun Gazette*, February 12, 1980.

4. HS correspondence with President Carter, Richard Gephardt, Paul Zorn, and others, February–April 1980, in HS archives.

5. Notes of Bill Lucas interview with HS, April 16, 1980.

6. Neal Russo, "Stephens: Owens Was Mr. Track," *St. Louis Post-Dispatch*, March 31, 1980. Also see *Globe-Democrat*, March 31, 1990; and *St. Louis Evening Whirl*, June 14, 1983.

7. Dan Balz, "Man or Woman? Ex-Olympian's Death Raises Questions about Her Biological Secret," *Washington Post*, reprinted in *Arizona Republic*, December 19, 1980. Also see Victor Cohn, "Famed Olympic Medalist Stella Walsh Wasn't a 'She,' Autopsy Finds," *Washington Post*, January 24, 1981. HS's *Playboy* issues of 1986–88, which she discarded in 1991, were retained by the author. Also see Elizabeth Price, "Walsh's Abnormality Is Rare Condition," and W. C. Miller, "Stella Walsh 'Lived and Died' a Female, County Coroner Says," *Cleveland Plain Dealer*, February 12, 1981, in HS archives; David Wallechinsky, *Complete Book of the Olympics* (New York: Penguin, 1988), 135; Michael Sampson, "Sports Devastated: Anabolic Steroids," *Sports News*, August 1991; Gretchen Edgren, "The Transformation of Tula," *Playboy*, September 1991; Hal

Higdon, "Is She or Isn't She?" *Runner's World*, January 1992; "City Councilwoman Disclosed Sex-Change," *Jefferson City Post-Tribune*, March 15, 1993; and author's 1993 correspondence and phone interview with Dr. Melvin M. Grumbach, Pediatrics Department, University of California, in author's archives.

8. Program, 1980 AIAW Championships, Columbia, Mo.

9. Dee Boeckmann to HS, January 16, 1981, in HS archives.

10. "42 Posts Compete in 1981 Explorer Olympics," *St. Louis Post-Dispatch*, June 18, 1981.

11. "Hazelwood Adds More Scholarships Because of Run," unidentified newspaper clipping dated July 7, 1982, in HS archives.

12. Herbert B. Leonard to HS, July 29, 1982, cc: Russ Barry, Paul Brenzie, July 29, 1982, in HS archives.

13. Author phone conversations with HS and Bud Greenspan, 1991. Also see *St. Louis Evening Whirl*, June 14, 1983; and film *Time Capsule: The 1936 Berlin Olympics*, written and produced by Bud Greenspan, Cappy Productions, 1984.

14. Howard Rosenberg, "High Moments of Truth," *Los Angeles Times*, July 4, 1984. Also see Sean Mitchell, "Paging Through an Album of Olympians, Special Puts Heroes in Historical Context, on Television," *Los Angeles Herald Examiner*, July 4, 1984.

15. Quoted in Thomas R. Raber, "Stephens, 68, Still Swift at Sr. Olympics," *St. Louis Globe-Democrat*, May 28, 1986.

16. Lisa Schmidt, "H/F Spotlight on Sportswomen," *Women's Sports*, October 1983, 10. Also see Joan Ryan, "Women's Sports Reach Milestone in New Agenda," *Orlando Sentinel*, reprinted in *Kansas City Star*, November 18, 1983.

17. Quoted in Mary Kimbrough, "How They Stay Fit," *St. Louis Globe-Democrat*, October 6, 1982.

18. HS to Jennifer Debo, December 2, 1982, quoted in "A Flash in History," *Fulton Sun Gazette*, January 19, 1994, 6.

19. Cliff Gewecke, "'Senior Olympics' Heads for Worldwide Arena," *Christian Science Monitor*, September 22, 1992.

20. Unpublished notes, in HS archives.

21. Author interview with HS, summer 1992.

22. Unpublished notes, in HS archives.

23. Unpublished notes, in HS archives.

14. Sportswomen: Pandora's Box

1. Author interview with HS, summer 1992

2. Author interview with HS, summer 1993.

3. Robert Burnes, *St. Louis Globe-Democrat*, June 5, 1989.

4. Quoted in "'Fulton Flash' Slowed Down by Broken Leg," *Fulton Sun*, February 3, 1988. Also see Donald E. Franklin, "Olympians Swap Stories of Victories," *St. Louis Post-Dispatch*, November 19, 1988.

5. Author and HS interview with David Weaver, November 26, 1990, Florissant, Mo.

6. Author and HS interview with Ann Morris, May 8, 1991, St. Louis.

7. Pam Miner, of the Missouri State Archives, worked with the author in the summer of 1991 in Jefferson City, Mo.

8. HS to author, 1991, HHS-1991 correspondence file in author's archives.

9. Author interview with HS, December 1993.

10. Author interview with HS, July 1993.

11. James Christie, "Genecological Checks Might Return for Women Athletes," *Toronto Globe and Mail*, reprinted in *Columbia Missourian*, May 8, 1991.

12. Karen Rosen, "Gender of '32 Gold Medalist Debated," *Atlanta Journal*, December 5, 1991. Also see Karen Rosen, "Visual Inspection for Gender Replacing Chromosome Test," *Atlanta Journal*, December 5, 1991; and correspondence from author to HS in author's archives.

13. Quoted in Mariah Burton Nelson, *The Stronger Women Get, the More Men Love Football: Sexism and the American Culture of Sports* (New York: Harcourt, Brace, 1994), 75. Also see Susan K. Cahn, *Coming on Strong: Gender and Sexuality in Twentieth Century Women's Sport* (New York: Free Press, 1994), 116, 262–65.

14. George Sherman, *The Lure and the Lore of Basketball in Missouri* (Virginia Beach, Va.: Donning, 1994), 72–73.

15. Obituary, *New York Times*, February 19, 1994.

16. Dave Dorr, "'Fulton Flash' Blazed Trail for Women Athletes," *St. Louis Post-Dispatch*, February 18, 1994.

17. Joan Wallner, "Fulton Says Farewell to Its 'Flash,'" and "Stephens: Great Tribute to Callaway Spirit," January 19, 1994.

SHARON KINNEY HANSON received a B.A. in English, journalism, and professional writing from Southern Illinois University, Edwardsville, and an M.Ed. in instructional media (TV/film) from the University of Missouri, Columbia. Her other books include *Katy Trail: Hiking, Walking, Biking Guide* and *Art Museums and Galleries in Missouri*. She is the editor of *Memories and Memoirs: Essays, Poems, Stories, Letters by Contemporary Missouri Authors* and *From Hog Alley to the State House: A History of the Jefferson City Police Department*.